TARGET AMERICA

TARGET AMERICA

The Soviet Union and the Strategic Arms Race, 1945–1964

STEVEN J. ZALOGA

PRESIDIO

Published by Presidio Press
505 B San Marin Drive, Suite 300, Novato, CA 94945

LIBRARY OF CONGRESS

Library of Congress Cataloging-in-Publication Data

Zaloga, Steve.
    Target America : the Soviet Union and the strategic arms race, 1945–1964 / by Steven J. Zaloga.
    Includes bibliographical references (p. 317) and index.
    ISBN 0-89141-400-2
    1. Soviet Union—Military policy. 2. Nuclear weapons—Soviet Union. 3. Arms race—History—20th century. I. Title.
UA770.Z346 1993
355.8'25119'0947—dc20   92-34207
                                                                        CIP

Typography by ProImage
Printed in the United States of America

To my parents, Muriel and John

Contents

Preface

FOR NEARLY FIVE decades, Soviet nuclear weapons sat in their missile silos, in the bomb bays of strategic bombers, and in the launch tubes of nuclear submarines, aimed at targets in the United States. It goes without saying that had these weapons ever been launched, they would have caused devastation too painful to imagine. How did these weapons come to be? This book describes how the Soviet Union became a superpower.

Until recently we took Russia's status as a superpower for granted, even after the tumult and changes that have been occurring there since the early 1990s. But in the years after World War II it seemed preposterous that the Soviet Union could challenge the United States in a technological contest like the strategic arms race. The Soviet Union had defeated Germany, but its technological capabilities were widely judged as being second rate, on a par with minor powers like Japan or Italy. Yet the Soviet Union did challenge the United States in the arms race and, on occasion, even managed to forge ahead. The Soviet Union launched the first intercontinental ballistic missile, orbited the first space satellite, put the first man in space, and fired the first submarine-launched ballistic missile. Even though its atomic bomb came four years after the American bomb, the gap narrowed with the detonations of the first hydrogen bombs.

This book examines the design and development of Soviet strategic weapons during the tumultuous decades from World War II through the end of the Khrushchev years. This time frame was selected for two reasons. First of all, it is the most interesting period from a technological standpoint. It was in these two decades that most of the critical innovations in long-range warfare occurred: the development of the atomic bomb, the thermonuclear bomb, the intercontinental bomber, the intercontinental missile, the submarine-launched ballistic missile, the submarine- and aircraft-launched cruise missile, the hardened missile silo, and many others. This was a period when technology most vigorously shaped the Cold War.

Secondly, this period was selected due to the availability of documentation on both the Soviet and American sides. Although there has been much talk about *glasnost* in the USSR since the late 1980s, in reality there are enormous areas of Soviet history that still remain off-limits. These limits have gradually rolled back, but so far as strategic weapons technology is concerned, Soviet documentation about events after the mid-1960s begins to peter out very quickly. The aim of this book was to rely, as much as possible, on Soviet accounts of these critical twenty years.

The catalyst for this book was my own curiosity about this subject. I grew up in the 1950s and 1960s, an era of Civil Defense shelters, the "bomber gap," the "missile gap," and, finally, the Cuban missile crisis. We lived not far from Westover Air Force Base in Massachusetts, and B-52 strategic bombers were not an uncommon sight over our home. I decided to study East European history while attending university in the early 1970s and did much research and traveling in the region as a result. During the past decade I have written more than a dozen books on the history of Soviet conventional weapons technology, an inevitable combination of my professional training and enthusiasms. I often found it difficult to reconcile the poverty and backwardness I saw in the villages of Eastern Europe with the technological sophistication of the Soviet weapons I was able to study and inspect. This paradox underlies the subject of this book.

What were these weapons that threatened America? For decades they have been so secret and so intangible, mere footnotes in the history books, bogeymen for the politicians. We didn't even know their real names, and instead gave them our own monikers: Bear, Sapwood, Shyster, Zulu. Until the late 1980s there just was not enough unclassified information to contemplate a book such as this. There were too many important gaps and too many unanswered questions. With glasnost, many of these gaps have been filled—at least partly.

There are no serious Soviet studies of this subject. There are no books on the Soviet atomic bomb, on the Soviet thermonuclear bomb, or on Soviet missile submarines. The development of military technology by the USSR remains a very sensitive area. This affects nearly all branches of the Soviet military, not only its most secret realm—the strategic nuclear weapons. For example, in the autumn of 1991, after the failed August coup, I was granted access to a previously closed Soviet Army tank museum. But l was told categorically that taking photographs of the exhibits, even the tanks of the 1930s, was not permitted; the facility was still too secret! The few Soviet books that *do* talk about the development of strategic weapons provide only tiny glimpses of the story: an anecdote here, an episode there.

What has made this book possible has been the emergence over the past decade of a scattered selection of memoirs, articles, and documents in the Soviet Union, and the declassification of a wide range of American intelligence materials on the Soviet strategic forces. The declassified U.S. intelligence reports have been used here to create the basic skeleton of this book, while Soviet accounts have been used to flesh out the details. There are still many missing pieces, both from the Soviet and American sides.

For example, there is no reliable data on the number of nuclear bombs built by the Soviet Union during the period covered here. The size of the Soviet strategic forces has never been detailed in any Soviet publication. Details of the Soviet espionage program against the U.S. atomic bomb effort are still very sketchy and new discoveries are likely to be made as the KGB, the Soviet special police, gradually opens its files. Even though Soviet espionage in Britain, the legendary "Cambridge Five," has resulted in scores of books on the subject, there are few reliabl studies on Soviet espionage in the United States. There is still hardly anything available on the operations of Soviet strategic forces in the 1950s and 1960s. How often and when did the submarines and bombers conduct training missions toward the United States? What were their tactics for strikes against the United States? How did the rapidly changing technology interact with the formulation of war plans? It will probably be some years before many of these questions can be answered. Russian military and political studies of this period are still steeped in the passions of the Cold War, preposterously denying the existence of Soviet war plans and feigning moral innocence.

This book examines the development of the Soviet strategic nuclear forces primarily from the perspective of the designers and the weapons technology, not from the perspective of the Soviet political and military leadership. This approach was taken both due to my own interests and to the general neglect of this subject in existing historical accounts. There is a wealth of fine scholarship on the political and diplomatic dimensions of the Cold War. I have limited my discussion of many of these issues, trying instead to provide landmarks that link the topics of this book with the broader issues. I have done so to keep this book focused on its primary and very complicated subject.

One of the most popular misconceptions about the Soviet Union's emergence as a superpower has been the assumption that the development of nuclear weapons alone accomplished this task. This book argues that the Soviet Union was not able to seriously threaten the United States until the early 1960s, nearly a decade after the development of atomic and thermonuclear bombs. The missing ingredient was delivery systems. The bomb alone, without a reliable means to deliver it to distant targets, is not an effective weapon. It was the challenge of developing long-range bombers, intercontinental missiles, and ballistic missile submarines that posed the most difficult hurdle to the USSR's emergence as a superpower.

This critical link between firepower and range is a characteristic yardstick for military technology in the twentieth century. Before that time, weapons could only hit targets within view of the front lines. The longest-ranged weapons, the cannons, seldom had ranges of more than a few miles. By the beginning of the century, technological advances in chemistry, metallurgy, and communications permitted the construction of long-range artillery that could hit targets in an opponent's rear area. This new capability had bloody consequences in the First World War.

The rise of military aviation further extended the depth of the battlefield from a dozen miles to hundreds of miles. By the end of World War II, it was no longer possible to think of the battlefield as some narrow little swath of land contested by uniformed soldiers. The strategic bomber had extended the breadth of the battlefield to thousands of miles. The industrialization of war, the central role played by military industries in creating and sustaining military power, had made the industrial cities of the opposing sides an inevitable objective of these new weapons.

The extension of the battlefield broadened the categories of targets deemed acceptable by the warring sides. Widespread attacks on cities meant that civilians were as likely as soldiers to become victims of the new technologies of war. While there is still debate as to whether the bombing of industrial targets played a significant role in winning the Second World War, the development of nuclear weapons ended the argument over the ultimate efficacy of strategic air power. The new weapons were so destructive that it seemed inconceivable that any city or nation could withstand their onslaught in an all-out war. In less than a century weapons had gone from breech-loading cannon, firing several hundred yards and able to destroy anything within a few yards of their projectile's impact, to thermonuclear-armed missiles, able to strike several thousand miles away and obliterate entire cities. Why the Soviet Union joined in this arms race is one of the underlying themes of this book.

This book is not organized in a strictly chronological fashion. Individual chapters focus on a particular aspect of the subject: nuclear weapons design, intercontinental missiles, strategic bombers, or submarine development. Each of these topics is so complex that a strictly chronological account, interweaving the separate weapons programs, might have proven too difficult to follow for readers not familiar with the bewildering assortment of Russian names and obscure technologies. I hope this approach will keep confusion to a minimum, even if it does require an occasional reiteration of some key points to place the individual topics in a broader context.

This book raises questions about the nature of modern military technology, especially the Soviet variety. An enduring controversy about Soviet weaponry is how important the copying of Western designs has been in order for the USSR to keep up with the West. As this book will show, there is no simple answer. In some cases, where the Soviet Union was significantly behind in a particular technology, there was a greater temptation to copy American weapons, or to use espionage to learn their secrets. Programs such as the atomic bomb and the Tu-4 strategic bomber were very heavily dependent on stolen technology. Others, such as the missile program, benefited from captured German technology, but quickly evolved into a truly indigenous Soviet effort. But Soviet engineers realized that the USSR would remain behind the West technologically if it continued to rely on espionage and copying; the pace of the development of military technology was simply too fast. As a result, many programs, including the early ballistic missile submarines, early cruise missiles, and some of the strategic bomber projects, borrowed very little from the West.

This raises the issue of another conundrum about modern weaponry and the arms race: the notion that a weapons program in one country triggers a similar program in a competing country. This was a common perception in the United States, and led to frequent calls for the termination of a particular American program in hopes that the absence of such a program would undermine the Soviet desire to build their own equivalent weapon. As will become evident in the later chapters of this book, the reactive paradigm of the arms race becomes less and less satisfactory when attempting to describe one where the technology is rapidly changing.

In the case of the strategic arms race in the late 1950s, technological advances were making new weapons possible at an incredible rate. New generations of missiles were spaced only three or four years apart. Under these circumstances, another catalyst triggered the arms race. There was the perception, both in the Soviet Union and the United States, that the other side would continue to press forward in its adoption of new technologies. Therefore, in order to keep pace, each side had to anticipate what the other side would design and deploy. In those circumstances, weapons development programs did not react to developments on the competing side, but instead forecast the opponent's plans and reacted to this forecast.

This predictive approach was often hidden by the need to obtain political endorsement before a weapons program progressed from development into production. Often, military and industrial leaders on both sides used the other side's development efforts to justify their own production programs. This created the false impression that the arms race was little more than a monkey-see/ monkey-do reaction, when in fact the new technology had already been developed in secret. The imperative to employ threat forecasting shaped the U.S.-Soviet arms race since the late 1950s in conventional weapons as well. It represents a cycle of modernization that is very difficult to interrupt, and which may only be interrupted by the collapse of one of the two competitors: in this case, the economic collapse of the USSR in the 1990s.

This book provides several clear examples of this predictive incentive in weapons design. In the case of the hydrogen bomb, the Soviet effort was pushed along on the presumption that the U.S. was working on a similar program; the Soviet Union did not wait for the United States to explode a hydrogen bomb to begin its own program. Soviet nuclear submarines, submarine-launched cruise missiles and submarine-launched ballistic missiles were all undertaken with little or no evidence of similar American efforts. Nor were the Soviet intercontinental missile programs begun in response to American efforts.

Besides illuminating the dynamics of the strategic arms race, this book also provides some insights into the Soviet and Russian dilemmas of the 1990s. A trademark of Soviet communism was the extreme militarization of its economy beginning with Stalin's industrialization program of the 1930s. This book suggests that the successes of the Soviet defense industries were central to the Soviet victory in the Second World War. Combined with the political imperative to match the United States in strategic weaponry after the war, this demanded the continued drain of enormous economic resources into the defense industries in the late 1940s and early 1950s. This occurred in spite of the need to rebuild the civilian economy, already bled white by war. After Stalin's death in 1953, Nikita Khrushchev desperately and ineptly attempted to lessen the military burden on the Soviet economy. His gambles and failures with strategic weaponry were an important element in his eventual overthrow by Leonid Brezhnev in 1964. Brezhnev returned to Stalinist economic priorities, continuing to devote a debilitating fraction of the national economy to military programs. In this sense, the two decades of weapons acquisition examined in this book and the failures of the Khrushchev years helped set the stage for the economic crisis confronting the former USSR in the 1990s.

But to see the strategic weapons program only in the light of later economic difficulties would be to ignore its real accomplishments. The Soviet Union, crippled by appalling war losses and the depredations of the paranoid and barbaric Stalinist political system, was able to overcome the severe limitations of its weak technological base and become a superpower. This stands in sharp contrast to the fate of other nations weakened by the war, Great Britain in particular. The Soviet strategic weapons program also had unintended consequences and triumphs, especially the space program. As this book suggests, the Soviet space program stemmed largely from the vision of one man, Sergey P. Korolev, the designer of the first Soviet ballistic missiles. Korolev, nearly unknown in the West, was able to initiate a space program with little government sympathy at first, one which eventually resulted in several of the most important Soviet technological accomplishments: the first *Sputnik* and the first human in space.

Indeed, Korolev's success in transforming his personal vision of space travel into a major government program conflicts with a widespread view in the West that everything of consequence in the Soviet Union was rigidly managed from the Kremlin. As this book shows, the Soviet system, even in the Stalin years, tolerated a limited measure of initiative by engineers and scientists. Both the first intercontinental missile and the Soviet hydrogen bomb program were pushed through by engineers over the objections of the central bureaucracy.

This book is just a beginning in the study of the Soviet Union's rapid climb to superpower status. Many aspects of the Soviet strategic weapons development program remain obscured by secrecy and the lack of serious research. It is my hope that this book will help to kindle interest in these fascinating questions.

A few technical notes are in order. I have made every effort here to use Soviet weapons designations, where they are known, in preference to NATO-assigned code names. The text uses a mixture of English and metric measurements. I have hesitated to be consistent in using one system or the other for a number of reasons. When discussing Soviet design requirements, the requirements frequently called for very general performance capabilities, for example a range of 8,000 km or a payload of 500 kg. These figures would seem oddly precise if converted to English measurement (4,971.1 miles, 1,102.2 lbs..) so l have left them in metric. l have chosen to give other measurements in English, especially many range and speed figures, since they will be more readily understood by readers.

A book like this requires the active assistance of many persons. l would especially like to thank David Isby for his long-standing encouragement of this project and his help in providing many of the documents on which this book is based. James Loop was generous, as always, in providing material from his extensive library. Dr. Norman Friedman has served as an unending source of insight on strategic technology and has been particularly helpful in naval matters. Joseph Bermudez passed along studies uncovered during his own archival searches. Charles Vick, the noted Soviet space expert, provided helpful comments and recommendations on some of the most difficult aspects of the Soviet rocketry program. Stephen "Cookie" Sewell provided valuable help with Russian translations when I reached the limits of my own Russian linguistic skills. Major George Cully, of the U.S. Air Force's Historical Branch at Maxwell Air Force Base, Ala., went out of his way to locate air force studies that helped illuminate the U.S. response to Soviet programs. Joshua Handler of Greenpeace was kind enough to send along studies on the environmental consequences of the Soviet nuclear programs. Gregg Herken, the chairman of the Space History Department of the National Air and Space Museum, provided some key material on the Soviet missile program. Charles Ziegler of Brandeis University helped clear up several misconceptions about American perceptions of the Soviet nuclear program, based on research for his forthcoming book on U.S. attempts to monitor Soviet atomic bomb tests. I would also like to thank the staff of the Federal Records Branch of the School of International Affairs library at Columbia University for their courtesy and help while I was doing research for this book. Special thanks are also in order for my colleagues in the former Soviet Union.

Chapter 1

The Uranium Bomb

THE MILITARY SITUATION in the winter of 1941–42 looked very grim for the Soviet Union. After a series of catastrophic defeats in the summer of 1941, the Red Army staged an unexpected comeback on the outskirts of Moscow. The German Wehrmacht drive, which had bogged down on the frigid steppes west of the capital, ground to a halt as Soviet reserves from Siberia helped bolster Moscow's defenses and push the Germans back in a few sectors. By February 1942 the front had stabilized and the Wehrmacht was forced to wait until the spring thaw before again attempting to crush the Red Army.

Lieutenant Georgiy N. Flerov, meanwhile, had other things on his mind. While his air force unit was assigned to the base at Voronezh, he decided to pay a visit to the local university. Heading for the library, he found the section devoted to foreign physics journals and began looking through American and British journals from 1940, searching for references to the spontaneous fission of uranium.

His interest was spurred on by more than pure academic curiosity. It was a matter of personal pride. Before the outbreak of the war, Flerov had been an aspiring young scientist specializing in nuclear physics. In late 1939 Flerov and his colleague, K. A. Petrzhak, had discovered the spontaneous fission of uranium. Their discovery was an important one and a short announcement about it had even appeared in the July 1940 issue of the American journal *Physical Review*.

Flerov and Petrzhak were nominated for the prestigious Stalin Prize. In a country where salaries were kept uniformly low as a matter of egalitarian communist doctrine, such prizes were especially important. They were not only a great honor, but they helped open the way to career advancement, better living quarters, and access to well-stocked shops closed to the general public. But Flerov and Petrzhak had not been awarded the prize because the committee had found that foreign physicists had shown no interest in the discovery. Although much of Soviet physics research was of world-class quality, there was a decided lack of self-confidence in the Soviet science community. In spite of all the public acclaim about the progress made by Soviet scientists, the accomplishments of German, British, and American scientists seemed so much more impressive. The acknowledgement of Soviet accomplishments in foreign journals was almost as great an honor as an award like the Stalin Prize.

Flerov, then twenty-nine years old, was determined to find an acknowledgment of his discovery in the American and British scholarly journals. If he succeeded, maybe then the Communist party would relieve him of the drudgery of his military duty and allow him to return to his first love, the study of nuclear physics. He did not find any references to his discovery in the foreign journals. In fact, he found no references at all to nuclear physics research. Names that had been prominent in the journals back in 1939—Szilard, Fermi, Wigner, Teller—were completely absent from their pages. It suddenly occurred to young Flerov that the problem was not that his discovery had not been recognized, but that the Americans and British had stopped publishing articles about nuclear physics altogether. It did not take him long to conclude there could be only one reason for this: the nuclear physics program had been declared a state secret and the Anglo-American scientists could no longer publish their work in this field. Flerov decided that the Americans and British must be working on a uranium bomb. In previous months, he had written to many of the top nuclear physicists in the Soviet Union, urging a new program to investigate the military potential of nuclear physics. His colleagues, themselves distracted from their research by the more immediate demands of the war effort, discouraged his attempts or simply failed to respond. With this new evidence in hand, Flerov decided to take the matter to the top. He wrote a letter directly to Joseph Stalin.

Soviet legends about the origins of the Soviet atomic bomb project claim that it was young Flerov's letter that prompted Stalin to initiate the Soviet A-bomb program. The idea of exploiting recent developments in nuclear physics to develop a bomb of unprecedented power was not entirely new, however. Soviet physicists had reached this conclusion as early as 1939. But there was no agreement that such a weapon was really feasible. Flerov's discovery of the missing articles in the scholarly journals was strong evidence that the Americans and British were working on such a bomb. According to standard Soviet accounts, Flerov's insightful analysis finally prompted Stalin to agree to a similar program, even though the Soviet scientific community had resisted the idea from the beginning. But more recent evidence suggests that the origins of the Soviet A-bomb project can more easily be traced to the shadowy world of espionage than to the ruminations of a young scientist in the musty shelves of a provincial library.

The Early Soviet Uranium Bomb Effort

In the late 1930s the idea that it might be possible to develop a weapon based on new discoveries in physics was reached by Soviet scientists at nearly the same time it occurred to American, British, and German scientists.

In December 1938, Dr. Otto Hahn discovered the first experimental evidence of nuclear fission in his laboratory in Germany. His discovery was reported in an article in the British scientific journal *Nature* in February 1939. Since the early 1930s, physicists in a dozen different laboratories had tried to unlock the secrets of the atom. They had already discovered unique transmutations of atoms caused by the bombardment of uranium by subatomic neutrons. Uranium was a particularly attractive element to study because it was the heaviest atom found naturally and its nucleus seemed particularly unstable. What was intriguing was the outcome of the splitting: the release of a considerable amount of energy. Enrico Fermi's lab, on confirming Hahn's discovery, concluded that 6 trillion times more energy was released by the fission process than was needed to initiate it.

Hahn's discovery that the uranium nucleus could be split in two was revolutionary enough. But it was quickly followed by related discoveries. In January 1939 Hahn and co-worker Fritz Strassman delivered a second article which concluded that the fission of uranium, induced by a stream of neutrons, resulted in nuclei of barium and krypton, as well as a new stream of subatomic particles. These subatomic particles were neutrons, the very same subatomic particles that were needed to induce the fission reaction in the first place.

The second paper suggested that a fission reaction might result in the release of sufficient neutrons to induce another fission reaction, cascading in an avalanche of reactions, and resulting in the release of enormous amounts of energy. So was born the idea of atomic chain reactions.

Soviet physicists first learned of the German discoveries in February 1939 when their subscription copies of *Nature* arrived. The article detailing Hahn's and Strassman's findings set off a flurry of activity. The initial Soviet study on the fission of uranium was a cooperative effort by a pair of young scientists working in two of Leningrad's premier research facilities: Igor V. Kurchatov at the Leningrad Physics Technology Institute (LFTI) and L. V. Mysovskiy at the Radium Institute of the Academy of Sciences (RIAN). Flerov worked in Kurchatov's LFTI laboratory. Kurchatov assigned Flerov and L. I. Rusinov the task of determining if the fission of uranium did in fact result in the release of significant amounts of neutrons. The young physicists concluded that the fission of each atom resulted in the release of two to four neutrons. The neighboring Institute of Physical Chemistry, headed by Nikolay N. Semenov, set up a team to determine under what conditions this release of neutrons might provoke a chain reaction. The young scientists involved in this study, Yakov B. Zeldovich and Yuliy B. Khariton, would later play critical roles in the design of the first Soviet nuclear weapons.

The younger physicists were not the only ones to become fascinated by the revolutionary implications of these discoveries. In 1939, a senior Soviet physicist, Igor Tamm, suggested that a "uranium bomb" might be capable of destroying a city out to a radius of ten kilometers. A conference held in Kharkov in November 1939 highlighted the generation gap. A. I. Leypunskiy, a senior physicist at the Kharkov Institute, concluded that more study was needed before the feasibility of a chain reaction could be proven. Leypunskiy had spent the previous year in prison, one of many scientists and engineers caught up in the hellish paranoia of the Great Purge.

The Great Terror

Stalin began the Purge in the mid-1930s to rid himself of political opponents, or potential opponents, in the Communist party. In 1937 the Purge spread into the military, leading to the execution of most of the military leadership. The military purge was allegedly rooted in a plot by Marshal Mikhail N. Tukhachevskiy and the upper ranks of the Red Army to stage a coup against Stalin with German connivance. At first the Purge was confined to the upper levels of party and military leadership ranks; it soon degenerated into institutionalized paranoia and mass murder affecting nearly all sectors of the government, industry, and the intelligentsia. Even in segments of Soviet society not directly enveloped by the Purge, its aura of universal suspicion poisoned nearly all aspects of creative endeavor.

By 1938 the violence had metastasized like a cancer in unpredictable directions. The repression of scientists and engineers connected with advanced military technology became widespread. Tank design bureaus, aircraft development centers, missile design teams, and radar development plants were subjected to cruel decimation as key personnel were accused of absurd crimes of treachery or sabotage. The lucky ones were detained for a few years and returned to civilian life shortly before the outbreak of the war. The unlucky languished in special prison design bureaus where they carried on their research under the scrutiny of the NKVD (*Narodniy Komissariat Vnutrennykh Del* or People's Commissariat for Internal Affairs) special police. The damned were thrown into the cruel world of the GULAG prison camps, dying of malnutrition, overwork, disease, or the brutality of the camp system.[1] The Purge can be described; it is still nearly impossible to logically explain outside the mindset of Stalin's barbaric despotism.

The Purge's impact on the scientific community was profound. The corrosive effects of fear gravely weakened the traditional collegial bonds of the many research centers. The NKVD's willingness to accept any denunciation, no matter how baseless, as evidence of treachery conferred tremendous power on the embittered, the jealous, and the unscrupulously ambitious. Petty bureaucratic vendettas between competing design centers degenerated into sordid connivery as one group sought advantage over another by denunciations to the NKVD special police.[2] Senior scientists were denounced by failed students. Once a single member of a scientific collective was in the clutches of the NKVD, it was a simple matter to extract further denunciations of his colleagues by bullying or torture. And when denunciations of certain scientists did not appear promptly enough, the NKVD seldom had problems creating a suitable source through intimidation.

The violence was often random and unpredictable. Biology and genetics were the hardest hit, due to the political repercussions of the fraudulent theories of Trofim Lysenko. Physics and mathematics, at the time relatively abstract and disconnected from the world of politics and the military, were less deeply scarred by the Purge. Lysenko's theories of biology contain curious parallels to the Purge. Lysenkoism rejected the accepted Mendelian views on gene mutation and their implications for the evolution of species.[3] Lysenkoism was a crude return to Lamarckian biology, linking evolutionary change to alteration of the surrounding environment, not to genetic change. Lysenko believed that a plant was subjected to a "shattering" of its hereditary characteristics when placed into a new environment. He argued that heredity was controlled by every bit of the plant and that genes were the fictitious invention of "bourgeois idealists." This shattering made the plant pliable to evolutionary change. The mere act of changing the environment created change in the plant, thus ensuring the continuation of the alteration in future generations.

Lysenkoist shattering was a crude analogy to the Stalinist Purge. By "shattering" the community, Soviet society was made pliable for changes in its very nature. Replacing one group of political and social leaders associated with a past regime with a new group of leaders sympathetic to the new regime is an age-old practice. What distinguished the Purge was its scale and brutality. Even in Nazi Germany, non-Jewish scientists were generally left unmolested so long as they did not openly challenge the new regime. During the Purge one's sympathy or antipathy towards Stalin was entirely irrelevant. Stalin was intent on shattering the existing society, no matter how illogical individual cases of repression might seem, with an aim towards creating a wholly new leadership class subservient to his demands. The policy does not appear to have been particularly subtle and, when put into practice, became one of the most grotesque experiments in societal engineering seen in an already brutal century.

The nuclear physics community, and Abram F. Ioffe's institute in Leningrad in particular, had been under fire from other elements of the science community since 1936.[4] Ioffe had been criticized at the 1936 general meeting of the Academy of Sciences for "breaking away from practical work." This meant that his institute was paying insufficient attention to practical military applications of scientific research and spending too much time on "fanciful" theoretical science, especially "useless" nuclear physics. When important government officials paid visits to the LFTI labs in Leningrad, they were shown P. P. Kobeko's lab where work was progressing on a cold-resistant rubber suitable for aircraft and truck tires in arctic conditions. The labs where world-class nuclear physics was being undertaken were avoided to prevent undue attention by hunters of "false science."

The campaign of denunciation continued. Other prominent senior physicists, including Igor Ye. Tamm, Lev D. Landau, and V. A. Fok, were denounced in the press as "idealists" and "smugglers of foreign ideas."[5] This was the first salvo in a campaign to unseat the physicists most closely involved in nuclear physics research for their "physics idealism."[6] The campaign against the Leningraders eventually fizzled out. The Kharkov Physics Institute, after the Leningrad institute the most important center for advanced nuclear research, was gutted. Its senior researchers were killed or tossed into the GULAG.[7] The most tragic long-term consequences for Soviet physics came when several of the up-and-coming young stars of the physics community were denounced and shot in 1938.[8]

It was not altogether surprising that the older generation of Soviet physicists was more wary than the younger generation of promoting the speedy exploration of new developments in nuclear physics, even after the Purge's fury began to subside in 1939. Nuclear physics, unlike some other forms of advanced theoretical study, was nearly unique at the time in its great demands for expensive specialized equipment and large budgets. Cyclotrons and other necessary equipment were so costly that they inevitably received the special attention of the power elite in Moscow. Attracting attention from the upper echelons of the Communist party and the NKVD special police was not a prudent course. Arguments over the priority of funding for physics programs between competing laboratories carried the risk of triggering denunciations. Requests for large amounts of state funds also carried the risk that if results were not immediately forthcoming, the principal scientists involved might be accused of "wrecking" or sabotage. The senior scientists, more vulnerable to the political risks of high-visibility programs, were more prudent than their juniors, who were less affected by the repression.

Senior physicists sought refuge from the political risks of sponsoring controversial programs by shielding their efforts behind the lofty respectability of major state institutions, especially the Academy of Sciences. The nuclear physics community lost its political naiveté during the Purge. Its members had learned that by cloaking their programs in the mantle of national security they would be shielded from charges of "idealism." Tamm's 1939 assertion about the potential of an enormously powerful uranium bomb was the first step in this direction. Although many senior physicists had serious doubts about the plausibility of this idea, the threat that the Germans might develop an atomic weapon was serious enough to gradually change the attitude of the Academy of Sciences towards the whole field of nuclear physics.

By 1940 theoretical work on nuclear fission had progressed to the point where costly experimentation was required. Deposits of uranium and other radioactive metals would have to be discovered, mined, and processed. A cyclotron or "atom splitter" would have to be constructed to actually study the properties of subatomic particles. It was wasteful to allow each individual institute to wander off on its own project; some form of coordination of the research effort would be needed. A central coordinating committee was formed in June 1940 under the leadership of a senior radiochemist, Vitaliy G. Khlopin, head of Leningrad's Radium Institute. The Uranium Commission was led by three of the most senior and prominent scientists of the time. Besides the 50-year-old Khlopin, there was Aleksandr Ye. Fersman, the legendary 57-year-old geochemist and explorer, and Vladimir I. Vernadskiy, the 80-year-old doyen of the physics community. The commission eventually recruited the most prominent physicists and chemists of the day, including such stalwarts as Ioffe, Tamm, and Semenov, as well as members of the younger generation, such as Petr L. Kapitsa and Kurchatov.

In the late 1930s the Soviet nuclear physics community was on the cutting edge of science, apace with Germany, Britain, and America. Articles by Soviet scientists appeared in prestigious Western publications and several key discoveries were made in the USSR. There was some collaboration between East and West. Both Kapitsa and Khariton had studied at the renowned Cavendish Laboratory under Ernest Rutherford in Britain. The Purge had curtailed these contacts but did not eliminate them entirely.

The Uranium Commission completed a tentative plan of action in the summer of 1940. The plan envisioned accelerating the study of uranium and its isotopes, constructing cyclotrons at several institutes, and stepping up the geological searches for uranium deposits under Fersman's direction.[9] As a first step, efforts were made to purchase a kilogram of refined uranium from the Soviet Union's erstwhile ally, Nazi Germany.[10] But the commission's program remained cautious and could not hope to satisfy the handful of young mustangs on the commission, led by Kurchatov.

Kurchatov continued to badger the Uranium Commission to take a more vigorous stand in support of research. He was especially keen to initiate the design of an experimental atomic pile where the concept of nuclear chain reaction could actually be investigated. At the Fifth All-Union Conference on Nuclear Physics in November 1940, Kurchatov presented a detailed exposition of his plan, including a list of the materials and equipment needed. He stressed the military implications of the research and, when asked if a uranium bomb could be built, boasted that it could. He estimated the cost of such a program as comparable to the expense of the massive Volkhov Hydroelectric Plant, one of the most ambitious engineering projects in Soviet history up to that time. Little could he know then how wildly he had underestimated the real cost.

Khlopin, the leader of the Uranium Commission, rebutted Kurchatov's presentation. He chided Kurchatov for failing to distinguish between "the possible and the practical" and reminded his younger colleague that the Academy's primary responsibility was to strengthen the "real defense capabilities" of the Soviet Union and not to fritter away precious resources on fanciful schemes.[11]

An even more damning assessment was offered by Ioffe, Kurchatov's mentor at the Leningrad Physics Technology Institute. Ioffe concluded that "if mastery of missile technology is a matter for the next fifty years, then the employment of nuclear energy is a matter of the next century."

The November conference took place in a somber atmosphere. In the summer of 1940, France had fallen to the German Wehrmacht, along with Belgium, Holland, Denmark, and Norway. Although Germany and the Soviet Union had signed a nonaggression pact preceding the 1939 dismemberment of Poland, few Soviet military leaders held much hope the alliance would last much longer. The Soviet Union was likely to be Hitler's next meal. Stalin, although denying the risk of a war with Germany, pressed for accelerated modernization of the Red Army. He placed increasing pressure on the Academy to assist the Red Army in a major modernization effort, emphasizing not adventurous schemes, such as nuclear research, but more prosaic studies, such as improved tank armor, ship antimine protection, and new radar technology.[12] Stalin insisted that the scientists shed their white lab coats and enter the grimy, practical world of weapons engineering. To protect Kurchatov's lab from these pressures, the neighboring lab at LFTI headed by Anatoliy P. Aleksandrov agreed to nominally collaborate on naval antimine technologies. But Kurchatov's lab remained focused on nuclear physics research, even if, on paper, it was engaged in the "practical" business of using electromagnetism to protect ships against magnetic influence mines.

The goal of Kurchatov and the other Leningraders was to prove the chain reaction theory through the construction of an experimental atomic pile. Realizing that this limited objective did not offer any immediate payoffs to the national defense effort, they tried to accentuate the military utility of their research. What was needed was a senior physicist, a full member of the Academy, to approach the government with this idea. Semenov, the director of the Institute of Physical Chemistry in Leningrad, agreed to sponsor such a letter, which was sent in late 1940 or early 1941.[13] It had no impact whatsoever. The guidance of the atomic research program remained in the hands of the commission's more conservative members. Planning for 1941 was undertaken by Khlopin and Leypunskiy. Although the plan may not have satisfied all of Kurchatov's requests, it represented a major step forward in the Soviet nuclear effort.

The plan had five main elements: the study of fission in uranium and thorium, the study of nuclear reactions in uranium isotopes, the investigation of techniques to separate uranium isotopes, the development of processing techniques for uranium metal, and the search for rich deposits of uranium and other radioactive metals, as well as techniques for extraction.[14] The plan was approved by the presidium of the Academy of Sciences on 15 October 1940. The Academy allotted the largest portion of the nuclear research budget to a special state fund to extract and process 300 kilograms of uranium as soon as possible, with the aim of mining and processing one-and-a-half metric tons in 1941. In the long term, the plan called for the extraction and processing of ten metric tons in 1942-43 under Fersman's direction. The second largest sum was allotted to the construction of a cyclotron at Khlopin's Radium Institute to complement the cyclotron already under construction at the rival LFTI.[15]

The Academy plan was stillborn. Fersman had set out with a team of geologists to explore mineral deposits in central Asia, but not a gram of uranium arrived at the labs in Leningrad and Moscow. With war imminent, all eyes were focused on preparing the armed forces to meet a possible German onslaught. The attack came on 22 June 1941. Physics research would go into limbo for the duration of the war.

Wartime Atomic Bomb Research

With the outbreak of war in the summer of 1941, nuclear research was all but abandoned. Khlopin's RIAN team lost many of its members to the draft. The scientists who remained were packed off on trains to Kazan. A small-scale program to study the chemical properties of uranium continued in Kazan but was severely hampered by the lack of laboratory equipment, instruments, and uranium. Ioffe's laboratories at the Leningrad Physics Technology Institute were also shipped to Kazan before the Germans surrounded Leningrad, leaving their unfinished cyclotron behind. Ioffe's teams were taken off nuclear research and split up between groups doing radar research and others involved in warship antimine protection. Kurchatov reluctantly gave up his cherished nuclear research and joined Aleksandrov's design team in the Black Sea area working on the naval antimine problem.[16]

Kurchatov assisted in the development of degaussing equipment for warships. The Germans had begun to employ naval mines with magnetic influence triggers. A sensor in the mine could detect the small disturbance in the ocean's electromagnetic field created by a ship's steel hull and would then detonate the mine. Naval mines were a particular problem for the Soviet Navy. The Germans were able to effectively bottle up the Baltic Fleet for nearly the entire war by using mines and other barriers. In early 1942, after a near fatal bout of pneumonia, Kurchatov received a letter from the irrepressible Georgiy Flerov. Flerov was still trying to drum up support for the atomic pile. Kurchatov, beset by doubts over whether work on the nuclear program made any sense in view of the life-and-death struggle going on between the Soviet Union and Nazi Germany, did not have the energy to reply to his young friend's letter.

It was after sending letters to friends and colleagues like Kurchatov that Flerov decided to write a letter directly to Stalin himself.[17] This was not an entirely unusual approach. Stalin and his cronies in the Communist party apparatus had created a cult of personality around the "Great Leader." Stalin was portrayed as an all-seeing and all-knowing demigod, a unique genius capable of understanding the most advanced concepts in politics, economics, and the sciences. There were ample examples in the press of letters dispatched to the Great Leader that resulted in Stalin's actions on behalf of the letter writer.

Of course Stalin read few of the letters himself. In Flerov's case, the letter was read by Sergey V. Kaftanov, the science plenipotentiary of the State Defense Committee (GKO). The GKO was the supreme governing body of the Soviet Union during the war. Headed personally by Stalin, it included all the most important Communist party, NKVD, and army officials. Kaftanov and the Scientific-Technical Council he directed offered the GKO advice on matters related to basic scientific research.

Flerov's letter to. Stalin forced Kaftanov to give the nuclear bomb idea more serious attention. Kaftanov, a chemist, was not heavily involved in the prewar discussions about nuclear research. But Kaftanov had visited Otto Hahn's lab in Germany before the war, and was personally acquainted with the fission concept. Furthermore, he had solicited the advice of other Soviet scientists on the matter and found that opinion was quite divided. Many scientists still believed that the harnessing of nuclear energy was off in the far distant future and so was of no relevance in winning the war with Germany. Leypunskiy, for example, judged that it would take fifteen to twenty years. Still others were even more pessimistic, doubting whether nuclear fission could ever be exploited for either military or civil purposes.

Spies and Stalin's Suspicions

While Soviet histories of the development of the atomic bomb have traditionally asserted that it was Fleiov's May 1942 letter that triggered the subsequent Soviet uranium bomb program, recent accounts by Soviet scientists, as well as studies of wartime Soviet espionage networks, suggest that the traditional account is not entirely accurate.[18] Espionage played a more important role than the Soviets were willing to admit.

On 4 November 1941, Lavrentiy Beria, head of the NKVD special police, received a coded telegram from "Vadim," the code name for A. V. Gorskiy, chief of the NKVD residency at the London embassy.[19] Gorskiy was the control agent for the legendary "Cambridge Five," the young British spies Kim Philby, Guy Burgess, Anthony Blunt, John Cairncross, and Donald Maclean. They provided invaluable service to the USSR from the late 1930s to the 1950s, when they were belatedly uncovered by British counterintelligence. Gorskiy reported that he had received top-secret material from one of his British agents indicating that theoretical work on a uranium bomb was being undertaken in England and that such a device would have enormous power, probably more than several thousand tons of TNT. This material came from John Cairncross, who at the time was private secretary to Lord Hankey. Lord Hankey chaired the British Scientific Advisory Council, which had discussed the British atomic bomb program in detail in October 1940. It was the notes of this meeting that Cairncross had handed over to Gorskiy.[20]

Beria went to the Kremlin to discuss the report personally with Stalin. Stalin's response was typically suspicious:

> The Germans are already at Volokolamsk [about sixty miles northwest of Moscow], and here you are launching into this fantasy! I do not believe this. And I advise you not to believe that it is possible to win a war using some kind of chemical element that no one has seen. Doesn't this seem like pure propaganda to you? Done deliberately to distract our scientists from work on new kinds of weapons for the army?

Beria parroted Stalin's suspicion. When Stalin asked what opinion the Soviet scientists had on the matter, Beria mentioned Ioffe's assessment that the program could take decades and might even then prove to be merely hypothetical. Stalin instructed Beria that the USSR would not undertake a similar program, but that the NKVD should keep track of any future reports on the subject.

In the autumn of 1941, Beria began to receive reports from the Soviet consulate in New York that the United States had entered the A-bomb race. In January 1942 Beria received a report from a tactical NKVD intelligence unit operating with the Red Army about a notebook that had been taken from a German prisoner. The notebook contained mathematical calculations relating to heavy water and uranium, as well as notes on uranium prospecting that indicated Germany was also working on an atomic bomb.[21] Beria decided against showing the material to Stalin due to his suspicious reaction to the November telegram from London. That spring, another telegram arrived from Gorskiy in London with further details of the secret British "Tube Alloys" project. Lord Hankey had been appointed to the new Tube Alloys Consultative Committee, which advised Churchill on the British atomic bomb program, in the autumn of 1941. As Hankey's secretary, Cairncross had access to the top-secret Maud Committee report, which predicted that an atomic bomb could be completed by the end of 1943. Cairncross's report to Gorskiy indicated that Britain did not have the resources to carry out the program alone and that efforts were underway, following an agreement by Churchill and Roosevelt, for a joint Anglo-American bomb program.

The new report placed Beria in an awkward position since Stalin evidently distrusted the reports coming from Britain. He decided to marshall his resources before reporting to Stalin. Beria was also aware that Red Army intelligence, the GRU, had its own agent network in London and its own contacts in the Tube Alloys project. There was a series of reports from the senior GRU intelligence officer in London, Simon Kremer, alias *Alexander,* who controlled a German émigré scientist named Klaus Fuchs. Fuchs, although a Communist and Soviet sympathizer, had easily passed through British security checks and was involved in the Tube Alloys bomb program.[22] Fuchs's material corroborated Cairncross's account. It also seems likely that the Soviets were aware of the German atomic bomb program via the Rote Kapelle spy network.[23] Beria was in no position to assess this material himself, nor was he willing to turn it over to scientists like Ioffe due to the sensitivity of the sources.

In April 1942 the thick file of highly classified NKVD reports was handed over to Mikhail G. Pervukhin. Pervukhin was the commissar of the Soviet chemical industry, but also held the rank of NKVD general, a far more important criterion so far as Beria was concerned. Pervukhin used his own sources to verify whether the reports seemed plausible. In May the legendary Flerov letter arrived in Moscow, further heating up the debate.

Flerov's discovery of the absence of articles on nuclear physics in Western scientific journals confirmed what Fuchs was saying: that Britain, the United States, and Germany were involved in vigorous research programs leading to the development of an atomic bomb. Beria was made aware of the letter but it was given to S. V. Kaftanov of Stalin's Scientific Technical Council, as mentioned earlier, for further work. Unlike the highly sensitive material handed over to Pervukhin, the Flerov letter could be openly discussed by scientists involved in the prewar Uranium Council. Kaftanov passed Flerov's letter on to the scientists attached to his Scientific-Technical Council, including Ioffe, Kapitsa, and Semenov. All of these scientists had been heavily involved in the prewar debate over the priority to be afforded nuclear research. Kaftanov reopened the debate.

In May 1942 Beria went to Stalin's office with the new evidence, as well as the evaluations by Pervukhin's staff. The new evidence changed Stalin's mind about the prospect for such a bomb. In short order the scattered legions of senior physicists—Ioffe, Kapitsa, Vernadskiy, and Khlopin—were all brought to Stalin's dacha at Volynskoye in the Moscow suburbs for consultation. NKVD officials, including Pervukhin, were also ordered to the special meeting. Stalin expressed his outrage that a junior scientist like Flerov, and not one of the vaunted Academicians, had foreseen the danger that would be posed if a foreign country, whether Germany, Britain, or the United States, developed a uranium bomb while the Soviet Union did nothing. Stalin ordered Pervukhin to initiate an atomic bomb program.

Young Georgiy Flerov's wish came true. In late May he was called back from his air force duties in the provinces to speak to Kaftanov about the atomic bomb idea. Consultations with other members of the physics community continued. The opinion of senior Soviet physicists quickly changed in favor of a uranium bomb project. Some, like Semenov, had long favored such a program on its own merits. Others were swayed by the foreign evidence that pointed to bomb programs in Britain, the United States, and Germany. The doubters, aware of Stalin's wrath directed against Ioffe and Vernadskiy, prudently changed their minds in favor of the program.

Pervukhin, the chemical industry commissar, was officially confirmed as the administrative head of the program by the GKO. By the summer of 1942 the issue was no longer *if* a uranium bomb project would be undertaken, but rather *how big* the program would be. In view of the constraints on the Soviet war economy and the sincere doubts of many Soviet physicists, Kaftanov proposed a very modest program totalling about a hundred scientists and a budget of 20 million rubles. This was not a very extravagant sum. It was only about one-tenth the size of the 1941 plan since it did not include any significant uranium mining effort. To put it into perspective, such a sum was the equivalent of buying a hundred T-34 medium tanks, or roughly $3 million.

One of the most important outcomes of the decision was its impact on Soviet espionage programs. From accounts of the wartime espionage rings, it is quite evident that nuclear bomb research became a major target of Soviet spies in Britain, Canada, and the United States. Beria heeded Stalin's earlier dictum and focused his efforts on keeping tabs on foreign atomic bomb efforts rather than assisting the domestic effort. On 14 June 1942, Pavel Fitin, Beria's deputy and the head of NKVD intelligence, sent out a coded radio message, number 834/23, to the intelligence posts in New York, London, and Berlin. The message read:

Top secret.
Reportedly the White House has decided to allocate a large sum to a secret atomic bomb development project. Relevant research and development is already in progress in Great Britain and Germany. In view of the above, please take whatever measures you think fit to obtain information on:
    -the theoretical and practical aspects of the atomic bomb projects, on the design of the atomic bomb, nuclear fuel components, and the trigger mechanism;
    -various methods of uranium isotope separation, with emphasis on the preferable ones;
    -trans-uranium elements, neutron physics, and nuclear physics;
    -the likely changes in the future policies of the USA, Britain, and Germany in connection with the development of the atomic bomb;
    -which government departments have been made responsible for co-ordinating the atomic bomb development efforts, where this work is being done, and under whose leadership.[24]

Soviet espionage efforts, though extensive, were not limitless. It would have been inconceivable for the Soviets to devote a significant fraction of their espionage resources in this direction unless it was deemed worthwhile by Stalin and Beria. The decisions in the spring of 1942 led the NKVD to expand its technological espionage work in both England and the United States. The scientific-technical espionage program was handed to one of Fitin's deputies, Leonid Kvasnikov (and later to Vsevolod Merkulov after Kvasnikov's departure to the New York station in 1943). Eventually two special agents were dispatched to coordinate these activities: Vladimir Barkovskiy, assistant *rezident* for intelligence in London, and Leonid Kvasnikov, rezident for intelligence in New York from 1943 to 1945.[25] These coordination efforts were needed because the espionage networks in these ostensibly "allied" countries were diffuse. In New York, for example, the NKVD ran operations not only from the consulate, but from the Amtorg trading company, and the Red Army's GRU had a separate network of its own. Outside New York, the Soviets operated espionage rings from the Washington embassy and in San Francisco.

Leadership of the scientific program was another issue. Although a senior physicist like Ioffe, Kapitsa, or Semenov might have seemed a logical choice, Stalin vetoed the idea. Stalin decided that a younger man, for whom the project would become "the main cause of his life," would be preferable. Other factors probably played a role in his decision. The selection of a senior physicist like Ioffe or Kapitsa would have made the program more visible to foreign intelligence agencies, exposing the Soviet program to discovery just as the lack of scientific papers had disclosed the existence of an American and British program. These senior Soviet scientists were well known in the Western physics community and their sudden disappearance into the secret world of weapons research would eventually become known. In addition, few of the senior physicists had shown any particular enthusiasm for the project. Nor could their services be wasted on a project that might eventually turn out to be an impractical pipe dream.

Ioffe suggested that Kurchatov and Abram I. Alikhanov be considered to head the project. Alikhanov was another of Ioffe's students at the Leningrad Physics Technology Institute before the war, running one of the labs next to Kurchatov's.[26] In October 1942, Alikhanov was ordered to report to Moscow from his scientific work in Armenia and Kurchatov was ordered back from Gorkiy, where he was involved in a new project to develop advanced tank armor. Both of the young physicists were interviewed by Kaftanov.[27]

Stalin selected Kurchatov to head the new program late in 1942 and Kurchatov accepted. Stalin's selection of Kurchatov over Alikhanov may have been due to the fact that Kurchatov was an ethnic Russian while Alikhanov was not. Stalin was becoming increasingly suspicious of the loyalty of the Soviet Union's non-Russian ethnic groups in his later years and eventually regarded them as security risks in top defense posts.

The relatively low priority afforded the uranium bomb program can be gauged by Kurchatov's activities. Although he was supposed to take up his new post in Moscow in January 1943, the navy still insisted he complete his work on the antimine degaussing system with a trip to the distant arctic navy base in Murmansk. The GKO confirmed Kurchatov's appointment in March 1943, but it wasn't until September that he was made a full member of the prestigious Academy of Sciences. The center of the uranium bomb research was a new organization in Moscow, code-named "Laboratory No. 2." Laboratory No. 2 was given space in the old Seismological Institute on Pyzhevskiy Lane, which had been evacuated in 1941 when there had been concern that the capital would be overrun by the Germans.

Kurchatov began taking steps to assemble a team of physicists to conduct the necessary research. His low rank in the hierarchy of the Soviet science community made it nearly inconceivable to recruit senior physicists like Ioffe or Kapitsa, and the NKVD security apparatus might not have agreed had he tried. It was just as well; physics is one of those fields in which scientists' early efforts are often their best. Kurchatov, forty years old at the time, chose younger scientists in their twenties and thirties. He began with colleagues from Ioffe's labs at the LFTI—Alikhanov and Flerov—and then turned to other Leningraders from neighboring institutes: Zeldovich, Khariton, and Lev A. Artsimovich. Nearly all of the candidates leaped at the opportunity to return to nuclear physics research after their exile from Leningrad to distant research stations in 1941.

The attitude of these young scientists was enthusiastic. Their nation was at war and many felt that their previous efforts on obscure weapons development efforts wasted their talents and minimized their contributions to the war effort. Some believed that they were malingerers compared to other young men of their age. Indeed, these scientists were among a very privileged group of draft-age men shielded from recruitment into combat units. The losses among colleagues in the same age groups were appallingly high. The draft cohorts of 1921 and 1922, young men who were 22 or 23 in 1943, suffered the highest casualties of any age group during the war: only 3 percent survived.[28] Half of all draftable Russian men were killed or wounded during the war. Compared to such sacrifices, the work of the privileged scientists seemed luxurious. The scientists were anxious to contribute to the war effort, and the nuclear weapons program seemed a much more productive use of their talents. From all the memoirs of the war years, it is evident that this program was undertaken with considerable enthusiasm and energy. Most of the scientists were given a nominal rank in the army to avoid draft problems. Kurchatov liked to sign his letters "Soldier Kurchatov," an affectation to assuage his conscience about his privileged position and a reminder that his efforts were not directed towards "impractical physics fantasy," but a worthwhile military program.

The team at Laboratory No. 2 in Moscow was very small. By the end of 1943, there were about fifty people on the staff, including only about twenty scientists. Kurchatov organized the work into three main areas. First, Laboratory No. 2 would have to prove the feasibility of a chain reaction by constructing an experimental "boiler," the contemporary name for a nuclear reactor.[29] One team, headed by Kurchatov himself, would develop a graphite-moderated boiler while another team under Abram Alikhanov developed a heavy-water–moderated boiler. The second aspect of the program would be

the development of techniques to extract uranium from uranium ore, especially the U-235 isotope. Three different techniques were to be studied by
three different teams. Issak K. Kikoin's team would examine gaseous diffusion,[30] Lev Artsimovich's team would study electromagnetic separation,[31] and
Anatoliy Aleksandrov would study thermal diffusion separation.[32]

The third and final phase of the program would be the design of the bomb
itself. Theoretical work in this direction was undertaken by Yakov Zeldovich
and Yuliy Khariton. The most obvious method for obtaining a critical mass
of uranium seemed to be a "gun configuration."[33] This was the same initial
approach taken by the American program. It isn't certain if this similarity in
approaches was due to espionage. It seems more likely that the gun technique was independently concocted in both the United States and USSR. Tests
began near Moscow on the dynamics of the interaction of metals striking each
other at high velocities using subcaliber guns. It was hoped to learn from
these tests what would occur in the microseconds of impact when a large
piece of uranium was fired into another piece.

Work on the uranium bomb was painfully slow due to staff shortages and
the lack of equipment. The unfinished LFTI cyclotron was eventually moved
from Leningrad after the siege was lifted in 1944 and reestablished in Moscow. But the bomb program had little priority, little funding, and little equipment.
The central problem was that there was no uranium to work with, not even
a microgram.

Central to the labs' work was the slow but steady flow of intelligence material
that was coming in. Beria insisted that the information be tightly compartmentalized. Kurchatov was given a small office in the Kremlin to view the
incoming reports. A special translator was assigned to the project to further
limit any possible leaks. Once Kurchatov read the material, he had to pass it
on to team members without revealing its source.

Code Name Perseus

The first espionage windfalls came from the New York station. An American
Communist, Morris Cohen, had been recruited by Soviet intelligence while
a volunteer soldier in the Spanish Civil War. Using the cover name "Luis,"
Cohen worked in the Amtorg bureau in New York after his return from Spain.
His wife, Leontine "Lona" Petka, also served as an agent for the USSR and
appears to have taken over her husband's "clients" after he was drafted into
the U.S. Army. The Cohens served as control agents for a number of spies
specializing in military technology.[34]

Morris Cohen had been contacted sometime in 1942 by an acquaintance
who had also fought in Spain. The acquaintance was a physicist working on
uranium isotope separation technology, a field of considerable interest to the

Soviets. Knowing of Cohen's contacts with the Soviets through the Amtorg trading company, the physicist offered his services. Like most of the atomic spies of the period, the physicist's motivation was ideological, a commitment to the Soviet cause and disdain for American society. He was given the code name "Perseus" and even in 1991 was still referred to in Soviet accounts by another pseudonym, "Arthur Fielding."[35] This spy's actual name is still not known. Soviet accounts state that he was alive and living in the United States in 1991.

The recruitment of Perseus was only a small part of the Soviet effort to infiltrate the American atomic bomb program. The physics department of the University of California at Berkeley had been the home of many of the central figures of the American atomic bomb program, including the head of the bomb design effort, J. Robert Oppenheimer, and the head of the electromagnetic uranium separation effort, Ernest Lawrence. As at many universities of the time, some of the physicists were Communist party members or leftists still sympathetic to the Soviet Union even after the 1939 Hitler-Stalin pact. In San Francisco they attempted to exploit the pro-Soviet sentiments on campus to gain access to American atomic bomb secrets. In 1943 George Eltenton, a British engineer apparently connected with the Soviet effort, tried to interest Oppenheimer in passing material to the Soviet Union. It is still not clear how the Soviets determined that Oppenheimer headed the bomb effort, though it was most likely through his former Berkeley connections. Oppenheimer had associated before the war with left-wing circles on campus, and so was viewed as amenable to such requests by the Soviets and their supporters. But Oppenheimer's attitudes towards the Soviet Union had changed dramatically since the 1930s and he refused to cooperate.[36] A number of Berkeley students were suspected of handing over material to the Soviets and the extent of the espionage may never be completely resolved.

The spies and their control agents were usually dedicated foreign Communists or fellow travelers—enthusiastic amateurs in the spy trade—who viewed the Soviet Union as mankind's last hope in the fight against fascism. Unlike many European and American Communists, the spies had not lost their faith in the wake of the Purge or the cynical Soviet-German accords of 1939. In contrast, the NKVD rezidents and senior intelligence officers who ran the operations were hardened professionals, mainly Russians, many with a first-hand taste of the Purge. They valued the work of their spies and control agents, but were privately disdainful of their motivations. Their attitudes were symbolized by the slang they used for foreign Communists: *govnoyed,* crap-eaters—people who would swallow any nonsense uttered by the Soviet leadership.

The first batch of material from Perseus was made available to Kurchatov in March 1943. Kurchatov judged it to be of "enormous, priceless importance for our government and our science." The material included descriptions of the use of centrifuges for uranium isotope separation. This was a new approach for the Soviets. Other material on the subatomic interactions in a nuclear detonation forced Kurchatov to revise his views of certain subjects, pointed out new approaches for the Soviet research program, and convinced Kurchatov that the development of a bomb could be solved earlier than anticipated.

As tantalizing as the new material had proven to be, Kurchatov had to face the fact that he still had no uranium. Pervukhin attempted to resolve this problem. Rather boldly, his staff initiated a request by the Soviet Purchasing Committee in the United States to win the approval of the American War Production Board to sell eight tons of uranium oxide ore and eight tons of uranyl salts to the USSR. Had this sale been permitted, it would have provided Kurchatov's team with enough uranium to construct an atomic pile similar in size to the first American one in Chicago.[37] The request for the uranium was passed on to Maj. Gen. Leslie Groves, the head of the Manhattan Project, code name for the United States bomb program. The Americans stalled, finally consenting in 1944 to the shipment of a thousand pounds of uranium salts and two pounds of low-grade uranium metal. The decision to supply this material was a curious attempt to help "smoke out" the scope of the Soviet program.[38]

The activity of the Soviet Purchasing Committee was symptomatic of U.S.-Soviet relations. Besides its legitimate role in facilitating the transfer of supplies to the Soviet Union, it also served as a front for military-industrial espionage against the United States, under the direction of the NKVD.[39] In April 1944, one of its agents, Viktor Kravchenko, defected to the United States, exposing its espionage functions.[40] Among the programs he disclosed was a clandestine effort to acquire uranium ore outside of official channels.

Although the Soviet Union and the United States were allies, the relationship between the military and scientific establishments of the two countries was neither friendly nor cooperative. There was nothing approaching the camaraderie and sharing that characterized the Anglo-American alliance. The British had realized from the start that they had more to gain than to lose by revealing their technological breakthroughs to the Americans. Britain had a decided lead in many new military technologies, such as radar, and freely shared these secrets with the United States early in the war.[41]

The Soviet-American relationship was far less friendly, severely poisoned by the pathologic xenophobia of the Soviet military after the searing experience of the Purge.[42] Contacts between Soviet and American scientists and military officers were shunned unless specifically sanctioned by the NKVD. Although the United States and Britain provided the Soviet Union with considerable new military technology under the Lend-Lease program, including advanced radars, the traffic was almost entirely one way. There was no sharing of Soviet technology.[43]

It was a popular argument that the alliance between the United States, Britain, and the Soviet Union mandated technological cooperation during the war. This viewpoint was widely disseminated after the war by apologists for Americans who spied for the USSR, such as the Rosenbergs. Their contention was that the Soviet Union, as an ally, should have had access to Anglo-American technological innovations, such as the atomic bomb and radar; that it is not "spying" if the recipient is an ally. But technological cooperation of the scope that existed between the United States and Britain during World War II was the exception, not the rule. The United States did not share technological research with its other allies, such as China, France, or Poland, nor has there ever been any presumption that it should have.[44]

The Hunt for Uranium

With Western sources limited by such distrust, Pervukhin's attention turned to possible domestic sources of uranium. It would prove to be one of the most important successes of the Soviet nuclear program during the war years. Foreign observers, including General Groves in the United States, were convinced that the Soviets would be unable to build an atomic bomb for decades owing to a lack of natural sources of high-grade uranium.

In 1940 the original Uranium Commission had set up a "State Fund for Uranium Metal" to hunt for uranium deposits. A geological expedition set out for central Asia to begin the search. Until the discoveries in nuclear physics, uranium had little industrial value, so there had been little interest in prospecting for it. Uranium had some marginal uses in ceramics manufacture and for some very specialized steel alloys, but there was not enough industrial requirement before the war to warrant serious mining efforts. The initial search was led by a legendary character in Soviet geology, Aleksandr Fersman. Fersman had spent much of the 1920s prospecting for new mineral deposits in the far reaches of Soviet central Asia, to the north of the Persian and Afghan borders.[45] Fersman recalled the intriguing discoveries made in the Fergana Valley and turned his attention there.

The Fergana Valley is a fertile refuge in the dry Uzbek lands of Soviet central Asia. Lying to the north of Afghanistan, the valley enjoys the rare riches of streams from surrounding mountains. By the time of the Second World War, mining had already begun in the northwestern reaches of the valley, mainly in Tadzhik areas, for a variety of rare metals, including bismuth, tungsten, and vanadium. All were critical to the wartime Soviet metallurgy industry. Fersman found that several mines in the Fergana Valley did have uranium deposits but in low concentrations. It would take a major effort to extract it.

Pervukhin's efforts to exploit Soviet uranium deposits were delayed by the pressures of the war and the stratified Soviet bureaucracy.[46] The Fergana

Valley was very remote and ill-served by railroads. Mining ostensibly came under Pervukhin's chemical industries, but the labor force necessary to conduct any substantial mining effort was stretched to the limit by the war effort. The largest available pool of potential miners was the forced labor camp system, the notorious GULAG controlled by Beria's NKVD special police. There were some limited efforts at the mines at Tuya-Muyun and Taboshar.

To coordinate Pervukhin's industrial and mining efforts with Kurchatov's scientific endeavors, Stalin assigned one of his closest aides, Vyacheslav Molotov, to serve as the nominal head of the uranium bomb program. It was not an entirely auspicious choice. Molotov was a key member of the GKO and one of his main industrial leadership roles was supervision of the vital tank industry. When it came to devoting time to industrial supervision, Molotov viewed tank output as far more important than some fairy-tale science project involving a few dozen young physicists. His role in expediting the bomb program was less than satisfactory.

Enter the Special Police

In late 1944 or early 1945 Kurchatov wrote a letter to Beria complaining that, after more than a year, the surveys for uranium deposits beyond the Leninabad deposits had not even been undertaken. The bomb project was desperate to get moving on the uranium hunt, since even after the deposits were located it would take months, if not years, to process enough uranium for the first reactors. It might seem that sending a letter to the head of the special police is an odd way to search for uranium. But the NKVD's Ninth Directorate was in charge of sensitive mining operations, controlling the enormous GULAG labor force. In addition, as mentioned earlier, Beria was a key figure in the attempts to obtain uranium overseas. Kurchatov would later come to regret involving Beria in the program, but at the time there was no other alternative.[47]

Lavrentiy P. Beria was one of the most sinister figures in Soviet history, leading the NKVD during a period when its powers were the greatest: from 1938 to the time of Stalin's death in 1953. Beria not only supervised the special police during some of the regime's bloodiest years, but he personally took part in the cold-blooded execution of many fellow government and military officials. Beria's Nazi counterpart was Heinrich Himmler, who headed the SS. Beria did not share Himmler's squeamishness. Himmler became ill when he witnessed the mass execution of Jews in Russia in 1941; Beria personally took part in scores of political murders and beatings. He was rumored to regularly carry a blackjack, even after he had become the chief administrator of the NKVD empire, to make it easier to take part in impromptu prisoner interrogations. Himmler was a fussy bureaucrat; Beria was a thuggish head basher. His chief skill was his ability to placate Stalin's paranoid delusions of treachery and sabotage. Beria "exposed" countless plots and managed the execution or incarceration of millions of "enemies of the people."

His insatiable and perverse pleasures were legendary in the NKVD. If later anti-Stalinist accounts are to be believed, he made a habit of having his men abduct attractive young women from the streets of Moscow. After he raped them, they were killed and their bodies dumped in the gutters.

Beria demonstrated his loyalty to Stalin by ruthlessly carrying out his cruel orders. Stalin in turn entrusted Beria with power over the vast NKVD empire. The NKVD was similar, but not identical, to Himmler's SS. Both organizations controlled the vast prison networks of their totalitarian states. Beria's subordinates supervised the massive GULAG system, which even at the height of the war included millions of prisoners. Both controlled large military and paramilitary forces. In Beria's case, the forces may have totaled as many as 2 million troops.[48] Unlike the Nazi SS's military arm, the Waffen SS, NKVD troops were not frontline soldiers. The NKVD troops were used to follow behind the Red Army, preventing troop desertion, routing out enemy stragglers, visiting retribution on anyone suspected of collaborating with the Germans, and destroying any signs of resistance among the recalcitrant minorities in the Soviet borderlands.

Beria's importance to the atomic bomb program was threefold: he controlled the slave labor force that would be necessary to carry out any extensive mining operations for uranium; he controlled the special prison design bureaus of incarcerated engineers and scientists who supplemented Kurchatov's meager staff;[49] and he controlled the foreign espionage network that was essential in stealing the secrets of the American and British nuclear bomb programs.

Beria's interest in the atomic bomb project was more than scientific. He headed the NKVD special police, one of the three great pillars of the Soviet state. The other two were the Communist party and the army. Beria had managed to extend his power into those two sectors as well by controlling security agents who verified the loyalty of all key personnel. As in the case of Heinrich Himmler, his counterpart in Nazi Germany, Beria constantly attempted to broaden his power by bringing additional government responsibilities under his wing. If the atomic bomb was indeed feasible, as it appeared to be judging from the Anglo-American effort, it would have a dramatic impact on military power.

Kurchatov had written to Beria hoping that he would step up searches for uranium. He got much more than he bargained for. Beria not only accelerated NKVD efforts to hunt out uranium, but he began to take steps to transfer control of the uranium bomb program from the industrial and political leaders of the GKO to the NKVD. Beria's usurpation of power over the bomb program was part of a larger effort to take control over all Soviet secret weapons. In 1938 many Soviet weapons designers had been accused of sabotaging their programs or selling out to foreign powers. What better way to supervise and control the most important programs than to place them directly under the NKVD! This led to a network of so-called "special design bureaus" with the engineers doing development work while within the confines of prison. Beria's attempt to control the atomic bomb program was another ambitious effort to expand his police empire. Not only did the atomic bomb program fall under his control, but advanced missile and electronic research eventually did as well. Beria's motives for taking control of the bomb program were also related to the vagaries of his relationship with Stalin. The growing power of the NKVD had worried Stalin, and he began steps to diffuse control over it. Although Beria continued to wield control over the NKVD even after its wartime reorganizations, he probably foresaw Stalin's intent of limiting his prerogatives. Leadership of critical weapons programs was a partial substitute for his diminishing control in other areas.

Beria's appreciation for the potential of the uranium bomb concept was based on his access to intelligence on foreign atomic bomb programs. Beria's NKVD controlled the major sources of intelligence information flowing into the Soviet Union about the American, British, and German atomic bomb efforts. By 1944 the German attempt had virtually collapsed and the independent British attempt had been largely folded into the American program. It was becoming quite obvious by late 1944 that the American project was of an enormous scale, and the Americans seemed quite confident of their ability to successfully complete it. The Soviets were very familiar with the progress of the American effort due to their success in penetrating the Manhattan Project with no fewer than three spy networks. From a scientific standpoint, the next important spy added to NKVD circles was Klaus Fuchs.[50]

Fuchs was originally controlled by the Red Army's GRU intelligence service, which had little appreciation of the significance of his information. The NKVD learned of his efforts in 1942 and eventually had him transferred to its control.

At first Fuchs was able to inform the Soviets about nearly all details of the critical gaseous diffusion process for extracting precious U-235 from the raw uranium. However, his help in this area was largely irrelevant at the time, since the Soviet Union had neither sufficient uranium nor the technological capability to build a gaseous diffusion system. Fuchs's revelations about uranium processing were premature, though eventually quite valuable.

In August 1944 Fuchs's value as a spy dramatically increased. Fuchs had been transferred to the American program in December 1943. The United States was in the process of manufacturing an enormous gaseous diffusion plant at

Oak Ridge, Tennessee, and Fuchs's assistance was deemed urgent and essential. He was given an American clearance on the basis of his existing British clearances, since the Americans little appreciated how thoroughly the British program had been compromised by Communists and pro-Soviet sympathizers.

In the summer of 1944, Hans Bethe, the head of the Theoretical Division of the Manhattan Project at Los Alamos, requested that Rudolf Peierls of the British nuclear program come to New Mexico to replace Edward Teller as the leader of the "Hydrodynamics of Implosion Group." This group developed the concepts behind the actual inner workings of the atomic bomb. Fuchs had worked for Peierls earlier in the war while still living in Britain. Peierls accepted the new posting with the American bomb program on the condition that he be allowed to bring along several of his younger colleagues from the British program, Fuchs among them. Fuchs arrived at Los Alamos in August 1944.

Fuchs was a quiet, industrious man who quickly won the respect of the team leaders. Hans Bethe labeled him "one of the most valuable men in my division." In a different environment from Britain, where pro-Soviet sympathies were commonplace, Fuchs kept his political enthusiasms to himself. He attracted very little attention except for favorable appreciations of his work effort. Through the winter of 1944–45, Fuchs's division assisted in perfecting the techniques for detonating the atomic bomb. In February 1945 Fuchs turned over several pages of notes outlining the process of assembling an atomic bomb, as well as several of the techniques being studied. The control agent who received the material was Harry Gold, alias *Raymond,* who worked for one of the top NKVD agents in the United States, A. A. Yakovlev, alias *John,* the vice-consul of the Soviet consulate in New York. In June 1945 another report was turned over to Gold with much more specific detail about the construction of the plutonium bomb scheduled to be test fired in July 1945.

Nor was Fuchs the only source of information at Los Alamos. A young American army private, David Greenglass, worked in the machine shop where the explosive lenses designed to detonate the bomb were manufactured. Although Greenglass did not have Fuchs's breadth of knowledge or wide access, Greenglass's practical technical knowledge of the actual bomb construction complemented Fuchs's material and helped confirm its validity. Greenglass's control agent was his brother-in-law, Julius Rosenberg.[51]

The material coming from Fuchs and Greenglass was important to Beria in 1944 primarily for making an overall assessment of American intentions. The Soviet program was too small and immature in 1944 to make much immediate use of the information. But the sheer scope of the Los Alamos project and the Oak Ridge uranium processing center made it quite clear to the Soviet intelligence chief that the Americans were convinced they could develop such a weapon.

Beria certainly did not reach this conclusion himself. He was not familiar with theoretical physics or the arcane technologies of uranium extraction. But some of his subordinates were well enough trained to appreciate the quality of the intelligence being received. Because of the NKVD's direction of a number of secret prison design bureaus, Beria had added a number of technocrats to his staff. General Avraami P. Zavenyagin, a metallurgist by training, was one of Beria's key aides on the nuclear program. He was astute enough to appreciate the scale of the American endeavor.

The importance of the espionage material was considerable. Given the very limited budget and staff available, Kurchatov's program was proceeding very slowly. The espionage material served as a substitute for experimentation and research that Kurchatov's lab was, as yet, unable to carry out. Kurchatov later stated that the work of the espionage agencies accounted for 50 percent of the success of the Soviet atomic bomb program.[52]

Ironically, Beria's suspicious nature nearly damaged the American spy network. Beria tended either to accept his agents completely, or doubt them totally, in which case their fate was sealed. Leonid Kvasnikov, code-named "Antonov," was one of those agents appointed by Beria's subordinates. Beria had little faith in Kvasnikov—for a very special reason. In 1940, while on assignment in Nazi-occupied Warsaw, Kvasnikov had been approached by a Georgian Catholic priest, Georgiy Peradze. Peradze had known Beria at the time of the 1919 civil war in Georgia. Peradze told Kvasnikov that Beria had maintained secret ties with British intelligence agents in the area. On returning to Moscow, Kvasnikov reported his contact with Peradze, but kept his charge of Beria's treachery to himself. He fully realized that if he accused Beria of complicity with a foreign intelligence service, Beria would have him killed to prevent his own exposure. Yet Beria remained suspicious of Kvasnikov. He continually questioned the reliability of Kvasnikov's reports, going so far in April 1945 as to demand his recall. During a meeting with Pavel M. Fitin, head of NKVD intelligence, Beria exclaimed, "I feel your Kvasnikov cannot escape the cellar. But have you recalled him from New York or not?"[53]

The "cellar" was NKVD slang for the sixth-floor interrogation cells at the Lubyanka NKVD headquarters, where suspects were physically broken. Fitin was reluctant to recall Kvasnikov back to Moscow, knowing Beria's plans and knowing that Kvasnikov was providing invaluable intelligence by his coordination of the atomic spies. Moreover, Fitin well knew that Stalin had begun to take personal interest in the atomic bomb issue. The recall of a key control agent could disrupt the whole operation and Fitin himself might be accused of subversion. Fitin had brought along several of Kurchatov's written assessments of Kvasnikov's reports. Kurchatov's remarks made it clear that Kvasnikov's material was of the highest state interest. Beria let the matter drop and Kvasnikov remained in the United States to control the atomic spies.

The success of the espionage ring, combined with Molotov's evident failure in administering the atomic bomb program, allowed Beria to solicit Stalin's approval to usurp administrative control over the atomic bomb program. The effects were dramatic. The NKVD's Ninth Directorate accelerated uranium mining operations in central Asia in the Fergana Valley area near Leninabad in the Tadzhik Republic. The new mining complex employed *zeks,* labor camp prisoners, from a GULAG camp at Sotsgorod.[54] The Ninth Directorate also began cooperating with the Ministry for Nonferrous Metals to discover additional deposits of uranium in the USSR. A "special regime camp" was set up on the outskirts of Chelyabinsk, near Kyshtym in the Urals, to begin work on a secret factory for uranium processing.

The NKVD Ninth Directorate, better known as the Guard Directorate, was an elite group responsible for guarding high Communist party officials and secret state installations. Mining operations related to the uranium bomb project were now added to its list of responsibilities.

The initial mining operations were disappointing. Uranium is relatively rare, and there had been little requirement for it before the war. The prospectors were forced to resort to tracking local Kazakh legends of the sources of medicinal water frequented by camels. By 1945 the major discoveries of uranium oxide were in the remote regions of Kazakhstan near the Chinese frontier.

The Bomb Explodes

Although Stalin had known about the uranium bomb concept since the 1942 decision to proceed with a Soviet equivalent, he had only a limited appreciation of the revolutionary nature of such a weapon. During the 24 July 1945 Potsdam conference with Winston Churchill and Stalin, Harry Truman, the new American president, informed the Soviet leader that the United States had a "new weapon of unusual destructive force." Truman was referring to the fact that the United States had successfully tested its first atomic bomb a week before. Stalin said that he was "glad to hear it" and hoped that it would be put "to good use against the Japanese." Truman and Churchill were left with the impression that Stalin did not appreciate the new weapon's significance.

Stalin's response was a charade. He feared that the Americans might attempt to blackmail him with the weapon at some later date. Only a handful of top government and military leaders were allowed to share his actual concerns over the bomb. To all others he pretended that the atomic bomb was just another trivial innovation in weapons technology.

Shortly after his encounter with Truman, Stalin met with Molotov and his top field commander, Gen. Georgiy K. Zhukov. Molotov agreed that they would "have to talk it over with Kurchatov and get him to speed things up."[55] Stalin did not express similar concerns to less important ranks of the military. General Shtemenko of the general staff recalled in his memoirs that Stalin had spoken to the chief of the general staff, Gen. Aleksey Antonov, about Truman's remarks. Stalin did not express much alarm, or even acknowledge the nature of the weapon discussed. Stalin would later forbid the armed forces to openly discuss the revolutionary strategic implications of atomic weapons in their journals and studies. To acknowledge the bomb's power would be to reveal the Soviet Union's weakness and vulnerability to blackmail.

Stalin telephoned Beria and castigated him for the failure of his intelligence network to predict the precise time of the first atomic bomb test. In fact, the spy network had disclosed the date of the anticipated test, but the timing at Los Alamos was thrown off by the weather. Stalin expressed his views to Beria over a scrambler phone:

> Truman is trying to exert pressure, to dominate . . . His attitude is particularly aggressive toward the Soviet Union. Of course, the factor of the atom bomb was working for Truman. We understand that. But a policy of blackmail and intimidation is unacceptable to us. We therefore gave no grounds for thinking that anything could intimidate us. Lavrentiy, we should not allow any other country to have a decisive superiority over us. Tell Comrade Kurchatov that he has to hurry with his parcel. And ask him what our scientists need to accelerate work.[56]

On returning to Moscow from Potsdam, Stalin summoned Kurchatov to a meeting at his dacha and accused him of demanding too little support and not sufficiently accelerating work on the bomb. Kurchatov, not foolish enough to accuse Stalin's close associates such as Beria and Molotov of failing to respond to his earlier requests, prudently weathered Stalin's wrath. His only retort was a lamentation about the sad state of the Soviet Union in the wake of the war: "So much has been destroyed, so many people have died. The country is on starvation rations, there is not enough of anything."

Stalin expected such groveling, and retained his practiced scowl. "If a child does not cry, the mother does not understand what he needs," Stalin snapped. "Ask for anything you like. You will not be turned down."[57]

The Soviet uranium bomb program was about to go into full swing.

Chapter 2

Building the Bomb

STALIN'S DECISION TO accelerate the uranium bomb program after the Potsdam conference in late July received further incentive in early August 1945 when the U.S. Army Air Force dropped two atomic bombs, one on Hiroshima and the other on Nagasaki. The atomic bomb was no longer the fanciful dream of "physics idealists." It had suddenly become a mandatory weapon in the arsenal of any nation aspiring to world power. In the middle of August, Stalin called the People's Commissar of Armaments, Boris L. Vannikov, to his Kremlin office. Already waiting there was Igor Kurchatov.

Stalin's message was simple: "Comrades—a single demand of you. Get us atomic weapons in the shortest time possible. As you know, Hiroshima has shaken the whole world. The balance has been broken. Build the bomb—it will remove the great danger from us!"[1]

The Soviet atomic bomb program started in earnest. It was given the code name "Operation Borodino." Borodino was the location of the famed 1812 battle between the Russian army and French forces led by Napoleon. Kurchatov was given the code name "Borodin."

The effect of the atomic bomb explosions was immediately felt in Moscow. It was apparent even to foreign observers. Averell Harriman, the U.S. ambassador, cabled Washington: "Suddenly, the atomic bomb appeared and [the Soviets] recognized that it was an offset to the power of the Red Army. This must have revived their old feeling of insecurity." The British ambassador was even more blunt: ". . . then plump came the atomic bomb. At a blow, the balance which had now seemed set and steady was rudely shaken. Russia was balked by the West when everything seemed to be within her grasp. The three hundred divisions [of the Red Army] were shorn of much of their value."[2] Alexander Werth, a correspondent in Moscow in

1945, recalled that news of the Hiroshima bomb "had an acutely depressing effect on everybody . . . some Russian pessimists dismally remarked that Russia's desperately hard-won victory over Germany was now as good as wasted."[3]

The official Soviet view of the situation was exactly the opposite. Stalin told Polish prime minister Stanislaw Mikolajczyk that "from a military point of view, [the atomic bomb] has no important meaning whatsoever." This charade was intended to hide Stalin's real concern over America's monopoly on atomic weapons. During a conference on the bomb program held at Volynskoye in late 1946, Stalin gave a more candid appreciation of the bomb's merit: "atomic bombs were the cheapest means of war."[4]

In the summer of 1945, the Red Army was the most powerful land force the world has ever seen: twenty thousand tanks, 11 million troops, and a tremendous crush of artillery. More than any other army, it had been responsible for the devastating defeat of Hitler's vaunted Wehrmacht in World War II.

But the August atomic bomb blasts changed the meaning of military power for all time. Traditional sources of military power—troops, weapons, and warships—were no longer sufficient. The Red Army's ability to impose Stalin's new world order was suddenly devalued.

Stalin would not accept the consequences of an American monopoly on strategic power. Acting on his orders, Soviet scientists and engineers began a frantic race to build an atomic bomb, as well as the means to deliver it to targets in the United States. The challenge was enormous. The Soviet Union emerged from the war in a perilous state. Human losses were staggering. Official estimates place the toll at some 27 million dead, although perhaps as many as 34 million Soviets died.[5] The agricultural situation bordered on catastrophe, especially in the western regions occupied by the Germans. Of 23 million pigs on farms in 1941, only 3 million remained. Of 11 million horses in the western USSR before the war, only 4 million remained—and many of those were still in army service. Half the housing in the western USSR was destroyed: 1.2 million homes in urban areas and 3.5 million homes in the villages.[6] People were living in holes in the ground and whole areas of the country were on the brink of starvation.

It was Stalin's nature to give priority to national defense. He left the people to fend for themselves. Famine and hardship would continue for years; the Soviet peoples' dreams of a better life after the sacrifices of the war would go cruelly unrewarded. Stalin remained every bit as ruthless as he had been before the war, and Beria's police network enforced his wishes. Millions of Soviet citizens had been swept up by the Germans to serve as forced labor. On their return to the Soviet Union they were viewed with suspicion. A portion of the returnees, as well as most returning prisoners of war, were hustled off to Soviet labor camps to wear off any signs of "Western contamination." The GULAG population swelled.[7] Ethnic groups deemed insufficiently enthusiastic in the Soviet war effort suffered decimation and deportation. The Tatars and other peoples of the Crimea were deported into the Siberian wastes. The same fate might have befallen the Ukrainian population but for Stalin's recognition that "there were just too many."

The Russian Secret Weapon

Stalin's postwar military programs focused on the need to reinforce the Soviet Union against the new weapons of mass destruction: the strategic bomber and its deadly payload, the atomic bomb. Stalin's great anxiety over the military importance of the bomb stemmed from his realization that it could strike at the heart of Soviet military power: the military industries. One of Stalin's proudest achievements was the impressive growth of the military industries in the 1930s. Soviet leaders had appreciated that Russia's humiliating defeat in World War I had at its roots the appalling backwardness of Tsarist industry.[8] A nation's military strength in the twentieth century is dependent on its industrial base, and Soviet leaders took that lesson to heart in the 1930s. The Second World War proved the wisdom of this view.

German soldiers who served on the Eastern Front in World War II, especially soldiers who fought in the savage battles of 1944 and 1945, attributed the Soviet victory over the German Wehrmacht to Soviet preponderance in weapons and troops. The same view can be heard over and over again in any number of memoirs by senior German commanders. It has become a monotonous refrain: "We were defeated because the Russians had more tanks, more artillery, and we did not have enough!"[9]

There is a measure of truth in this assertion. By the end of the war the Red Army *did* have a numerical advantage over the Wehrmacht in most critical weapons. For example, in 1945 the Red Army had a threefold advantage in tanks. Yet recent studies by British and American military historians have begun to question the Germans' "brute force" view of the war, pointing out the considerable skill of Soviet field commanders in the final years of the war.[10] But the new revisionism in histories of the war has not addressed whether Soviet operational skills would have led to victory if Soviet military industries hadn't been able to provide substantial numerical superiority in weaponry? Could subtle advantages in tactical and operational skills alone have compensated for less than overwhelming differences in weaponry? Or would the war on the eastern front have been a grim repeat of the Russian World War I experience?

The Soviets clearly drew their own lessons from the war, continuing to devote a massive portion of their gross national product (GNP) after the war into maintaining numerical superiority over NATO in most categories of conventional and strategic weapons. The Russian experience in World War I demonstrated the risks of materiel inferiority; the Soviet World War II experience demonstrated that the lesson had been learned and confirmed.

At the heart of this controversy is a question that has seldom been asked. How was the Soviet Union able to produce vast quantities of tanks and other weapons? How was it able to outproduce Germany? Many historians have taken for granted that the Soviet Union was a great economic powerhouse, while Germany, hobbled by the relentless Anglo-American strategic bombing campaign, could not hope to compete with the Soviet Union in weapons production and was inevitably doomed to fail in the face of hordes of Russian tanks and fighter planes.

This view does not withstand careful scrutiny. In the years before the Second World War, Germany had a greater industrial output than the Soviet Union in most important sectors, and after the stunning victories of 1939–40 the Germans added the substantial industrial resources of continental Europe.[11] The Soviet Union gained no significant industrial power in this period. Worse yet, with the German invasion of 1941 the Soviets suffered appalling losses in their war industries and general economy. The German blitzkrieg of 1941 was enormously destructive to Soviet war potential. It is important to remember that in 1941, 40 percent of the Soviet population fell under German occupation, along with 63 percent of coal production, 71 percent of iron ore production, 58 percent of steel production, and 42 percent of electrical plants.[12] These figures go on and on. The Soviets managed to salvage a fraction of their industrial potential by evacuating some vital war plants before their capture by the Germans. But by the beginning of 1942, the Soviet Union's war potential was in desperate shape.

The Soviet Union's secret weapon in its war with Germany was its remarkable, yet little known, success in rebuilding its war potential. In 1942–43 the war industries were reconstructed in the Russian hinterland to the east of Moscow and deep in the Ural Mountains region. By 1943 the Soviets were outproducing the Germans in tanks, fighter aircraft, artillery ammunition, and small arms. The Soviets were able to accomplish this miraculous recovery by draconian means. Production of goods for the civilian economy was halted, a measure Hitler was unwilling to take until too late. Only the most essential military goods were produced. The production of railroad cars and locomotives, trucks, agricultural tractors, and buses virtually ended. Many military sectors also suffered drastic cutbacks. Warship production was radically curtailed, as was production of military trucks, artillery tractors, and infantry transporters. At its peak in 1943 the armaments industry absorbed 33 percent of the Soviet GNP, while Germany's peak armament production in 1944 absorbed only 18 percent of its GNP. The human costs of this program in the Soviet Union were high. Famine, exhaustion, and disease wreaked a high toll on the neglected civilian work force.

If the success of the Soviet war industries in turning out vast quantities of essential equipment was critical to winning the war, the German failure to halt or slow this production was one of the reasons for Germany's defeat.

Unlike the German war industries, which were pulverized by American and British bombers, the Soviet war industries were largely untouched by German bombers. The German Luftwaffe frittered away much of its best advanced aviation research on revenge weapons, such as the V-1 buzz bomb and V-2 missile, instead of developing an effective long-range strategic bomber.[13] Even as early as 1939, a third of German basic aerodynamic and technical research was devoted to the missile program.[14] American intelligence experts after the war concluded that the Germans had spent nearly three times as much to develop these futuristic revenge weapons as the United States had spent to develop the atomic bomb. The German effort, though technologically brilliant, was futile. It profoundly weakened other branches of the aviation industry by diverting talent and resources and contributing little to the war effort. In spite of the punishing effect of strategic bombers on their own war industries, the Germans devoted very little attention to weakening the Soviet industries until it was too late. Attempts to bomb Soviet tank factories in 1943 enjoyed modest success, but it was too little, too late.

There has been considerable historical controversy in the years after World War II regarding the effectiveness of the Anglo-American bombing campaign. Many historians argue that it did not live up to the extravagant claims of its most vociferous advocates: that strategic bombing alone could decide the outcome of the war. Certainly, in the German case, the traditional military means of ground invasion was needed to defeat the German armed forces. But critics of strategic bombing—focused on denying the most extreme promises of its advocates—often overlook the profoundly crippling effect that it had on Germany and, to an even greater extent, on Japan.[15]

Although most military historians have recognized the central role that the overwhelming quantities of Soviet weapons played in determining the outcome of the German-Soviet war of 1941–45, few have considered whether Germany's failure to plan and conduct a strategic bombing campaign against the brittle Soviet war industries was a decisive lost opportunity.

The Soviet war industries were especially vulnerable for a variety of reasons. The devastating losses of 1941 reduced the pool of machinery in the civilian economy that could be diverted to reinforce the military economy.

One of the reasons that the German war economy could continue to expand until 1944, in spite of Allied air attacks, was the substantial reservoir of machine tools and facilities in the German civilian economy that could be taken over to bolster military production. In the Soviet Union, this reservoir simply did not exist after 1942. The Soviet Union was particularly dependent on foreign machine tools before the war, and not as self-sufficient as the German economy in this critical sector.

The Soviet transportation network, especially its rail system, was much more limited than the German network. Allied planners eventually learned during the war that transportation was such a critical bottleneck that attacks against key transportation facilities had a disproportionate effect in weakening military production. Soviet industry was heavily concentrated, to economize on transportation and to increase efficiency. For example, a single factory, the Ural Railcar Plant in Nizhniy Tagil, accounted for nearly 30 percent of total Soviet tank production. This combination of weak transportation infrastructure and heavy industrial concentration made Soviet industry particularly vulnerable to air attack.

Although the Soviets have heralded the successes of their war industries during the Great Patriotic War, Soviet historians have been reluctant to provide any detailed statistics. Until the late 1970s, many of the basic statistics relating to war production were still classified, and there are still no definitive statistics for many sectors of the war economy. The reason is quite simple: the fundamental role of the war industries in the Soviet victory underlined a significant vulnerability of Soviet military power.

The reason that the American atomic bomb so terrified Joseph Stalin was its capability to devastate the wellspring of Soviet military power. It wasn't simply the atomic bomb itself that worried the Russian leadership. The American and British style of war was fundamentally different from that of continental powers like Germany and the Soviet Union.

Both the United States and Britain devoted considerable resources and talents to the creation of large strategic bomber forces suitable for waging air campaigns against enemy war industries. Unlike the Soviet and German bomber forces, which were tied to flying tactical support missions for the ground forces, the American and British bomber forces were dedicated to strategic missions, largely focused on obliterating an opponent's military industries.

For Soviet military leaders, who were well aware of how narrow the margin of victory had been in World War II, the American monopoly on the atomic bomb posed a terrible military threat. Not only did the Americans have a weapon which could devastate the heart of Soviet military power, but American military doctrine was inclined to use it in precisely that fashion. American B-29 bombers could reach the Urals factories from bases in Europe, and American military planners had access to captured German intelligence documents and to their own wartime observations that pinpointed most of the major Soviet wartime production centers.

The Soviet response to the American atomic bomb was twofold. On the one hand, Stalin ordered a crash program to develop a Soviet atomic bomb and the means necessary to deliver it to targets in Britain and the United States. By possessing its own bomb, Stalin expected that the Soviet Union would be better able to resist American or British pressure in the international arena and deter them from attacking the USSR. On the other hand, Stalin also ordered a crash program to devise a means to defend the Soviet Union against strategic air attack. The focus here is the first part of the program, the atomic bomb program.[16]

Cold War

The arrival of the atomic bomb coincided with continued deterioration in relations between the wartime allies. The alliance between the Soviet Union, Britain, and the United States had been one of convenience, not one of trust. In the eyes of Truman and Churchill, Stalin shared responsibility with Hitler for starting the Second World War in 1939. The Red Army had invaded Poland in 1939 to claim its spoils after the initial German invasion. This had been followed by further Soviet territorial aggrandizement against neighboring Romania and Finland in 1939–40 and by the conquest of the three tiny Baltic republics in 1940. Britain contemplated going to war with the Soviet Union in 1940 over Finland. Royal Air Force reconnaissance aircraft flew over Soviet oil fields around Baku in 1940 in anticipation of air raids aimed at denying Soviet oil to their German allies. The German invasion of the Soviet Union in 1941 put an end to such schemes. With Britain beleaguered and alone, Churchill welcomed the Soviet Union as an ally out of sheer desperation. Many Britons, especially those on the left, welcomed their new Soviet allies with a great deal more enthusiasm. American attitudes towards the Soviets were equally mixed. Concern over the brutality and mendaciousness of Stalin's regime was glossed over due to the importance of the Red Army to the wartime Allied coalition.

The necessity for the alliance diminished as the end of the war approached. The uneasy relationship between the Anglo-American side and the Soviets began to show serious fissures in the summer of 1944, beginning with the diplomatic crisis over Poland's future. Stalin attempted to secure Anglo-American approval of his territorial aggrandizement from the years of his alliance with Hitler.[17] The disintegration of the wartime alliance became almost inevitable owing to Stalin's plan to create a buffer of satellite states with pro-Soviet governments in east-central Europe, and Truman's and Churchill's resistance to total Soviet domination of the region. In view of the paranoid nature of internal Soviet politics under Stalin, most clearly evidenced by the Purge, suspicions over the intent of the United States and Britain were unavoidable. Stalin needed little to find a quarrel. There was no better barometer of the relationship than the Soviet special police; from the end of the Second World War, the United States began to be referred to in NKVD/NKGB documents as "the Main Adversary."[18] In March 1946 Churchill fatefully noted that "an iron curtain" had descended in central Europe. It was the most lucid rhetorical broadside to mark the beginning of the Cold War.[19]

The First Chief Directorate

The long-awaited defeat of Nazi Germany meant that defense resources devoted to the mundane munitions essential for prosecuting a conventional war could be turned towards exotic weapons, such as the uranium bomb and long-range missiles. Due to the high priority attached to Operation Borodino, a more elaborate bureaucratic infrastructure was erected to support it. The mining and chemical processing operation would cost billions of rubles and require the labor of tens of thousands of workers.[20] At first the program was placed under the control of the Ministry of Agricultural Machine Building, a postwar attempt to camouflage the wartime munitions industry. In June 1946 a new organization was formed, entirely separate from the rest of the munitions industry, under the innocuous title of "First Chief Directorate of the USSR Council of Ministers." NKVD Gen. B. L. Vannikov, the former head of the munitions industry, was transferred to head the First Chief Directorate. Vannikov reported directly to Beria, who in reality was the head of the program. Vannikov's two deputies were Kurchatov, responsible for the scientific aspects of the bomb program, and Mikhail Pervukhin, responsible for the enormous uranium mining and processing effort. As a sop to Molotov, he was assigned as the head of the program representing the party. Georgiy Malenkov was put in charge of personnel, another party post. In practice, neither Molotov nor Malenkov had much input into the program due to Beria's dominance.

Stalin gave Beria two years to carry out the program, with a test explosion set for 1948. At the same time the atomic bomb program was formalized, a Second Chief Directorate was organized under Gen. Dmitriy F. Ustinov, responsible for developing the means to deliver the new atomic bombs. Ustinov, then thirty-eight years old, was the brilliant head of the wartime weapons industry and, arguably, one of the most important, if least heralded, architects of Soviet victory.[21]

Beria's control over the uranium bomb program was counterbalanced by the continuing diminution of his control over the special police. Stalin, never one to tolerate too much power in the hands of any of his henchmen, was worried by Beria's gradual accretion of power, so he decreed yet another reorganization of the special police in an attempt to diffuse police power. In 1943 the NKVD was divided into the NKVD and NKGB, both of which Beria controlled. In 1946 they became, respectively, the MVD (Ministry of Internal Affairs) and MGB (Ministry of State Security). Stalin installed Sergeiy Kruglov, his personal bodyguard, as head of the MVD and V. S. Abakumov, former head of the wartime SMERSH counterintelligence service, as head of the MGB. Neither was from Beria's entourage. The 1946 shakeup marked the beginning of a gradual eclipse of Beria's police power.

Yet Beria's control over the bomb program remained strong. Beria was finally given full Politburo membership and he became deputy chairman of the Council of Ministers. It was the Council of Ministers that took over most government functions from the wartime GKO and which controlled the bomb program in the postwar years. As head of the bomb program, Beria retained control over the vital intelligence network in the United States, Great Britain, and Canada. His position on the Council of Ministers also allowed him a great deal of control over other aspects of the program, including the recruitment of German scientists and the uranium mining operations.

Beria kept a tight rein. Information on the progress of the program was limited to a handful of top government officials, and the military was largely excluded from any extensive discussion. The critical role played by forced labor in creating the facilities for the bomb program allowed Beria to exert control over that sphere as well. The GULAG was now under the command of the MVD headed by Kruglov, who was more vulnerable to Beria's wiles than was Abakumov of the MGB. Beria also supervised the exploitation of occupied eastern Germany, particularly any scientific or engineering booty related to his high-technology programs.

The German Connection

Defeated Germany contained a wealth of resources useful for Operation Borodino: scientists, laboratory equipment, and uranium deposits. Although the Germans had not managed to create a uranium bomb themselves, several of their scientists had made key breakthroughs in uranium processing technologies.[22] German uranium deposits had been more thoroughly exploited than those in the USSR. Beria was in an ideal position to take over this war booty, with many of his men in key positions within the Soviet occupation authorities, the so-called SVAG.[23]

Beria placed two of his aides, Col. Gen. Avraami Zavenyagin, and Col. Gen. V. Makhnev, in charge of the German effort. Zavenyagin arrived in Berlin in April 1945 and set up an office in the Berlin-Gruenau district. With the help of specialists from Kurchatov's team in Moscow, including Flerov, Artsimovich, and Kikoin, Zavenyagin began recruiting likely German scientists. The Soviets did not have a particularly difficult time.[24]

Some of the captured German physicists, such as Gustav Hertz, were ardently anti-Nazi and happy to aid any of the countries that had helped bring about Hitler's defeat. Some of these scientists' leftist political beliefs inclined them to aid the Soviets, but for many anti-Nazis it was the luck of the draw: they happened to be captured by the Soviets or were located in the Soviet zone of occupation when the war ended. Hertz later said that he thought that his talents would be better appreciated by the Soviets since so many of the top German physicists had already gone to the United States before the war.

The opposite was the case with other German scientists. Physicists like Peter-Adolf Thiessen had been compromised by their high-level association with the Nazi party and were fearful that the victors would treat them harshly. They quickly found that the NKVD did not share the uncompromising moralism evident in some British and American occupation officers. Zavenyagin and his men were willing to turn a blind eye to wartime "indiscretions" in return for German assistance in "pure, basic, scientific research."

A third group of German scientists had less choice in the matter. Other branches of the NKVD had made wholesale arrests of key German industrial personnel and thrown many prominent German industrial engineers into concentration camps. The entire leadership of the Siemens company, for example, was thrown into a camp at Poznan in Poland. Many of the older men, including von Siemens himself, died in the camp from malnourishment and disease, while others barely avoided the same fate. Zavenyagin's team discovered several prominent engineers in the camps, such as Max Steenbeck from Siemens, and recruited them for the uranium bomb program. The choice between dying in a concentration camp or being released to work for the Soviets was an easy one to make.

The most difficult recruitments involved German scientists living in western Germany, outside the Soviet-occupied zone. In 1946 attempts were made to lure Werner Heisenberg, the head of the wartime German nuclear program, to the Soviet Union. This attempt and several others directed at scientists in western Germany failed. In explaining why these recruitment attempts failed, Heisenberg recalled, "The fox notices that many tracks lead into the cave of the bear, but that none come out."[25] By 1946 it was becoming evident Soviet recruitment entailed greater sacrifices than Zavenyagin's sugar-coated pitch suggested.

In spite of these failures, by the summer of 1945 Zavenyagin had already managed to recruit several dozen German scientists. At first they worked in small teams inside occupied Germany. Another destination soon awaited them. Baron Manfred von Ardenne, a wealthy physicist who owned his own physics laboratory in Berlin, was an early and prominent catch. Von Ardenne and his lab were best known for their work in electromagnetic isotope separation. On 19 May 1945 he was visited by General Zavenyagin, who offered him the leadership of a large research lab that would conduct nuclear research for the Soviet Union. Von Ardenne readily agreed. On 21 May 1945 he flew to the USSR, accompanied by his Soviet counterpart, Artsimovich, for "two weeks of talks." The two weeks eventually proved to be ten years.

Von Ardenne was the first of the German nuclear scientists to become trapped in the so-called First Circle of the GULAG concentration camp system.[26] The First Circle shared little in common with the hellish brutality of most Soviet slave labor camps. The First Circle labs were not much different from the scientific institutes elsewhere in the Soviet Union—except that there was no doubt that the scientists were prisoners and would only be freed at the whim of the NKVD. No sooner did von Ardenne leave Berlin than General Zavenyagin's NKVD troops raided his Berlin lab, bundled up his equipment for shipment to the USSR, and herded his staff onto special trains for transport to their new home.

The new lab was located at Sinop, near the city of Sukhumi on the Black Sea. The lab was code-named Object A, the A referring to von Ardenne. Later in the year other German scientists followed, including Thiessen and Steenbeck. The Soviets set up another prison lab at nearby Agudzeri, called Object G, and headed by Gustav Hertz.[27]

In the end, German scientists had very little impact on the successful completion of the first atomic bombs. Their skills lay in specialized areas, such as uranium processing, which would prove marginal to the needs of the atomic bomb effort. Their main contribution would come in the late 1940s in the effort to develop more advanced nuclear weapons.

Nor was Germany the only defeated Axis power with an atomic bomb program. Japan also had an active atomic bomb program, much of it based in Korea to avoid the devastation of the American strategic bombing campaign. As in Germany, the program had faltered. Soviet recruitment of Japanese scientists does not seem to have occurred, if for no other reason than the stubborn refusal of the Japanese, who vowed to commit suicide rather than cooperate with the Soviets.[28] As with the Germans, the Japanese had enjoyed far greater success in obtaining working stockpiles of uranium and other radioactive materials during the war than the Soviets. This was of special interest to the Soviets because many of the mines were in occupied Korea.

Soviet troops attempted to occupy the main Japanese A-bomb development center at Konan on the Hamhung plains in the summer of 1945. Japanese resistance was much fiercer than in the Manchurian battles, as the area contained a prized concentration of undamaged military industrial facilities. Skirmishes continued to rage until November, some two months after the war had officially ended. After preliminary surveys by MGB teams in 1946, Soviet engineers visited the mining sites in Korea in 1947 with the help of Dr. Chao Yong, formerly with the Japanese Imperial University. In 1948 a barter agreement was reached between the North Korean government and the Soviets, with a major extraction program beginning in September 1949. The program was similar to that in the Soviet Union itself, relying on primitive mining techniques and forced labor. By 1951 about 49,000 tons of monazite, containing some 3,000 tons of thorium oxide, had been extracted. The program to secure fissionable material from Korea was interrupted by the Korean War, but continued afterwards. Although the Korean sites were nowhere near as rich as the German and Czech deposits, the Soviets were unwilling to ignore any potential source of valuable fissionable material.[29]

The Plutonium Bomb

By 1946 Kurchatov and his team were no longer referring to the product of the bomb program as a uranium bomb. A comprehensive overview of the American bomb program had become available through Beria's spy network towards the end of 1945 thanks to Perseus, Klaus Fuchs, and others. The Americans had developed two distinctly different types of atomic bombs. The first type, using uranium as its fissile material, had a "gun" configuration in which one piece of uranium was fired into the other to create a critical mass. This was the most obvious approach to the problem and had occurred to Kurchatov's team during the war.[30] The second bomb type used plutonium as the fissile material and detonated the device using the implosion technique. Implosion uses high-explosive charges to compress a ball of plutonium to reach critical mass. This technique was learned through espionage. Kurchatov and his team quickly appreciated that implosion using plutonium would offer far speedier results. The discovery that plutonium instead of U-235 was used as the primary fissile material in one of the types of American atomic bombs was one of the most important outgrowths of the NKVD's World War II spy network.

Klaus Fuchs provided the details about this second type of bomb. His first package of materials explaining the plutonium implosion bomb was turned over in February 1945, followed by additional data later in the year. For Kurchatov's program, plutonium was a more attractive choice than U-235 for the bomb since it would be much easier to manufacture within the time frame set by Stalin. Plutonium could be produced by nuclear reactions within a "boiler," the early reactor that Kurchatov was already building in Laboratory No. 2 in Moscow. The plutonium could then be chemically extracted from the reactor output rather than relying on costly and complex uranium isotope separation techniques, such as those being developed by the captive German scientists. This chemical processing technique presented less of a technological hurdle than the very difficult methods of enriching uranium that had been undertaken by the Americans.

Kurchatov's team became aware of the enormous difficulties in the manufacture of enriched uranium not only from its own research efforts, but from espionage as well. Klaus Fuchs's first reports to his Soviet spymasters in 1943 had been on the subject of uranium isotope separation by means of gaseous diffusion. Kurchatov had several teams working on the uranium isotope separation problem and none were anywhere near developing a successful method. The addition of German teams at the prison design bureaus in Sinop and Agudzeri certainly helped, but these teams also faced formidable challenges. Kurchatov realized that enriched uranium would probably not become available from these efforts until the early 1950s. These factors reinforced the decision to give priority to plutonium. The first quantities of enriched uranium great enough for a bomb did not become available until early 1951. If Kurchatov had continued the initial plans for a uranium bomb using the gun configuration, it would have delayed the program by two years.

The plutonium bomb could not use the gun configuration being developed by Kurchatov's team. The plutonium Pu-239 extracted from a nuclear pile was contaminated with trace amounts of Pu-240, a plutonium isotope. This particular isotope had a high rate of spontaneous fission. If plutonium had been substituted for uranium in a gun-assembly bomb, the bomb would suffer from premature detonation. As the two pieces of plutonium merged with one another in a gun-assembly bomb, the neutrons emanating from the Pu-240 would start the chain reaction before the critical mass had been attained. The sudden release of energy would destroy the bomb in a small, low-order explosive burst before a full-scale fission reaction could take place.

This did not concern Kurchatov, as Fuchs had also provided a detailed description of the internal layout of the American plutonium bomb. A ball of plutonium at the center of the bomb was surrounded by several layers of explosive lenses. When detonated, the explosives crushed the plutonium, thereby reaching sufficient density to create a critical mass. At the very center of the bomb was an "urchin," a neutron initiator consisting of a small ball of polonium encased in beryllium. When crushed in the implosion, it squirted out a vital flux of neutrons, initiating the chain reaction. This was a brilliant solution and not as immediately apparent as the gun configuration had been. Many

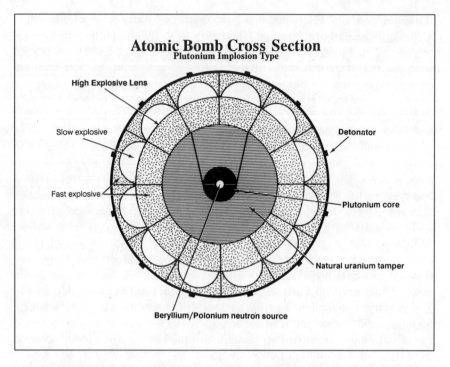

Atomic Bomb Cross Section
Plutonium Implosion Type

High Explosive Lens

Slow explosive

Detonator

Fast explosive

Plutonium core

Natural uranium tamper

Beryllium/Polonium neutron source

American scientists had been skeptical of the idea when it was first proposed in 1943. They likened the idea to trying to compress water between two hands: the water squirts out in all directions. It took major breakthroughs in explosive design to come up with a configuration that would crush the plutonium fuel *and* the neutron initiator together quickly enough and uniformly enough to create a nuclear explosion.

Not only had Fuchs provided a very detailed explanation of how this "crushing," or implosion, could be accomplished, but another spy, David Greenglass, provided further details on the configuration of the explosive lenses that were used to initiate the chain reaction, as well as the urchin. The Greenglass material was useful in two respects. On the one hand it had intrinsic technical value since it provided engineering details of a type not provided by Fuchs. Secondly, and perhaps most importantly, it corroborated the material Fuchs had provided in several key respects.

This was not an unimportant detail so far as Beria and the Soviet intelligence network were concerned. Stalin was intensely suspicious of foreign spies. In 1941 he had dismissed many of the intelligence reports from the NKVD and GRU networks warning of the German invasion, leading to one of the greatest military debacles of the twentieth century. Illustrative of his suspiciousness are the few documents from his personal papers released in recent years. One of these is a report from an agent warning of the German preparations for war in 1941. In the margins, in Stalin's handwriting is the notation, "To Comrade Merkulov [of the NKVD]. You can tell your 'source' at the German aviation headquarters to go fuck his mother. This is not a source, but a disinformer."[31] Stalin's original suspicions about the atomic bomb program in 1942, when the first material became available, had been gradually quieted as more and more evidence of the Anglo-American effort surfaced.

The Greenglass material, although not the most important revelations of the Soviet spy network, would eventually become the most notorious. Greenglass's control agent, his brother-in-law Julius Rosenberg, was discovered after the war when decrypted NKVD material helped the FBI track him down.[32] Although Rosenberg and his wife were portrayed in the newspaper headlines as "atom bomb spies," the Rosenberg spy network appears to have been aimed at other high technology efforts, primarily advanced military electronics, such as radar. Radar was one of the greatest technological accomplishments of British and American technology during the war, and the Soviets appear to have placed as much priority on uncovering secrets of this program as they did the A-bomb program. Of particular interest was radar technology that the Americans refused to turn over to the Red Army via Lend-Lease, such as the proximity fuze. The proximity fuze, a miniaturized radar device fitted to antiaircraft artillery projectiles, dramatically increased the effectiveness of antiaircraft fire.[33] The new fuzes, given the deceptive cover name VT for "variable time," were so secret that their combat use was restricted, even in 1945, for fear that an unexploded device would be captured by the Germans or Japanese. Rosenberg managed to provide the Soviets with a proximity fuze, a point which has not been adequately appreciated in most accounts of this case, and that was not widely understood at the time due to the secrecy surrounding the VT fuze.[34] One of the most curious outcomes of the Rosenberg case was its impact on Soviet computer technology. Two suspected spies implicated in the case fled the United States. They would play an important role in early Soviet computer development, so essential to the early Soviet missile program.[35]

Information provided by Fuchs was amplified by others. Recently released KGB documents about Perseus's revelations seem to indicate that his material may have rivalled Fuchs's. Two other spies working for the Soviets on the atomic bomb project were active in Canada in the closing year of the war. Dr. Allan Nunn May, a British physicist, had begun to work on the British Tube Alloys program in 1942. Following his transfer to the Atomic Energy Division of the Canadian National Research Council in Montreal, Nunn May was under GRU military intelligence guidance. Rather remarkably, in the first half of 1945 the Soviets asked for samples of enriched uranium, a clear example of how limited Soviet technological capabilities still were at that time. Nunn May provided the GRU with uranium samples, as well as reports on atomic research and the bombs dropped on Hiroshima and Nagasaki.[36] Nunn May was uncovered shortly afterwards, but a second voluntary agent, Italian physicist Bruno Pontecorvo, offered his services to the NKGB in Ottawa late in the war. Pontecorvo continued his work in Canada until 1949 before transfer to the British program at Harwell. KGB agents familiar with the case claim that Pontecorvo's efforts were valued almost as highly as Fuchs's, which suggests he was a very important source of material.[37] Three of the "Cambridge Five" spies in Britain served as diplomats in the United States after the war and continued their spying for the Soviet Union there. Donald Maclean in particular was able to pass along data on the American nuclear program.[38]

The data provided by the spy network had critical repercussions in the planning of Operation Borodino. Recent memoirs confirm a very cogent CIA assessment made in 1951: "if outside information [from espionage] had not been made available, the Soviets simply could not have had the time to do the required basic research in reactor and weapons design and produce a weapon in the period it was accomplished."[39] Nikita Khrushchev, in the third installment of his memoirs, recalls that Stalin and Molotov had both said that spies, the Rosenbergs specifically, had "provided significant help in accelerating the production of our atomic bomb."[40] Kurchatov himself would later give half the credit for Operation Borodino's success to the espionage rings.[41]

Espionage saved the Soviets considerable time in the basic research and advanced development phases by removing the need to explore fruitless, expensive, and unproductive alternative technologies. Reports from Fuchs and others about the American program helped direct the Soviet development teams into the most productive avenues of development, steering them away from blind alleys. The Soviets could thus pursue proven engineering technologies, having complete confidence that they would eventually prove feasible since they had already done so for the Americans. For example, by making it clear that a bomb could be produced using plutonium rather than enriched uranium, the Soviets did not have to embark on a crash uranium isotope separation system, as was done in the United States. Such a program, concurrent with the plutonium extraction program, would have put enormous strain on the limited technological resources available in the USSR in the late 1940s. Instead, the Soviet teams could develop plutonium on a crash basis while pursuing enriched uranium processing sequentially.

But the role of espionage should not be exaggerated. The location, mining, and processing of sufficient uranium is a gargantuan process involving tens of thousands of workers and scientists and requiring considerable technological competence. Spying made it possible for the Soviets to design the bomb sooner and develop it less expensively than had they undertaken Operation Borodino without the aid of espionage. The Soviets could have developed an atomic bomb without the espionage material, but it probably would not have been available until the early or mid-1950s.

This raises the intriguing question of whether the possession of the atomic bomb by 1949 influenced Soviet policy. For example, did the possession of the bomb in 1950 affect Stalin's decision to provide aid to the North Koreans for their attack on South Korea? The evidence would suggest not. Even though the Soviets had the atomic bomb by 1949, they did not have a reliable means to deliver it to targets in the United States. Nor would they have such means until later in the decade, after Stalin's death. This key issue will be examined in detail later.

The Uranium Problem

The main problem facing Operation Borodino in 1946 was the continuing lack of sufficient uranium. The decision to use plutonium as the bomb fuel did not remove the need for uranium. Uranium was still required to fuel the first nuclear reactor, which would in turn produce plutonium. But the uranium needed for the reactor was not the highly enriched uranium of the type needed for the bomb (with a high percentage of U-235) but rather uranium with a low U-235 content that could be produced using chemical extraction techniques.

The uranium problem was so severe that some American military leaders, including the head of the Manhattan Project, General Groves, believed that it would take the Soviets twenty years to build their first bomb. Wartime assessments had erroneously concluded that the combined Soviet and Czech deposits would total only about 5 percent of the world's uranium supply. Groves believed that the USSR lacked sufficient high-grade uranium deposits and hoped that his teams operating in Germany in 1945 had managed to scour up all the German uranium supplies before the Soviets could get their hands on them. To further stymie the Soviet effort, Groves initiated an Anglo-American effort to buy up the world's high-grade uranium stocks to preempt Soviet purchases.[42]

In fact, Groves was mistaken. There were substantial uranium deposits in the USSR. The real problem was their remote location. The main Soviet uranium mining effort was concentrated in the Fergana Valley area of Uzbekistan, near Tashkent and the Chinese frontier. Mines were started at a dozen locations, all coordinated by an MVD operation code-named Combine 6.[43] The labor for Combine 6 came from neighboring GULAG forced labor camps, such as Sotsgorod in Tadzhikstan and Khaidarovka in Kyrgyzstan.[44]

GULAG facilities providing labor for the uranium mines in central Asia became virtual death camps. Uranium is extremely dangerous to handle, not only because of its radioactivity, but also due to its chemical toxicity. It is a heavy metal and, like lead, can cause appalling medical problems when inhaled as dust or accidentally eaten from uncleaned hands. The miners worked without any form of protection or decontamination equipment and used mining equipment that was crude in the extreme. CIA reports talk about the use of simple wooden shovels. Soviet accounts refer to the efforts as the "Neanderthal age" of Soviet nuclear energy. Camp buildings were constructed of cement and concrete made from tailings from the mines, further exposing the camp inmates and their guards to persistent low-level radiation doses. By 1950 about a hundred thousand miners and other workers were involved in uranium mining in the USSR, nearly all from GULAG forced labor camps.

But extraction efforts in the Fergana Valley were still insufficient for the first reactor. The Soviets, aware that Germany had begun to explore for uranium for its own failed bomb program during the war, turned their attention from the steppes of central Asia to the mountains of central Europe. In the spring of 1946, Col. Gen. Ivan Serov was transferred from his post in the state security apparatus to head the so-called Geologic Prospecting Group No. 1. Serov's MVD teams began exploring mines in occupied Czechoslovakia and began shipping uranium oxide back to the USSR for processing. Czechoslovak deposits would eventually fulfill about 15 percent of total Soviet uranium needs up to 1950.[45] About twenty thousand people in Czechoslovakia were involved in these mining operations.

Both the Czech and the Soviet mining operations were soon dwarfed by efforts in occupied Germany. Serov's men, heading teams from the Chief Directorate of Rare Metals and the Ninth Directorate of the MVD, began exploring the Erzgebirge region of Saxony in eastern Germany in July 1946. Several deposits had been mined before the war for radium, such as the high-grade ore deposit at Radiumbad Oberschlema. The Soviet teams soon discovered significant deposits all through the area. At first the Soviet teams began shipping previously mined material back to refining plants in the USSR. New mining operations began in 1946, eventually totalling 250 mine shafts. In June 1947 the mining operation was consolidated under a German-Soviet front company called Wismut A. G. In German, *Wismut* refers to bismuth, a metal used in alloys and pharmaceuticals, so this appears to have been an attempt to disguise the operation as an ordinary mining venture. The German mining program was headed by one of Serov's men, Maj. Gen. M. M. Maltsev of the MVD. By 1950 the German operation had become the single largest source of uranium for the Soviet bomb program, about 45 percent according to later CIA estimates. Wismut A. G. operated eight concentrating plants, which took the low-grade ore coming from the German mines and used chemical and mechanical means to raise the uranium oxide concentrations to at least 1 percent. The German uranium mines employed about 175,000 workers by 1950.

Occupied Germany played an important role in the atomic bomb program for other reasons as well. Purified calcium was a critical ingredient in processing the uranium oxide ore into uranium of sufficient purity for a nuclear reactor. The Soviet Union lacked the capability to manufacture it. However, one of the largest calcium plants in the world, the I. G. Farben plant at Bitterfeld, was in the Soviet occupation zone and its production was sequestered beginning in April 1946.

As quickly as uranium was mined and processed it was shipped to Kurchatov's team at Laboratory No. 2 in Moscow. There were two possible approaches to the design of a nuclear boiler suitable for conducting experiments on nuclear chain reactions. The world's first nuclear pile in the United States used purified graphite as the moderator. The term *moderator* refers to a material that will slow the speed of neutrons, making them more efficient in splitting other atoms. The other reactor design would have involved the use of heavy water as a moderator. Kurchatov's team explored both alternatives, with one team under Kurchatov and V. Fursov designing a graphite-moderated reactor called the F-1 and A. I. Alikhanov designing a heavy-water–moderated reactor called the TVR. Since Kurchatov wanted a nuclear reactor not only for experiments but for the production of plutonium, the proven graphite reactor was given priority.

The design of the F-1 graphite-moderated reactor appears to have been based on the American Hanford 305 test reactor. Since information about the Hanford reactor was not declassified until 1953, presumably the design information was obtained through espionage.[46] The Hanford reactor was chosen as a model because it was suitable for plutonium production while the first American pile, the Fermi pile in Chicago, was not.

The problems facing the boiler designs were not confined to uranium supplies. Fursov's reactor required graphite of extraordinary purity. Prior to the war, the Soviets had managed to construct the Dneprovskiy Electrode Plant, which used petroleum coke to manufacture purified graphite. This plant was overrun by the Germans in early 1942 and was not rebuilt until after the war. During the war, the Soviet Union received over 4,000 metric tons of graphite annually from the United States for various industrial requirements. These supplies were shut off in 1946 owing to their utility in nuclear programs. Plants in occupied Germany, including the I. G. Farben plant in Bitterfeld and the Siemens plant in Plania, took up the slack until a new Soviet facility in Chelyabinsk became available.

Although Kurchatov's team may have relied on an American design for the F-1 reactor, it was already very familiar with the conceptual aspects of operating such a facility from independent research. Actual design of the F-1 reactor began under Kurchatov's direction in July 1943 and the majority of

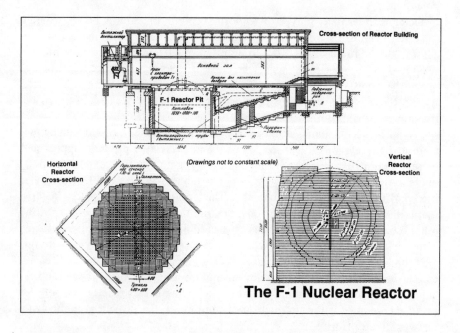

The F-1 Nuclear Reactor

the studies on reactor functioning were completed by the summer of 1945. Kurchatov's team waited impatiently for the supplies of critical graphite and uranium to begin work on its actual construction.[47] In the meantime, a 1.5-meter cyclotron was assembled in a new building in the Laboratory No. 2 complex. Completed in the late summer of 1945, the cyclotron was extremely valuable in experimental research. Kurchatov's brother, a chemist, managed to isolate the first samples of plutonium based on experiments with the device.

The first supply of refined uranium, formed into cylindrical slugs, became available to Kurchatov's team in January 1946. By July, 850 of the slugs had been fabricated, weighing some 1.5 metric tons.[48] As the year wore on, graphite that had been precast into standard blocks began to arrive from plants in occupied Germany, Chelyabinsk, and other Soviet facilities. About 500 tons of graphite blocks were supplied during 1946. When combined with existing supplies, this gave Kurchatov's team the needed graphite by August. By that time, a foundation pit and shelter for the F-1 physics boiler had already been prepared at a new Laboratory No. 2 facility using forced labor from nearby GULAG prison camps. As the graphite and uranium became available, a series of scale models of the pile were constructed for experimental purposes. The first, completed on 1 August 1946, contained 1.4 metric tons of uranium and 32 metric tons of graphite. The final of four models, completed on 15 October 1946, contained 24.6 metric tons of uranium and 290 metric tons of graphite.

With the pit ready, and sufficient graphite finally available, assembly of the full-scale graphite pile began. Insertion of the uranium fuel rods began on 15 November 1946. Kurchatov and his team watched with fascination as their instruments began to record the first fission reactions in the F-1. The first controlled chain reaction in the USSR took place on 25 December 1946.

The construction of the F-1 reactor consumed most of the attention of Kurchatov's team at this time. It was an enormously expensive undertaking, costing about $120 million—about half the Soviet nuclear weapons budget in 1947, according to CIA estimates.

With the successful completion of the F-1, Kurchatov invited Beria to a demonstration. Beria showed up at Laboratory No. 2 along with his aide, General Pavlov. Kurchatov brought them to the control room and demonstrated the operation of the control system. The loudspeaker was hooked to a Geiger counter in the reactor room and, as Kurchatov initiated the chain reaction, the slow clicking on the loudspeaker escalated into a noisy hum. Beria was skeptical of the whole operation, expecting something grander than the simple racket of a Geiger counter. He suggested that they visit the reactor room itself to see the device firsthand. Kurchatov dissuaded him from doing so, citing the health risk posed by the radiation. Beria, not easily convinced, asked to see more tangible evidence. Kurchatov mentioned that in a few months they would begin to make plutonium as part of the experimental program. When Beria asked how much, Kurchatov admitted it would be only a few micrograms.

Beria persisted. "And when can we see that this isn't a deception, not just your fantasy?" he asked.

Kurchatov admitted that the proof would come only when they detonated the plutonium bomb.

Beria insisted on hard evidence. Ever suspicious, he questioned why Kurchatov was now promoting plutonium instead of uranium as the fuel for the bomb. Kurchatov tried to convince him by citing the Danish physicist, Niels Bohr. Beria jumped on the remark. After clearing the other scientists from the control room he instructed Kurchatov to write a personal letter to Bohr asking him to confirm the American use of plutonium in the bomb. Kurchatov consented, if only to end the hectoring.[49]

Beria subsequently had the letter delivered by hand to Bohr through the MVD special police network. Bohr was unable to provide details because he had never been privy to any bomb secrets. It was a pointless exercise, as Beria had ample evidence from several Soviet spies that one of the American bombs did in fact use plutonium at its core. Beria's badgering of Kurchatov was typical of his suspicious nature. Soviet scientists close to Kurchatov believe that the stress placed on him by his unholy alliance with Beria was the cause of Kurchatov's premature death in 1960.

The F-1's successful completion represented the first of three key hurdles the Soviet bomb program had to surmount. The operation of the F-1 reactor permitted Kurchatov's team to begin critical experiments needed to finalize the design of plutonium production reactors and to test their bomb design concepts. The next two stages of the program were already well underway: the production of sufficient fissile material to manufacture the first bomb and the design of the bomb itself.

Feeding the Bomb

Kurchatov and Pervukhin were well aware of the theory behind plutonium production in 1946. They next had to face the substantial engineering efforts required to actually build a plutonium production facility.

The site chosen for the new plant was the small village of Kyshtym in the Ural Mountains region. The site was selected for a variety of reasons. To begin with, it was close to the industrial city of Chelyabinsk. Chelyabinsk would be critical to the facility, since it was the home of the Chelyabinsk Electrode Factory, the Soviet Union's primary producer of purified graphite. It made no sense to transport tons of purified graphite to a distant location when the plutonium plant could be built near the source. Kyshtym was selected from other possible locations around Chelyabinsk due to its proximity to the water in nearby lakes. Large quantities of water would be needed to cool the reactors.

The new nuclear reactor facilities at Kyshtym were known only by their post office box address: Chelyabinsk-40.[50] The related plant for chemically separating the plutonium from the Chelyabinsk-40 reactors was code-named Chelyabinsk-65.[51] Stalin was quite concerned that Soviet atomic facilities might be bombed by the Americans, so special precautions were taken to harden the plants against American air attack. Parts of the Chelyabinsk-65 plant were to be built partly under one of the neighboring lakes, with massive concrete reinforcement to further harden them against air attack.

The MVD special police in charge of constructing the facility established twelve GULAG camps in the area employing some seventy thousand *zeks* (prisoners), including many German prisoners of war.[52] The technology for creating the underground bunkers was based on the Moscow subways' construction group, the Metrostroy.

The Lake Irtyash area is located on a solid slate rock bed. The forced-labor teams first drained the lake adjoining the new plant, then blasted an enormous cavity into the slate below. The main facility was constructed as a huge tunnel, 30–40 meters (100–130 feet) under the lake's surface with steel-reinforced concrete roofs over some vital areas as much as 7 meters (25 feet) thick. The zeks then refilled the lake with water from the nearby Techa River. All that showed from the plant was a smokestack.

As the Chelyabinsk-65 plant was being constructed, work was also underway on the new production reactor. One of the main technological problems was the chemical processing of graphite sufficiently pure for such a reactor. In a plutonium-producing reactor, the graphite serves to slow down the neutrons released by uranium before they reenter other uranium atoms to form plutonium or to continue to trigger the nuclear reaction. The presence of impurities in the graphite amounting to only a few parts per million will drastically reduce the reactor's plutonium production capacity and can even stop its operation. The Soviets managed to get some graphite of sufficient purity from occupied Germany and also contracted with the Cece Graphit Werk A. G. in Zurich, Switzerland, for a small amount. Beria was insistent on developing indigenous Soviet supplies, so the Chelyabinsk Electrode Factory continued to expand.

Kurchatov dispatched V. Fursov to Chelyabinsk-40 as his chief representative. Fursov had collaborated with Kurchatov on the design of the F-1 nuclear reactor and was responsible for the new reactor, code-named Object Zero, at Kyshtym. Design of the new nuclear reactor had been completed by a young engineer, Nikolay Dollezhal. Dollezhal would later design many subsequent Soviet reactors, including the ill-fated one at Chernobyl. The Object Zero reactor was soon given a less fearsome nickname by the scientists, the A-Reactor or *Annochka* [Little Anna]. Construction of the A-Reactor began in early 1948 and it was ready by summer. In anticipation of the reactor becoming operational, all the forced laborers and German prisoners of war were removed from the Kyshtym area in the spring of 1948 and several MVD special rifle divisions were moved into the area to cordon it off. Soviet scientists working at the site labored under extremely tight security restrictions. A scientist who worked there at the time recalled that there was an air of suspicion hanging over the place and a thoughtless comment could mean a death sentence. The complex took eighteen months to assemble and the reactor finally became operational on 10 June 1948.[53]

The scientific director at neighboring Chelyabinsk-65 was Vitaliy Khlopin.[54] Khlopin had headed the original Soviet atomic bomb program in 1940–41 and had rebuffed Kurchatov's efforts to accelerate the program in the early, prewar years of the atomic program. But he was a highly skilled chemist and previous disagreements were forgotten. Khlopin and the other Chelyabinsk-65 staff members were working on a vast chemical processing plant to handle the fuel rods once they had become suitably enriched inside the hot belly of the Annochka reactor.

The uranium slugs in the Annochka reactor were subjected to intense neutron bombardment and then were carefully extracted. The engineer responsible for developing the technology to extract plutonium from the blocks was B. Nikitin.

The work was messy and dangerous. Due to the pressures placed on Kurchatov's team by Stalin and Beria to hurry the development of the bomb, safety precautions were minimal. Although the safety standards of the day limited a worker's radiation dose to 30 rem per year (lax by today's standards), workers at the Annochka reactor in fact received average doses of 93.6 rem in 1949. The worst exposures were suffered by workers at the Chelyabinsk-65 processing plant where, in 1951, they *averaged* a whopping 113.3 rem annual dose. In comparison, Soviet radiation standards since 1970 have been set at 5 rems per year.[55] Environmental concerns were all but ignored. The radioactive waste from the Chelyabinsk-65 plant was dumped directly into the Techa River. In 1951, less than three years after the reactor became operational, radioactive material from the site was found in the Arctic Ocean, hundreds of miles away. The extent of the contamination of the Techa River forced the Soviet government to evacuate villages downriver from the plant and to create reservoirs in an attempt to isolate local ground water from the spread of deadly radionuclides.[56]

The urgency of the atomic bomb program caused Soviet nuclear engineers to be careless. On at least one occasion in the early 1950s, a nuclear reactor at the Chelyabinsk-40 complex nearly went out of control. The operators panicked and it was only the presence of mind of Kurchatov's old friend and colleague, Anatoliy Aleksandrov, that prevented an accident that might have rivaled Chernobyl.[57] Kyshtym's luck finally ran out in 1957 when the intermediate waste facility exploded.

A second major facility for the manufacture of fissionable materials quickly followed on the heels of the first near the small Siberian village of Zhelenogorsk. Code-named Krasnoyarsk-26, its GR-100 plutonium production reactors were placed in bunkers deep underground. The construction of the underground shelters involved the work of more than 100,000 soldiers and 65,000 GULAG workers.[58] The Krasnoyarsk facility was a backup for the Chelyabinsk complex, and production began several years later than at the first facility.

Designing the Bomb
The third and final phase of Operation Borodino was the design of the bomb itself. In a sense, this was the least formidable of the tasks due to the espionage material provided by Fuchs, Perseus, Greenglass, and the others. Nevertheless, there was considerable experimentation to be done to fill in major gaps in the espionage material. What Fuchs had provided was a very rough recipe for the bomb. He provided very few details about key components, such as the devices that triggered the high explosive lenses, the exact amounts of various materials employed in the bomb's construction, the chemical composition of the various explosive elements, and so on. Soviet engineers had to determine these details by careful experimentation.

In 1945, Kurchatov formed a special team to perfect the design of the bomb. The team was eventually given the code name KB-11, a Russian abbreviation for Design Bureau-11. The scientist in charge of the program was Yuliy Khariton, one of the young Leningraders Kurchatov had recruited back in 1943.[59] Khariton had done some of his early research at the Cambridge lab of noted British physicist Ernest Rutherford. On his return to the Soviet Union, Khariton had become a protégé of Nobel Prize winner Nikolay Semenov. The administrative head of the bomb design effort was Pavel M. Zernov, later called "the Soviet Groves" by his colleagues after his American counterpart.[60]

The team's first task was to develop a model of the bomb for display to Stalin and Beria. Based on the espionage material, as well as Soviet research, a one-tenth scale model was completed in 1946 and delivered to the Kremlin. One of the issues discussed was the bomb's delivery. A decision was made that the weapon should be designed as an aircraft bomb suitable for the new Tupolev Tu-4 strategic bomber. Stalin approved the project, authorizing the establishment of a top-secret facility in an isolated location. Khariton's technical requirements document for the atomic bomb was submitted to the Council of Ministers on 25 July 1946.[61]

KB-11 was assigned to a new top-secret facility on the grounds of the old Sarovskiy Hermitage Monastery near the town of Sarova, outside the industrial city of Gorkiy (restored to its traditional name of Nizhniy-Novgorod in 1991). The monastery had been one of Russia's most sacred pilgrimage sites, housing the relics of St. Seraphim. It was closed and partly destroyed by Soviet security forces in 1927 as part of the Communist party's atheism drive.[62]

The new design center was known by its post office box number, Arzamas-16, or by such cover names as Kremlev City and Installation N. This center was considered so secret that in Andrey Sakharov's memoirs Arzamas-16 is referred to simply as the "Installation," and KB-11 is not mentioned at all. General Nikolay L. Dukhov was brought in to handle the actual manufacture of the bomb. Although he held a military rank, Dukhov was in fact an engineer best known for his highly successful heavy tank designs during World War II. The industrial head of Operation Borodino, Boris L. Vannikov, insisted on having an experienced engineer like Dukhov at the head of the bomb manufacturing program, as he felt that the scientists were too inexperienced and amateurish in the complex processes of mass production. The aim of Operation Borodino was not only to design a bomb, but a bomb that could be mass produced.

Khariton's KB-11 design team was organized into departments. The bomb's engineering design was undertaken by a team first headed by V. Turbiner. Yakov Zeldovich, a brilliant young physicist and another member of the original Leningrad group, was responsible for theoretical research. Zeldovich had been diverted from his physics research during the war to help improve the famous Katyusha "Stalin Organ" artillery rockets until his rescue by Kurchatov in 1943. Among Zeldovich's team members was Georgiy Flerov, who, as noted earlier, had helped trigger the Soviet atomic bomb program with his 1942 letter to Stalin. Flerov was responsible for studying the breeding of fast neutrons in the plutonium mass. This work was essential to an understanding of how the explosive chain reaction would occur and how much plutonium would be required. Flerov was entrusted to conduct a number of experiments to prove his conclusions. The experiments were so dangerous that Beria forbade Kurchatov to observe them.[63] Similar experiments in the United States had led to the first American casualty of the atomic bomb program.

K. Shchelkin's department designed and tested the critical explosive charges called lenses, which were needed to compress the plutonium fissile material. Even with the espionage material that had been made available, considerable effort was needed by Soviet chemical engineers to devise the technology to manufacture such large castings of homogeneous high explosive. Moreover, extensive testing was needed to ensure that the explosive charges detonated uniformly and predictably.

Closely linked to this problem was the matter of detonating the many charges simultaneously. The best Soviet blasting caps could be expected to detonate within a hundred microseconds of one another. This was not accurate enough to ensure the uniform compression of the plutonium mass. V. Komelkov's department designed advanced krypton devices that would ensure all the charges would detonate within a tenth of a microsecond of one another. V. Davidenko's department developed the urchin neutron source from polonium and beryllium that would trigger the chain reaction after the plutonium had been compressed by Shchelkin's charges and Komelkov's detonators.

Beria's representatives were evident throughout the facility. The Arzamas-16 compound was surrounded by MVD guard units, manning the watchtower and patrolling the neighboring terrain. Inside the compound, Gen. A. Aleksandrov of the MVD special police supervised security arrangements. Unlike the relatively loose and cooperative atmosphere inside the Los Alamos design site, Arzamas-16's departments were tightly compartmentalized to prevent security leaks. These measures succeeded. The name and location of the facility did not become public until 1990, some forty-four years later, after the KGB decided to relax security. Khariton later recalled, "These were the times when a slip of the tongue could cost you your life."[64]

Another Purge?

In spite of the rapid technological progress being made on the atomic bomb, Operation Borodino was nearly scuttled by another episode of Stalin's vicious paranoia. Rumors of a new purge began circulating in Moscow in the wake of yet another round of political infighting following the suspicious

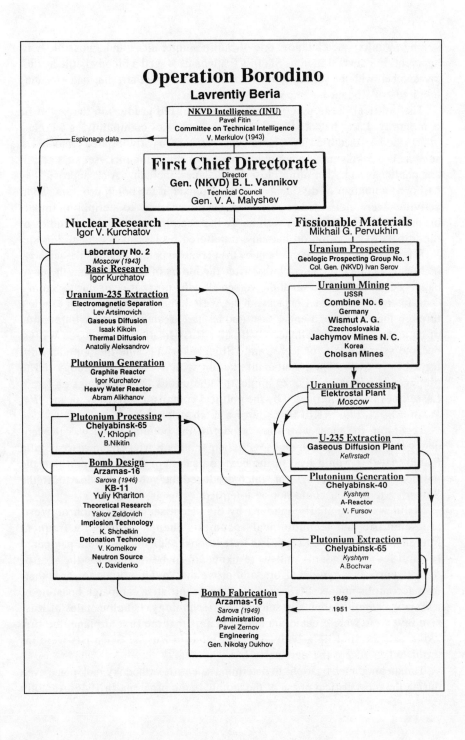

death of Andrey A. Zhdanov, one of Stalin's chief aides and a possible heir-apparent. For several months Stalin's lieutenants waged a bloody battle against one another, with the various elements of the special police arresting and executing hundreds of Zhdanov's supporters.

The political purge precipitated a revival of old grudges in the scientific community. Party hacks viewed the nuclear physics community as a hotbed of unorthodox scientific views, particularly resistant to party-inspired orthodoxies, such as Lysenkoism. Kurchatov had made his revulsion of Lysenko's activities public, as had other of his closest colleagues, including Aleksandrov. They harbored a number of dissident young biologists in the bomb program. Their activities were motivated in part by disgust over Lysenko's crippling impact on biology in the USSR, as well as by the need to foster biology studies of the impact of radiation on humans, unfettered by Lysenko's quack ideas.

Scientific quarrels, brought about by the pervasive politicization of the sciences, had festered since the late 1930s. After the hiatus of the war years, the campaigns began again. The situation worsened in the postwar years due to Stalin's "anti-foreign" campaign. Contact with the West during the war years, for example through the supply of Lend-Lease goods, had created a popular impression of its technological excellence. "Villis," a Russification of the name Willys, became synonymous for jeeps, and "Studebaker" became the popular word for a heavy truck. The popular infatuation with Western technology led to propaganda campaigns. For example, the ubiquitous USA markings on Lend-Lease trucks were interpreted by the political commissars to really mean *"Ubit Sukin-syna Adolfa"* (Kill that son of a bitch Adolph)!

To Stalin, the most worrisome aspect of the popular mood was the tendency to contrast Western items with their shoddy Soviet counterparts. Stalin feared that this would lead to the next logical step: the conclusion that the political and economic system which produced the goods was superior to the Soviet system. That could not be tolerated.

Stalin was particularly annoyed by the scientists' appreciation of Western scientific and technological accomplishments, evident by frequent references to non-Soviet scientists in textbooks. Scientists lived a pampered life by Soviet standards and were expected to be models for the rest of the citizenry. In a cynical effort to improve the Soviet attitude towards their own accomplishments, Stalin had his cronies initiate a campaign boasting of Russian accomplishments in science and technology. Fabulous tales of Russian invention were created, including claims that the first airplane, the first radio, and the first light bulbs were invented in Russia. Scientists were intimidated to accept the new party line.

Threatening interrogations to determine scientific orthodoxy took place even during the most critical phase of the atomic bomb program. In 1946, Anatoliy

Aleksandrov was called into a party Central Committee meeting and confronted by an impromptu board that included several staff members from Moscow State University. They began to pester Aleksandrov with leading questions about quantum theory and Einstein's theory of relativity. These ideas were deemed "foreign" in some of the darker corners of Soviet academia, a particularly damning charge given Stalin's insistence on accenting Soviet contributions to science and technology in his propaganda battles with the West. Aleksandrov retorted, "Reject quantum mechanics and make the bomb yourselves!"[65] Aleksandrov realized that the bomb program and the key scientists connected with it were protected from most of these depredations. Nevertheless, attempts to intimidate the scientists continued.

It is not at all clear who instigated the campaign, but it must have been countenanced by someone close to Stalin himself. At the end of 1948 S. I. Vavilov, president of the Academy of Sciences, and Sergey Kaftanov, Stalin's former wartime science adviser and then Minister of Higher Education, sought permission to hold a national session of researchers from the physics and mathematics branches of the Academy of Sciences. It would, of course, have included nearly all of the scientists working on the atomic bomb. The purpose of the session was to correct "evident shortcomings" among the physicists. The instigators of the purge complained with the usual Marxist pseudo-scientific twaddle:

> . . . Physics is being taught with no regard to dialectical material-
> ism. Lenin's work of genius "Materialism and Empiricocentrism" has
> not been used to the full . . . Idealistic philosophical trends which seek
> corroboration from modern physics are not uncovered and duly criti-
> cized. Idealistic philosophical conclusions from concepts of theoreti-
> cal physics [quantum physics and relativity] are particularly dangerous
> for students' minds . . . Manuals on physics unacceptably underestimate
> the role of Russian scientists in the development of physics. Instead,
> these books abound in the names of foreign scientists.[66]

A series of prepared speeches was written for various participants that blasted the "idealism" and "cosmopolitanism" of many physicists. Denounced as "underlings, menials, and traitors," there could be little doubt what the fate of these men would be if the session was allowed to occur. Among the senior physicists singled out for abuse were Abram Ioffe and Igor Tamm, whose young protégés were now building the Soviet atomic bomb. Although some of the scientists targeted by the "orthodox" physicists were Russians like Kapitsa, many were Jews. The expression "cosmopolitan" was often used at the time as a synonym for Jews. The attacks were directed primarily at those working in the field of theoretical nuclear physics. Even before the scheduled March 1949 session, word of the papers leaked out to scientists in the Moscow area. Those supporting orthodox physics began proving their bona fides with insipid editorials calling for the support of all physicists in the ideological struggle underway between the Soviet Union and its enemies abroad.

Beria had been one of the primary instigators in the Zhdanov purges, but he was alarmed by the unexpected threatened spread of the slaughter into the scientific community, especially into the ranks of *his* nuclear physicists. At one of his periodic meetings with Kurchatov, Beria coyly asked if quantum theory and relativity really were idealist concepts that had best be cast off as such. Kurchatov replied, "The A-bomb is based on the theory of relativity and quantum mechanics. Should we discard them, the project will have to be discarded as well." Beria was dumbfounded by the bluntness of Kurchatov's response. He said that all the talk about physics was so much rubbish and that the atomic bomb project was all that mattered. Beria quickly got in touch with Stalin and the proposed conference was cancelled.

Testing the Bomb

By the spring of 1949 sufficient plutonium for the first bomb was shipped from Chelyabinsk-65 to Arzamas-16. Kurchatov made the familiar train ride from his headquarters at Laboratory No. 2 in Moscow to the Gorkiy train station, where he was met by an MVD chauffeured limousine that took him to Sarova. A brief meeting with Khariton and his teams convinced him that the bomb was ready for testing. Stalin insisted on a meeting in Moscow before the bomb was detonated. Khariton and Zernov accompanied Kurchatov back to Moscow, bringing with them the plutonium core for the bomb.

The meeting was held in Stalin's Kremlin office. Kurchatov made an overall report on the progress of Operation Borodino and solicited permission to go ahead with the test, scheduled for June 1949. Kurchatov showed the plutonium charge to Stalin, who inquired how many more were ready. When Kurchatov explained it was the only one, Stalin frowned.

When told that the second would not be ready for another four months, Stalin remarked, "We may bully the Americans while having nothing in reserve in the warehouse. What if they press on with their atomic bombs and we have nothing to contain them? After exploding a first charge, we've got to have a second, and even a third one. It would be fine if we could make two charges out of this ball. Add some chemical explosive and let there be two bombs, even if of smaller power."

Kurchatov was flabbergasted. Stalin didn't have the slightest appreciation of the nature of nuclear weapons. His suggestion would result in a bomb that would fail to achieve an explosive chain reaction. If the bomb failed, Kurchatov knew that there would be lethal recriminations against himself and his team. Thinking quickly, he explained to Stalin that two small bombs would not have sufficient critical mass to create a chain reaction.

"Critical mass . . . critical mass. It is also a dialectical notion!" Stalin shouted, covering his own ignorance by falling back on Marxist incantations. "And how can one be sure that it's plutonium and not a mere glittering piece of iron?"

Kurchatov suggested that if one of Stalin's guards would touch the ball, it would be warm, not cold to the touch like iron. The scientist explained that the heat was due to the spontaneous alpha-decay of the plutonium. Stalin seemed convinced and finally approved the test, insisting, however, that a second device be prepared immediately.

A major discovery in 1949 helped accomplish this. It was learned, possibly through espionage, that a reactor could be operated with only about half the uranium throughput as had previously been considered necessary. This reduced the ore requirements by half and lessened the need for additional chemical separation facilities. Additional reactors were soon under construction at Chelyabinsk-40, bringing the total to three by 1952.

The Poligon

A site to test the bomb was chosen in 1948. Located on the left bank of the Irtysh River, in the deserts south of Semipalatinsk in Kazakhstan, the test site was nicknamed the *Poligon,* the Russian word for a military proving ground. Its official code name was Semipalatinsk-21. The specific portion of the Poligon reserved for the first bomb test was code-named *Moskva* (Moscow).

Originally, the KB-11 team had been instructed to design the "article" as an actual aerial bomb with an aerodynamic body, fins, and an internal power supply. However, consultation with Soviet aircraft designers revealed that there was no Soviet aircraft capable of lifting a device of the expected size and five-ton weight.[67] This led to the decision to follow the American pattern and detonate the article on a tower. The bomb was code-named *Tatyana,* a popular female name in Russian. It was also nicknamed *Tykva* (pumpkin) by the KB-11 crew—probably because of the segmented appearance of the shaped charges.[68]

Kurchatov went to the Semipalatinsk proving ground in May 1949 to supervise the final preparations. Months of work had already been devoted to ensuring that proper measurements of the test could be taken. Special aircraft were fitted with Petryakov filters to scoop up airborne debris samples after the test. This would show what percentage of the plutonium fuel had been con-

Key Soviet Strategic Weapons Facilities

Anadyr
(Bomber Base)

OKB-1
Kaliningrad
(Missile Design)
●Moscow

●Leningrad-300
Plesetsk
(Missile Base)

Arzamas-16
Sarova
(Nuclear Bomb Design)

Kapustin Yar ●
(Missile Test)

Chelyabinsk-40
Kyshtym ●
(Plutonium Production)

Chelyabinsk-65
Kyshtym
(Plutonium Processing)

Tashkent-50
Tyuratam ●
(Missile Testing)

Poligon
● Semipalatinsk
(Nuclear Tests)

Combine No. 6
Fergana Valley
(Uranium Mining)

Scale ├─────┼─────┤ Kilometers
0   500   1000

sumed in the blast. Tanks were modified to carry sensors into the explosion site after the blast. A set of observation bunkers was built ten kilometers from the blast site. MVD guard units under Gen. V. Bolyatko patrolled the area.

The test bomb was mounted in an elevated, fifty-meter-high steel tower, sheltered inside a ferro-concrete blockhouse at the top. A variety of weapons such as tanks and aircraft were placed around the tower, as well as a number of concrete structures to determine the effects of the blast. Construction of the tower and several other buildings was slipshod. The test program suffered a temporary setback when the tower developed an alarming tilt due to the shifting of its concrete foundation.

Anxious to meet the schedule promised to Stalin and Beria, Kurchatov's team considered detonating the bomb at ground level. It was against their better judgment to do so and the decision was made to erect another tower, delaying the first test by two months.

By the end of August 1949 all was ready. A rehearsal was conducted to make certain that the detonation circuits running to the bomb were functional. The detonation, code-named *Pervaya Molniya* (First Lightning) was scheduled for 0600 on 29 August. On 27 August, Beria arrived from Moscow to witness the event, along with General Zavenyagin, the representative of the First Chief Directorate. Beria remained as suspicious as ever and insisted that special observers witness the event. The Americans had invited a Soviet delegation consisting of M. G. Meshcheryakov, D. V. Skobeltsyn, and MVD colonel

Aleksandrov to witness a nuclear explosion at Bikini Atoll in 1947. Beria directed that they would witness the first Soviet test from one of the bunkers overlooking the test site.

In the dark early morning hours of 29 August, Kurchatov and Beria supervised the final preparations for the test. Four hours before the scheduled blast, both were ordered to leave the site as the explosives were being armed. The administrative head of KB-11, Zernov, and the designer of the explosive charges, Shchelkin, were the last to leave the site, checking a final relay station three kilometers from the tower, where the final safety and arming device was activated.

Kurchatov anxiously awaited the explosion, fully aware of his fate if the bomb failed to detonate. He consulted with Flerov. There was some worry that there might be an excess flow of neutrons inside the device, leading to a premature, partial detonation. Flerov checked his instruments and reported that there were only two to three neutrons per fifteen minutes, an acceptable level.

Around 0550, Beria scornfully remarked to Kurchatov, "Nothing will come of it, Igor Vasiliyevich!"

Kurchatov's face turned red and he tried to reassure Beria. After an interminable wait, the countdown finally began.

"Desyat, devyat, vosem, sem, shest, pyat, chetyre, tri, dva, raz, Start!"

The blast was immediately evident to everyone in the bunker. With a sweeping gesture, Kurchatov began shouting, "There it is, there it is, there it is!" An enormous smile spread over his face. In an explosion of emotion, he raced for the door and ran up a protective earthen berm near the bunker for a better view. Flerov dashed after him. In dismay, Flerov could see the shock wave racing towards them through the distant grass. He grabbed Kurchatov's hand and forced him back into the bunker.

The men closest to the blast were sitting in two modified T-34 tanks of the Radiation Safety Service. One of the crew, A. Burnazyan recalled:

From the little knoll one could see neither the field nor the tower. But it was clear to everyone inside that the light from the glow of the atomic blast had reached our periscopes. The little knoll just ahead of us was glowing with incredibly bright light, incomparable to anything. In the incinerating light, we could see how the shock wave was spreading and bringing the clouds down from the sky over the spot of the nuclear blast. The tanks were tossed around like feathers. On one of them, the attachment for holding the sampling arm up didn't hold. It fell down, damaging one of the ionization chambers as it hit the ground. For a few minutes, we watched the formation of the radioactive cloud. Through the binoculars, one could see a "frying pan" of glazed earth sparkling maliciously in the rays of the setting sun at the epicenter of the blast. The two tanks started up at the same time . . . Literally within 10 minutes after the explosion, our tank was at the epicenter. A broad vision of annihilation was spread before our eyes. The steel tower where the bomb had been hoisted and its concrete base had vanished into thin air. An immense crater gaped in place of the tower. The yellow sandy soil all around had been baked and glazed. It crunched in a terrifying way under the tank's caterpillar tracks. Small melted shards of shrapnel flew off in all directions, emitting invisible alpha, beta and gamma rays.[69]

The crowd inside the observation bunker was jubilant. Beria hugged and kissed Kurchatov. But even in victory, Beria could not help being menacing. "It would have been a great misfortune if it hadn't worked!" he told Kurchatov.

Beria, still not satisfied, even though he had seen the blast with his own eyes, telephoned M. G. Meshcheryakov, one of the Bikini witnesses, and asked, "Did it look like the American one? Very much alike? We didn't screw it up? Kurchatov isn't pulling our leg, is he? Everything the same? Good!"

Finally, convinced that the explosion had indeed been a real atomic detonation, Beria telephoned Stalin over a special line.

"Joseph," he reported, "all is well. The blast was the same as the Americans'!"

Stalin, still in bed, answered curtly, "I already know," and hung up the phone.

Beria was furious. He had been robbed of his moment of glory, reporting the first news back to Stalin. He was supposed to be the head of the bomb program but some spy had reported back to Moscow before him. He stormed back into the bunker and shouted at the design team.

"Even here you put spokes into my wheels, traitors! I'll grind you into powder!"[70]

Chapter 3

Beria's "Brick Bomber"

THE EXPLOSION OF the first Soviet atomic bomb in 1949 set Russia on the road to becoming a superpower rival to the United States. There was still one problem, though: the Soviet Union had no means to deliver atomic bombs to targets in the United States—its long-range bomber force was basically nonexistent.

The Soviet Air Force's backwardness in strategic bombers in 1949 was all the more ironic considering Russia's earlier aviation history. Russia had been the pioneer of strategic bombers. On the eve of the First World War, Igor Sikorsky designed a large, four-engined aircraft that would become the Ilya Muromets bomber. The Russian Army possessed one of the earliest and most capable bomber forces of the First World War, the legendary "Squadron of Flying Ships."[1] The Russian revolution and subsequent civil war demolished much of the aviation industry and it took a decade to recover. Many of Russia's finest aviation designers, including Sikorsky, emigrated in the face of Bolshevik terror. Sikorsky went on to found a major American aviation company and in the 1940s perfected the world's first practical helicopters.

The turmoil of war and revolution did not leave the infant Soviet Union entirely bereft of creative aircraft designers. A talented young Russian designer, Andrey N. Tupolev, had laid the groundwork of the new Soviet aviation industry in 1918, amidst the confusion and turmoil of civil war. Tupolev, then thirty years old, convinced Lenin to permit him to establish the TsAGI, a Russian acronym for the Central Aerodynamics Institute. Tupolev was the son of a prominent lawyer jailed for revolutionary activity by the Tsarist police, and the younger Tupolev had himself been incarcerated in 1911 for the same offense. Impressed with Tupolev's credentials—both the political and engineering variety—Lenin consented to the establishment of TsAGI. Tupolev's

63

TsAGI went on to become the heart and soul of Soviet aviation, existing to this day in the Moscow suburbs. TsAGI is as familiar to Russians as NASA is to Americans.

The infant Soviet Union of the 1920s lacked the resources to compete with Britain, France, and America in aircraft design. But TsAGI kept alive that dream. The Soviet aviation industry reached full blossom in the mid 1930s with Tupolev as its premier designer. Stalin's industrialization program needed a motif and aviation was it. Aeromania gripped the popular imagination as Tupolev turned out a string of monstrous record-breaking aircraft. Tupolev aircraft soon held world records for long-distance flights and Tupolev's ANT-20 was the largest aircraft of its day.

Stalin's industrialization program was spurred on by a massive military modernization effort. After their humiliating defeat by Germany in World War I, the new Soviet military leaders were determined to build a modern armed force capable of defeating any other European power. Soviet military leaders realized that the backwardness and poor performance of Russian industry in World War I had been a major factor in the Russian Army's defeat.

Tupolev's contribution to this effort was in the field of bomber design. Stalin's encouragement of massive propaganda aircraft and record-breakers helped to support the development of large long-range bombers like Tupolev's TB-3. Appearing in the early 1930s, the TB-3 heavy bomber was the finest of its day. At the time, most foreign heavy bombers were still fabric-covered biplanes. Tupolev's design was an all-metal monoplane.[2] Tupolev also designed the SB-2, a remarkable light bomber that clearly displayed its superior design when it was committed to battle with Soviet "volunteer" pilots during the Spanish civil war in 1936.

The TB-3 heavy bomber was scheduled to be replaced by a more modern bomber by the end of the 1930s. Tupolev had assigned one of his most promising young engineers, Vladimir Petlyakov to the design, the ANT-42 heavy bomber.[3] The ANT-42, later called the TB-7 or Pe-8, was a Soviet counterpart to the American B-17 Flying Fortress and the British Halifax bombers. The ANT-42 made its first flight in December 1936, a year and a half after its American counterpart, the B-17.

In spite of the remarkable accomplishments of Soviet aviation in the 1930s, in no small measure due to Tupolev's brilliant leadership and administrative skills, Soviet strategic bomber design was destined to be delivered a crippling blow in 1937. It was not a foreign enemy who would accomplish this, but the nemesis within—Stalin's Purge.

In June 1937, the NKVD special police arrested Marshal Mikhail N. Tukhachevskiy, the head of the Red Army's rearmament program. Tukhachevskiy was closely associated with most of the novel military technologies of the day—bomber aircraft, artillery rockets, and new tank designs. His arrest and subsequent execution on trumped-up charges initiated a wholesale purge of the Soviet military leadership. On 23 November 1937, Gen. Ya. A. Alksnis, head of the Red Air Force, was thrown into Lubyanka prison in Moscow. Alksnis was one of the foremost proponents of the Soviet strategic bomber program.

Tupolev's own arrest preceded that of Alksnis. In the summer of 1937, NKVD special police began arresting some of the younger designers working for Tupolev, including Petlyakov, the head of the heavy bomber design unit. Convinced of their innocence, Tupolev appealed directly to Stalin for their release. On 21 October 1937 the NKVD responded by dispatching three agents to Tupolev's lavish home in Moscow. The agents ransacked his papers and arrested him on the charge of passing new aircraft design technology to the German Messerschmitt firm. The charge was obvious nonsense, but this was of no consequence in the face of the sadistic madness of the Purge.

The aircraft designers did not suffer as gruesome a fate as their military counterparts, however. Some of the younger aeronautical engineers thrown into the GULAG were executed or died of exhaustion, malnutrition, or disease in the forced labor camps. But most of the senior engineers, including Tupolev and Petlyakov, were spared. Tupolev was deposited into Lubyanka prison, Moscow's premier hellhole. After a short stay to provide him with a taste of how much worse things could get, Tupolev was transferred to Butyrki Prison. Butyrki was only one step out of hell.

Tupolev had been accused of the preposterous charge of providing the Germans with the plans on which they based their Bf 110 twin-engined fighter. On the advice of friends already in the prison, he decided to confess rather than face torture. Humiliation and self-abnegation were more prudent choices than heroic attempts to prove one's innocence. There were other prices to be paid. His NKVD wardens insisted that he prepare a list of his other colleagues already in jail. Tupolev was afraid that if he inadvertently listed one of his designers who, despite rumors to the contrary had not been imprisoned, the colleague might very well be apprehended and tossed into jail as well. He was saved from this sordid task by the NKVD when agents handed him a list of the names of more than two hundred aeronautical engineers.

Although he was not entirely certain of it at the time, Tupolev presumed that the list was intended to form the basis of a prison design team, a practice with which the NKVD had experimented in the past. Besides his own acquaintances, Tupolev added the names of other engineers who might be saved by his intervention, even though they were not from his bureau. Among these engineers was a young rocket scientist consigned to the bleak arctic gold mines at Kolyma. This engineer, Sergey Korolev, will figure prominently in a later chapter.

As a reward for his cooperation, Tupolev's wife was allowed to join him in his cell in Butyrki, a rare privilege. The usual alternative was to send the family to the GULAG. He was even allowed a drawing table in his cell to amuse himself.

Beria, "the father, intellect and guiding spirit of the sciences," had decided to exploit the talents of his prisoners in a series of special design bureaus, nicknamed *sharashki* by their inhabitants. Tupolev was assigned to TsKB-29-NKVD (Special NKVD Design Bureau-29) in Butyrki Prison.[4]

Tupolev had been spared, but Beria was not interested in fostering his former leading role in the aviation world. Rather than heading the bureau, Tupolev was simply named the head of one of four smaller design groups. To further humiliate Tupolev, the other group heads were markedly junior to him in experience. One of the other groups was led by his protégé Petlyakov, a very talented designer. But the other two were headed by junior engineers, Dmitriy L. Tomashevich and Vladimir M. Myasishchev, neither of whom had any substantial experience. The head of TsKB-29 was Col. Grigoriy Kutepov, a former NKVD guard whose expertise in aircraft design was limited to some work as an electrician in one of the Moscow aviation factories in the early 1930s.

Even if the NKVD did not recognize his authority, the younger designers most certainly did. Tupolev soon exhibited his old authoritarian manner in dealings with his younger colleagues. There was never any doubt who was really in charge of the design work. It was clearly a situation of master and students. Few of the younger designers rebelled at his insistence on being treated as the senior team leader—he was, by far, the most talented and experienced engineer in the bureau. Also important in maintaining their respect was Tupolev's willingness to accept the less pleasant responsibilities of leadership. Given the tendency of the NKVD to lace the teams with informers, Tupolev on occasion was faced with the problem of one of his team being denounced on various trumped-up charges. As one of his aides later recalled, Tupolev would fight the NKVD for his team members "like a lion."

The new head of the Red Air Force, a former rifle brigade commander named Aleksandr Loktionov, was not at all keen on Tupolev's ANT-42 heavy bomber idea. Loktionov wanted a smaller bomber, patterned on the German Ju 88, more suitable for close support of the Red Army. The new aircraft was code-named "103."[5] Stalin reportedly told Tupolev, "You are aware of the Ju 88. Now design something better!"

Conditions in the prison design bureau, while certainly better than in the forced labor camps, were still very difficult: barracks housing, daily walks in the prison compound to the sound of baying guard dogs, poor food, cold quarters, arbitrary rules, and impossible work schedules. Tupolev was assigned a number—0011—and his engineering drawings were so identified. By February 1940, models of Project 103 were completed, and in June the GKO ordered three prototypes constructed. The decision to proceed to the actual construction phase meant that Tupolev's team, code-named *Otdel* 103 (Unit 103), was transferred from Butyrki Prison to the Plant No. 156 aircraft factory on the outskirts of Moscow. The first flight of Tupolev's new twin-engined bomber took place in April 1941, a month before the outbreak of the war with Germany.

With the German invasion of the Soviet Union on 22 June 1941, the modernization of the Red Air Force took on a new urgency. Tupolev's earlier creations, the SB-2 light and TB-3 heavy bombers, suffered the same fate as the rest of the air force. The German Luftwaffe smashed many of the bomber units on the ground in the first days of the war and shot down the few aircraft that managed to get into the air. The Red Air Force, which had outnumbered the Luftwaffe by a substantial margin at the outbreak of the war, was blasted into oblivion. New aircraft, of better technical quality, were desperately needed.

Aircraft Plant No. 156 was too close to the German lines, well within range of German bombers. So, in the autumn of 1941, Tupolev and his small band of fellow prisoners were transferred to a new factory in the Urals industrial region at Omsk, called Plant No. 166. The conditions in Omsk were every bit as appalling as those in Butyrki Prison. The factory was crude and unfinished. Machinery and raw material were difficult to obtain. Critical engines were slow to arrive and often suffered from serious manufacturing flaws. But police control over the designers was relaxed, and a degree of normality returned.

It was nothing short of miraculous that an improved version of Project 103, now called the ANT-60, was completed in the summer of 1942. Tupolev had been forced to substitute wood and bakelite for aluminum in the new version, owing to severe shortages of advanced metals during the war. The program received little support and languished for years. When the final Red Air Force trials of the ANT-60 took place in April 1943, they proved a stunning success. The ultimate compliment was offered by one of the test pilots: "It flies like a fighter and can turn with the best of them!" The aircraft was far superior to any twin-engine bomber in Soviet or German service. The design was so good that in 1943 Tupolev was awarded the Stalin Prize and a cash bonus of about $25,000. Stalin reportedly apologized to Tupolev for his rough treatment in prison and, in honor of his accomplishment, ordered that the new plane be designated Tu-2, the *Tu* signifying Tupolev.

The prison experience left Tupolev embittered and cynical. He turned to that most traditional of Russian escapes, vodka. In 1937 he had been at the very pinnacle of the aviation industry in Moscow: head of a massive design bureau, enjoying every luxury the state could bestow upon him. In 1943 he lived near a grimy factory in a remote mill town in the Urals. His access to the corridors of power was circumscribed. After his downfall, a young fighter designer from the rival Polikarpov bureau, Aleksandr S. Yakovlev, gradually took his place. In 1940, Yakovlev took over as the deputy commissar of the aviation industry—the head of the industry's design bureaus—a role formerly belonging to Tupolev. There was no love lost between the two men. Yakovlev was a single-engine fighter designer who favored small tactical aircraft over the multiengine monstrosities of Tupolev's prewar bureau. Yakovlev shut down production of the Tupolev/Petlyakov TB-7/Pe-8 heavy bomber, arguing that the enormous resources squandered on multiengine heavy bombers were better spent on single-engine fighters and attack aircraft.

Although Yakovlev was no fan of the heavy bomber, Stalin began to think otherwise. In 1941 a handful of the Pe-8 heavy bombers were used on a bombing raid against Berlin. The raid by Soviet bombers did little damage but held enormous propaganda value for Stalin.[6]

In the summer of 1943 German heavy bombers raided the Soviet tank factory at Gorkiy, causing extensive damage. The Germans, like the Soviets, devoted very little attention to long-range strategic bombers during the war. But the Gorkiy raids reminded Stalin of the harm that could be done by these bombers. Stalin was also aware of the enormous resources that his Anglo-American allies were devoting to strategic bombers. Although Stalin no more favored diverting resources to heavy bombers than did Yakovlev, he foresaw their use after the war as a means to extend Soviet military power beyond Soviet borders.

Stalin made at least three requests to the United States for the best of its bombers, the Boeing B-29 Superfortress, through Lend-Lease.[7] All these requests were ignored. Stalin lowered his sights and made a formal request for 240 B-17 Flying Fortresses and 300 B-24 Liberators, far less capable aircraft than the B-29. These requests were also turned down, even as late as 1945.[8] Stalin had no recourse but to attempt to have a similar bomber built in the Soviet Union.

There were only two designers in the Soviet Union capable of creating such an aircraft, Andrey N. Tupolev and Sergey V. Ilyushin. A third, Tupolev's young protégé Petlyakov, had been killed in an aircraft accident in 1942. But Ilyushin's successes had mainly been in the area of single-engined attack aircraft, such as his legendary Il-2 *Shturmovik*. His larger bomber designs were far less successful. Soviet pilots loathed his Il-4 medium bomber, dubbing it the "flying coffin" due to its weak defensive armament and sluggish performance.

This left *Starets,* the "Old Man," Andrey Tupolev. In early 1944, with Tu-2 production well underway, Stalin ordered Tupolev to begin designing a four-engine bomber capable of reaching targets 3,000 km (1,850 miles) away with a 5,000 kg (5 ton) bomb load. The new aircraft was called Project 64 and was based in part on data obtained by Beria's spy network in the United States. At the same time, Arkadiy Shvetsov's Engine Design Bureau was ordered to start designing a new engine with a turbosupercharger capable of powering such an aircraft. This was no small feat; Germany's failure to deploy an effective heavy bomber was due primarily to its inability to design a lightweight engine with sufficient power, reliability, and fuel economy for this challenging role.

The Eastern Gift

On 29 July 1944 a B-29 from the U.S. Army Air Force's 771st Bombardment Squadron was hit by flak while attacking the massive Japanese Showa Steel Works near Anshan in occupied Manchuria. The B-29 had taken off from one of the new American bases in south-central China near Cheng-tu, which had been organized for attacks on the extensive Japanese war industries in occupied China and Korea. The bomber's pilot, Capt. Howard Jarrell, realized that the damaged aircraft would never make it back to friendly Chinese soil and set course for the USSR. The American crews had been briefed that, in the event of trouble, nearby Soviet bases could be a safe haven.[9]

Although the Soviet Union was allied with the United States and Britain in their war with Germany, the Soviet Union maintained strict neutrality in regards to Japan. The Japanese and Soviets had fought a series of savage border battles near the Manchurian and Chinese borders in 1938–39, and Stalin wanted to avoid a second front with the Japanese while fighting Nazi Germany. American aircrews landing at Soviet bases in the Far East after raids on Japanese targets were officially interned for the duration of the war, though in fact the Soviets often managed to arrange secret escapes.[10] Jarrell steered his damaged bomber toward nearby Vladivostok, the main Soviet naval base in the Pacific region. As it flew over Vladivostok harbor Soviet antiaircraft batteries began firing. The bomber was soon intercepted by Soviet Yak-9 fighter aircraft of the navy's Fifth Fleet Air Force. Jarrell ordered his gunners to hold their fire. Fortunately the Soviet squadron commander realized that the B-29 was not hostile and waved his pilots away from their attack. The Soviet pilot signaled the bomber to land at its base near Tavrichanka, a simple grass strip north of Vladivostok. After landing, the crew was interrogated and interned.

To the Soviet fighter pilots, the B-29 looked like something from the future. Their own fighters were almost primitive in comparison. Shortages of aluminum had forced Soviet manufacturers to make extensive use of plywood sheeting and fabric, so the B-29's silvery metallic finish was an impudent boast that the American bombers had nothing to fear from Japanese, or any other, fighters. The Soviet Yak-9s, on the other hand, wore a muted camouflage.

Soviet officers from nearby air bases were especially curious about the function of the many systems inside the B-29. It was like nothing they had ever seen before. Not only was the B-29 far larger than any aircraft in Soviet service, its technology was startlingly more advanced. The gun turrets were unmanned and lacked the normal Plexiglas dome. They were remotely controlled from central gunners' stations. The aircraft had many electronic systems that had no Soviet counterpart, including navigation radars.

In late August, Jarrell and his men were flown to Khabarovsk and would never see their aircraft again. Theirs was not the last B-29 to visit the Soviet Union, however. On 20 August 1944 a B-29 piloted by Richard McGlinn crashed in rugged terrain north of Khabarovsk. The crew parachuted and stumbled out of the woods days later. On 11 November a B-29 piloted by Weston Price was blown off course and landed at the main Vladivostok airfield. On 21 November another B-29 from Price's 794th Bombardment Squadron also encountered severe weather over its target in Japan and was forced to divert to Vladivostok. The Soviets now had three of the world's most advanced strategic bombers in their hands, and parts of a fourth were scraped up from the crash site.

On Stalin's orders the first of the three B-29s was flown to the central USSR by S. Reydel, one of the top Soviet Navy test pilots. This was followed by the other two aircraft later in the year. Tupolev was one of the first engineers allowed to inspect the huge bombers. He was called to Moscow for a special meeting with Stalin in 1944 and asked his opinion about how long it would take to produce a copy of the B-29. Tupolev said that he guessed it would take about three years. He pointed out that not only did the aircraft represent significantly more advanced aviation technology, but that many of the subsystems, such as its electronics and engines, were beyond contemporary Soviet capabilities.

Tupolev was allowed to continue work on the B-29 analog, the Project 64 bomber. But by 1946, with the aircraft only in the mock-up stage, Stalin began to lose patience. The head of the air force, Marshal A. A. Novikov, and the head of the aviation industry, A. I. Shakhurin, were subjected to special police investigation and imprisoned for failing to push the program along quickly enough.[11]

Stalin, over Tupolev's protests, ordered the Project 64 bomber to be scrapped and the American B-29 bomber copied instead. The new project began under the code name B-4, which signified "Bomber with 4 engines." Stalin ordered the bomber to be copied exactly, so that the resulting Soviet version would be as alike "as two peas in a pod."

The B-4 program was given the highest state authority. To give special bite to his order, Stalin ordered Lavrentiy Beria to supervise the B-4 program. Beria was given extensive powers to divert design bureaus and factories from existing assignments to this new, high-priority venture. By the time the program reached fruition, some sixty-four design bureaus and research institutes, as well as nine hundred factories, were involved in the development and production of the B-4. It soon became dubbed "the brick bomber" since it was assembled bit by bit, with all the various components coming from factories scattered across the breadth of the USSR.

The first of the three B-29s was taken apart to serve as a model for the copying effort. The second was used to train crews and to conduct actual flight trials. The third was kept in reserve "just in case." The components from the first aircraft were soon scattered across the Soviet Union. The massive turbocharged Wright Duplex Cyclone engines were sent to Arkadiy Shvetsov's Engine Design Bureau and the gun turret systems to I. I. Toropov's Experimental Design Bureau-134 in Tushino.

The decision to copy the first B-29 was not entirely fortunate. An early production machine (in fact the fifty-second off the line), it had a fair number of bugs. But Stalin had insisted that the aircraft be copied exactly and Beria took the order literally. The duplication effort sometimes took on ridiculous dimensions. There was a tunnel running from the forward pressurized cabin to the aft pressurized gunners' stations. The interior of the tunnel was painted, partly in zinc-chromate green antirust paint and partly in white, probably due to an oversight of the assembly teams at Boeing's Wichita plant. Tupolev ordered the paint scheme to be copied exactly.[12]

The program took on a new urgency in August 1945 when two American B-29 Superfortress bombers dropped the atomic bombs on Japan. No longer was the B-29 just another aircraft project; it suddenly became wrapped up in the entire Soviet atomic bomb effort. It was the only aircraft program that required Stalin's signature on key requirement and certification documents.[13]

The B-4 program required major technological innovations in the Soviet aviation industry. The original Boeing design made extensive use of lightweight aluminum as well as magnesium spars and internal components—techniques never before attempted in the Soviet Union. Although Soviet engine designers had attempted to develop turbochargers for aircraft engines, none approached the complexity or performance of the General Electric systems on the B-29's engines. Copying the engines was made easier by the fact that the Shvetsov Engine Design Bureau was familiar with Wright engines, having built the Wright Cyclone 18 radial engine for Soviet fighter planes under license.

Even seemingly minor issues proved difficult to resolve. Take, for example, the aircraft's aluminum skin. On the B-29, the panels were made out of one-sixteenth–inch aluminum sheet. Soviet machine tools and measuring instruments were calibrated in metric, not in the English measurements used in American industry. As a result, the one-sixteenth–inch skin translated out to 1.5875mm thick—not a realistic objective given the limitations of aluminum tooling technology of the time. The Tupolev team was concerned that if it adopted 1.5mm-thick panelling, it might not give the aircraft sufficient structural rigidity. On the other hand, if they used 1.6mm-thick skin, it would add considerably to the overall weight of the aircraft. Unbeknownst to Beria's watchdogs, Tupolev's team decided to use aluminum sheet varying from 0.8mm to 1.8mm—depending on where the panels were located. The same problem affected the thickness of the copper electrical wiring, not an insubstantial problem since there was nearly a mile of wiring in the aircraft. Inevitably, the overall weight of the aircraft rose when only thicker, metric wiring was available. Difficulties with the landing gear and large-diameter tires proved so severe that Tupolev was forced to request that Beria use his spy network in the United States to attempt to buy up those components from the war surplus market in 1946.

Stalin made only a few concessions on the matter of precise copying. Rather than adopting the American .50-caliber machine guns used on the B-29, he agreed to allow the designers to use standard Soviet machine guns. Tupolev, not wishing to incur Stalin's wrath, asked Beria whether the copying instructions extended to the matter of national markings. Beria thought it was a good joke, but still believed it prudent to ask Stalin. Stalin smirked and agreed that red stars could be substituted for the American insignia.

Series production of an initial test batch of twenty aircraft was assigned to the aviation plant in Voronezh, rebuilt shortly after the war. Components began flowing in by the autumn of 1946 and the first prototype was ready in the spring of 1947. The first test flight occurred in July 1947 with N. S. Rybko at the controls. In recognition of Tupolev's central role in the program, the B-4 bomber was dubbed the Tupolev Tu-4 bomber by the Soviet Air Force. Tupolev also managed to use the components from the disassembled B-29 to create a transport version, called the Tu-70.

Three of the new Tu-4 bombers and the Tu-70 transport were ready in time for the annual airshow over Tushino airbase on 3 August 1947, Soviet Aviation Day. The aircraft created a sensation. They came screaming over the crowd at a height of only six hundred feet, caused by a mistake by the air traffic controller who had the bomber flight at the same altitude as an approaching flight of other display aircraft. An enormous aerial collision was avoided, but the low altitude of the bomber flight made it all the more exciting to the crowd below.

The display was startling in a very different way to American and British observers. By 1947 the Cold War was well underway and Anglo-American military leaders were very concerned about the strategic capabilities of the Soviet Union. Attempts to recover the three B-29s from the USSR were to no avail. Until the 1947 air display there had been little reason for concern over the threat of Soviet bomber attack against either the United States or Britain. Although there had been reports from German prisoners returning from camps in the Soviet Union that work had begun on a copy of the B-29 Superfortress, and one such report appeared in Berlin newspapers in November 1946, U.S. Air Force leaders initially dismissed them all as preposterous. The magnitude of such an effort was deemed to be outside the capability of Soviet industry. American liaison officers stationed in the Soviet Union during World War II were familiar with Soviet bomber design. While newer medium bombers like the Tupolev Tu-2 were of good quality, the Soviet Union possessed only a handful of archaic Petlyakov Pe-8 heavy bombers. The Soviet Air Force's strategic air arm had been reorganized after the war, but its aircraft were pathetically ill-equipped to carry out long-range bombing missions of the type conducted by the U.S. Army Air Forces and the British Royal Air Force during the war.[14]

With the appearance of the first Tu-4 bombers, later dubbed Bull by NATO, a new assessment of the threat was clearly in order. The short-term threat was not as alarming as the long term. The 1947 Tushino display had included only three bombers and the Tu-70, a transport derived from the B-29. Considering that the Soviets were known to possess three interned aircraft, it seemed likely that the display included only prototypes. It was assumed that it would take some time before the new design could actually be produced in any quantity, and before the organizational and technical bugs were worked out.

Indeed, that was the case. The first twenty Tu-4 bombers were not completed until the end of 1947 and testing was not completed until the summer of 1948.[15] Even then, the bomber was plagued with teething problems. There were significant technical shortcomings in the performance of the early Tu-4, not altogether surprising in view of the revolutionary technology of the systems incorporated in the design. The powerplants were a major source of trouble, as were the extremely large variable-pitch propellers. The radar bombsights, code-named Kobalt, were not ready for the initial test flights and were not completed until 1948.[16] The advanced radio navigation system was unlike any system in Soviet service and took extensive practice by its new crews.[17]

Of the first five aircraft produced, three were involved in accidents during testing. The third Tu-4 prototype was lost when an engine fire and failure in the aircraft hydraulic systems led to a belly landing. The second aircraft suffered an engine breakup during full-power testing, but the pilot managed to land it safely. The fourth likewise suffered an engine breakup and, in the ensuing fire, the propeller was ripped off. Once again, pilot skill saved the aircraft. There were other near tragedies. The Soviet factories had problems with the Tu-4's deicing system and, during high-altitude testing, one aircraft was nearly lost due to severe ice buildup on the wings. Another particularly troublesome problem was the large Plexiglas cockpit panels and gunners' domes. The Soviet plastics industry was very backward and the material used in the Tu-4 had a tendency to turn opaque and scratch easily, making it very difficult for the pilots to get a clear view out of the aircraft.[18]

Some of these problems were rectified before series production began, but the Tu-4 remained a difficult aircraft for its crews. The first Tu-4 strategic bomber regiments didn't enter service until 1949, almost two years after the completion of the first test flights. By the time of the Korean War in 1950, the Tu-4 strategic bomber force was expanding rapidly. By 1953 it began to peak, with more than a thousand in service. The Long-Range Aviation force deployed three air armies and one independent bomber corps. One of the air armies was located in the Far East with six regiments and about 220 Tu-4 bombers. The other two air armies were located in the western Soviet Union, as was the independent bomber corps.[19]

The Tu-4 Threat

The Tu-4 by itself did not alarm U.S. military leaders. It did not have sufficient range to pose much of a threat to the United States using conventional bombs. At the time, the U.S. Air Force believed that the Soviet bomber force, without the atomic bomb, was capable of little more than harassment attacks against the United States.[20] What did cause concern was the combination of the new Tu-4 bomber and the new Soviet atomic bomb. American military leaders did not know if the Soviet bomb was small enough to be carried by the Tu-4, but they had to presume that it was. The Air Force chief of staff sounded the alarm, noting that there was "a desperate need for a vastly more effective air defense for the United States."

Until the 1949 Soviet atomic bomb explosion, air defense had received a very low priority in the United States. In 1948 the army had only two air defense gun battalions, although air force plans cited the need, even without the threat of the Soviet A-bomb, for as many as 325 battalions.[21] Air force assets were equally paltry, consisting of only four squadrons of F-61 Black Widow propeller-driven night fighters and nine squadrons of F-80 and six squadrons of F-84 jet day fighters. Air force efforts to win congressional approval for a network of early warning radars, code-named Supremacy, had floundered due to the perception that there was no short-term air threat. A temporary network called, appropriately enough, Lash-Up, was underway in its place. In the summer of 1949, as Kurchatov and his team were beginning to prepare the first Soviet A-bomb for testing, U.S. Air Force intelligence concluded that the first Soviet bomb would not be ready until 1952. As a result the emphasis was on the development of a deterrent force of B-36 strategic bombers and the slow construction of a partial radar screen that would be operational by 1953. The unexpected detonation of the first Soviet A-bomb quickly changed those priorities.

Even *with* the A-bomb the Soviet bomber threat was limited. Under normal operating conditions, the Tu-4 could reach targets 1,700 miles away from its base on a roundtrip flight.[22] The optimal location for bomber attacks on the United States would have been the upper Chukotskiy peninsula in the northern Pacific area, such as the airbase at Anadyr. This was the closest point from the Soviet Union to the United States. The problem was that the Tu-4 did not have adequate range to reach the United States from this base and return, even under optimum conditions. From Anadyr a Tu-4 could have reached central Alaska and portions of northwestern Canada, but not even as far as northern Washington state.

In order to strike at targets in the United States with the atomic bomb, there were basically two methods of attack that could have been used. The most obvious was a one-way mission. The Tu-4's maximum range with a five-ton A-bomb was 3,100 nautical miles. A Tu-4 taking off from Anadyr on a one-way mission could attack targets located in most of the western United States, an area contained in an arc ranging from San Diego to Lake Superior. The northeastern United States could not be reached on one-way flights, even those launched from bases in the northernmost portions of the European USSR, such as the Kola peninsula. One-way missions were a credible threat to U.S. Air Force planners who, in later years, planned one-way missions against the USSR for their B-47 medium bombers.

The more alarming alternative was aerial refueling. An aircraft consumes a disproportionate share of its fuel capacity during takeoff and the climb to cruising altitude. By refueling the Tu-4, its combat radius for a roundtrip attack on the United States could be extended to about 2,150 nautical miles and its one-way range could be increased to 4,000 nautical miles. A refueled Tu-4 taking off from Anadyr could reach only the northern tip of the contiguous United States, covering such cities as Seattle. This offered little advantage over unrefueled attack plans. If, however, the refueled aircraft was on a one-way mission, it could reach targets virtually throughout the entire United States. The only area not vulnerable to attack would be Florida and some of the southern states.

For many years it was a great mystery whether the Soviet Air Force ever managed to develop aerial refueling technology for the Tu-4 bomber. U.S. intelligence agencies concluded that aerial refueling was within the technological grasp of the USSR, but found no evidence that it existed.[23] The mystery was not solved until 1989, when the Soviet aviation magazine *Krylya Rodiny* (Wings of the Homeland) finally disclosed the first detailed information on the Soviet program.[24]

By 1948 the ambitious Tu-4 copying effort seemed well on its way. Realizing that the Tu-4 could not realistically cover most major targets in the United States, two different programs were initiated. Tupolev's team was assigned the task of modifying the Tu-4 to give it greater range by increasing internal fuel. Another design bureau, headed by V. S. Vakhmistrov, was assigned the task of developing a method of refueling bombers in the air.

Vakhmistrov had an interesting career in the aviation field. His specialty was one of the most outlandish and peculiar: designing parasite aircraft. In the 1930s Vakhmistrov had developed a system to allow a large bomber aircraft, like Tupolev's TB-3, to carry several smaller fighter aircraft. The idea behind carrying several fighters was to protect the bomber. The Soviet fighters of the day lacked the range to follow the big TB-3 all the way to its target. By carrying the fighters most of the way, they could be launched when enemy fighters were encountered. Vakhmistrov actually managed to design and test such contraptions, but they had little more than propaganda value. Only one of these parasite combinations, called *Zveno,* was ever used in combat. During the early years of the war, the Red Air Force used Zveno combinations to attack vital targets located too far behind German lines for attack with conventional aircraft. The massive TB-3 bomber would carry aloft a pair of small Polikarpov I-16 fighters, releasing them some distance from the target. The fighters would swoop in, bomb the target, and return to the mother ship. It was a hair-raising process for all involved—more an act of desperation than a practical technology.

Vakhmistrov's solution to the refueling problem was similar to the British method of the time.[25] The tanker aircraft, a converted Tu-4 bomber, would spool out a fuel line from one wing tip. The line was stabilized by a small parachute. The normal Tu-4 was modified to include a fuel receptacle and small hook on its left wingtip. The pilot of the receiving aircraft would maneuver his bomber behind the tanker and catch the fuel line with his wingtip hook. Once secure, the fuel line was winched into the fuel receptacle and refueling could begin.

The first test of this contraption took place on 16 June 1949. It was deemed too risky for the new and expensive Tu-4 bombers, so two smaller Tu-2 bombers were substituted. Two of the most experienced Soviet test pilots, Amet-khan Sultan and Igor Shelest, took the controls of the experimental aircraft. The system required substantial improvements, with test pilot and engineer Viktor Vasyanin playing a prominent role. The refueling system eventually proved practical for the Tu-4 and some ten test flights were conducted. A portion of the Tu-4 fleet was suitably modified to use the system.

Even with the refueling system in place, the capability of the Tu-4 bomber force was very limited. The first limitation was the size of the Soviet atomic arsenal. Throughout the early 1950s it was quite small. Following the successful detonation of the first atomic bomb in 1949, the First Directorate set up a state commission under Pavel Zernov to begin the construction of the first five series-production bombs. These were apparently completed in 1950. Later that year they decided to test one of the series-manufactured bombs. It failed to detonate.[26] Work to correct the bomb defects took time. Furthermore, the nuclear reactors at Kyshtym were being diverted to work on the secret new thermonuclear bomb. As a result, the Soviet nuclear stockpile in the early 1950s was quite small, on the order of 20–30 bombs.[27]

The marginal range of the Tu-4 forced the Strategic Aviation Force to use very remote bases. The airbases in the northern Chukotskiy area were in the Arctic, with severe weather conditions for much of the year. Rail lines to support the base with fuel and equipment were nearly nonexistent. Sustained tanker operations to support a surprise attack would have been difficult to conduct under these conditions.

As a result, Soviet strategic bombers were not permanently stationed in the Arctic regions. Their main operating bases were located in central Russia and Kazakhstan, where the temperate weather conditions and ground support facilities permitted a more active training routine. In the event of war, selected aircraft would have been shifted forward to the Arctic bases to carry out their missions.

Although *glasnost* has brought out much new detail on the early Soviet technology for nuclear war with the United States, we still lack a clear picture of the human element of the war machine. Strategic bombing operations require well-trained crews and an elaborate infrastructure to coordinate operations. So far, little has been declassified by the Soviets on such issues as the extent of Soviet aircrew training for missions against the United States. Given the poor record of the Soviet long-range force in World War II, one is inclined to doubt that the Tu-4 air armies became capable intercontinental bombers in the few short years after 1949, when nuclear attacks became technically feasible. A more optimistic view of Soviet capabilities was offered by the CIA in 1953:

> There can be little doubt that Soviet air crews would have the ability to navigate with sufficient accuracy to reach the major population and industrial centers of the United States, and to achieve bombing accuracy, by either visual or radar means, generally within the effective [blast] radius of the [atomic] weapons available.[28]

American strategic intelligence after World War II varied widely in its estimates of Soviet strength. The U.S. intelligence agencies were almost totally ineffective in placing agents into the Soviet Union and, until the advent of technical intelligence gathering systems in the late 1950s and early 1960s, the United States was forced to rely on educated guesswork with little hard evidence. Immediately after the war, the intelligence groups tended to dismiss the Soviet Union as hopelessly backward. Some predicted it would take the Soviet Union twenty years to develop an atomic bomb. Others argued that copying the B-29 bomber was outside the capabilities of the Soviet aviation industries. The first Soviet atomic bomb and the first flights of the Tu-4 were a shock to U.S. analysts, who thereafter tended to overestimate Soviet strategic capabilities.

In hindsight, the 1953 CIA assessment quoted above appears to be overly optimistic about Soviet capabilities. A Soviet bomber attack on the United States in 1953 or 1954 would have been an extremely chancy proposition. So few bombs were available that the attack force would have been quite small. A significant portion of the force, probably 20 percent, would fail to reach its objectives due to mechanical and other problems. This fraction would have been much higher in the event of severe weather conditions over the Arctic or over northern Canada. Surviving aircraft would have faced growing air opposition from U.S. Air Force air defense squadrons, and this would have caused the loss of additional aircraft.[29] The 1949 Soviet atomic bomb detonation had led to a crash U.S. air defense program that was beginning to take shape by the summer of 1954. There were 800 of the new F-86D Sabre interceptors, 300 F-94C Starfire interceptors, and almost 100 of the new F-89D Scorpion missile-armed interceptors. The first five army Nike antibomber missile battalions had been installed and over fifty more would be added during the next three years.[30] Finally, the Pinetree radar line was in place.

The Tu-4's most serious shortcoming was the time it would take to traverse Alaska or Canada to reach targets in the United States. Depending on its routes, the Tu-4 bomber would have cruised for more than ten hours over Canada and the United States to reach its targets, greatly increasing the probability of interception by U.S. units. Unlike the U.S. Air Force, which had extensive experience in electronic warfare to confuse enemy radars, the Soviets were novices with no practical experience. It is conceivable that ten to fifteen Soviet bombers could have leaked through American defenses in 1954 and delivered atomic bombs against American cities and military bases, but only under the most optimistic of circumstances. But the consequences of such an attempt no doubt prevented Stalin from seriously considering such an attack.

In 1953 the U.S. Air Force's Strategic Air Command (SAC) had significantly fewer strategic bombers than the Soviet Air Force, about 760 vs. 1,000.[31] But 185 of these were B-36 bombers, able to hit targets nearly anywhere in the Soviet Union from bases in the United States. Furthermore, SAC did not share the basing problem suffered by Soviet strategic aviation—it had bases in Europe and the Pacific that put even medium-range bombers within striking distance of many Soviet targets. The most critical difference was in the nuclear arsenal. In 1953 the United States had about 1,350 nuclear bombs, compared to about 20–30 Soviet bombs.[32] An attack on the United States, as destructive as it might have been, would undoubtedly have resulted in a retaliatory strike of unimaginable horror on the USSR.

Building a Better Bomber

The Tu-4 bomber was an essential step in the creation of the Soviet strategic forces. But the Soviet Union clearly had a great deal of catching up to do if it expected to reach nuclear parity with the United States. The Tu-4 first flew in 1947, a year after the much superior American B-36 heavy bomber.

Immediately after series production of the Tu-4 began in 1947, Andrey Tupolev and his design bureau shifted their attention to extending the aircraft's range. Their first attempt, the Tu-80 bomber, was uninspiring. The Tu-80 added about 15 percent more fuel than the normal Tu-4, which was not a significant enough improvement to warrant manufacture. It first flew in December 1949. It was followed by a far larger and more ambitious evolution of the Tu-4 design, called the Tu-85. The Tu-85 employed a new generation of piston engines and, more importantly, incorporated massive new fuel cells that gave it much greater range than the Tu-4. Tupolev was so enamored with the new design that he and his design team pushed it forward with great vigor. The original plans had called for test flights to begin in 1951, but the first prototype flew in early 1950. The design offered an effective unrefueled combat radius of 3,500 miles, sufficient to reach most industrial cities in the northern United States. With refueling the Tu-85 could have reached virtually all of the United States and returned to base. Several Tu-85 prototypes were under construction, but in 1951, the project was abruptly terminated.

The reason for the cancellation had to do with an air war far distant from Andrey Tupolev's design offices in Moscow. In 1950, following the repulse of the North Korean invasion of South Korea, Stalin consented to the dispatch of Soviet fighter pilots to the war zone. Stalin had been pressured by his Chinese comrade, Mao Zedong, to contribute to the defense of North Korea against the combined U.N. forces headed by the United States. Stalin was not at all anxious to get involved in a direct confrontation with the United States. The last thing he wanted to do was to provoke the United States into a war with the Soviet Union, especially considering the sizeable American advantage in strategic nuclear arms. The contribution of new jet fighter aircraft and pilots seemed like a modest risk, since the pilots were restricted to flying defensive missions over territory held by North Korean and Chinese troops. In fact, while it was long known that Soviet "volunteer" pilots had flown during the Korean War, it wasn't until 1989 that the Soviets removed the subject from the list of state secrets and began revealing the full extent of their participation in the war.[33]

Stalin authorized the shipment of the latest Soviet jet fighter to Korea, the legendary MiG-15. The MiG-15 had been designed specifically as an antibomber interceptor capable of destroying the best of the U.S. Strategic Air Command's heavy bombers. Over Korea it faced older Boeing B-29 bombers and not the latest types, like the B-36. Large-scale battles with B-29 formations took place in April and May 1951. On Bloody Thursday, 12 April 1951, several of the big American bombers fell to the guns of Soviet MiG-15 pilots. Later in the year the threat posed by the MiG-15 proved so great that B-29s were withdrawn from daylight bombing missions and restricted to night attacks.

The lessons of Bloody Thursday were not lost on the Soviet Air Force. The B-29s had been escorted by American jet fighters, which managed to minimize the loss of bombers. Had no American escort fighters been present, the slaughter of the B-29 bombers would have been even greater. In the event of strategic bomber operations against the United States, there would be no escort fighters. The American bombers had not managed to shoot down a single Soviet jet fighter over Korea, a failure that had obvious implications for any intended missions by Soviet bombers against the American air defense network.[34] The experience of Bloody Thursday made it very clear that the slow bombers of the Tu-4/B-29 generation were no match for jet interceptors.

The Tu-85 had many advantages over the Tu-4, but its speed was not much greater. It would be nearly as vulnerable to jet interceptors as the Tu-4. What was needed was a modern jet-powered bomber. With some alarm, Beria's intelligence agents in the United States began reporting that the Americans were working on just such an airplane. This was soon confirmed in international aviation journals such as *Interavia*. It was the Boeing B-52 Stratofortress.

The B-52 rivalled the jet fighters in speed, and its normal flight regime, high in the stratosphere, well above the altitudes normally used by the B-29 and Tu-4, made it all the more difficult to intercept.

In the spring of 1951 Andrey Tupolev was called into a meeting of the Communist party Central Committee chaired by Stalin himself. Stalin outlined what was known about the American bomber and asked if Tupolev could design a long-range strategic bomber powered by jet engines. Tupolev answered quite firmly that he could not. Stalin sharply pointed out that Tupolev was already working on a jet-powered medium bomber, the Tu-16, for attacking American and British bomber bases in Europe. Tupolev responded that jet engine technology in the Soviet Union was not mature enough to produce an engine with fuel efficiency and power suitable for a strategic bomber able to reach the United States. He proposed a turboprop bomber instead, which his bureau was already working on. Stalin was furious. The American program had been underway for two years and Tupolev, the premier bomber designer, claimed that a Soviet counterpart was impossible!

The prison term in the GULAG had hardened Tupolev. He was not as easily bullied into projects, realizing full well that unsuccessful aircraft would only lead to recriminations later. He suspected that the worst Stalin would do to him was to send him back to the GULAG. But he doubted that Stalin would even do that. The Tu-4 program and its evolutionary improvements had given Tupolev and his team unmatched experience in the design of heavy bombers. No other Soviet design bureau was prepared to undertake such an effort, not even his competitor, Ilyushin.

Stalin was not about to be denied, however. Rebuffed by Tupolev, yet not wishing to again deprive the Soviet Union of the best of its bomber designers, Stalin decided his only recourse was to give the jet design program to another team. But whose? The Ilyushin team had been beaten by Tupolev's in the design of the new jet-powered medium bomber. And Ilyushin was likely to voice the same objections as Tupolev. Stalin instead turned to a highly unlikely candidate: Vladimir M. Myasishchev, Tupolev's son-in-law.

Myasishchev had not yet emerged from the bush leagues of Soviet aircraft designers, although he had worked under Tupolev in the 1930s and had been in the same NKVD special prison as Tupolev during the war years. Myasishchev graduated to leading his own design teams, working mainly on medium bombers. None of his designs offered a radical enough break from existing designs to warrant production. In the postwar years he had worked on an improved B-29 equivalent, called the DVB-202 and DVB-302, which did not progress beyond paper studies. He was one of the first Soviet designers to work on a conceptual long-range jet bomber, the RB-17, which would have used captured German jet engines had it actually been built. Like so many of his other projects, it never left the drawing board. Myasishchev too often made rosy-eyed assessments of upcoming propulsion technology and designed his aircraft around new powerplants that were not yet proven. His lack of realism proved to be a fatal flaw in most of his designs.

It might seem peculiar for Stalin to have placed so much faith in such a comparatively young designer with so few real accomplishments. Yet in the postwar years some of the other obscure designers who had been in the shadows during the war, Artem Mikoyan and Pavel Sukhoi, for example, began to emerge as the new stars of Soviet aviation design, outshining such wartime heroes as Yakovlev and Semen A. Lavochkin. Stalin no doubt saw parallels between Myasishchev and Tupolev, hoping to replace the crusty and obstinate older designer with a younger, more pliable, and more adventurous new designer.

Myasishchev was given permission to start his own design bureau in March 1951, and he began recruiting some of the cream of young aviation engineers at the Moscow Aviation Institute, from the legendary TsAGI research institute and from friends from his prison days in TsKB-29. Myasishchev soon attracted more than fifteen hundred engineers, mostly former design engineers languishing as instructors or researchers in the aviation institutes. Many wished to return to the more exciting world of real aircraft design and readily agreed to join the new team. The design bureau set up shop in the Fili aviation plant, a legendary facility in Soviet aircraft history. The head of the factory was S. M. Leshchenko, the former head engineer of the defunct Petlyakov bomber design bureau and an old colleague of Myasishchev.

The new jet bomber went by the name of SDB 103M (Strategic Bomber 103-Myasishchev). As design work progressed, Myasishchev quickly realized why Tupolev had refused the assignment. The air force requirement called for the delivery of a five-ton bomb load with a maximum range of 9,950 miles. Myasishchev consulted with the engine designer, Aleksandr Mikulin, and came to the conclusion that it might be possible using eight of Mikulin's AM-3 turbojet engines. But Mikulin's engines were massive and thirsty. Rough calculations indicated that such an aircraft would weigh a whopping 250 tons. There was no way that such an aircraft could be designed within the given timeframe. Myasishchev and his team settled on a far less radical design employing only four AM-3 engines. What the design lacked in power would have to be made up in aerodynamic excellence.

Myasishchev's team already had a head start in that direction. In the 1940s Myasishchev had taught at the Moscow Aviation Institute and had been closely associated with the TsAGI research institute. Under his tutelage students had worked on a number of advanced swept-wing designs. He had become familiar with current developments in jet engine technology by assisting on the Tu-4LL project, a flying laboratory used to test new engines like the

AM-3 turbojet. While working with the Tupolev bureau on the design of the new Tu-16 medium jet bomber, TsAGI aerodynamic engineers had developed a particularly elegant and streamlined design. Unlike American jet bombers of the time, which had their engines suspended from pylons under the wings, the TsAGI design placed the engines close to the fuselage, blending them into the wings.

The design process went quickly and the final drawings went to the experimental assembly facility at Fili in May 1952. Stalin approved the design, although there was marked skepticism on the part of many aircraft designers over whether it would meet its projected requirements. As a result, in 1952 Tupolev was given permission to begin development of a turboprop bomber to serve as a backup in the event that the 103M failed to meet expectations.

The first 103M prototype was completed in January 1953, barely twenty-two months after the start of the program. Although well-known test pilot Mark Gallay had normally flown earlier Myasishchev designs, the new bureau had a new chief test pilot, Fedor Opadchiy. Opadchiy took the 103M up for the first time on 20 January 1953. The flight proceeded smoothly and, on landing, Opadchiy remarked that it had performed well—except for a tendency to slide laterally. Some thirty test flights followed. As Tupolev had predicted, the aircraft's range was well below the air force requirements. In fact, its maximum range was barely half the requirement, only 5,600 miles. Such a range made it incapable of flying a two-way mission to the United States unless it was refueled in flight. And, since the requirement had called for a 9,500-mile range, no thought had been given to equipping it with aerial refueling equipment.

In spite of its shortcomings, the 103M was placed into production at the Fili plant, although on a small scale. It was designated the M-4 *Molot* (Hammer) in Soviet Air Force service. If it didn't fulfill the requirement to bomb America, at least it could serve in good stead for propaganda. The prototype flew over Red Square during the 1954 May Day parade, giving the U.S. Air Force a good scare. American intelligence analysts were asked to determine how long it would be before the M-4, code-named Bison by NATO, would enter production. They concluded four years, or roughly 1956.[35] They were in for another shock in 1955. Western military attachés in Moscow were invited to the annual Aviation Day air show at the Tushino airbase in the Moscow suburbs on 13 July 1955. A wave of ten M-4 Molots passed over head, followed later by a second wave of nine aircraft and a third wave of nine aircraft. This suggested that the Soviets might have more than two dozen of the bombers already in service, indicating it had reached quantity production.

As some of the more skeptical Western attachés suspected at the time, it had all been a ruse. In fact, only ten aircraft had been ready for the air show

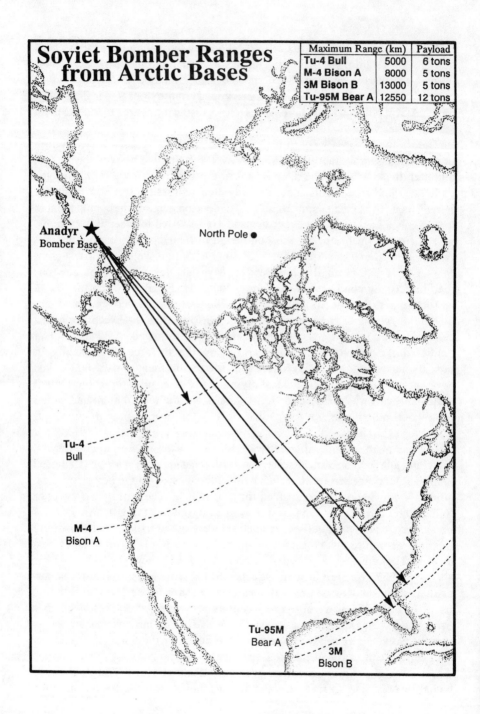

Soviet Bomber Ranges from Arctic Bases

Maximum Range (km)		Payload
Tu-4 Bull	5000	6 tons
M-4 Bison A	8000	5 tons
3M Bison B	13000	5 tons
Tu-95M Bear A	12550	12 tons

Anadyr
Bomber Base

North Pole ●

Tu-4
Bull

M-4
Bison A

Tu-95M
Bear A

3M
Bison B

and they had simply been flown around in circles to create the illusion of greater numbers.

The M-4 triggered a significant controversy in the U.S. intelligence community. The U.S. Air Force believed that the M-4 would form the basis for a new Soviet strategic strike force. The CIA estimated that by 1960 the Soviet Strategic Aviation Force would possess 400–600 heavy bombers, of which a portion would serve as dual role tankers/bombers. The air force strongly disagreed, saying that the 1960 force would be 400–600 bombers, plus an additional 300–350 bomber aircraft tasked for the midair refueling role.[36]

In fact, there was widespread disenchantment with the M-4. The Myasishchev bureau was instructed to redesign the aircraft to get greater range from it. In 1954 it began a new bomber project, called the 201M, to improve its performance. The Mikulin AM-3 engines were deleted and four new VD-7 engines from the V. Dobrynin design bureau were substituted. The 201M made its maiden flight in March 1956 with Mark Gallay back at the controls. The new version, called the M-4A in Soviet Air Force service, proved to be more satisfactory than the existing M-4. The flights went so smoothly that the 201M prototype flew over the 1956 May Day parade. The new engines extended the plane's range to 8,000 miles. It was also the first variant of the bomber capable of aerial refueling. Its range was still short of the government requirement, but the bomber was capable of reaching portions of the United States and returning to base even without refueling. Production was very slow and was eventually cancelled. By 1960, instead of having hundreds of strategic jet bombers, the Soviets had only fifty-six.[37]

The Bear Backup

By 1952 it was becoming obvious that Myasishchev's attempt to develop a satisfactory intercontinental bomber was likely to come up short. As a result, Stalin relented and authorized the further development of a turboprop intercontinental bomber project that spring.

In fact, Tupolev's bureau had taken initial steps to consider such a bomber as early as 1950, realizing that the existing piston engines and conventional turbojets would not give the fuel economy necessary to reach targets in the United States except on one-way missions. The turboprop option was a new one in bomber design. Such a powerplant uses a jet engine at its core, but derives its thrust from a conventional propeller, driven off the rotational energy of the jet's spinning turbine blades. Soviet work on the turboprop concept was in fact an outgrowth of German technology.

Towards the end of World War II German aircraft engineers were working on a number of projects to develop a bomber capable of reaching the United States. One of these teams, under an Austrian engineer, Ferdinand Brandner, was working with the Junkers firm. As in the case of German engineers working on the uranium isotope separation program, many German aviation engineers ended up in prisoner-of-war camps or forced labor camps in the Soviet Union. In 1948, to better utilize the talents of these engineers, an effort was undertaken to sort through the camps looking for engineers with specific skills. German aircraft engine designers were recruited for a new aviation engine project headed by Nikolay Kuznetsov, based in Kuibyshev in the Urals industrial belt.

In all, some eight hundred German and Austrian engineers were located and sent to Kuibyshev. The incentive was quite simple. If the Germans succeeded in developing a turboprop engine with 6,000 shaft horsepower, they would be returned home. Brandner was appointed head of the design team and the Germans set off to build the turboprop engine. Little did they realize it, but the effort was a competitive one, with a Soviet team under Vladimir Ya. Klimov developing a similar engine at its lab in Leningrad. The German engine was completed and successfully tested in the summer of 1950.

The completion of the NK-6 turboprop was duly reported to Stalin, and the first group of German engineers was allowed to depart from Kuibyshev. But the Tupolev design bureau, on learning of the details of the engine, inquired whether a 12,000 shaft horsepower engine could be designed for a planned strategic bomber. Work on this project started in the late summer of 1950 and a test model of the Kuznetsov engine, called the NK-12, was ready by 1951.

Design of the bomber itself had proved much more straightforward. Called the Tu-95, the new aircraft was a further elaboration on the Tu-85 bomber. The most significant change was the wing layout. The Tu-85 had used fairly conventional straight wing and tail surfaces. By 1950, when the Tu-95 design began, the Tupolev bureau had developed enough experience in sweptwing design to add this feature to the new aircraft. The first airframe was finished in 1952 and was fitted with the original NK-6 turboprops. The first flight, on 11 November 1952, demonstrated that they were not powerful enough for an intercontinental bomber. Substantially more power was needed, so the Tu-95 returned to the drawing board.

The first NK-12s were mounted on a Tu-4 testbed for trials. Problems with the new propellers—a unique eight-bladed, contra-rotating pair—would soon have tragic consequences. The Tu-4, called the Tu-4LL (LL being the Russian acronym for "flying laboratory"), had engaged in only a short series of tests before one of the propellers broke up, hurling a huge blade into the cockpit and killing the test pilot, A. D. Perelyet. The first satisfactory combination of NK-12 engines and propellers was not ready until 1954. Test flights of the Tu-95 with the NK-12 engines, called the Tu-95M, took place in late 1954.

The Soviets had hoped to demonstrate the first Tu-95Ms at the 1955 May Day parade, but the engines were not deemed ready. The first public display came in July 1955, when seven appeared at Tushino as part of the annual Aviation Day airshow.

If American observers were impressed by the sleek new M-4 Molot, the same could not be said for the Tu-95M, christened Bear by NATO. The Bear appeared nearly a decade after the U.S. Air Force's last propeller-driven bomber, the B-36. Admittedly, the Tu-95 used more efficient turboprop engines. But the U.S. Air Force had considered the turboprop when designing its new strategic bomber, the B-52, and had rejected it.[38] Most air force analysts assumed that the Tu-95 was a low-risk backup for the more advanced Bison, which in fact was the case. But the U.S. Air Force, not yet aware of the substantial difficulties facing the M-4 bomber, presumed that it represented the future of the Soviet strategic forces.

The Soviets themselves were not entirely happy with the Tu-95M when it was accepted for bomber service in 1956. The early aircraft proved nearly as troublesome as the M-4, due mainly to the overstressed engines. Once the bugs were worked out by the late 1950s, the Soviet Air Force came to appreciate the incredible range offered by the new bomber. But even if its range was impressive, its speed was not. The Tu-95M's top speed was quite remarkable for a propeller-driven bomber, more than 500 miles per hour. But for maximum endurance, such as during an attack on the United States, it would have to fly at more economical cruising speeds. By the late 1950s American air defense interceptors were already supersonic. Not only were they much faster than the Tu-95M, but they were armed with missiles.

Back in 1951, when Soviet MiG-15 fighters tore up American B-29 bomber formations over Korea, the bomber crews had some success defending themselves against the fighters using their machine-gun turrets. The advent of missiles meant that bombers could no longer protect themselves in the event they were intercepted by fighters while carrying out their mission. Even the early American missile types, such as the Falcon, could hit the bombers from ranges outside the defensive armament of the Tu-95M Bear bomber. Equally alarming, the U.S. Army had begun fielding surface-launched missiles to act as a final layer of defense against bombers surviving the fighter onslaught. These missiles, including the Nike-Ajax and Nike-Hercules, could strike at bombers from dozens of miles away from their intended targets.

In spite of its puny size and troubled equipment, the Soviet strategic bomber force had an impact on the balance of power out of all proportion to its actual resources. The United States had no idea there were so few bombers. The U.S. Air Force, seeing the Soviet bombers on public display, presumed that the Soviets would follow the American path to strategic power and base their nuclear delivery force on long-range bombers. This created the famous "bomber gap," which led the U.S. Air Force to demand an even larger Strategic Air Command. The 1954 CIA National Intelligence Estimate predicted that by 1957, there would be five hundred Bear bombers.[39]

The possibility that the Soviets might launch a surprise attack with their bomber force prompted the United States to erect an elaborate and expensive network of radars, interceptors, and missiles to protect American cities and bases from bomber attack. The threat of bomber attack was exaggerated by inaccurate American intelligence estimates.[40] In the mid 1950s, as Myasishchev was struggling with the flawed M-4 and Tupolev with the outdated Tu-95, the North American Air Defense Command was erecting a network of long-range radars, the DEW (Distant Early Warning) line, across Canada and the United States, numerous fighter squadrons were deployed to meet any incoming Soviet bomber, and many cities were ringed with Nike-Hercules, Nike-Ajax, and Bomarc missiles. The air defense network erected by the United States in the 1950s to keep out Andrey Tupolev's bombers cost tens of billions of dollars.

It was only in the late 1950s that American military leaders learned just how limited the Soviet bomber threat really was. Lacking human intelligence sources on the ground, the United States turned to aerial reconnaissance. The first attempt—Project Moby Dick—using balloons, was unsuccessful.[41] But, beginning in 1956, the CIA began to conduct overflights of key Soviet bases using the new U-2 spy-plane. It quickly became evident that the Soviet bomber force was far smaller than predicted. The 1957 National Intelligence Estimate placed the Soviet heavy bomber force at 90 to 150, instead of the 500 predicted earlier.[42] But so strong was the presumption that the Soviets would follow the American pattern of strategic forces that the intelligence forecasts continued to speak of a large bomber force in the immediate future. The 1957 National Intelligence Estimate predicted 400 to 600 heavy bombers by 1960.

All the while, unknown to and largely unobserved by the Americans, the Soviets were racing ahead with another nuclear delivery system—the ballistic missile.

Chapter 4

Building a Better Bomb

WITH THE FIRST Lightning atomic bomb test a success in 1949, Operation Borodino turned in the direction of perfecting nuclear devices as weapons of war. Tatyana, the first Soviet A-bomb, was a cumbersome affair, not suitable as an actual weapon. Real bombs needed to be compact enough to fit into the long slender bomb bays of Tupolev's new Tu-4 "Brick Bomber." Beyond tinkering with the first bomb design, Kurchatov and his team continued to press ahead to increase the bomb's power. This took two forms. On the one hand, theoretical calculations had shown that a bomb using uranium could be built which would have considerably more explosive power than a plutonium bomb. On the other hand, theoretical physicists like Zeldovich had suggested that new approaches to bomb design, relying on the energy potential of nuclear fusion rather than nuclear fission, would create bombs that would dwarf Tatyana in destructive power.

Following the First Lightning test explosion in 1949, Stalin ordered the first series of nuclear weapons into production. Pavel Zernov, the administrative head of the secret bomb design center at Arzamas-16, was appointed head of the state commission responsible for the program. Only five bombs were built during the initial production run because of the continued shortage of plutonium. Of course there was still the need to divert a substantial portion of the production from the boilers at Kyshtym to support Kurchatov's bomb design experiments.

The first five serial-production atomic bombs, like the prototype, were implosion bombs. There were no fundamental design changes; rather the focus was on ways to reduce the weight and bulk of the bomb. In 1950, with production under way, Beria decided that the new bomb designs should be subjected to a test. One of the new bombs was transferred to the Poligon at Semipalatinsk. It was placed on a tower, just like the First Lightning test.

Zernov, Beria at his side, awaited anxiously in the bunker. He knew what fate awaited him if he failed. The timing sequence began again. *"Desyat, devyat, vosem, sem, shest, pyat, chetyre, tri, dva, raz, START!"*

Nothing happened. The bomb had fizzled.[1]

Zernov had a heart attack on the spot. It was not fatal and, strangely enough, may have saved his life. Beria's usual fee for failure was the death penalty. For whatever reason, Beria allowed a cardiologist into the top secret testing zone to administer to Zernov. Not only was Zernov spared, but he was allowed to continue as the chief administrator of Arzamas-16. Perhaps Beria was satisified that Zernov's heart attack was adequate demonstration of the fear in which he was held by his subordinates.

The design team at Arzamas-16 set about the task of determining why the bomb had failed to detonate and to this day the cause remains a Soviet state secret. But the Arzamas-16 team managed to clear up the problems and "Second Lightning" was scheduled for 24 September 1951. To the relief of the hapless Zernov, the bomb detonated.

The Uranium Problem

In the rush to build their first atomic bomb, Kurchatov's team had taken many shortcuts. The greatest shortcut was the 1946 decision to deemphasize the processing of weapons-grade uranium in favor of the simpler and less costly approach of relying on plutonium alone. This was an acceptable short-term solution, but it placed too many limitations on future bomb design. Uranium has a number of advantages over plutonium in bomb construction. Besides its suitability for more varied bomb designs, both gun and implosion types, uranium's different properties make it possible to design atomic bombs with far greater explosive yields than is possible with plutonium. The first bomb had a yield of about 15 kilotons.[2] Given the technology of the period, it was possible to improve a plutonium implosion bomb to the point where the plutonium would be consumed efficiently enough to yield an explosion on the order of 70 kilotons. But for the truly destructive potential of the fission bomb to be realized, uranium U-235 would be needed. Uranium fission bombs held the potential for an explosion on the order of 750–1,000 kilotons.

Kurchatov had included a uranium processing project as part of Operation Borodino from the outset. But the technological hurdles were formidable. Three separate teams had been working on the problem since 1943: Lev Artsimovich's team on electromagnetic separation technology; Isaak Kikoin on gaseous diffusion; and Anatoliy Aleksandrov on thermal diffusion technologies. The U.S. program had attempted all three methods as well. The electromagnetic separation plant was used to provide uranium for the first bomb, but after the war it was diverted from uranium production due to the enormous cost.[3] The thermal diffusion method was not successful in producing weapons-grade uranium, but it did enrich U-238 to a point where it could increase the efficiency of the electromagnetic separation plant. Of the three methods used by the United States, the gaseous diffusion process proved to be the most effective and was the only technique in use after the war. But it was neither a simple nor a cheap approach. The gaseous diffusion plant at Oak Ridge, Tennessee, code-named K-25, was a half mile long and covered forty acres of floor space. It was also the most advanced automated industrial plant in the world at the time and the most expensive single element in the U.S. atomic bomb program.[4]

Kurchatov learned of the American attitude toward the separation technologies from the Smyth report, which was published in 1945.[5] In addition, Kurchatov presumably verified this information using espionage material collected by Beria's spies in the United States and Canada. All three approaches were undertaken in the Soviet Union after the war, but priority was given to the gaseous diffusion process.

The uranium separation problem was organized as a competitive effort between the Soviet teams at Laboratory No. 2 and the German teams located at the Black Sea labs in Agudzeri and Sinop. The parallel efforts were undertaken in part to keep the Germans isolated from the top-secret work going on in Moscow, as well as to best take advantage of the skills of both groups. The groups did not work entirely in isolation from one another, however. When the Germans developed a particularly successful technique, or when the skills of a particular German scientist were needed, they would be brought to Moscow to participate in the work there. In some cases, the Soviets found it easier to work with leading German scientists than the Germans found working among themselves. For example, when Professor Thiessen and Max Steenbeck arrived at Manfred von Ardenne's lab at Sinop, they refused to be subordinated to his group, forcing the Soviets to set up separate design teams.

Based on the evidence from the United States regarding the utility of the gaseous diffusion method, as well as some limited successes by Kikoin's Soviet team in Moscow and Thiessen's German team at Object A in Sinop, the Soviets decided to begin constructing a massive uranium separation plant in the fall of 1947.[6]

The main problem in separating U-235 from U-238 is that their only significant difference is a minute difference in weight. These isotopes cannot be chemically separated. In a gaseous diffusion system, the uranium metal is first chemically converted into a gas—uranium hexafluoride. The gas is then passed into a tank. The tank walls are lined with a thin, slightly porous metallic sheet. A larger portion of the lighter U-235 passes through the barrier than the heavier U-238. The process has to be repeated in a series of

cascades, since at no one stage does the barrier isolate the U-235 to a sufficient degree of purity. As Kurchatov explained, "It's like coming out of the
theatre after a performance—the small, agile people make it to the exits faster
than the slow-moving, fat spectators."

The gaseous diffusion process presents an enormous engineering challenge
due to the materials being used. Not only does it require a major chemical
processing facility to transform the uranium metal into uranium hexafluoride, but the uranium hexafluoride gas is extremely toxic and corrosive. The
main problem in developing a suitable barrier material for such a plant was
to locate a metal that was sufficiently porous, while at the same time sufficiently durable, to withstand the destructive effects of the gas. The material
developed by Thiessen's team was a form of sintered nickel sheet.

Even after the system's basic design is developed, the industrial engineering
aspects of the separation plant are equally formidable. The plant requires thousands of cascade tanks and its energy requirements were prodigious. The American
Oak Ridge plant consumed about 0.5 percent of total American electricity
production in 1945—roughly equivalent to the needs of a city of 1 million
people.

The Soviets, like the Americans, decided to proceed with the separation
plant in 1948 before the technology had been perfected.[7] They felt confident
in doing so because their spy network had made it clear that it was the preferable approach. The lead time in constructing the plant was so long that
the Soviets felt it prudent to initiate the effort even before Kikoin and
Thiessen were finished with their work. The site selected for the plant was
the small village of Rusnoy near Kefirstadt (Verkhniy Neyvinskiy), northwest of Sverdlovsk in the Urals industrial region. It was given the military
code name Sverdlovsk-45.

One of the main technological hurdles was the production of sufficient
barrier material for the plant. Manufacturing was underway by mid-1948 at
the Elektrostal Plant No. 12 south of Noginsk, resulting in delivery of the
first small quantities of sheet by year's end. The 1949 program called for
the delivery of about 30,000 square meters, an objective that was not met.
Nevertheless, the program was stepped up, with a requirement for a further
75,000 square meters in 1950.

The first gaseous diffusion cascade was assembled at Sverdlovsk-45 in 1949.
Its initial operation was a nightmare, with serious corrosion problems in the
cascade, uranium hexafluoride gas leaks, and bungled construction. Thiessen
spent much of his time with Kikoin at the Verkhniy Neyvinskiy plant trying
to resolve the difficulties. They finally succeeded in early 1951.[8]

The problems plaguing the Sverdlovsk-45 project forced Kurchatov to continue
the search for alternative methods of isotope separation. Knowing that the

Americans had succeeded in extracting weapons-grade uranium using the electromagnetic separation process, Kurchatov continued to support Lev Artsimovich's efforts on this program at Laboratory No. 2 in Moscow. The conscripted German scientists played a key role in this project, too, with von Ardenne's secret Object A lab in Sinop focusing on electromagnetic separation at the same time.

When Lev Artsimovich learned that the reknowned physicist Max Steenbeck was located at the secret Sinop facility, Artsimovich won Beria's approval to have him transferred to Moscow, an arrangement that the special police had previously resisted.

After recovering from malnutrition and illness caused by his incarceration in the Soviet camp at Poznan, Steenbeck had been assigned to von Ardenne's group. Steenbeck proved less pliant than many of the German scientists. He refused to work for von Ardenne on the electromagnetic separation project, remarking, "I am the physicist of us two!" He refused to negotiate with General Zavenyagin over conditions of his employment in the Soviet atomic program. Steenbeck grasped the fact that the German scientists were crucial to the effort and insisted on negotiating with Beria himself. Surprisingly, the special police agreed, and Steenbeck quickly came to an understanding with Beria.

If he found his relations with von Ardenne strained, Steenbeck found a more congenial environment in the heart of the Soviet program. For a year and a half he served as a consultant to Artsimovich. Their relationship was nearly unique in the history of Soviet-German collaboration on the atomic bomb. Steenbeck quickly appreciated that Artsimovich was not like the low-grade Soviet physicists he had become accustomed to at Sinop. Artsimovich was a world-class physicist, and the proud Steenbeck had less difficulty working in harmony with him than with his fellow German, von Ardenne.[9]

In 1949 the technical council of the Soviet atomic program, chaired by Vyacheslav Malyshev, met to determine whether Artsimovich's or von Ardenne's separation system would be selected for construction. The council judged Artsimovich's overall design to be superior, but found that von Ardenne's ion source was the better of the two. Construction of an electromagnetic separation facility incorporating the best features of both designs began in 1950 and lasted for a year and a half.

By the time the electromagnetic separation facility was ready, the problems with the gaseous diffusion plant had been overcome. Diffusion thus became the standard method for uranium enrichment for the Soviet program. Electromagnetic separation was undertaken only as a potential backup in the event that the lingering problems with the diffusion cascade at Sverdlovsk-45 continued to persist.

The Soviets also examined the possibility of using centrifuges instead of gaseous diffusion in the early 1950s. Steenbeck headed a team that developed a successful laboratory model by 1952. The centrifuge process was attractive because it used considerably less electrical energy. However, the Soviet bomb program had such a high priority that its inefficient use of the electrical power grid in the Sverdlovsk area was of little concern to Stalin. By the time Steenbeck had his laboratory model working, the diffusion cascades at Sverdlovsk-45 were producing large amounts of weapons-grade uranium and the conservative Soviets opted to stick with this proven technology.

The first large quantities of enriched uranium from the diffusion cascade at Sverdlovsk-45 became available in early 1951. Yuliy Khariton's team at Arzamas-16 began to develop a "composite core" bomb that would include a mixture of about 7 kilograms of uranium and 3.5 kilograms of plutonium as its fissile material. Such a bomb design offered the possibility of more efficient burning of the plutonium in the bomb, and a higher yield than any of the all-plutonium bombs tested up to that stage.[10]

The first composite bomb, called "Ivan," was ready for trial in the autumn of 1951. The test was significant for two reasons. Not only was it the first Soviet bomb using the new composite design, but it appears to have been the first Soviet atomic bomb successfully dropped from an aircraft. It was detonated on 18 October 1951 over Semipalatinsk. Its yield, about 50 kilotons, was almost triple that of the first Soviet A-bomb.[11]

Building the Superbomb

By the early 1940s U.S. physicists, most notably Edward Teller, were working on the notion of exploiting nuclear fusion as a more potent alternative than nuclear fission. Fusion is the opposite of fission. In fission, an atom of one of the heavy elements like uranium or plutonium splits into two lighter atoms, giving off energy in the process. Fusion takes place when the atoms of a light element, typically hydrogen, fuse together to form a heavier element, such as helium. The best known natural occurrence of fusion is in the sun, where the fusion of light atoms under conditions of extreme heat and compression gives off immense amounts of energy. Unlike fission, fusion does not occur naturally on the earth. Fusion is known to occur only in extreme conditions of heat and compression, as on the sun. The 1990 "cold-fusion" controversy was precisely over this issue of whether fusion might occur under conditions other than the known regime of high temperature and compression. As physicists in the early 1940s quickly appreciated, fusion produces even more massive amounts of energy than fission. Indeed, per unit mass, a fusion bomb would release 40 million times more energy than conventional explosives. But designing a fusion bomb is a great deal more complicated than designing a fission bomb.

The Soviet Union probably came up with the idea of fusion bombs through espionage channels. Klaus Fuchs became aware of the early concepts developed by the Americans while he was at Los Alamos. Noted Soviet nuclear physicist Andrey D. Sakharov suggests that espionage reports inspired the early Soviet efforts.[12]

The early American H-bomb concepts had substantial flaws that were not resolved until the early 1950s, so the lead provided the USSR through espionage was substantially less than in the case of the fission bomb. Given the technological and time limits, the early Soviet nuclear weapons program necessarily concentrated on building the first fission bombs and perfecting the technology required to begin quantity production. Beria realized that the decision to proceed with fusion bomb fabrication would slow fission bomb manufacture, not only by the diversion of scientific and engineering talent, but also the diversion of fissionable metals production to the processing of materials unique to the fusion bomb, such as tritium. This attitude lingered well into the 1950s, years after atomic bomb production was underway.

The idea for a fusion bomb was sketched out in a letter to the government by Khariton, Zeldovich, and others in the late 1940s. The concept was tempting enough to prompt Kurchatov to initiate small-scale research into the concept. The initial work on the Soviet thermonuclear fusion bomb was undertaken by Yakov Zeldovich and his groups at the Institute of Physical Chemistry and at KB-11 in 1947–48. Zeldovich quickly concluded that such a bomb was feasible and that its energy output would be considerably greater than that of a fission bomb. In June 1948 the Council of Ministers ordered the formation of a special advanced nuclear bomb research group at the Physics Institute of the Academy of Sciences (FIAN), to be headed by the distinguished academician, Igor Tamm. Tamm, who taught many of the prime movers of the Soviet atom bomb program in their student days in Leningrad, had only peripheral contact with the bomb development program up to that time. Beria had been reluctant to allow senior, world-reknowned physicists to be closely connected to the program since their disappearance from public view would provide information to Western intelligence agencies about the scope of Soviet nuclear development efforts. With work on the first bomb nearing completion, Beria's attitude began to soften.

Tamm's small group was involved in theoretical research and, at first, was not stationed at the design center at Arzamas-16. Among the early recruits to Tamm's group was a promising young physics graduate, Andrey Sakharov. The group's initial effort was devoted to verifying and refining Zeldovich's calculations.

Zeldovich's original thermonuclear bomb design envisioned using an atomic bomb as a trigger to provide the needed heat and compression to initiate the thermonuclear reaction. The initial concept was to place a layer of liquid deuterium between the fissile material and the surrounding chemical high explosive. Tamm's group concluded that a lack of sufficient heat and compression of the deuterium would result in an insignificant fusion of the deuterium fuel.[13]

Work on the fusion bomb revolved around gas dynamics. The basic concept of fusion was well enough understood. What was critical was to study the interaction of the blast wave from the atomic bomb triggering the fusion event and the hydrogen fuel that would be fused. If the shock waves reached the hydrogen fuel too soon, it would simply be blasted away before the fusion reaction could begin. The other problem was the nature of the hydrogen fuel itself. The most likely candidates were two hydrogen isotopes, deuterium and tritium. In a pure natural state, both are gases. This complicated the bomb design. Eventually it became clear that a liquid or solid hydrogen compound would be suitable, so long as the compound did not absorb neutrons or absorb too much of the energy of the fission explosion.

Sakharov's study group at FIAN in 1948 came up with a refined concept, nicknamed the "First Idea," in August or September of 1948. Sakharov suggested adding a shell of natural, unenriched uranium around the deuterium. Besides increasing the deuterium concentration at the uranium-deuterium boundary, the shell added to the overall yield of the device as the natural uranium would capture neutrons and itself undergo fission as part of the thermonuclear reaction. This idea of a layered fission-fusion-fission bomb led Sakharov to call it the *sloyka,* or layer cake. Other members of the team called it "sugarization"—a play on Sakharov's name, which is derived from the Russian word for sugar.

As Sakharov was developing the layer cake approach, other members of the group explored the use of different light isotopes for the fusion fuel. Tritium seemed the most promising. Tritium's main drawbacks were its production cost and its radioactive composition. It decayed more rapidly than deuterium, and so would have to be replenished in the bomb periodically. Before this issue was settled, Sakharov's layer cake was modified by the "Second Idea," based on improvements devised by Vitaly Ginzburg, also of the FIAN team. Ginzburg proposed the substitution of lithium deuteride ($^6Li^2H$) in the bomb for ordinary deuterium. During a thermonuclear reaction, lithium deuteride generates tritium, which in turn serves as the fusion fuel.[14]

The work of Tamm's FIAN team was examined by the Technical Council of the First Chief Directorate sometime in 1949. The council was so impressed by the team's efforts that in March 1950 several of the key scientists, including Sakharov, were transferred to the Arzamas-16 nuclear weapons design bureau.

The Second Idea bomb was not a fully evolved thermonuclear bomb in the contemporary sense, but an intermediate step between pure fission bombs and the thermonuclear "supers." The bomb's energy output was further enhanced by lining the center of the fission bomb with layers of lithium deuteride. The heat of the fission explosion created momentary fusion of part of the lithium deuteride fuel, thus boosting the explosion's power by more than a third.

The Architect's Downfall

As the KB-11 design bureau was perfecting the first Soviet thermonuclear bomb, the specter of new threats loomed in the world outside of Arzamas-16's barbed-wire fences. Although Kurchatov had managed to keep the nuclear physics community free from the depredations of show trials, the pressure continued. In the summer of 1950 a special government commission visited Arzamas-16 to check up on the political purity of the scientists and engineers working there. Among the questions was their attitude towards Lysenkoism, the politically correct orthodoxy that had crippled Soviet biology. Andrey Sakharov recalls in his memoirs that he spoke unfavorably of Lysenkoism to the commission members. Sakharov was spared any dire consequences due to his importance to the thermonuclear bomb effort. But Lev Altshuler, a less prominent physicist, had answered as forthrightly as Sakharov. Lacking Sakharov's prestige, he was threatened with dismissal, which was narrowly averted by Sakharov's intervention.[15]

The tension subsided shortly afterwards, but there remained the fear that Stalin planned a repeat of the 1937–38 purges. Beria did little to allay these fears. Then, in November 1952, the United States detonated its first true thermonuclear superbomb. This placed even greater pressure on the Arzamas-16 bureau. Beria added to the tension by dispatching two members of the Academy of Sciences, Mikhail Lavrentiyev and Aleksandr Ilyushin, to Arzamas-16. It was no secret that they had been sent to replace Khariton if his thermonuclear bomb failed.

The tempo of political plots and propaganda picked up in early 1953 with the revelation of the so-called Doctors' Plot, an alleged scheme by Kremlin doctors to kill Communist party leaders, including Stalin himself. The campaign of denunciation had a distinctly anti-Semitic ring to it. A lead article for *Pravda* was already typeset, cynically entitled "The Russian People Are Rescuing the Jewish People." Reportedly, Stalin had ordered plans for the mass deportation of Moscow's Jews to labor camps. The byzantine nature of the intrigues has led others to suggest that Beria was behind the campaign, intent on isolating an increasingly ill Stalin from his trusted medical staff.

At Arzamas-16, the campaign of denunciation was more muted than in Moscow, but present nonetheless. At least one doctor on the medical staff was dismissed. The campaign was alarming to the scientists not only because many were Jewish, but because most believed it to be the forerunner of another purge that would affect everyone.

On 5 March 1953 Stalin's death was announced. Younger and more naive scientists like Sakharov expressed genuine sorrow at the startling news. To those scorched by the purges, however, Stalin's death offered the promise of better times ahead for the Soviet Union.

The news had no immediate impact on the atomic weapons program, since Beria was one of the political leaders jockeying for Stalin's position. Much to the relief of the scientists, it was announced in April that the doctors arrested on Stalin's orders had been exonerated and freed. To many, it seemed as though rule by terror was finally ending in the Soviet Union.

In July 1953 the signs on Beria Street in the Arzamas-16 compound were removed and replaced with new signs identifying it as Kruglov Street. Later, it was announced that Beria and his immediate associates had been arrested. The final obstacle to reform had been removed.

At the time of Stalin's death, four principal figures had emerged as possible successors: Georgiy Malenkov, the premier; Nikita Khrushchev, first secretary of the Communist party; Nikolay Bulganin, the minister of defense; and Beria. At first, Malenkov supported both Beria and the merger of the MVD with the MGB—all under Beria's control. But Beria's consolidation of power, as well as his growing arrogance, alarmed party and army officials. The military leaders, in particular, had a grudge with Beria. There had been a series of arbitrary dismissals of top army and navy leaders in the late 1940s and early 1950s. Beria and the MVD had made continuing efforts to interfere with military affairs, the police control of the atomic bomb program being one of many examples. Khrushchev coordinated the support of the key military leaders, including marshals Zhukov and Konev and generals Moskalenko and Batitskiy.

On 26 June Beria activated two of his MVD paramilitary police divisions inside Moscow in anticipation of a coup attempt. But the military was already in the process of moving far more formidable forces into the city's outskirts, thanks to Zhukov.[16]

A late night meeting of the Presidium was held, and Zhukov managed to secretly move himself and other senior army officials into the Kremlin without being noticed by Beria's MVD guard force. In the early morning hours of 27 June Khrushchev denounced Beria in front of the assembled national leaders and summoned in the military officers. Zhukov and his group stormed into the room, arrested Beria, and sneaked him past the cordon of MVD troops around the Kremlin.

Beria was kept at Lefortovo Prison and later at the Ministry of Defense building while the military meticulously removed Beria's allies within the

MVD. Once control over the special police was reestablished by the military and the Communist party, the campaign of denunciation began. By the end of July a document nicknamed the Red Book was prepared to chronicle Beria's crimes.

Beria was accused of secretly serving the intelligence services of the anti-Soviet Moslem Mussavat party in 1919 at the time of the civil war and, in later years, murdering loyal Soviet intelligence officials aware of his civil war treason. He was also accused of personally murdering a number of people during his tenure as the head of the NKVD in Georgia during the 1930s. Various sordid personal crimes were added to the list, including his rape and murder of young women in the Moscow area after he became NKVD chief. Copies of the Red Book were made available to senior Communist party and army leaders, as well as selected members of the intelligentsia and scientific community, including members of the atomic bomb team.

Beria was tried in a special closed court in the Ministry of Defense building, with no one attending except the tribunal and the group of senior Soviet Army officers who had arrested him. Also in the dock were several of his closest associates, themselves accused of an equally gruesome array of crimes. The court judged the group guilty and ordered the death sentence for Beria and his cronies. A young army officer grabbed Beria and led him into a bunker in the basement of the building. At first Beria did not seem to realize that the army officers intended to execute him immediately. But, after they took off his tunic and began to tie his hands behind his back, he seemed to grasp reality. He broke away from the young officer, fell at the feet of the chairman of the court, Marshal Ivan S. Konev, and pleaded for mercy.

The judge ordered the sentence carried out. The head of the Special Guard Detachment, Col. Gen. Kirill Moskalenko, said to his aide Lt. Col. V. P. Yuferev, "You're the youngest, will you do it?"

Yuferev pulled his Tokarev pistol from his holster, but was shaken by Beria's hysterical behavior. General P. F. Batitskiy, several of whose friends had been killed or tortured by Beria's NKVD during the war years, stepped forward.

"Permit me," Batitskiy said. He then drew a war-trophy German Parabellum pistol from his holster and shot Beria at point-blank range. Beria's corpse was taken into the courtyard of the building and burned. His henchmen soon shared the same fate. It reminded some of those present more of an exorcism than an execution.[17]

Ministry of Medium Machine Building

Beria's death in 1953 marked an important step in the de-Stalinization of the Soviet Union. But it would not be until the Twentieth Party Congress in February 1956 that Stalin himself would be attacked.

The most immediate impact on the scientists of Arzamas-16 was a change in leadership. Boris Vannikov, too closely associated with Beria, was removed as head of the First Chief Directorate. In his place came Vyacheslav Malyshev, and the organization was renamed the Ministry of Medium Machine Building, a name that it kept until just recently. Malyshev was an ally of Georgiy Malenkov, the head of the Presidium and the apparent "first among equals" in the Kremlin's new collective leadership. Malyshev was not without his own accomplishments, however. During the war years he had headed the vital tank industry and was credited by many with its tremendous success.

The leadership change in the atomic program also had a curious impact outside the top-secret world of the bomb program. Beria had kept the program as his personal preserve, reporting only to Stalin. Although Stalin had informed some of the military's senior leaders of the general details of the bomb program, the military in general was quite ignorant about many of its aspects. Party and military leaders were told only what they needed to know in connection with the program. Stalin had gone so far as to forbid discussion of the tactical and strategic applications of nuclear weapons to modern warfare as part of his campaign to reduce the vulnerability of the Soviet Union to nuclear blackmail by the West. With the change in leadership, the restrictions began to relax.

The military began to openly discuss the actual combat potential of atomic weapons and to incorporate them into their strategic planning. In 1954 sole control of the atomic bombs passed from the MVD, which entered into a joint-control arrangement with the armed forces.

Boosted Bomb

By the late summer of 1953 the Arzamas-16 team was ready to test its first thermonuclear bomb, the so-called article (*izdeliye*). In July 1953 Khariton and the bomb's design team, which included Sakharov, Tamm, and Zeldovich, left for the steppes of Kazakhstan. Like the first atomic bomb test, it was scheduled to be detonated on a high tower. On arrival at Semipalatinsk-21, the team was faced with an unexpected problem. The blast was expected to be significantly greater than in previous tests. Consulting the "Black Book," an American textbook on nuclear weapons effects, they realized that there was a good possibility that fallout from the bomb would contaminate neighboring Kazakh villages. Much to the consternation of Malyshev and the military, the bomb designers insisted on staging a precautionary evacuation of the surrounding area, amounting to tens of thousands of people. The army finally relented and provided trucks.

A week before the tests, Georgiy Malenkov made an important speech outlining new government policies before the Supreme Soviet in Moscow. He concluded the address by boasting that the Soviet Union already had the hydrogen bomb.

Malenkov's remarks caused a sensation around the world, since it was widely doubted that the Soviets would have a thermonuclear bomb so soon after the United States.

With the evacuation complete, final preparations for the test were made and the device was detonated on 12 August 1953. The weapon's yield was somewhere from 200 to 300 kilotons—about six times more powerful than any previous Soviet test.

The scene at the observation bunkers was very different from the scene four years before when the first bomb had been detonated. Although there was a great deal of anxiety before the blast due to concerns over whether the device would detonate as predicted, there was none of the foreboding that accompanied Beria's presence. Following the detonation, the new head of the program, Malyshev, rushed from his bunker to the Arzamas-16 bunker and warmly congratulated the scientists. He had telephoned Malenkov with the news and Malenkov asked him to single out Sakharov in particular for praise.

Malyshev assembled a group of dignitaries and scientists to visit the blast site. The group was issued protective clothing and dosimeters and set off for the epicenter in a small convoy. At Ground Zero, Malyshev got out of his truck and Sakharov followed, the black crust of fused soil crunching under their feet like glass. All that was left in the immediate blast area was a portion of one of the steel girders that had formed a leg of the test tower. Suitably impressed, Malyshev and Sakharov mounted the trucks and returned to the base camp.

Rewards soon followed. Both Sakharov and Igor Tamm were awarded the Hero of Socialist Labor decoration, the highest Soviet award for civilians, along with a state prize valued at 500,000 rubles. Both men also received *dachas* (summer homes) in the exclusive Zhukovskiy suburb of Moscow. Kurchatov, Khariton, Zeldovich, and Shchelkin received their second Hero of Socialist Labor awards for their role.

There was considerable confusion in the United States about exactly what sort of bomb the Soviets had detonated. American reconnaissance aircraft, fitted with special "sniffers" to pick up traces of the fallout, detected traces of lithium deuteride in the atmospheric debris. Some intelligence analysts interpreted this to be the sign of the successful development of a so-called dry thermonuclear bomb. American thermonuclear bomb design had already gone through two stages and was on the verge of a third. The initial stage was boosted bombs, the first of which was the "Item" detonation on 21 May 1951. This was very similar to the 1953 Soviet bomb, although the yield of the American bomb was considerably smaller. The next stage was a true superbomb, code-named "Mike," on 1 November 1952. It had a yield of 10.4 megatons, about fifty times greater than the Soviet 1953 boosted bomb. However, the Mike device was a "wet" design that used deuterium kept in a liquid state by an enormous refrigeration system. Although it proved the "superbomb" concept, the Mike design was much too large to convert into a practical weapon. The only way to transport it would have been by ship. The third stage in the American program was a dry bomb design using lithium deuteride as the fusion fuel, a radically different approach in bomb design.

Some American analysts concluded from the airborne debris that the Soviets had skipped the first two stages and were already testing a third-stage device, a true dry super. The interpretation of the fourth Soviet bomb test led to controversies that have continued to this day over whether the United States should have tested the Mike superbomb. Those who opposed the test argued that it would provide the Soviets with evidence useful in perfecting their own super.[18] However, the military and the intelligence community soon realized that the fourth Soviet test was a boosted device, not a super.[19]

The Third Idea

In the early part of 1954, after Sakharov had returned to his laboratory at Arzamas-16, he began work on what he called the "Third Idea." The Third Idea was a third-generation thermonuclear bomb, basically similar to the American dry super. Actual authorship of the concept is in some dispute. Sakharov admits that the idea occurred nearly simultaneously in the Theoretical Department at Arzamas-16, with Yakov Zeldovich and Yuriy Trutnev coming up with similar concepts. It is still not clear if the inspiration came from assessments of the atmospheric debris from the Mike test or the later American "Castle" test series in March 1954.

Did the Soviets obtain the "secret" for the hydrogen bomb by studying American tests or through espionage? Soviet accounts have skirted the issue. Sakharov insists that his team failed to isolate samples from the tests due to a simple lab error. But other Soviet organizations may very well have isolated atmospheric samples and passed the results on to the Arzamas-16 team. Interpreting these samples would have required a sophisticated bomb design already well on its way toward completion.[20] This question has been quite controversial over the years due to its connection with political arguments in the American scientific community occurring at the same time. There were bitter disputes between American nuclear weapons designers over whether the thermonuclear bomb program should be pushed ahead at all. J. Robert Oppenheimer clashed with Edward Teller on this issue, a controversy that cost Oppenheimer his leadership position in the nuclear program. Acrimony over this dispute has spilled over into assessments of the importance of the bomb tests in inspiring Soviet bomb designs.

The conditions under which the Soviet thermonuclear bomb was being designed were very different from the conditions under which the earlier atomic bomb was designed. In 1943, Kurchatov's team was small, poorly supported, and woefully ill-equipped. A decade later, the Arzamas team was supported by every resource available to the Soviet government. By the mid-1950s, the Soviet Union was actually beginning to outstrip the United States in the number of scientists employed in the nuclear program.[21] The atomic bomb team was forced to rely on foreign espionage due to its own poverty of resources; the thermonuclear design team did not have espionage coups to rely on, but its own scientific resources were infinitely richer. To some extent, the argument that the Soviets relied on samples of the earlier American test to design their own bomb is based on the dismissive attitude towards Soviet science widespread in the United States in the pre-*Sputnik* years, reinforced by the political passions of the Oppenheimer-Teller dispute. In view of later Soviet successes in fusion research, such as the design of the tokamak fusion research reactor, it is entirely plausible that the Soviet thermonuclear bomb was an entirely indigenous effort.

The Third Idea was based on the concept of using the radiation of a fission bomb to trigger the fusion—not simply the heat and compression of the initial nuclear explosion. Unlike the boosted bomb, which placed the fusion fuel inside the primary A-bomb trigger, the thermonuclear super placed the fusion fuel in a secondary structure a small distance from it. The fusion fuel was compressed and ignited by the energy from the trigger caused by the x-ray radiation. Substantial theoretical work was required to understand how the initial blast could trigger the fusion explosion before obliterating the fusion fuel cell. These studies were aided by the use of one of the earliest Soviet computers.

As intriguing as the Third Idea was to the scientists, the Kremlin had other thoughts. Sakharov and the Tamm team were supposed to be developing a refined version of the boosted bomb detonated in August 1953, suitably modified for use on a new R-7 intercontinental ballistic missile being developed by Sergey Korolev's design bureau. But the head of KB-11, Yuliy Khariton, was so impressed with the potential of the Third Idea that he tacitly supported the development effort in spite of the fact that it contradicted government mandates.

Malyshev and the Ministry of Medium Machine Building eventually learned that KB-11 was proceeding with the development of a radically different thermonuclear device, even though it had only been authorized to develop a refined "classical" first-generation thermonuclear device. Infuriated, Malyshev personally flew out to Arzamas-16. He immediately called for the convocation of a Technical Commission meeting, bringing together all the critical development leaders, including Kurchatov.

Malyshev was very critical of the KB-11 team for embarking on such a stunt. He considered it flagrant insubordination. But he was trapped between the designers, who were committed to developing a refined classical bomb for Korolev's new missile, and the Kremlin leadership, to whom he had promised to deliver a device by 1955. Tempers flared and the conferences dragged out indecisively. Kurchatov stood by the KB-11 scientists. Malyshev eventually arranged a severe Communist party reprimand for Kurchatov for "anti-state behavior." That Kurchatov got by with a reprimand is a clear indication of how radically changed the political atmosphere was in the Soviet Union. A few years earlier, under Beria, "anti-state behavior" would have been rewarded by a bullet in the back of the head.

Malyshev's attitude towards the unauthorized superbomb may seem strange in retrospect. But his management style was heavily shaped by his wartime experiences in the tank industry. Malyshev had learned to his detriment that constant tinkering and improvements in tank designs disrupted production and decreased the number of tanks leaving the factory. To maximize production, he placed very strict limits on tank modernization efforts until forced to remove them by German advances.[22] This management style worked very well. Indeed, the German industrial style was almost the opposite, with constant incremental changes in tank design and a much lower production rate.

The Kremlin was unhappy with the whole superbomb affair. An effort was underway to set up a competitor to the unruly group at KB-11. Even before Beria's downfall, efforts had been made to replace Kurchatov with a more pliable leader. Beria had offered the post to Abram Alikhanov, the head of the heavy water reactor program at Laboratory No. 3 and Kurchatov's rival, in 1943. Alikhanov, who was far less enthused than Kurchatov about working for Beria and the military on such a bomb, refused the offer.[23]

The new effort was aimed not at replacing Kurchatov but at setting up an entirely separate second design team. Ostensibly, the second nuclear weapons design bureau would generate new ideas and leaders and accelerate thermonuclear weapons research. Malyshev disagreed, arguing that a second center would simply dissipate limited talent and resources. One of the unspoken objectives of the effort was to reduce the influence of Jewish scientists. The leaders of KB-11—Khariton, Zeldovich, and others—were Jewish. Even after Stalin's death there was a general trend toward reducing the number of Jews in critical defense industry leadership posts.

In February 1955, during another round of Kremlin infighting, Malenkov lost his post as head of the Council of Ministers. Malyshev had been appointed by Malenkov and was regarded as one of his protégés. The new Council of Ministers quickly ordered Malyshev's removal as head of the Ministry of Medium Machine Building, ostensibly due to his failure to establish the second nuclear weapons design bureau.

The new head of the ministry was a familiar face to many of the scientists, Avraami P. Zavenyagin. Zavenyagin had been one of Beria's deputies in the First Chief Directorate and had played a prominent role in the atomic bomb program since 1945. In spite of his past NKVD rank, Zavenyagin was not so much a special policeman as a technocrat with past ties to the police. He was, by training, a metallurgist.

Zavenyagin succumbed to pressure to open a second nuclear weapons design center in Synezhinsk near the Kyshtym processing center. Code-named Chelyabinsk-70, it was headed by Yevgeniy I. Zababakhin. The original bomb design center, KB-11, was soon dubbed "Israel," and the new Zababakhin design bureau, "Egypt"—a precursor of the 1956 anti-Zionist campaign.

The decision to open a second nuclear bomb design center presents a curious parallel to events in the United States at about the same time. As in the USSR, a second bomb design center, the Lawrence Livermore Laboratory, was added to the existing Los Alamos facility, owing to arguments over the development of the hydrogen bomb. However, in the American case, the addition of a second lab was due in no small measure to the perception that J. Robert Oppenheimer and many of the Los Alamos scientists were less than enthusiastic about proceeding with so destructive a weapon as the hydrogen superbomb due to moral concerns. In the Soviet Union, the second bureau was added in large measure because of the scientists' overzealous efforts. Few Soviet scientists shared the moral pangs of conscience over their bomb efforts that so pained Oppenheimer and many of his associates. This would change with time. After designing the Soviet superbomb, Sakharov later reconsidered his attitudes toward further bomb work. He later became one of the most outspoken opponents of Soviet policies in the Brezhnev years.

Super or Classical?

Zavenyagin reopened the whole debate about the first-generation classical device versus the Third Idea second-generation superbomb when he took over the nuclear program. Zavenyagin suggested that both weapons be tested in the autumn of 1955, with the classical device tested only if the Third Idea bomb failed. The Presidium agreed.[24]

The accelerated test date put enormous strain on Sakharov's design group. The new thermonuclear bomb design required elaborate mathematical calculations associated with the gas dynamics of the explosion. Until then, most mathematical computations had to be done by hand in the traditional manpower-intensive and laborious fashion. In 1955, access was finally opened to the new Soviet second-generation computers, the BESM. Soviet computer technology had stagnated under Stalin due to the repression of certain branches of mathematics, such as Boolean algebra, which was viewed as "Western deviationism." After Stalin's demise, mathematicians were able to proceed with advanced research needed for developing programs of use to the nuclear physicists. A team from the Academy of Sciences headed by Izrail Gelfand assisted Sakharov in the calculations for the new bomb, using the new computers.[25]

Contrary to the initial promises, the Kremlin decided to go ahead and test the classical device anyway. It was successfully dropped from an aircraft and detonated on 6 November 1955 at Semipalatinsk. It differed in design from the initial first-generation thermonuclear bomb in configuration, being more suitable for military use than was the initial 1953 device, which was of an experimental configuration.

On 18 November 1955, a Tu-95 bomber dropped a simulated thermonuclear superbomb over Semipalatinsk to test the parachute retarding mechanism designed for the real bomb test. The actual test of the device was scheduled for 20 November, but low clouds prevented the drop. The test of the second-generation Third Idea superbomb finally took place on 22 November 1955. It exploded as planned, yielding a whopping 1,600 kilotons—about a hundred times greater than the first Soviet atomic bomb.

There was a temperature inversion in the weather patterns over the test site that day, altering the pattern of the shock waves near the ground and causing more damage than anticipated. Zavenyagin emerged from the bunker with a bump on his head caused by a chunk of plaster knocked free from the ceiling by the shock of the blast. But the crowd was jubilant. The weapon had performed as predicted. The Americans had exploded such a device over a year before. But the gap between the United States and the Soviet Union was closing. More to the point, with a weapon of this magnitude, the race was over. Thermonuclear bombs might be tinkered with and perfected, but the Soviet Union finally had a weapon that could detroy any target in the United States.

Chapter 5

Missile War

THE DETONATION OF the first Soviet superbomb in 1955 was proof that the strategic weapons gap between the Soviet Union and the United States was closing. But the Soviet Union still had no dependable way to deliver atomic weapons to targets in the United States. In the mid-1950s the Soviet bomber force, even with its sleek new Tu-95 bombers, was still puny. Furthermore, American air defenses were keeping pace with this challenge.

The Soviet bombers represented the threat that the American armed forces had anticipated for years, since they mirrored the American bomber force controlled by the air force's Strategic Air Command. The appearance of M-4 strategic bombers in the 1954 May Day celebration spurred the United States and Canada to greatly expand the coverage of the North American Air Defense Command (NORAD). Any Soviet bomber venturing toward American targets would run a gauntlet of long-range detection radars, followed by missile-equipped jet interceptors, and, finally, a layer of Nike antibomber missiles. The mission of any Soviet bomber would be an unenviable one. No matter where a Tu-95 entered American airspace—Alaska, Iceland, or straight over the North Pole—the bomber would have to traverse thousands of miles of territory under radar scrutiny. NORAD would literally have hours to vector fighters towards the incoming Soviet bombers.

Nor were the new interceptors anything like the types of fighters used by the German Luftwaffe to challenge American bombers in the skies over the Third Reich. Bombers like the Tu-95M had progressed little over their ancestors like the B-29. But fighters had evolved considerably. The new American interceptors were much faster than their predecessors, with newer types approaching and surpassing the sound barrier. Their weapons were also far more potent. Nuclear weapons could be used not only for attack, but for defense as well. Some of the new interceptors were being armed with the Genie, an unguided rocket armed with a nuclear warhead. The Genie did not require guidance because it did not need to *hit* its target. If it could just get to within a few miles of its intended victim its explosion would prove lethal.

The Soviet armed forces were not as committed to the strategic bomber as were the Americans, however. In fact, since the end of World War II they had placed their hopes primarily on new missile weapons. In the summer of 1945 Stalin authorized a crash missile program to enable the Soviets to devastate targets in the United States from bases deep inside the Soviet Union. And, unlike bombers, nothing could stop these new missiles.

Rocket Man

If any one man symbolized the Soviet effort to develop intercontinental ballistic missiles, it was Sergey Pavlovich Korolev. Korolev was responsible for developing the first Soviet ballistic missiles, the first intercontinental ballistic missiles, the first satellite, and the rocket that put the first man in space.

As a youngster, Korolev became wrapped up in the romance of space flight and rocketry. The 1920s were a time in Russia where anything seemed possible—even the fanciful schemes of a visionary writer like Konstantin E. Tsiolkovskiy. Tsiolkovskiy inspired Korolev and many other young dreamers with tales of spaceships and interplanetary travel. His writings were more scientific than those of writers like H. G. Wells, but imaginative enough to hold the attention of young enthusiasts. Tsiolkovskiy is sometimes compared to early rocket pioneers like Robert H. Goddard in the United States. But this is not an entirely apt comparison. Goddard was a practical engineer who realized his dreams through experiments with actual rockets. Tsiolkovskiy's dreams never left paper. Korolev, and many others like him, saw it as their mission in life to translate Tsiolkovskiy's dreams into reality.

In the late 1920s and early 1930s, rocket clubs sprang up in the larger Soviet cities, especially Moscow and Leningrad. The most famous of these were the Moscow and Leningrad GIRDs. GIRD was a Russian acronym for "Group for the Investigation of Jet Propulsion." Korolev graduated from the N. E. Baumann Higher Technical School in Moscow in 1931 and was a pupil of aircraft designer Andrey Tupolev. Korolev worked mainly with sailplanes, but his contact with a young rocket enthusiast, Frederikh Tsander, sparked his interest in using a rocket engine to power a glider. GIRD eventually won some state funding from the OSOAVIAKHIM, the government agency responsible for sponsoring preinduction military training and sports among Soviet youth. OSOAVIAKHIM's mandate was fairly broad and included sponsorship of glider clubs, skydiving, auto racing, and a host of other sports which taught young Soviet men skills that would prove useful in military life. In spite of the support, the GIRD staff was motivated by its enthusiasm for rocketry. The pay was so poor that staff members joked that GIRD really stood for *Gruppa inzhenerov rabotayushchaya darom* (Group of Engineers Working for Free).

Korolev was one of the principal leaders of the Moscow GIRD when the organization's success attracted the attention of Marshal Mikhail N. Tukhachevskiy, the charismatic Soviet army commander and head of Soviet weapons development at the time. Tukhachevskiy's office was already funding a small rocket research center called GDL (Gas Dynamics Lab), but the young Moscow amateurs were achieving more promising results. In 1933 Tukhachevskiy convinced GIRD's leaders to amalgamate with GDL and, in return, receive military funding for their efforts. The new institute, called RNII (Scientific Research Institute for Jet Propulsion) was headed by Ivan Kleymenov of the GDL, with Korolev as his deputy.[1]

The RNII's work paralleled similar efforts in Germany and America. Experimental liquid-propelled rockets entered flight tests in 1933, and the young engineers continued to tinker with ever more elaborate and sophisticated rocket engines. The rockets were still too primitive for military applications, but received Tukhachevskiy's continuing endorsement and modest financial support. RNII engineers like Korolev, Glushko, and Kleymenov were given money to pursue development of liquid-fuel rocket engines even though there was little promise of immediate military applications. At the same time, less ambitious solid-propellant rockets were also developed by a team under Georgiy Langemak. These rockets had better prospects for short-term application to military uses.[2]

The advent of the Purge in 1937 had devastating consequences for the rocket program. Virtually all of the RNII's senior leaders were arrested and most of the young engineers were put up against a wall and shot. The close ties between the RNII and Marshal Tukhachevskiy, the alleged ringleader of the military treason plot, may have been the ultimate cause of the RNII's destruction. However, the immediate cause was the unscrupulous activities of several new members of the RNII staff. In particular, Andrey G. Kostikov, an ambitious air force political officer and communications specialist, supported the NKVD charges against the RNII leadership and provided fabricated evidence. Kostikov accused RNII's leaders of organizing a Trotskyite sabotage and spy ring in 1930 that was wrecking the Soviet rocket program.

Kleymenov, Langemak, and Nikolai Ya. Ilyin were all arrested. Under torture, they implicated other members of the RNII. To curry favor with the NKVD, other members of the RNII staff wrote letters to the Communist party committee of the RNII denouncing still other members of the organization's staff. The next person to be brought up on wrecking charges was Valentin P. Glushko,

one of the RNII's most successful young liquid-fuel rocket engine designers. Glushko's colleagues were forced to sit in judgment of him, and almost
unanimously agreed with a resolution that he was "unreliable." He was arrested in early March and imprisoned. Korolev continued to work on his rocket
projects, but it was only a matter of time before he too was jailed. Glushko
had been forced to denounce him. Korolev was put in an isolation cell in
March—shortly after Glushko's arrest—and finally charged in June. The top
RNII leaders, including Kleymenov and Langemak, were shot, while Glushko
was thrown into prison with the other defense industry "wreckers," including Tupolev and his design team.[3] The informer, Kostikov, was appointed to
head the RNII in place of the senior engineers he had betrayed to the NKVD.[4]

In September 1938, Korolev was convicted as a "Trotskyite enemy of the
people" and sentenced to five years of hard labor at the Nagayevo mine in
the Kolyma arctic death camp.[5] Of all the hellholes in the GULAG system,
Kolyma was the most notorious. Aleksandr Solzhenitsyn called it the "pole
of cold and cruelty" of the GULAG archipelago. During the height of its operations
before and during World War II, its camps claimed an estimated 3 to 4 million lives, a greater toll even than the Nazi death camp at Auschwitz. Until
1937 Kolyma had been an ordinary forced-labor camp. There were deaths—
not unexpected, considering the arctic working conditions. But after 1937,
although gold mining remained an important activity, the camp's central aim
was to kill off the prisoners. There were no gas chambers in the Kolyma system—
there was no need for them. Although there were mass executions, most of
the deaths were caused by overwork, famine, exposure, and the harsh arctic
climate. The rule of thumb in the GULAG death camps was that a zek was
good for about six months of work before malnutrition, exposure, or illness
took its fatal toll. The zeks were worked to death in the gold mines or simply froze from lack of adequate clothing. Korolev had the misfortune to be
sent to Kolyma during its worst year, 1938—a year that went down in Kolyma
history as "the year of the tempest."[6]

Korolev survived nearly a year in the Kolyma mines. His earlier association with Andrey Tupolev saved his life. As the NKVD special police began
rounding up Tupolev's associates in the GULAG system, they noted in the
files that Korolev had studied aircraft design under him. At the end of 1939
Korolev was rescued from Kolyma and shipped by train back to the Tupolev
prison design bureau in Moscow.

Few other designers went through so harrowing an experience as Korolev.
Most were either killed outright, like Langemak and Kleymenov, or sent directly
to prison design centers. Korolev's incarceration at Kolyma left him broken,
embittered, and cynical. In the first years after his release, he wandered around
the Tupolev prison offices repeatedly muttering, "They'll just wipe us out

and the newspapers won't even notice." Tupolev assigned him to help work on wing design for the Tu-2 medium bomber. But as Korolev's spirit gradually returned, he continued to turn his attention to the potential of rocket engines for aircraft.[7]

Glushko also joined the Tupolev team in Moscow. Then, after the outbreak of war in 1941, Glushko was allowed to resume his work on rocket engine development as the head of a small design office in Kazan, named GDL after the lab Glushko had belonged to in Leningrad prior to the founding of the RNII. The new GDL was concerned with developing rocket engines to boost the speed of existing propeller-driven warplanes.

Korolev began petitioning Lavrentiy Beria to allow him to continue his work on rocket propulsion almost immediately after his release from Kolyma.[8] Toward the end of 1942 he was transferred to Kazan to help the Myasishchev bureau work on a new long-range bomber. Finally, at Glushko's request, he was transferred to the GDL to work on rocket propulsion. Though he officially remained a convict, Korolev was placed in charge of the flight-test program. It was an awkward position for him to hold, since his status as a prisoner convicted of treason made it very difficult for him to travel unescorted. Glushko could do little to alleviate this situation, since he too remained under criminal sentence.

The GDL's rocket-assisted aircraft propulsion program was one of a number of disconnected rocketry efforts during the war.[9] By far the largest effort was connected with the design and manufacture of solid-fuel artillery rockets, the legendary *Katyushas*. Katyusha development had been under Langemak's direction at RNII before the Purge. The engineer who had betrayed them, Andrey Kostikov, was elevated to the rank of major general and headed the program throughout the war. The main design effort was undertaken at the Kompressor Factory in the Moscow area.

The Katyusha artillery rocket was one of the proudest achievements of Soviet military engineering during the war—to the point where most Soviet accounts refer to the rocket weapons as the "legendary" Katyushas. The Katyushas consisted of a rail-launcher mounted on a truck, most often a Lend-Lease two-and-a-half–ton Studebaker, which could fire several artillery rockets in quick succession. The nickname Katyusha means "little Katie" and comes from a popular wartime tune. The official code name for the weapons was "Guards Mortars"—a deliberate deception intended to fool the enemy. Today, these types of weapons are called multiple-rocket launchers.

The Red Army was enamored of such weapons for two reasons. On the one hand, Guards Mortars could pulverize an enemy target—with enormous psychological effect. This type of massed bombardment fit in very nicely with the Soviet style of artillery employment during the war, which placed greater emphasis on volume than on accuracy. The second reason for their appeal was the nature of their construction. Conventional artillery weapons required special foundries and tube-boring machines to manufacture howitzer barrels. Guards Mortars were of very elementary construction and could be built at small machine shops that were incapable of producing the more sophisticated conventional artillery. The two main disadvantages of the Katyushas were that the rockets consumed far more propellant per warhead than normal howitzers, and they were not as accurate as conventional artillery. So Katyushas supplemented, rather than replaced, conventional howitzers during the war.[10]

During the war years, evolution of the Katyushas stagnated, in no small measure due to the killings of the RNII leadership and the incarceration of many of the other more creative engineers like Glushko and Korolev. Only incremental improvements were made in the artillery rockets, and no serious attention was paid to larger, liquid-fueled missiles. New rocket types, such as the M-28, were copies of similar German rocket weapons. One measure of the severity of the decay of Soviet rocket technology was the fact that the Red Army was one of the few major World War II armies not to develop an infantry antitank rocket akin to the American bazooka or German *Panzerschreck*.

A third rocket effort, centered around NII-1 (Scientific-Research Institute-1) under Lieutenant General Fedorov, concentrated on developing liquid-fueled rockets to propel small fighter aircraft. One such aircraft, the BI-1, was built in small numbers during the war but did not prove to be practical enough to actually enter series production.

The Soviets never seriously entertained the idea of pursuing a major ballistic missile program comparable to the wartime German V-2 effort. To begin with, the potential research staff for such an effort had been crippled by the Purge. Beyond that, the wartime Soviet industries were too hard pressed to be able to afford such an expensive effort. This attitude was hardly unique. The United States and Britain, both of which had far more advanced aviation industries during the war, never seriously contemplated a major missile program either.

The spur to the development of ballistic missiles and other advanced missile weapons by the Soviet Union was the appearance of German secret weapons in the summer of 1944. When the Germans began to bombard London with V-1 buzz bombs, the Soviet leadership, including Stalin, feared that such a weapon would be turned on Soviet cities.

As a precaution, the commander of the Red Army's artillery force, Gen. N. N. Voronov, began moving some one hundred additional antiaircraft batteries to bolster the defenses around Leningrad, the only major Soviet city still in range of German missiles at that time. Taking a cue from the British, Voronov also ordered that two hundred barrage balloons be deployed in a ring around the city.[11] The barrage balloons trailed cables underneath them that could shear the wing off any V-1 that flew into them.

As it transpired, the Germans never did launch a V-1 attack on Leningrad, though Otto Skorzeny developed a hare-brained scheme to launch piloted V-1s against key Soviet industries in the Urals. Skorzeny, the architect of Benito Mussolini's rescue by glider troops in 1944, proposed that 250 V-1s be delivered as close to the Urals as possible by bomber and then released. The "volunteer" pilots of the flying bombs would steer the missiles toward important tank plants and other targets, then bail out moments before crashing into their targets. The project was assigned to SS *Gruppenführer* W. Schellenberg, and the targets selected included Kuibyshev, Chelyabinsk, and Magnitogorsk. This scheme also came to naught.

Russian Buzz Bomb

The first serious Soviet effort to develop a long-range rocket weapon began after the first V-1 attacks on London. On 13 June 1944, Stalin called in Gen. Aleksandr Novikov of the air force and A. I. Shakhurin, the head of the aviation industry, and ordered them to start a crash program to develop a Soviet buzz bomb.[12] Shakhurin was aware of the work of a young engineer, Vladimir N. Chelomey, who was developing a pulse-jet engine of the type used in the German missile.[13] Chelomey had proposed such a missile in 1943, and was allowed to develop the pulse-jet engine even though a missile had not been authorized.[14]

Chelomey went through ten designs before settling on a configuration basically identical to the German V-1. For this reason, he named the missile 10X and the engine that powered it D-10.[15] The first tests were made from a ground-launched version, dubbed the 10XN, at a field near Moscow. Flight tests began in March 1945 with the 10X suspended from a Pe-8 bomber. The missile proved cheap and effective, according to Soviet accounts. These sources claim that the missile could have gone into production in 1945, but it did not. To date, the Soviets have not even released a photo or drawing of the 10X. There were probably two reasons for its failure. To begin with, even though the 10X missile may have been aerodynamically acceptable, Chelomey had been unable to develop a satisfactory guidance system for it. Secondly, by 1945 the Red Army had captured intact German V-1 buzz bombs, the design of which was superior to the 10X. Chelomey's work on pulse-jet cruise missiles continued after the war, and was based on evolutionary improvements of the German V-1, not his own 10X.[16]

The V-1 assault on London was followed by V-2 ballistic missile attacks beginning in September 1944. The Germans attempted to move V-2 launch equipment toward Leningrad but, by the time it arrived, the front had been pushed back too far. Even if there was no immediate threat, the V-2 presented a more serious dilemma to Soviet security in the long run. Unlike winged cruise missiles like the V-1, there was no means within existing defense technology to shoot down a ballistic missile. Stalin insisted that work begin on duplicating both weapons to equip Soviet forces.

Red Army intelligence was alerted to search for V-2 components, in no small measure due to the efforts of Winston Churchill. British intelligence had long known of the V-2 program and had kept a wary eye on its progress in the hopes of delaying its eventual deployment. By the summer of 1944, the main British concern turned to developing methods to counteract the V-2. The British at the time were under the mistaken impression that the V-2 employed a radio command link for guidance during at least part of its flight.[17] They hoped this would prove to be the missile's Achilles heel, since such a command link could possibly be jammed electronically. In order to speed up development of an electronic jamming system, Churchill wrote to Stalin on 13 July 1944 requesting that British officers be allowed to examine any captured V-2s the Soviets might encounter in their summer offensive in central Europe.

Following the bombing of the German missile development center at Peenemünde by the Royal Air Force, the Germans moved the test range to eastern Poland, near Blizna, well out of range of the British bombers. In the second week of July 1944, however, the few remaining German troops at Blizna were pushed out by a Polish partisan unit. The Germans managed to retake it on 20 July. The following week, the Red Army captured the proving ground once and for all.

Following Churchill's request, Stalin allowed an Anglo-American team of missile specialists to examine the German test site in hopes of picking up clues about the V-2 missile. The Soviets delayed the team for nearly a month, by which time other evidence captured by the Polish underground had already reached London. Nevertheless, the team persevered and packed up some one and a half tons of material and parts. The crates were to be delivered to the Royal Aircraft Establishment at Farnborough by Soviet authorities. On arrival in Britain, the RAF engineers were surprised to find that the Soviets had removed all the German missile parts and substituted miscellaneous bits and pieces of aircraft![18]

The Soviets had already combed the site before the British and Americans arrived. The V-2 parts that the Anglo-American team had so carefully gathered were delivered to a secret study group, named *Raketa*, Russian for missile.[19] The Raketa group was formed by the Peoples Commissariat for Aircraft Production in the summer of 1944 to study the whole issue of ballistic missiles. Its chairman was V. F. Bolkhovitinov, an aviation designer who had spent the war working on rocket-powered aircraft. The team included other young engineers associated with wartime rocket and jet research, including Mikhail K. Tikhonravov, Yuriy Pobedonostsev, and Alexey M. Isayev. Besides the haul from the Blizna test site, the Soviets also captured a number of launch platforms and other equipment from a German missile launch team code-named R-13. This group had been moved into position in the Pskov region, as well as around Tallinn, in preparation for the use of V-2s against Leningrad. Their efforts were disrupted by local partisan activity as well as the general collapse of the German war effort.

While the Red Air Force's Raketa group was beginning its studies of the captured V-2 bits, the Red Army was considering its future role in the whole missile business. It had not escaped the attention of the Red Army's artillery branch that the V-1 buzz bomb was under the control of their counterparts in the German artillery branch. In the late summer of 1944, the Military Council for Artillery appointed Gen. L. M. Gaydukov to head a special project to assess the future of missile weapons. He appointed Lt. Col. A. I. Semenov, an army engineer, to head a field investigation team. To provide him with some experience in army missile needs, one of the most experienced Katyusha operations officers, Lt. Col. G. Tyulin, was assigned to his group.[20]

Tyulin examined the available material on the V-1 and was not impressed. It was apparent to him from reports coming from England that conventional antiaircraft defenses could deal with such missiles since they were little faster than conventional aircraft. Captured documents indicated the Germans were placing greater emphasis on the V-2 ballistic missile.[21] Tyulin recommended that the Red Army pay more attention to ballistic missiles than cruise missiles.

The issue of who would lead the missile program was still up in the air in the spring of 1945 when Soviet troops began occupying the main German missile test and production sectors. Both the test center at Peenemünde and the main V-2 production center at Nordhausen were in the Soviet occupation zone. The decision regarding which branch of the armed services would head the exploitation of this booty was made in the summer of 1945 following the Potsdam conference. After the organization of the First Chief Directorate under Boris Vannikov to accelerate the development of the Soviet atomic bomb, Stalin also authorized the formation of the Second Chief Directorate, under the command of wartime defense industries head, Dmitriy F. Ustinov. Ustinov would be responsible for developing delivery systems for the bomb. High on the list of potential for delivery systems was the ballistic missile.

By order of the Council of Ministers and the Central Committee of the Communist party, the Raketa group was dissolved and its members attached to the new Second Chief Directorate. While the Soviet aviation industry would play a central role in the development of the new missile technology, the Soviet Army and its artillery branch, not the air force, would be in charge. A similar debate occurred in the United States in the 1940s and 1950s, but with opposite results: the U.S. Air Force eventually emerged in control of the main ballistic missile program.

Ironically, the two engineers who would play the most prominent role in the Soviet ballistic missile program, Sergey Korolev and Valentin Glushko, were not involved in these initial efforts. They were still officially criminals under long-term sentence. With the revival of interest in missiles in the summer of 1944, friends and associates of both Glushko and Korolev tried again to convince Soviet authorities to release them. Finally, on 27 July 1944, Korolev's sentence was suspended. Glushko also was freed. Glushko was put in charge of the design bureau at Aircraft Plant No. 16 in Kazan, with Korolev as his deputy. Officially, they were involved in the same fruitless endeavor as before, the adaptation of rocket propulsion to propeller-driven aircraft. But Korolev soon began studies of the future of long-range missiles.

The rocket engineers attached to Ustinov's new command were assigned the task of studying captured German missile technology and initiating its production in the USSR.[22] The missile engineers formed a new group, the MTK, or Interdepartmental Technical Commission (*Mezhvedomstvennaya Tekhnicheskaya Komissiya*). The destination of the group was Germany; its mission: to recover as much material as possible about the German wartime missile program.

Even before the MTK set foot in Germany, the British and Americans had made considerable strides in the race to ferret out missile information. The Americans enjoyed an enormous windfall when key leaders of the German missile program, including Wernher von Braun, fell into their hands. This was not purely by chance. Von Braun had moved the key members of his team into Bavaria with the express idea of surrendering to the Americans rather than to the Soviets. This was not an unusual attitude in Germany at the time. The war on the eastern front between the Soviets and Germans had been waged with appalling brutality. As the Red Army advanced into Germany, horrific tales emerged of the fate of civilian populations left behind by the retreating *Wehrmacht*. The Red Army's conscious policy of brutal retaliation against the German civil population for the horrors of German occupation backfired in this case. It greatly hampered Soviet recruitment of key German engineers, who were terrified at the prospects of being captured in Soviet-occupied Germany.[23]

Two major missile centers fell into Soviet hands: the test center at Peenemünde and the underground production facility at Nordhausen. Peenemünde was less impressive a gain than might be expected. Since the British bombing raids of 1943, the development efforts were shifted to less obvious locations—the test range into Poland and the development offices to other locations.

Furthermore, the records at Peenemünde had been carefully sifted by members of von Braun's team, who carefully took the most important documents with them. Nordhausen, likewise, was something of a disappointment. Although ultimately in the Soviet occupation zone, the Americans and British managed to reach the site in advance of the Soviet forces. The Americans grabbed significant amounts of equipment, sufficient to build more than a hundred V-2 missiles, along with some documentation. However, they left behind much of the production equipment.

The initial Soviet effort was directed toward collecting as much documentation as possible about the German missile effort, its production centers, and its key scientists and engineers. The first members of the team arrived in Berlin in August and Sergey Korolev arrived shortly afterwards, wearing the uniform of a Red Army colonel.

The MTK was headed by Gen. L. M. Gaydukov on the army side, and Yuriy Pobedonostsev on the engineering side. Pobedonostsev was a close friend of Korolev from the Moscow rocketeer days, and came to rely on him for his advice on the conduct of the missile search. Korolev and Glushko were by far the most competent members of the MTK in assessing German missile technology. Other members, such as the air force's Georgiy Tokady-Tokayev, had very little practical experience with missile design. Still other members, including Nikolay A. Pilyugin and Vladimir P. Barmin, were there to study specific aspects of missile technology, such as guidance and launch systems.

Contact with their Anglo-American counterparts was wary and not entirely friendly. The British missile teams, part of Operation Backfire, decided to stage test firings of captured V-2s in October 1945. A Soviet delegation of three was invited for the third launch on 15 October; five showed up. General Gaydukov, his deputy, Pobedonostsev, and Valentin Glushko were allowed into the launch site. Korolev was politely but firmly turned away. During the preparation of the V-2 for firing, Pobedonostsev approached some of the American officers. He complained that they had "cleaned out" Nordhausen, making his job a great deal more difficult. He then offered to allow them to inspect Peenemünde if a Russian team could visit the new American test site at White Sands, New Mexico. The Americans turned down the request.[24]

One of the members of von Braun's team who refused to join the Americans was Helmut Grottrup. His reasons were never made entirely clear, even in his later writings, although conflicts with other members of the design group probably played a more important role than ideological leanings. In May 1945, a member of the Soviet MTK, Maj. Boris E. Chertok, visited Grottrup in the American occupation zone. Grottrup made several clandestine trips into the Soviet occupation zone, negotiating a contract to return to the eastern zone to assist the Soviets in reconstructing the Nordhausen production facility.

Grottrup had been the assistant director of the guidance and control lab of the German ballistic missile program and would emerge as the most senior German engineer to agree to work for the Soviets.

Gaydukov established the *Institut Rabe* as the German wing of the MTK program in occupied Germany. Rabe was an acronym for *Raketenbau und Entwicklung* (Missile Production and Development). It consisted of the main V-2 production facility at Nordhausen, called the *Mittelwerke,* as well as several subsidiary factories and development agencies. The main aim of the MTK and Institut Rabe was to reestablish V-2 production at Nordhausen and to prepare sufficient documentation to permit the establishment of V-2 production inside the Soviet Union.

In March 1946 the Supreme Soviet approved a new Five-Year Plan that contained an ambitious top-secret rocket program to complement the atomic bomb effort. The details were worked out at a Council of Ministers special session on 13 May 1946.[25] The program envisioned establishing German V-2 missile production in the Soviet Union as the first stage of a program to develop a long-range missile capability. It was still not at all clear that missiles could be designed to reach intercontinental targets such as the United States. But it did seem likely that weapons could be built in the near future which could reach targets in western Europe from the Soviet Union, a range over five times that of the existing V-2 missile. The plan also called for the creation of the first Soviet missile units, to acquaint the army with the characteristics and performance of these new weapons. The plan expected that by the end of the decade a new generation of indigenous Soviet missile designs would be ready to carry the new atomic bomb.

The Grottrup team managed to reconstruct a limited assembly line for V-2 missiles at the Mittelwerke. One of the main stumbling blocks was the dispersion of component plants. The Allied bombing campaign in 1944–45 had necessitated this dispersion to reduce the vulnerability of the rocket manufacturing effort. In 1946, many of these component manufacturers were in the British or American occupied zones. Grottrup and Gaydukov's teams managed to locate these suppliers. By barter and theft they managed to acquire enough parts to assemble thirty V-2 missiles by September 1946.

While working on the reconstruction of the production facilities, Institut Rabe was also assigned the task of assembling two FMS trains. FMS (*Fahrbare Meteorologische Station* or Mobile Weather Station) was the cover name for a V-2 launching train. Von Braun's group had come up with the idea in 1944 as a more practical way to move the large assortment of support equipment needed to fuel, test, and launch V-2s against England. By the summer of 1944, however, the railroad lines in western Europe were too dangerous due to the activities of Allied fighter-bombers, so the concept was abandoned. Not faced with the same problem, the Soviets found the idea attractive since it would concentrate the equipment in one location. The two FMS trains were to form the basis for the first Soviet missile units.

The Soviet Army formed its first ballistic missile unit, the BON (*Brigada osobogo naznacheniya* or Special Purpose Brigade) in July 1946 on the basis of an existing Guards Mortar (multiple rocket launcher) regiment. Commanded by Maj. Gen. A. F. Tveretskiy, the unit was equipped with the two special V-2 FMS missile-launcher trains. Tveretskiy's men accompanied the MTK engineers, learning the operation of V-2 missiles from German veterans. This unit was mainly intended to serve as a teaching establishment to form additional rocket units once quantity production of missiles began in the Soviet Union. It would also serve as the basis for the troops needed to fire test missiles once the program had matured sufficiently.

The activities of the Soviet Technical Commission in Germany also gave the leadership of the Soviet Army a better appreciation for the talents of the various Soviet engineers. If any one engineer's performance stood out, it was that of Sergey Korolev. Korolev had broad experience in aircraft and missile design, which gave him a good perspective on the accomplishments and shortcomings of the German missile program. So too did his former bureau chief, Valentin Glushko. But what separated Korolev from the other engineers was his administrative abilities. He worked well with other engineers, and they respected his judgment, and found it easy to cooperate with him in the very complex tasks that the commission faced. Korolev's understanding of German also helped, enabling him to deal freely with the Germans. If Korolev's disgust with the Communist party political officers and MVD security snoops showed, it was an attitude shared by many of the military officers as well.

Glushko, although a more talented engine designer than Korolev, was not as adept as Korolev in working with the other members of the commission. Glushko was a perfectionist, insisting on overseeing every last detail of the rocket engine studies himself. He had difficulty delegating responsibility to other design groups or even to his subordinates. Nor did he get along very well with the Germans—neither appreciating their contributions nor soliciting their help. His brilliance as a rocket engine designer made him an invaluable asset, but his shortcomings as a team leader led to the reversal of his wartime relationship with Korolev, who soon became the overall program head.

In the summer of 1946, Korolev was put in charge of the first serious attempt to modernize the German V-2, a project called K-1. The idea was to extend the V-2's range by expanding the fuel tanks. (Curiously enough, the Iraqis used the same idea nearly fifty years later to extend the range of their Soviet Scud missiles to hit Saudi Arabia and Israel.) Korolev also oversaw the completion of the multivolume study *Guide to the Materials for the Study of*

Captured Missile Technology, a series that became the bible of Soviet missile research in the years to come.

Meanwhile, in the Soviet Union, work was proceeding on the construction of facilities in which to house the German missile production equipment. Appropriately enough, the site chosen was the former site of Artillery Plant No. 8 in Kaliningrad in the suburbs of Moscow.[26] The plant had been erected in 1926 by Rheinmetall-Borsig under a secret cooperation plan between Germany and the Soviet Union.[27] The artillery manufacturing equipment had been evacuated to Sverdlovsk in 1941 during the German onslaught on Moscow, so in 1946 the plant site was abandoned. The new plant was under the direction of Gen. Lev Gonor, who had managed an artillery factory during the war. The missile program by this stage was largely under the administrative control of the Soviet Army's artillery branch, and its highly respected research arm, the GAU.[28] A second facility for rocket engine development was organized at Plant 456 in Khimki.

Korolev was appointed chief designer for NII-88 (Scientific Research Institute-88) at Kaliningrad in August 1946 while still in Germany. In the Soviet Union, chief designer (*glavnyy konstruktor*) was a prestigious rank reserved for the heads of engineer design bureaus. Korolev's design bureau at the NII-88 complex was eventually called OKB-1 (Special Design Bureau-1).[29] Glushko, already a chief designer from his wartime days heading the GDL-OKB, was put in charge of the new rocket engine development center at Plant 456. Korolev returned to the Soviet Union from Germany in January 1947, but he didn't stay in Moscow long. He had already suggested that the Soviet Army conduct a series of experimental V-2 launchings to acquaint Soviet engineers and military personnel with the procedures. The army agreed and a large area of sparsely inhabited steppe near Kapustin Yar, to the east of Stalingrad, was selected as the launch site.

Although OKB-1/NII-88 was nominally under the control of the Soviet Army's artillery branch, it formed a part of the network of research establishments tied to the new special police KB-1 design bureau (not to be confused with OKB-1). KB-1, based in Moscow, was responsible for all guided missile and high technology research. As was typical during this period, control of these programs was taken over by the NKVD state security forces. KB-1 was headed by Beria himself, and his son was one of the chief designers. Part of the reason for NKVD control was the high priority given to the ballistic missile program by Joseph Stalin. The program was threatened with entanglement in an unusually complicated set of bureaucratic ties since it was managed by the army's GAU but relied primarily on the Ministry of Aircraft Production (MAP) for its engineers and production facilities. NKVD control facilitated activities across ministerial lines.

With the Technical Commission mission in Germany largely finished, the Soviets began to consider the future of their German staff. This issue not only affected the five thousand German engineers and workers of the Institut Rabe missile program, but jet engine design groups, aircraft designers, and nuclear research teams. To date, the Germans had worked mainly on reestablishing German wartime technology. The Soviets were interested in soliciting German help in advancing the technology beyond the level of wartime programs, but they were concerned about the limits of security in occupied Germany. All of these high-tech groups were under the direct control of Beria's MVD special police. A plan was formulated to secretly move about twenty thousand of the most important German engineers and their families into the Soviet Union in October 1946 to continue their work there under tighter security. The forced transfer of the German engineers was given the code name Operation Osoaviakhim.[30] The evacuation was under the control of one of Beria's men, Col. Gen. Ivan Serov, the deputy special commissioner of the Soviet Military Administration of Germany and a first deputy in the MVD special police. Serov had only recently completed another high priority mission for Beria in Germany: the establishment of a uranium mining operation for the atomic bomb program.

On 21 October 1946 the key German missile engineers were invited to a meeting at General Gaydukov's residence in Bleicherode near the Mittelwerke missile production center. Gaydukov outlined the plans for further missile development. The meeting was followed by a party that lasted until 4:00 A.M. In the early morning hours, as the party was still going on, teams of Soviet special police began rounding up the Germans on the invitation list and depositing them on special trains. The roundup was made in haste. The Germans were appalled at the deception, but had little recourse but to obey the Soviet police. The trains arrived in Moscow on 28 October and the Germans were informed that they would become a part of Korolev's NII-88.

For all intents and purposes, the Institut Rabe had been enveloped wholesale into the First Circle of the Soviet GULAG system. Conditions for the Germans were far better than for the average Soviet zek. Grottrup and his wife were allotted a private villa, an automobile, and a chauffeur. Accommodations for the remaining German staff members were dependent on their rank. But there was no doubt that their freedom was substantially curbed. No one would be permitted to return to Germany until the group's work was completed.

The Antipodal Bomber

While the Soviet Army's artillery branch was working on the V-2 program, the Soviet Air Force was pursuing a more ambitious scheme. During the 1945 meeting of Truman, Churchill, and Stalin at Potsdam, Soviet intelligence officers had first learned of a secret German program to develop an intercontinental manned rocket bomber capable of reaching from Europe to the United States. The Sanger-Bredt bomber design was the work of Dr. Eugen Sanger and Dr. Irene Bredt. Sanger was one of a number of prewar rocket enthusiasts employed in the German aviation industry during the war. In the years before the war he had come up with the idea of building a manned aircraft that would be propelled into the edge of space using a rocket sled. The aircraft would skip like a flat stone along the upper reaches of the atmosphere and would offer a phenomenal range: on the order of 14,600 miles. Sanger was working on a 100-ton–thrust engine for the boost system in 1942, but the program was cancelled. Sanger and Bredt continued to pursue the idea without official Luftwaffe support. In 1944 they submitted a secret report which suggested that the aircraft could be used as a bomber capable of striking New York.[31] This highly fanciful project failed to stir much enthusiasm in the Luftwaffe, which was plagued by more pressing problems.

When Stalin learned of the project in 1945 he insisted that it be pursued in the Soviet Union. The project was assigned to the air force, and a young engineer, Georgiy Tokady-Tokayev, was given the task of hunting for documentation on the program. Tokady-Tokayev, one of a number of Soviet engineers assigned to study the German aviation industry, had little experience in rocket design. The material was forwarded to the reconstituted RNII rocket propulsion institute, where it received the attention of Mstislav V. Keldysh. A report on the prospects for such a weapon was prepared by RNII under Keldysh's direction and was finished in 1947.[32] Neither Keldysh nor Tokady-Tokayev held out great prospect for a short-term realization of such a project. It represented a far greater leap in technology than was realistic at the time. The rocket booster engine envisaged was several times more powerful than the most potent rocket engine yet built, the V-2's engine. The aircraft design would have to overcome enormous technological hurdles, such as the heat buildup difficulties experienced by high-speed aircraft in the earth's atmosphere.

In spite of their skepticism, there was a child-like fascination with such bizarre projects in the upper reaches of the Soviet leadership of the time, Stalin included. The considerable success demonstrated by the Germans in realizing many of their secret weapons programs convinced technologically illiterate men like Stalin that nearly anything was possible. It was an era of huge strides in military technology. The Sanger-Bredt antipodal bomber seemed no more fanciful to Stalin than the V-2 missile or the American atomic bomb.

On 13 April 1947 a meeting was held in the Kremlin in anticipation of another meeting scheduled for the following day to complete the outlines for a new Five-Year Plan. The engineers and scientists connected with the

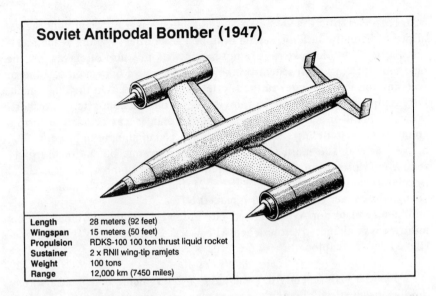

Soviet Antipodal Bomber (1947)

Length	28 meters (92 feet)
Wingspan	15 meters (50 feet)
Propulsion	RDKS-100 100 ton thrust liquid rocket
Sustainer	2 x RNII wing-tip ramjets
Weight	100 tons
Range	12,000 km (7450 miles)

program, including Keldysh and Tokady-Tokayev, were brought to the office of N. A. Voznesenskiy, chairman of the State Planning Committee (Gosplan). Present at the meeting was the entire upper leadership of the aviation industry, as well as Stalin's prominent Communist party associates, including Georgiy Malenkov.[33]

Lieutenant General Timofey Kutsevalov was a hotshot young fighter pilot who had won the top Soviet military decoration, the "Hero of the Soviet Union" medal, after he became an ace fighting against the Japanese in Manchuria in 1939 during the border battles there. Only forty-three years old, he was a rising star in the Soviet Air Force, although he was better known for his flying exploits than his appreciation of high technology. As the head of the Aviation Department in occupied Germany and Tokady-Tokayev's immediate superior, Kutsevalov made the initial reports to Stalin about the antipodal bomber. Kutsevalov assured Stalin that the bomber could indeed reach the United States with a large payload and return to the Soviet Union.

The head of the Soviet Air Force, Marshal Konstantin A. Vershinin, was apoplectic with rage at Kutsevalov's performance. "Never did I believe before such a blockhead could exist! Kutsevalov . . . had been babbling such twaddle in there that I burned with shame." Unfortunately, the damage had been done. Stalin was convinced of the program's feasibility.

The main meeting was something of an anticlimax. Both Tokady-Tokayev and Keldysh explained to the prestigious audience that the German designer,

Sanger, was a gifted theoretician, but not an engineer in touch with the re-alities of actually building such a design. The political leaders at the meet-ing, particularly Malenkov, were not happy with this turn of events. On the one hand, Stalin was insistent on the development of a weapon capable of reaching the United States in the shortest possible time. On the other hand, the existing rocket program, Korolev's V-2 reconstruction, offered no short-term prospects of accomplishing this. In the end, it was decided to form a commission, paralleling the Technical Commission already in place in Ger-many studying the main German missile programs, but more narrowly focused on preparing the Sanger-Bredt antipodal bomber. It was called Special Technical Commission-2 (STK-2), the other missile commission in occupied Germany having been renamed STK-1.[34]

When Minister for Aviation Production M. V. Khrunichev whined that his ministry was already overburdened with work, including STK-1's V-2 mis-sile, Malenkov exploded:

> I paid a visit recently to [where the V-2 was being built] and I was most dissatisfied. You don't seem to make any progress at all—it's still only the same old V-2. What are you thinking of Comrade Khrunichev? We are not going to fight a war with Poland! We have to remember there are vast oceans between ourselves and our potential enemy.[35]

The plan to proceed with the antipodal bomber was incorporated into the Five-Year Plan at Stalin's insistence. But Stalin's wishes or not, the project was technologically infeasible at the time. In the wake of continued prob-lems with the program, Stalin even ordered the Soviet special police to at-tempt to kidnap Dr. Sanger, at the time working for the French government. Nothing ever came of the scheme. During the kidnap attempt, Tokady-Tokayev used his visa to France as a means to defect.[36]

In October 1947 the Soviet report was handed over to several of the German scientists working under Korolev at NII-88 outside Moscow. They concurred with Keldysh and Tokady-Tokayev, labeling the scheme infeasible with the current level of technology available in the USSR.

The antipodal bomber program eventually petered out. Keldysh soon be-came wrapped up with the more practical work being undertaken by Korolev's team at NII-88. But the concept never entirely died. The antipodal bomber program is the ancestor of a number of later Soviet programs, eventually leading to the space shuttle *Buran* (Snowstorm).[37] Furthermore, the U.S. Air Force was inspired to begin developing an intercontinental cruise missile, called the Navaho, that flew within the atmosphere rather than in space. The American Navaho program sparked a revival of the Soviet program, as we shall see later.

The R-1 Missile

Despite Malenkov's dismissal of the Russian V-2 production program as being suitable for little more than bombing Poland, Stalin directed that it be continued. Korolev was called to Moscow for a personal meeting with Stalin on 14 April 1947, the same day as the antipodal bomber meeting was completed, and made a presentation on his group's progress. Korolev indicated that work was complete on the assembly of the first V-2s from German components. These would henceforward be called the R-1 missile in Soviet service. At the same time, production facilities were being set up in the Moscow suburbs to assemble V-2s using Soviet-manufactured components. These would be called R-1A missiles. Korolev also promised Stalin that the first test launches of the R-1 missile would begin that year in the Soviet Union.

After a year of training in basic missile handling, General Tveretskiy's special missile unit, the BON, was moved to the new Kapustin Yar proving ground to conduct the first launches. In anticipation of the launch, a static test firing of an R-1 engine took place on 17 September 1947 under Valentin Glushko's direction.

The test site at Kapustin Yar was still quite primitive at the time. There were few buildings, so most of the accommodations were being located in Lend-Lease U.S. Army tents. As one participant later recalled, the area had more camels than cars. The top official to arrive for the tests was the minister of the defense industry, Dmitriy Ustinov, who also headed the top-secret Second Main Directorate. Accompanying him were most of the senior officers of the Soviet Army's artillery branch. The German engineers were also brought to Kapustin Yar to observe the tests.

The first missile was ready on 18 October 1947 and was launched at 9:47 A.M.[38] Ustinov was delighted. He gave Korolev a bear hug, danced about, and bear-hugged the surprised head of the German team, Grottrup, as well. The Soviets had been very lucky. What they hadn't realized at the time is that the missile hadn't functioned properly. It lifted off the launch platform in good order, but the control system malfunctioned and the missile impacted a considerable distance from its intended target. The vagaries of the V-2 were expected by the Germans, who remembered all too well its finicky performance. This became obvious the next day when the second V-2 went awry shortly after launch, in a fashion all too familiar to the German engineers. There was some muttering from Soviet officials about the possibility of "sabotage," but Korolev pushed ahead with the test program. Most of the V-2s that had been assembled back in Germany in 1946, some twenty in all, were test fired from the end of October to the beginning of December 1947.[39]

Most of the engineers returned to the Moscow area following the tests. The ballistic missile efforts in late 1947 concentrated on two principal objectives, production of the R-1A in the Soviet Union and development of an improved derivative of the R-1. It was the Germans under Grottrup who did the pioneering work on the improved R-1. The German team was located at a separate facility at Gorodomlya Island. Under the code name R-10, Grottrup's team suggested three main innovations in the design. The fuel tanks, rather than being constructed as separate items, would be modified to use the outer walls of the missile fuselage itself. This type of construction, called monocoque, was already in use in more advanced aircraft designs, such as the American B-29 bomber, and had the advantage of considerable weight savings. The engine would also be modernized to increase its thrust. Finally, the warhead section would be made separable. This had several advantages, most notably in missile accuracy. The problem with the V-2 design was that during its descent, the missile could become unstable. Its weight was contained in the extreme forward end (the warhead) and in the extreme tail end (the rocket engine), since the fuel in the massive central section was largely expended. Under certain conditions this configuration could suffer from axial sway, causing the missile to wobble to either side and thus decrease accuracy. Under extreme conditions the axial sway could degenerate into a "barbell" effect, with the missile toppling end over end and finally disintegrating. By releasing the warhead near the top of the trajectory, these problems could be avoided and the warhead's flight path made much more accurate and predictable.

While Grottrup's team was working on the R-10, Korolev's team was involved in establishing the indigenous Soviet production lines for the V-2, called the R-1A. This was a formidable task given the backwardness of the Soviet aerospace industry at the time. Many of the materials and subcomponents required for the missile were nearly impossible to obtain. The effort eventually involved thirty-five research institutes and eighteen factories.[40]

Korolev had quickly appreciated that missile design and manufacture would require more than one design group and a single factory. Modern industrial technology is no longer the domain of a single inventive genius—there are simply too many fields that need to be mastered. It was Korolev's rare insight into the changing nature of technology that made him so successful a leader in missile design. In 1946 he had helped to arrange an informal working group made up of the chief missile designers. Such a group was an aberration in the Soviet Union at the time, the preferred managerial style being highly centralized through government-sponsored organizations. Given the pressures of the time, Korolev's approach proved far more efficient. The Council of Chief Designers, nicknamed the "Chiefs' Council" (*Sovet glavnykh*) consisted of the "Big Six" of Soviet rocketry: Korolev of OKB-1 (missile design), Glushko of the GDL-OKB (rocket engine design), Vladimir P. Barmin at the Kompressor Factory in Moscow (ground support and launching equipment), Viktor I. Kuznetsov (command and control), Nikolay A. Pilyugin (inertial guidance), and Mikhail S. Ryazanskiy (radio-command guidance).[41] The Chiefs' Council would play a central role in Soviet missile and space development over the next two decades.

Other Soviet engineers and scientists shared Korolev's ambitions but had neither the talent nor government support to carry them out. There were a score of small efforts to develop ballistic missiles, cruise missiles, sounding rockets, and other advanced missile weapons. But, working in isolation, they progressed far more slowly—or not at all.[42]

Production of the V-2 missile in the Soviet Union did not take place in quantity until 1950 due to the enormous difficulties in manufacturing and quality control. At the time, the aviation industry was attempting three crash programs simultaneously: the new strategic bombers (Tu-4 and Tu-16), a new jet interceptor (MiG-15), and the missile program. Its production capabilities were stretched to the limit. The first missiles became available in the fall of 1950, permitting the formation of the first Soviet missile unit at Kapustin Yar. The unit was given the cover name of 23d Special Purpose Engineer Brigade of the RVGK, and was commanded by Col. M. G. Grigoryev.[43]

The next step for Korolev's engineers was the design of an improved V-2 derivative, called the R-2. Grottrup's engineers had led the way with their study of the R-10. However, for security reasons, the German efforts were always kept separate from those of the Soviet team. The Soviet team used many of the concepts proposed for the R-10, but the Germans were never permitted to get a detailed picture of the Soviets' activities.

Development of the R-2 by Korolev's engineers began in earnest in April 1947. The process for approving a new development effort was the convocation of a special meeting of the Scientific and Technical Council at Kaliningrad. These meetings were attended by members of the Chiefs' Council, as well as critical government officials, such as Dmitriy Ustinov, the head of the Second Chief Directorate. After critical discussion of the program's objectives, the R-2 missile was approved.

The aim of the program was to double the range of the R-1A from 300 km to 600 km and, in the process, to gain the experience needed to develop a truly indigenous Soviet ballistic missile. The R-2 was longer than the R-1 in order to enlarge the propellant tanks, and used a monocoque fuselage and separable warhead as proposed by the Germans. The launch weight of the R-2 was 151 percent of the R-1 (20.4 tons vs. 13.9 tons), but the structural changes and engine improvements provided the intended performance enhancements. The first test flight took place on 26 October 1950, revealing several design problems. A modified R-2 design underwent test flights in 1951 and series production began in August 1951. The R-2 entered Soviet Army service in 1952.

Nature played a cruel trick on the Soviet rocketeers the following year. The main storage depot for the R-1A and R-2 missiles was in one of the central

districts of the Russian Republic. January 1953 was unusually warm, leading to a sudden thaw. A huge snow melt followed, causing a river near the
depot to overflow and flood the fields near the depot buildings. The missile
depot managed to survive the inundation, but the flooding also caused the
thousands of mice and voles in the neighboring fields to flee to the comfort
of the depot buildings. The rodents soon discovered the R-1A missiles in the
storage sheds and found the fabric insulation of the electrical wiring to be
quite tasty. By the time Soviet troops realized what had happened, a large
portion of the Soviet Army's missile arsenal had been ruined. General Gaydukov
personally visited the depot and relieved the commander, General Volkodav,
on the spot. Korolev, on hearing of the incident, reportedly laughed himself
to tears. OKB-1 sent a delegation of technicians in an attempt to rectify the
problem—along with a special detachment of cats.[44]

The successful completion of the R-2 missile marked the end of the ap-
prenticeship stage for Korolev's team. It was the last Soviet missile in which
the basic design was German or based primarily on German innovations. Future
designs, though certainly influenced by German technology, would take on
an increasingly Soviet character. The completion of the R-2 also marked a
watershed in the applications of missiles for the Soviet Army. Both the
R-1A and R-2 were basically improved V-2s, with similar operational quali-
ties. The next generation of missiles would be more carefully tailored to the
operational requirements of the Soviet Army, and they would be capable of
carrying nuclear weapons.

Nuclear Missiles

In July 1949 Korolev was called to an evening meeting in Stalin's Kremlin office to discuss the future of the missile program.[45] Stalin's much
desired antipodal bomber idea had proved to be a chimera and the intercontinental bomber program was floundering. With the atomic bomb program
nearing completion, Stalin wanted a method to deliver it to distant targets.
Stalin insisted that the First and Second Chief Directorates hasten their work:

> We want long, durable peace. But Churchill, well he's warmonger
> Number One. And Truman, he fears the Soviet land as the devil's own
> stench. They threaten us with atomic war. But we're not Japan. That's
> why we, Comrade Kurchatov, Comrade Ustinov, and you others as well,
> that's why things must be speeded up![46]

The new missile program gradually took shape in 1950. Rather than proceeding with a single missile design, three separate designs eventually emerged—
with three different applications. The Soviet Army was not entirely happy
with the R-1A and R-2. Both missiles were extremely cumbersome to use in

the field. The main problem was the cryogenic (super-cooled) fuel. The use of liquid oxygen as a propellant was a major inconvenience because it had to be maintained at very cold temperatures. Not only was this difficult to do in the field, but the missile could not be left on the pad for very long before launch as the oxygen would start to boil off. A more practical propellant was needed. This led to a new tactical ballistic missile called the R-11, similar in range to the R-1A, but easier for Soviet artillery units to operate.

The second missile under development, the R-5, was intended for operational-level targets deep in the enemy rear, to distances as far as 1,200 km away. Although the Second Chief Directorate's primary objective was the United States, Britain had also developed its own independent nuclear force. Besides British targets, there were a number of forward American strategic bomber bases in Europe that had to be targeted. The R-5 missile was essentially a much improved V-2, using cryogenic fuel. Although no easier to launch than the R-1A or R-2, the fueling complications were not a concern in a missile like this and the superior characteristics of liquid oxygen more than compensated for the inconvenience.

The third missile under development, the R-3, was the most ambitious, a 75-ton missile with a range of 3,000 km. The R-3 was intended to be the first Soviet strategic missile. Although it could not reach targets in the United States, it could reach American bases in England, Japan, and elsewhere. It was believed at first that this range was at the outer limit of the existing technology.

Korolev's approach to the accelerated program was to delegate much of the design work to his younger colleagues. He was probably influenced by his experience in the Tupolev design bureau before the war. Andrey Tupolev had favored large design bureaus, containing several teams of capable engineers. He viewed the other approach—a plethora of small design bureaus, each with their own chief designer—as costly and inefficient. Korolev's approach would make the Kaliningrad OKB-1 design bureau the training ground for many of the Soviet Union's most talented future missile designers.

The short-range missile, the R-11, was, in most respects, the least troublesome. The smallest of the three missiles, weighing about five tons on launch (compared to twenty tons for the R-2), its design team was headed by Korolev's assistant, Vasiliy Mishin. The R-5 missile, an evolutionary outgrowth of the R-2, was handled by a rising star in the missile design field, Mikhail K. Yangel. Korolev himself focused on the most challenging of the three, the R-3 strategic missile.

The Scud Missile

The R-11, which would gain fame in later years under its NATO code name, SS-1b Scud,[47] was the first Soviet ballistic missile to use hypergolic fuels. Hypergolic fuel, instead of using liquid oxygen to burn the propellant, uses a chemical oxidant, in this case nitric acid. Nitric acid reacts violently with hydrocarbon fuels such as kerosene. While it does not offer the efficiency of cryogenic fuels, such as the traditional alcohol/liquid oxygen combination, it is easier to use under battlefield conditions because both the propellant and oxidant remain at room temperature. The Germans had been designing such engines at the end of the war, though none entered quantity production. The R-11 used a rocket engine developed by one of the smaller Soviet teams under Aleksey Isayev. Isayev's new engine was based on a German design intended for the unfinished *Wasserfall* (Waterfall) antiaircraft missile. In 1949–50, the Soviet fighter design bureau under Semen Lavochkin was building a Soviet derivative of the Wasserfall for Soviet use as the R-101 antiaircraft missile. The R-11 ballistic missile would use essentially the same engine, but with a new fuselage design more suitable for a ballistic missile. The R-11 was ready for flight tests in 1953, and the first missile was launched on 28 April. It took nearly two years to work the bugs out of the system and prepare it for mass production, which finally began in 1955. It was produced in larger numbers than any previous Soviet ballistic missile. In its later versions, most notably the R-17 *Zemlya,* it would see more extensive combat use than any ballistic missile since the German V-2. Scud missiles were first fired in anger during the 1973 Arab-Israeli war, and are best known for their use in the Iran-Iraq war in 1987–88, in the Afghanistan war since 1988, and during the 1991 Persian Gulf war.

The R-5 missile was another step forward in the basic V-2 evolution. It would weigh only about 9 tons more than the R-2 (29 tons vs. 20 tons) but would nearly double the effective range. This was accomplished in no small measure by the use of a more efficient engine, the RD-103, being developed by Valentin Glushko's bureau. Like earlier Soviet ballistic missiles, the R-5 used the V-2 technique of graphite vanes in the rocket efflux for steering, rather than the more advanced engine gimballing concepts beginning to be examined in the United States at the time. Korolev favored proven technologies, particularly due to the marginal reliability of missiles at this time. The R-5 design progressed quite rapidly, with the first static test firing of the new RD-103 engine on 15 March 1953 and the first test flight of the prototype R-5 missile on 2 April 1954.

Korolev's R-3 program was a far more difficult proposition. The missile was expected to weigh about seventy-five tons on lift-off, more than three times heavier than any previous design. This necessitated a major leap forward in engine design. As was the case with strategic bomber design during the period, the limiting factor was engine design. The engine needed to be powerful enough to not only lift a given warhead off the launch pad, but to get the warhead to its intended target.

Glushko's bureau had been working on a variety of new approaches to improve liquid-fuel rocket engines.[48] However, none of these designs offered enough thrust to propel a missile of the type envisioned by the R-3 program. Glushko's GDL-OKB had been working on the RD-110 100-ton–thrust engine since the late 1940s. The design was a failure and a major setback in the development of intercontinental missiles.[49] Soviet metal technology of the time was simply not advanced enough to permit large volume combustion chambers able to withstand the heat, shock, and vibration of an engine developing so much thrust.

Korolev took a look at German intercontinental missile concepts, including the A9/A10. The A9/A10 was a two-stage design using a V-2 as the second stage. The first stage would lift the V-2 into space, at which time the V-2's engine would ignite and separate the rocket from the first stage. Although multistage missiles would later become standard in long-range strategic missile design, Korolev was not entirely happy with the idea in the 1950–51 period. The reasons had to do with missile engine reliability. Up to this point, engine reliability was not very great, even on simple single-stage missiles. Launch failures were commonplace. In the case of a two-stage design, the reliability problem had a potentially crippling effect since not only must the first stage perform perfectly, but the second-stage engine as well. The probability of both stages operating flawlessly was much lower than the probability of a single stage operating as planned. The other problem was uncertainty about the performance of rocket engines in the low-gravity environment of space. Most missiles built before that time used engines which largely exhausted their fuel by the time they reached their apogee in the upper atmosphere. The R-3 would travel higher and farther than any previous design.

Korolev's work on the R-3 program marked the beginning of his collaboration with Mstislav V. Keldysh, the brilliant young Soviet mathematician whose calculations helped torpedo the Sanger-Bredt antipodal bomber program. Keldysh had been appointed to head the RNII, so he and Korolev began examining the various options for long-range missile flight. The product of their collaboration was a twenty-volume study, *The Principles and Methods of the Design of a Long-Range Missile*. Keldysh completed the first stage of his study in 1951, and presented his findings to the Mathematics Institute of the Soviet Academy of Sciences.[50] The effort to develop an intercontinental ballistic missile was soon dubbed the "Three K" project for its three principal figures: Korolev, Kurchatov, and Keldysh.

The R-3 proposals considered a wide variety of approaches. One approach considered the possibility of a two-stage design using exotic new fuels, such as oxygen-difluoride, as the oxidant. A second design considered a missile with a central pair of propellant tanks feeding a single engine cluster with two or more external fuel tanks that could be jettisoned after they had been exhausted. The third option examined a multiple engine design fed by a single set of propellant tanks. The fourth called for a multiple engine design fed by separate propellant tanks with the exterior engines firing first, followed by the ignition of the remaining central engine cluster once the outer engines had exhausted their fuel. The fifth design study called for a multiple engine design, with all engines firing on launch. But the central cluster would be fueled from the tanks of the adjoining exterior engines and thus begin using its own fuel supply only after the exterior engine pods had exhausted themselves and dropped free. The sixth and final option called for a multiple engine design with all engines firing at launch, but a central engine remaining after fuel exhaustion by the exterior engines due to the greater capacity of its propellant tanks.[51]

The Cruise Missile Diversion

In December 1951 and January 1952 a series of meetings was held in Moscow to discuss the outcomes of these studies. Korolev noted that such designs could be scaled upward to surpass the requirements of the R-3 design, offering true intercontinental ranges on the order of 7,000 km. The sticking point still remained the engines. The technology of the day was still not mature enough to render any of these designs feasible.

Intelligence about American ballistic missile programs further interfered with the program. The U.S. Air Force was not pursuing intercontinental ballistic missiles with the single-minded purpose of the Soviets; it was still convinced that manned bombers were the only reliable delivery system for thermonuclear bombs. Unlike the Soviets, the Americans had bombers with sufficient range to reach their targets.

But a missile program *was* underway in the United States. The intercontinental system farthest along in the early 1950s was the XSM-64 Navaho, which had been under development since 1946. The Navaho was a ballistic rocket that boosted a supersonic cruise missile high into the atmosphere. The cruise missile was powered by a pair of ramjet engines. In some respects it was reminiscent of the Sanger-Bredt antipodal bomber, except that the final missile portion was powered and would fly the final leg of its flight inside the upper atmosphere.

The idea of using an atmospheric cruise missile was attractive for one principal reason: if an air-breathing ramjet was used to power it, it would not have to carry its own oxidizer, thereby reducing the missile's weight. By lowering the weight of the missile, a smaller rocket engine could be used in the first stage. In the case of the Navaho, the first-stage rocket engine had a thrust of twenty-five tons—well within the means of both American and Soviet rocket technology at the time.

The Korolev bureau began to take a look at a similar design as a fallback in case its own ballistic missile designs continued to be stymied. The Korolev proposal differed from the American Navaho in configuration, but the basic concept was the same. It was a two-stage missile launched with a liquid-fuel rocket engine on the bottom and a ramjet-powered cruise missile for the second stage. The only significant difference between this idea and the Navaho was that the Korolev design placed the cruise missile on top of the first stage, while the Navaho mounted the cruise missile on the side. Korolev's design envisioned keeping the missile in the atmosphere throughout its flight, with the ramjet providing the boost needed for extended ranges.[52] The oxidant would come from the atmosphere: ordinary oxygen.

Korolev suggested that work should begin first with a test missile with a half-ton warhead and a range of 900–1,300 km before the full-scale design was attempted. This was agreed to, and the work began in 1952.

The Korolev intercontinental cruise missile never proceeded beyond the design phase. In April 1953 the project was taken out of his hands by the state commission so that his design bureau could concentrate on ballistic missiles. Two other designers were given the assignment of developing an intercontinental cruise missile: Myasishchev and Lavochkin.

Myasishchev's bureau had no experience at all in missile design. But it was widely assumed that the real trick would be the cruise missile portion, not the basic first-stage rocket booster. Myasishchev, as noted earlier, raided key Moscow institutes and schools and collected one of the largest groups of bright new aviation designers to help on his M-4 Molot strategic bomber project. Furthermore, his bureau had also scooped up a number of key engineers who had been involved in the design of cruise missiles at Vladimir Chelomey's bureau.[53] Inside the bureau, the Myasishchev missile was code-named "Product 40," although it was better known by the Russian word for forty, *Sorokovka*.[54]

Lavochkin's design bureau was famous for its most successful World War II fighter aircraft designs, the La-5 and La-7, arguably the finest Soviet fighter aircraft of the war. Lavochkin had not fared as well in the postwar years. With the advent of the jet engine, it was the upstarts—Sukhoi and Mikoyan—who won most of the fighter design contests. Lavochkin and his team retained enormous prestige and continued to earn a reputation for adventurous, ground-breaking research. In 1949–50, Stalin personally ordered Lavochkin to take over the top-secret R-101 antiaircraft missile program. Stalin, deeply fearful of the consequences of American nuclear attacks on Soviet cities, insisted on a crash program to develop such a weapon. Work on the R-101 project gave Lavochkin his first experience with missile design. The Lavochkin project was given the designation La-X, although it was better known by its code name *Burya* (Tempest).[55]

The Lavochkin and Myasishchev strategic cruise missile designs were essentially similar. They planned a conventional, liquid-fuel rocket for the first stage. This would boost the cruise missile up to an optimum altitude of between 12 and 22 km. It was up to Keldysh's RNII to determine these requirements.[56] The upper stage, the cruise missile portion, would be powered by one or more ramjet engines being developed by M. M. Bondaryuk's design bureau. The main difference between the designs was the payload. Myasishchev's missile would have a payload some 150 percent of Lavochkin's. As a result, Myasishchev's first stage would require a larger booster. The rocket engine for the first stage of the Myasishchev missile was undertaken by Valentin Glushko's bureau. Lavochkin was already working with the Isayev rocket engine design bureau for the development of the R-101 antiaircraft missile's engine, so Isayev was given the task of developing the engine for Lavochkin's missile.

The Myasishchev design followed the basic layout of the earlier Korolev project with the cruise missile mounted above the first-stage rocket booster. But it looked considerably different. Rather than a single rocket in the first stage, the Sorokovka had four boosters. The cruise missile also differed in appearance, having a slender delta wing rather than the more conventional wing of the Korolev design.

The Lavochkin Burya was, in many ways, the more advanced of the two designs. The boosters were a pair of simple liquid-fuel rockets with a combined thrust of 140 tons. The cruise missile stage resembled a large aircraft with stubby swept wings and conventional tail surfaces. Its propulsion was by ramjet. The missile was remarkable for a variety of reasons. It pioneered the use of advanced metals, notably titanium, for an aerodynamic vehicle. Titanium was attractive for its strength, light weight, and resistance to the high-temperature buildup that could be anticipated in the atmosphere at speeds of Mach 3. Equally innovative was the guidance method selected: astronavigation. On the spine of the fuselage were two optical ports that collected data on star locations and fed them into the missile's computer navigation system.[57]

The Race Is On

The development of the Sorokovka and Burya cruise missiles completely changed the complexion of the Soviet strategic missile program. Korolev realized that he was in a race with not only the Americans, but other Soviet designers as well. He had already been leaning toward abandoning the R-3 in favor of a true intercontinental ballistic missile, one with a range capable of reaching the United States. The initiation of the competitive cruise missile program in April 1953 forced his decision. He determined he must leapfrog ahead.

The main stumbling block remained the matter of propulsion. The failure of the GDL-OKB to develop a 100-ton–thrust rocket engine was a serious setback, since an intercontinental missile would need an even bigger engine. The limiting factor in the engine design was the combustion chamber. The state of metallurgy and welding technology in the early 1950s did not permit the construction of a chamber large enough for 100 tons of thrust since no existing design could withstand the tremendous heat and vibration for any period of time. The experimental chambers that were built simply disintegrated in the fiery onslaught.

But Glushko was not totally dismayed by the failure of the 100-ton engine. Design studies in 1952 suggested a different approach. By clustering several small combustion chambers together, all fed by the same turbopump, an engine of considerable thrust could be created that would offer greater efficiency and reliability than several larger single-chamber engines. This idea was subjected to further discussion in the Chiefs' Council. Korolev was already leaning in the direction of a so-called packet design. This would take the engine cluster idea one step further. Not only would a clustered engine be used, but five "clusters of clusters." The five-clustered engines would provide a tremendous amount of thrust: 400 metric tons.

Stalin's death in March 1953 led to a general reexamination of the conduct of strategic weapons programs. In the summer of 1953 the Interdepartmental Committee overseeing the First and Second Chief Directorates' programs was convened to examine the progress on the R-3 missile. The meeting was attended by the new head of the nuclear weapons program, Vyacheslav A. Malyshev, and the head of the strategic missile and bomber program, Dmitriy Ustinov. Korolev summarized the conduct of the R-5 strategic missile program and the R-11 tactical missile. As Malyshev and Ustinov listened attentively, Korolev shocked his audience by suggesting that the R-3 program be cancelled. Korolev argued that the R-3, with its range of only 3,000 km, was not what was really needed. What was needed was a true intercontinental missile, with a range of 7,000 to 8,000 km, capable of delivering a thermonuclear bomb all the way to the United States.

Malyshev was particularly flabbergasted by the proposal. So far, Korolev's team had managed only to fire missiles to ranges of about 500 km with 35-ton–thrust engines, and now they were talking about 8,000 km–range missiles with 250-ton–thrust rockets! It seemed too good to be true. Malyshev preferred the certainty of a less capable missile, with a 3,000 km range available in the short term, rather than a possible 8,000 km missile in the far distant future. Korolev argued that 3,000 km or 8,000 km was not the issue. Given the design studies, either missile would take approximately the same amount of time to develop and test. Malyshev was deeply suspicious of Korolev's motives in suggesting the new missile. He accused Korolev of attempting to develop a space booster disguised as a military missile.

Since the inception of the missile program, Korolev had carefully supported a small-scale space research program as an adjunct to the military program. Small numbers of R-1 and R-2 missiles had been requested by the Academy of Sciences to conduct tests in the upper atmosphere.[58] Korolev's personal ambitions were more closely tied to the dreams of visionary Russian space enthusiasts like Tsiolkovskiy than to the military programs of Stalin and his successors. Korolev had already sponsored studies to place a man in space using the R-2 missile as a booster.[59] Malyshev knew of these interests and suspected that they were at the heart of Korolev's proposal.

As mentioned earlier, Malyshev was inclined toward a more conservative approach in weapons development, preferring less ambitious but more certain efforts over risky gambles. Deep down, he was suspicious of any revolutionary improvements in weapons technology. From bitter wartime experience, he had learned that incremental, evolutionary improvements were more suited to Soviet industry.

However, Malyshev was not in charge of the strategic missile program; Ustinov was. And Ustinov had a great deal more faith in Korolev. Ustinov was under considerable pressure to develop a weapon system capable of reaching the United States. The bombers under development were having serious teething pains. Ustinov was surprised by Korolev's proposal but, on reconsideration, it made sense. The ultimate objective of the Second Chief Directorate had always been to develop a missile capable of reaching the United States. If Korolev thought that it was feasible to make the leap forward, skipping the R-3 stage, Ustinov was willing to trust his judgment.

The meeting concluded with several tentative agreements. Malyshev insisted that Korolev complete his work on a medium-range missile capable of carrying an atomic bomb. This project, the R-5, was due for test flights in 1954. Until then, any talk of intercontinental missiles was nothing but boastful promises. Ustinov and Malyshev agreed to set up a governmental commission to decide the fate of Korolev's intercontinental missile. A success with the R-5 was necessary if Korolev hoped to win their confidence.

The genius behind the Soviet space and missile program, Sergey P. Korolev, shown here after World War II following his release from prison on trumped-up treason charges. *Sovfoto*

Stalin and his entourage walk to Red Square during World War II. To Stalin's right is Vyacheslav Molotov, nominal head of the Soviet A-bomb program until 1944. To Stalin's left is Marshal Klimenti Voroshilov, whose inept performance early in the war led to his removal from positions of responsibility. Immediately over Voroshilov's shoulder is Georgiy Malenkov, Stalin's erstwhile successor in 1953, and beside him, the sinister NKVD chief, Lavrentiy Beria. *Sovfoto*

The man behind the Soviet atomic bomb program, Igor V. Kurchatov. Not surprisingly, his subordinates nicknamed him "the Beard." *Sovfoto*

Andrey N. Tupolev, the grandfather of Soviet aviation, while in the prison design bureau at Omsk in 1943. Behind him is his wartime medium bomber design, the Tu-2.

Mstislav Keldysh, the mathematical genius behind the Soviet strategic weapons program, played a crucial role in the scientific research behind the atomic bomb, early ballistic missiles, and the first strategic bombers. *Sovfoto*

Kurchatov (left) chats with Yuliy B. Khariton, head of the nuclear bomb design team at Arzamas-16.

The wartime administrator of the A-bomb program, Mikhail G. Pervukhin. An NKVD officer, he was responsibe for the vital uranium production effort after the war. *Sovfoto*

The head of the ill-fated OKB-23 bomber design bureau, Vladimir M. Myasishchev, shown shortly before his death in 1968. In front of him is a model of his failed 3M Molot (Bison) bomber.

General Dmitriy F. Ustinov, head of the wartime Soviet armaments industry. After the war, he headed the Second Chief Directorate, responsible for developing nuclear-armed bombers and missile systems. *Sovfoto*

Gen. Vyacheslav A. Malyshev, wartime head of the tank industry, and head of the nuclear weapons program after Beria's downfall. *Sovfoto*

Vladimir N. Chelomey, head of the upstart OKB-52 missile design bureau, which challenged both Korolev and Yangel in the mid-1960s.

Mikhail K. Yangel, head of the SKB-586 missile design bureau.

The Tupolev Tu-4 was the first postwar Soviet strategic bomber. It was a direct copy of the Boeing B-29A Superfortress. *P. Butowski*

The first Soviet ballistic missile was the R-1A, a carbon copy of the German V-2. It was too small to carry the early Soviet A-bomb.

As a matter of national prestige, Stalin insisted on a strategic jet bomber. The result-ing M-4 Molot (Bison) bomber proved to be too short-ranged for nuclear strikes against targets in the United States. *P. Butowski*

The first series-produced Soviet A-bomb was code-named "Tanya." The disarmed version shown here is currently preserved at a formerly secret museum on the grounds of the Arzamas-16 design center. *Sovfoto*

The Tu-95 Bear bomber outlived all its Soviet competitors with production continuing into the 1980s. It proved very adaptable. Shown here is a Tu-95RTs Bear D long-range naval patrol bomber. (U.S. Navy)

The first Soviet nuclear missile was Korolev's R-5M, the last Soviet design based on wartime German missile technology. The R-5M was too short-ranged to strike vital targets in Europe and Asia, so it was not produced in significant numbers. *Sovfoto*

This photo, taken from an American U-2 spy-plane, was the first clear evidence of strategic missile launchers at the Tashkent-50 base. The enormous chasm beside the launch pad was called the "Stadium" by its soviet designers. It deflected the hot rocket exhaust away from the launcher.

The Lavochkin La-350 Burya intercontinental cruise missile was one of the most technologically advanced Soviet designs of the 1950s. This illustration from the Lavochkin design bureau shows the cruise missile portion separating from its two rocket boosters. *National Air & Space Museum.*

The first successful Soviet ICBM was the R-7 Semyorka. During launch preparation it was held in place by the massive girder structure of the Tyulpan launcher system shown here.

The final product of Myasishchev's OKB-23 design bureau was the M-50 Bounder supersonic bomber. As was too often the case with Myasishchev's designs, the M-50 proved incapable of effectively engaging targets in America.

The first SLBM was Korolev's R-11FM, a version to the famous Scud family. Here one is being prepared for loading into a Project 611AB submarine.

The Yangel R-12 missile was at the center of the Cuban missile crisis. Seen here on parade in Moscow, the R-12 used a simple pad launcher, which the Soviets believed would be easy to conceal. *Sovfoto*

This Project 611AB (Zulu V) submarine was forced to the surface near Iceland in May 1959 by U. S. Navy subhunters. Its two R-11FM missiles are contained in the two domed launch tubes visible at the rear of the conning tower. *DIA*

The Project 629 (Golf I) submarine used the nuclear-armed Makayev R-13 missile. This diesel-powered submarine was the backbone of the Soviet Navy's SLBM force in the early 1960s. *DIA*

Photos like this convinced the CIA something was afoot in Cuba in the late summer of 1962. This star-shaped deployment pattern is characteristic of the Soviet V-75 Volkhov antiaircraft missile, the type used to shoot down Francis Gary Powers's U-2 spy-plane over the USSR in 1960. *U.S. Air Force*

The Yangel R-14 was a longer ranged missile scheduled for deployment in Cuba. The U.S. blockade prevented ships carrying these missiles from ever arriving there. *Sovfoto*

The most worrisome photos to U.S. intelligence agencies were like this one, taken near the San Cristobal missile site. This prefabricated shelter was a standard Soviet nuclear warhead storage and handling structure.

Nikita Khrushchev displays evidence from Francis Gary Powers's U-2 spy-plane, shot down over the USSR on 1 May 1960. The photo in his hand is a contact sheet showing several pictures taken by the spy-plane's cameras during its overflight. *Sovfoto*

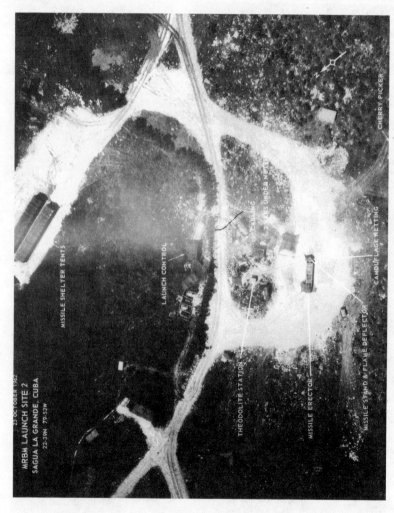

An aerial reconnaissance photo of the Soviet R-12 ballistic missile site at Segua la Grande, Cuba, during the missile crisis. The half-hearted Soviet attempts to camouflage the missile sites allowed the United States to discover them before they were ready for operation. *U.S. Air Force*

Chapter 6

Technological Pearl Harbor

WITH THE ADVENT of the new year, Korolev faced the challenge of convincing the government of the feasibility of his ambitious plan for an intercontinental ballistic missile. Ironically, his hopes for this venture rested on the performance of a far less ambitious missile, the R-5, code-named *Pobeda* (Victory).

The R-5 was the first ballistic missile of indigenous Soviet design. Although it was an evolutionary outgrowth of the R-2, it was considerably more sophisticated and refined, having nearly double the R-2's range, some 1,200 km. The most important element of the design was its engine, the new RD-103 developed by Valentin Glushko's GDL-OKB design bureau. Engine static test firings began on 15 March 1953 and continued for the rest of the year. As confidence in the new engine soared, plans were begun to launch the first R-5 missile at Kapustin Yar. The migration of designers and workmen from the plants in the Moscow area to the southern steppes began in early 1954, and the first successful R-5 launch took place on 2 April. It was an important milestone for the Soviet missile program. It provided the Soviet Army with the first missile capable of reaching American bases near the Soviet frontier. Earlier missiles, such as the R-2, had been dismissed as "good for nothing but firing at Poland." The R-5 was also the first Soviet missile with sufficient throw weight to carry an atomic warhead.

Work on a version of the R-5 suitable for carrying the atomic bomb began in 1954. Called the R-5M, there was nothing fundamentally different between it and the R-5. The changes were entirely a matter of reliability. The early Soviet missiles, like missiles elsewhere at the time, were not particularly dependable. All too often they blew up on the launch pad, veered wildly off course after launch, or otherwise managed to do something other than what was expected. This was in part due to the novelty of the technology and in part to the rough-and-ready engineering style of Korolev and his associates. There was so much urgency to the program that shortcuts were often taken to push the program forward. Korolev preferred to test a concept with actual hardware, not to depend on lengthy paper studies. This technique would ultimately prove successful, but it did lead to a recurring string of launch-pad explosions at Kapustin Yar.

The R-5M would have to be different. Lack of reliability would be totally unacceptable with a nuclear weapon resting atop the missile. A single malfunction, and the entire launch area would be obliterated. Special care was taken during the manufacture of the R-5M to ensure that each component worked flawlessly. Extra attention was paid to the guidance and control system. A new system was developed by Nikolay A. Pilyugin which had duplicate and, in some cases, triplicate, control channels. If one channel failed, another could be used.

Work on the R-5M was completed in the late summer of 1954 and a third set of R-5 tests was conducted in August at Kapustin Yar to ensure that the new R-5M components worked as predicted. The first actual R-5M missiles were manufactured at the new Dnepropetrovsk plant in the winter of 1954–55 in time for trial launches in the summer of 1955.

For more than six months, from the summer of 1955 to early 1956, twenty-eight R-5M test launches were conducted. A special restricted test range was set aside at Kapustin Yar, code-named Range 4N. The special test area was used not only by Korolev's men, but a team of Kurchatov's atomic bomb specialists from the Arzamas-16 development center. Aleksandr P. Pavlov and Vladimir K. Lilye were assigned the task of developing a modified fission bomb suitable for mounting on the R-5M missile. As was the case with the missile itself, the new bomb design had to have redundant safety and arming systems to ensure that it did not prematurely detonate, yet would detonate reliably when scheduled to do so.

During the R-5M missile tests in 1955, the plutonium fissile material in the dummy bomb was replaced by a special steel model. Even though the warhead impacted against the ground with considerable force, the steel marker could be recovered. From close inspection of the steel marker, the atomic bomb designers could determine whether the explosive lenses of the bomb had detonated properly. In the twenty-eight test flights, only one of the missiles exploded on the pad, a remarkable achievement for its day. But there were a number of cases where the missile failed to launch, as well as a number of cases where the missile missed its intended target by a considerable distance. The final state classification launch took place on 11 January 1956 and was entirely successful.

Operation Baikal

A state commission was formed to organize and supervise the first launch of an R-5M missile with a nuclear warhead. Head of the commission was Pavel M. Zernov, who had been the administrator in charge of Soviet atomic bomb production. Representing the main customer for the new missile was Marshal Mitrofan I. Nedelin. Nedelin was a crusty artillery officer who after the war headed the GAU, one of the most powerful agencies in the Soviet Army. Nedelin's GAU represented the army in all matters related to missiles and atomic weapons. Nedelin was the driving force behind the army's interest in the missile program. Following Stalin's death and Beria's execution, there was a diffusion of power. For expensive weapons programs like Korolev's, support was needed not only from the Party, but the military as well. It was forceful advocates like Nedelin who ensured a constant stream of funds for Korolev's missiles.

Also present for the R-5M launch were the members of the Chiefs' Council —Korolev, Glushko, Pilyugin, Ryazanskiy, Barmin, and Kuznetsov—and Pavlov, as a representative of the bomb designers. The launch was scheduled for 18 February 1956. The skies over Range 4N at Kapustin Yar were sunny and bright, but the impact area was clouded over. The test was postponed for two days. Korolev got very little sleep during the interlude, and his aides recall him being a nervous wreck. Korolev had witnessed hundreds of test launches and dozens of failures. This launch was especially critical. Missiles without nuclear warheads offered little over conventional aircraft, but a successful nuclear-armed missile would take the Soviet armed forces one step closer to their ultimate objective: a weapon that could strike directly at the United States.

The skies over the impact area cleared on 20 February, and Zernov agreed to initiate the test. The missile design teams were located in a bunker six miles from the launch site as a precaution in case the R-5M's atomic warhead blew up prematurely. The launch went smoothly. The missile lifted off and quickly disappeared into the low cloud cover lingering over the launch site.

Minutes later, observers at the impact area telephoned to announce: "We observed Baikal."

The test was a success.

Number 7

While Korolev and his teams of engineers in Kaliningrad were perfecting the R-5M, work on a far more ambitious missile was underway. Due to strong opposition to Korolev's idea of dropping the R-3 missile program in favor of a true intercontinental missile, Ustinov had agreed to establish a state commission to study the matter. The commission was headed by Konstantin N. Rudnev. Rudnev at the time was the deputy defense minister and chairman of the State Committee for Defense Technology. The committee sponsored and coordinated advanced high-technology research efforts in place of Beria's old KB-1. Rudnev was very familiar with the missile programs, having served as director of the NII-88 research center in Kaliningrad in 1950. The commission included representatives from the army and the aerospace industry.

Rudnev's deputies on the commission were Marshal Nedelin, representing the GAU, and Gen. G. Tyulin, a ballistics expert from the Academy of Artillery Sciences. The military was suspicious of Korolev, sharing Malyshev's concern over his obsession with space research and his arrogant independence from state control. But Korolev's proposal to embark directly on an intercontinental missile design without an intermediate medium-range missile was supported by Keldysh's mathematical analysis. Further evidence came from Valentin Glushko, who argued that the clustered engine concept was within the state of the art. In spite of the initial skepticism of Malyshev and the military, Korolev's bold approach looked more and more attractive. In May 1954 Korolev received final governmental approval to begin construction of the new intercontinental ballistic missile (ICBM).[1] The new missile was labeled R-7, but it was better known to its designers as *Semyorka* (Little Old Seven).

By the time he got the green light in 1954, Korolev and his team were well along in the design process. Earlier studies of various configurations had led them to select the basic design for the R-7, which consisted of a central fuselage with its own propellant tanks and engine. Attached to this central core were four "packets," each containing a complete engine and propellant system. The central engine, as well as the four packets, would be ignited simultaneously on the ground. The packets would have an endurance of 130 seconds and would drop away from the central core after burnout. The remaining central core would continue to be propelled by the remaining engine, which had an endurance of 320 seconds.

One of the major technological hurdles in the development of the R-7 ICBM was the matter of propulsion. The design requirement called for a missile capable of delivering a thermonuclear warhead to targets in the United States. Early Soviet thermonuclear devices, with their fuzing and arming system, ablative shield, and container, weighed up to 4.5 metric tons. Even with the innovative clustered engine configuration, the task was extremely formidable. Besides the weight of the warhead, the R-7 was burdened by a relatively heavy structure due to Soviet backwardness in aviation materials and metallurgy. For example, the contemporary U.S. Atlas missile design incorporated a lightweight stainless-steel skin so thin that it had to be kept "inflated" by internal positive overpressure to keep it from collapsing. In contrast, Korolev's design was so robust that workmen could actually walk along the outer skin of the missile when unfueled. The launch mass of the R-7 without fuel was 23 metric tons; with fuel it was 267 metric tons. Therefore, the total thrust requirement was on the order of 400 metric tons. The thrust of the largest Soviet rocket engine before that time (the RD-103 on the R-5 missile) was a mere 40 metric tons.

Earlier efforts on the 100-ton–thrust design forced Glushko to adopt an engine cluster with four separate combustion chambers but only a single turbopump to feed them. It was an ingenious solution, but it required the design of a turbopump of considerable complexity. The individual chambers on the new engine did not offer much more thrust than those of the German V-2 engine, but they were only a third the weight and far more efficient.[2] Two slightly different engines were designed for the R-7: the RD-107 for the four packets, and the RD-108 for the central sustainer. The main difference between the two engine types was that the RD-107 had two vernier thrusters, used to steer the missile, while the RD-108 had four—and a longer burn time. These engines still used vernier thrusters, as the more advanced method of steering the engine by gimballing the main combustion chamber proved to be beyond Soviet capabilities at the time. The attempt to develop the R-110 gimballed engine for the original R-3 proposal had been a failure.

Guidance and trajectory planning also presented a significant technological challenge. Never before had a missile been fired over such enormous distances. An inertial guidance system of the type used by the V-2 was suitable for flights of a few hundred miles, but its inherent inaccuracies, acceptable at short ranges, would lead to gross navigational errors at the ranges contemplated for the R-7. Even if it was armed with a powerful thermonuclear weapon, it would still have to land within a few miles of the target.

Development of the guidance system was a cooperative effort between the Ryazanskiy and Pilyugin design bureaus. Ryazanskiy's bureau was responsible for the radio-command guidance portions, and Pilyugin's developed the inertial guidance elements. Following launch, the missile would be tracked by radar, with radio-command guidance signals transmitted to the guidance unit to make modest corrections using the vernier chambers until the proper ballistic trajectory was reached.[3] At this point, the inertial guidance system could take over. A crucial role in the study and planning of over-the-pole trajectories was undertaken by Mstislav Keldysh.

Tashkent-50

As important as the missile and its subsystems were to the program, it was the surrounding infrastructure that proved so costly. The missile represents only 15 to 20 percent of the cost of an intercontinental missile system.[4] The real cost comes from launch pads, missile preparation facilities, fuel systems, tracking and telemetry stations, and a host of other construction programs.

The Soviet government decided to erect a new and more elaborate test center for the R-7 missile program. Three sites were studied. Makhachkala in Dagestan on the Caspian Sea seemed attractive because boosters from the missiles would fall harmlessly into the sea. The forested area of the Mordovian Republic in the Urals was also studied.[5] But the site finally selected was near the Tyuratam railroad station in the Kazakhstan desert. It was isolated enough to discourage spying and the area was sparsely populated. The new launch site was code-named Tashkent-50. In later years, when the Soviet Union publicly announced the site of origin of the first space flights, it was called Baikonur—even though the town of Baikonur is 400 kilometers from the missile launch pads. The misnaming of the site was typical of Soviet security precautions of the time.

Prior to the R-7, Soviet ballistic missiles had employed wheeled transloader trailers and simple launch deflector pads. These were clearly inadequate for so large a missile. In 1955 the Barmin OKB was assigned the task of developing the new launch site at Tashkent-50, including the enormous launch complex itself and related support facilities, such as the huge assembly and preparation hangars.[6] Support facilities for missiles of this size usually absorbed at least half of the funding for the program. This program led to the legendary *Tyulpan* (Tulip) launch structure that is characteristic of Soviet launch sites even today.[7] Tyulpan got its name from its shape. The R-7 missile sat in the center of the complex, stabilized on all four sides by enormous "petals." The petals contained the work gantries and other structures needed to fuel and test the missile before launch. When the launch was initiated, the petals would fold back away from the missile, allowing it to lift off unimpeded. At the base of the Tyulpan was a gigantic concrete foundation and exhaust trough, nicknamed the "Stadium." This deep chasm vented hot exhaust gases from the rocket engines away from the launch pad. The excavation of the Stadium required the removal of more than a million cubic meters of earth.[8]

Until the advent of the Semyorka, facilities for tracking the missile over long distances were lacking in the Soviet Union. Such facilities are needed for two reasons. First, telemetry equipment is used to monitor the performance of the missile's subsystems in flight. This is absolutely essential in so complex a weapon as an ICBM. There are hundreds of onboard systems that could cause missile failure. Even minor devices, such as fuel pumps, can lead to engine shutdown and loss of the missile if not performing properly. The telemetry devices monitor their performance and transmit the data to a ground station. In the event of missile failure during testing, these devices help the engineers determine what went wrong so that corrections can be made. Second, tracking devices monitor the missile's flight path. Radar is the traditional method of missile tracking, though in the crucial initial launch stages, optical devices also follow the missile's path.

Korolev and the other chiefs had relied on captured German telemetry equipment for the R-1 and R-2 programs. New equipment was developed for the R-5, but it was not adequate for an ICBM. A network of command and telemetry posts had to be established and proper equipment developed. It was not until the early 1960s that an adequate tracking network began to take shape.[9] Until then, the missile programs relied on a haphazard mix of ground stations and telemetry devices to track missiles in flight.

The first static test firings of the R-7 engines began in February 1956. The engines were the single most likely source of missile failures, and special attention was needed to ensure their reliability. The government program for the R-7 was much too ambitious. Korolev wrote in a report to the government, "The preparatory operations for the first launches of the rocket are proceeding with significant difficulties and behind schedule."[10] The first launch was pushed back several times and finally scheduled for March 1957.

Test Launch

Even though his own missile program was proceeding with great difficulty, Korolev's competitors working on the winged cruise missile program were even farther behind. The Myasishchev Sorokovka project was still in the paper phase; the bureau was simply too overwhelmed by work on the M-4 bomber and the newer M-50 supersonic bomber project. Lavochkin's remarkable La-X Burya transitioned from paper to metal first. But the first La-X launch, in 1957, went awry. Fortunately the missile crashed some distance from the pad. An enormous amount of money was being pushed into the program. The cruise missile portion itself was made partially of titanium, a very expensive metal even in the USSR. Additionally, the fabrication of the cruise missiles required revolutionary engineering discoveries, further driving up the cost.

The ballistic missile designers proceeded in full knowledge that the cruise missile designers were hot on their heels. Korolev and his team began preparing for their first launch at Baikonur in February 1957.[11] Erection of the first missile for launch was a time-consuming and tedious process. The R-7 ICBM was much too large to be transported in an assembled state. This was done at Baikonur itself, inside a huge hangar called the MIK-KA (Space Vehicle Assembly-Test Building).[12] The four strap-on boosters were carefully mated to the missile's central core stage. Tests were conducted to determine whether all of the interstage connections were correctly fitted. The missile, mounted on a giant railroad transporter, was then moved to the Tyulpan launcher.

When it arrived at the Tyulpan launch pad, the enormous girder petals were folded back like an open flower. The railroad transporter erected the missile, placing it carefully over the blast hole. The petals of the Tyulpan were then raised, snaring the missile in their grasp. Electrical and telemetry cables were fastened to the missile, connecting it with the launch control center. In essence, the missile was suspended in the clutches of the Tyulpan's petals. This was no minor engineering feat. The strong desert winds around the Baikonur launch site could wreak havoc on an insufficiently restrained launcher.

Following erection, the next task was to fuel the missile. By far the most sensitive aspect of the fueling was handling the liquid oxygen (LOX). Liquid oxygen must be maintained at a frigid temperature of -190° C. It cannot simply be pumped directly into the missile fuel tanks in bulk, as a sudden change in temperature could damage the tanks. Instead, a small amount of LOX was sprayed into the tanks, gradually chilling them. This wash was then bled off. Only after the tanks were chilled was the bulk of the LOX pumped into the missile. The LOX hoses remained attached to the missile until the final countdown. In the hot sun, the missile body gradually heated up, as did the LOX inside. As the oxygen became gaseous again from the heat, it was bled off and replaced by fresh, chilled LOX. In contrast to the delicate oxidizer process, using kerosene fuel was a relatively straightforward process because it remained at ambient temperature for loading.[13]

The whole process of attaching the hosing to the missile and fueling it took about five hours. The launch scheduled for March was unsuccessful and had to be halted before lift-off. The fuel in the missile then had to be laboriously drained and the many subsystems dismantled. The first missile wasn't ready again for nearly a month, until the first week of April. Ill fortune dogged the second launch attempt as well. The missile did not lift off. Once again the missile crews at Baikonur laboriously unloaded the fuel, checked and rechecked the many pumps and onboard systems, and prepared the missile for a third try.

To the joy of Korolev and his team, the third attempt was more successful. On 15 May 1957, the first R-7 finally lifted off the pad. The missile's engines worked as promised and it began to accelerate skyward. But at T-plus-50 seconds, with all five of its engine clusters firing, the missile exploded over the test range.

Korolev sent Pilyugin and Barmin back to Moscow to explain. Korolev himself refused to return to Moscow until a missile was successfully launched.

He wrote to his wife at the time, "When things are going badly, I have fewer friends. . . . My frame of mind is bad. I will not hide it. It is very difficult to get through our failures. . . . There is a state of alarm and worry. . . . It is a hot 55 [131° F] degrees here."

Another launch followed on 11 June 1957 and Korolev wrote to his wife, "Things are not going very well again." Problems continued to dog the program. In mid-July Korolev wrote simply, "Things are very, very bad."

There was enormous pressure on Korolev from the government and the military. Not only had the R-7 program cost stupendous amounts of money, but there was considerable evidence that the competing American program, the Atlas missile, was forging ahead. Nikita Khrushchev insisted that the Soviet Union reach parity with the Americans. If the next launch failed, Khrushchev threatened to close the design bureau and cancel the R-7 program.

Finally, in the early morning hours of 21 August 1957, an R-7 lifted off from Pad 1 and successfully continued downrange toward the Pacific Ocean. All systems worked properly, marking the first flight ever of an intercontinental ballistic missile. The R-7's dummy warhead impacted in the Pacific some 6,400 km downrange.[14] Korolev was ecstatic. He gathered the rest of the chief designers around and for hours talked about the future of the Soviet space program. He was so excited he didn't go to bed until 3 A.M.

The Soviet government publicly announced it possessed an ICBM on 26 August 1957. Washington hardly paid any attention. Many defense officials doubted the Soviet accomplishment and assumed it was more of Khrushchev's bluster.

Nevertheless, the intelligence agencies knew the launch was not a fluke. The United States' radars and other sensors based around the periphery of the Soviet Union had been tracking the test program and on 7 September picked up traces of a second successful launch. They had no way of knowing that Soviet Premier Nikita Khrushchev was standing beside Korolev in the launch control center with a broad smile on his face as the second R-7 hurtled into space.

Khrushchev was less happy about the progress of the cruise missile effort. Myasishchev's Sorokovka was still on the drawing board, with little to show after three years of effort. Khrushchev ordered it cancelled in November 1957 after witnessing the R-7's successful flight. The Lavochkin Burya project was plagued by serious shortcomings in a wide range of technologies: materials able to withstand atmospheric heat buildup, computers and guidance systems to compensate for the eccentricities of atmospheric flight, and dependable separation systems. The cruise missile itself was horribly expensive because of its titanium construction. More Burya tests followed, but few fulfilled their objectives. In all, some seventeen Burya launches were made, of which four had some measure of success. The final test, shortly before Lavochkin's death in 1960, flew 9,000 km, finally reaching its design objectives. But by 1960 the missile was too expensive, too complicated, too unreliable, and too late.[15]

Sputnik

The 7 September launch of the second R-7 was to have a profound impact on future Soviet defense policy. Although Khrushchev had supported the missile program from the outset, it was just one of a number of major Soviet defense initiatives, including the competitive cruise missile program. The spectacle of the 7 September launch deeply impressed Khrushchev. He became obsessed with the potential of missile technology. The back-to-back successes of the R-7 missile led Khrushchev to reward Korolev by allowing him to pursue one of his fondest dreams—the launch of a space satellite.

For the Soviets, the R-7 was a critical step in developing a super-weapon capable of reaching targets in the United States, as it moved them farther down the road to strategic parity with the Americans. For Sergey Korolev, the successful flights by the R-7 served as the first step toward putting a man in space. As the military had correctly assumed back in 1953, Korolev was more interested in spaceflight than in nuclear missiles.

Korolev never forgot his imprisonment in Kolyma or his treatment during the war years. Yet his hatred of Stalin's regime did not overcome his fascination with rocketry and spaceflight. To the contrary, his study of the German missile program in 1946–47 convinced him of the feasibility of the dreams of his idol, the visionary space enthusiast Konstantin Tsiolkovskiy. Korolev participated in the Soviet Army's missile program with enthusiasm, not necessarily for its military consequences alone, but because of the prospects of realizing his own dreams of spaceflight. Korolev's experiences during the Purge did not cause him to retreat from contact with the Soviet state. To have done so would have forced him to abandon his own ambitions. But he used his missile successes to extract small concessions from the Soviet Army to further the Soviet space program.

Korolev maintained strong ties to members of the Academy of Sciences interested in space exploration, such as Mikhail Tikhonravov. With the successful launch of the early R-1s, Korolev won army approval to divert small numbers to scientific research of the upper atmosphere. He even studied the possibilities of launching a man into the edge of space using one of these early missiles.[16] Korolev continued to sponsor further space programs, including launching dogs into space to study the possible effects of spaceflight on humans.

The military attitude towards these efforts was not enthusiastic. In the summer of 1948, Tikhonravov asked permission to present a paper on the possibility of an artificial earth satellite to a scientific session of the army's Academy of Artillery Sciences. The academy head, Anatoliy Blagonravov, was reluctant at first, fearing that the army officials at the academy would accuse him of fostering unrealistic science-fiction projects instead of the serious business of war. Blagonravov was intrigued by Tikhonravov's research and allowed him to present the paper. As feared, the army officers at the conference were not amused. A senior general rebuked Blagonravov, "The institute hasn't enough to do and switched to the realm of fantasy?"[17]

Korolev, who was present at the conference, did not share the military's view. He approached Tikhonravov and began a collaborative effort to study such a satellite in more detail. The program remained in limbo for many years, as Korolev realized that the army would not countenance an all-out effort until an ICBM was in the Soviet arsenal. But in May 1954, with the R-7 ICBM project officially underway, Korolev wrote to the USSR Council of Ministers, seeking approval of a plan to develop an artificial satellite. He received tentative approval.

On 29 July 1955 President Eisenhower announced that the United States would begin efforts to launch an artificial satellite in conjunction with the International Geophysical Year in 1957. "Eisenhower's Moon" would be further evidence of America's primacy in advanced technology. Soviet government officials became more interested in Korolev's space project. An earth satellite suddenly seemed vital as an assertion of Soviet technological prowess. Spurred on by the American announcement, Korolev won Khrushchev's approval to start a state commission to consider an artificial earth satellite, chaired by himself and Keldysh.[18] Several days after Eisenhower's announcement, the Kremlin authorized Leonid I. Sedov of the Academy of Sciences to announce that the Soviet Union would also launch a satellite in 1957. Few Americans paid much attention to the boast.

Given the green light to develop a satellite, Korolev proceeded to recruit a large number of top Soviet scientists. As he was soon to learn, academic excellence does not necessarily translate into practical results in the world of engineering. The satellite designs that were proposed were grossly unrealistic given the time frame and monetary restraints. Tikhonravov, aware of Korolev's frustrations, proposed that the first satellite incorporate a very elementary design; more sophisticated satellites could follow. If the Soviets' first satellite beat the Americans into space, government funding for future ventures was far more likely. Korolev agreed. Ignoring the feckless, fanciful academics, he turned to the engineers for help. Three design bureaus began long-term satellite efforts: a team under G. Babakin at the Lavochkin design bureau to study interplanetary spacecraft, a team under M. Reshetnev at OKB-1 to study communication satellites, and a bureau under D. Kozlov to study scientific satellites in earth orbit.[19]

Korolev applauded Tikhonravov's idea for a simple satellite and began work on PS-1 (*Prosteyshiy Sputnik-1*, or Elementary Satellite-1). Instead of weighing a ton, the satellite would weigh only about ninety pounds. It was little more than a metal sphere containing a small radio transmitter—just enough to prove that a satellite had been launched, though not large enough to contain any real scientific instruments. His staff at Kaliningrad preferred to call it the SP, which also happened to be Korolev's nickname among his staff (based on his initials: Sergey Pavlovich).

Khrushchev's glee at the successful launch of the second R-7 prompted him to authorize the use of an R-7 for the launch of the PS-1, but at the earliest possible opportunity. A modified R-7 was prepared, with a simple ballistic nosecone replacing the usual warhead.[20] Erection of the missile began in mid-October, and the PS-1 *Sputnik* was launched into space on the night of 4 October 1957. An hour after launch, PS-1 *Sputnik* had completed its first orbit around the earth, its characteristic *beep-beep-beep* being picked up at stations around the Soviet Union and the rest of the globe.[21] Korolev called together his engineers and gave an impromptu speech: "Today, the dreams of the best sons of mankind have come true! The assault on space has begun."

The Kremlin's goals were less lofty. For Communist party propagandists, the lessons of *Sputnik* were obvious. Superiority in space meant superiority on earth. Long accustomed to the dismissive tone of Western reporting on Soviet technological accomplishments, the Soviet press relished the opportunity to rub American noses in their own failures.

Nowhere was *Sputnik*'s impact greater than in the United States. The American satellite program had been a string of embarrassing failures. Missile after missile exploded on the pad, giving American television viewers and moviegoers a constant string of spectacular disasters. The newspapers soon spoke of American "Flop-niks." Not content to belittle America's own satellite program, some journalists continued to doubt the Soviet triumph. A number of papers suggested that "We got the wrong Germans," when, in fact, it was the other way around.

Nor was the first *Sputnik* a fluke. It was followed in quick succession by much larger and more sophisticated satellites. First there was PS-2 on 3 November 1957, with a dog as a payload, and then, on 15 May 1958, PS-3, a massive 1,325 kg geophysical satellite.

Sputnik represented a "technological Pearl Harbor" for the United States in the view of Lt. Gen. James M. Gavin. Even after the shocks of the earlier-than-expected Soviet A-bomb and H-bomb, there still was widespread doubt about the Soviet Union's technological competence. *Sputnik* shattered this complacency. American public opinion began to shift to the other extreme. The Soviets were soon regarded as being nearly irretrievably ahead in space technology. America's school system was blamed for its lack of attention to mathematics and science. The American intelligence system was blamed for providing insufficient warning of the Soviet accomplishments. America's own missile programs were denigrated as backward and inept. Politicians began to speak of a "missile gap" between the United States and the Soviet Union.[22]

In fact, a technological gap between the United States and the Soviet Union did not really exist. If anything, America had the edge and could proudly point to its enormous technological advantages over the Soviet Union. America's aerospace industry was considerably richer in resources of every kind: advanced materials, novel computers, sophisticated telemetry equipment, unequalled chemical engineering. But what had separated the United States and the Soviet Union was the *will* to commit these resources to an ICBM program. The U.S. Air Force, which might have been the primary advocate of such a program, remained fixated on the manned strategic bomber as the best vehicle for delivering thermonuclear weapons. The Atlas and Navaho missile programs, although proceeding at a steady pace, did not have the high priority afforded Korolev's R-7 Semyorka program.

That would soon change. The shock of the *Sputnik* launch led President Eisenhower to authorize a stepped-up American ballistic missile program. It was the beginning of the great strategic arms race of the 1960s. *Sputnik*'s challenge set in motion an accelerated American weapons development program not seen since the days of World War II. The Atlas ICBM was first tested months after *Sputnik*. It was quickly followed by the much larger and more powerful Titan missile. Hardly had the Titan reached service than yet another design, the versatile Minuteman, appeared. Nor was the effort confined to land-based missiles. The U.S. Navy sponsored its own strategic missile design, the Polaris. Any one of these programs rivalled the R-7 in complexity, and several of them, especially Polaris and Minuteman, were beyond the technological capacity of the Soviet Union at the time. But, given the poor level of United States intelligence during the period, this was not appreciated.

One of the most important outcomes of the *Sputnik* launches, and one not recognized at the time, was the effect they would have on reducing tensions between the United States and the Soviet Union. Khrushchev had adamantly refused to consider Eisenhower's Open Skies program, which sought to allow unarmed reconnaissance flights over one another's territory. In his haste to beat the Americans into space, Khrushchev did not realize that *Sputnik*'s flight path would set an important precedent. By orbiting over the United States, *Sputnik* acknowledged that there was no national sovereignty in space. This meant that the United States could fly reconnaissance missions over the USSR, but in space, not within the atmosphere. This helped spark the deployment of spy satellites. It was these satellites, following in the wake of the U-2 flights, which would help American intelligence services learn that the strategic balance between the United States and USSR was less alarming than feared. Likewise, in later years the Soviets found that their own spy satellites helped quash exaggerated fears about the progress of American arms programs.

From Test to Missile Base

In spite of *Sputnik's* success, the R-7 was still not a true weapons system. It had not been tested with an actual nuclear weapon. Nor was its reliability sufficient to warrant mass production. From the end of 1957 to the spring of 1958, about a dozen more R-7 missiles were test launched. The program was intended to clear up remaining bugs in the design and to verify that corrections did, in fact, cure the problems. Failures continued, but at a reduced rate. There was a hiatus in the tests after April 1958.

In the wake of *Sputnik's* phenomenal impact on world public opinion, Khrushchev's attitude towards Korolev's private space program changed dramatically. Khrushchev became an enthusiastic and insistent supporter of space spectaculars. The military's concern over the diversion of engineering talent into space fantasies continued. But, with Khrushchev's backing, the military's attitude was irrelevant.

After a string of earth satellite successes, Korolev's next surprise was a moon-orbiting satellite, the Luna 1. It was launched on 2 January 1959 aboard a new version of the R-7, fitted with a true second stage. This was a significant technological advance, because it paved the way to longer-ranged ICBMs.[23] The Luna 1 mission signalled a maturation of the R-7 design. Two months later, in March 1959, a final series of military R-7 acceptance trials was conducted at Tyuratam. For the next few months, R-7s were launched at a rate of one a week. This was the final step before the R-7's deployment as a true weapons system.

While Korolev was supervising the final adjustments to the R-7, steps were underway to create the first Soviet intercontinental missile base. The range of the R-7, some 8,000 km, was not sufficient to reach the whole of the United States from the southern launch pads at the Tyuratam proving ground. Instead, a dedicated military launch site was under construction farther to the north and, therefore, closer to the United States via the polar trajectory. The secret base was known only by its code name, Leningrad-300.[24] The site selected was in a sparsely populated forest region near Plesetsk, to the south of the arctic port city of Arkhangelsk. Work began on Leningrad-300 on 15 July 1957 under the command of Gen. M. G. Grigoryev. The new base was eventually given the cover name *Severniy Kosmodrom* (Northern Cosmodrome) some years later when civil space launches began to take place from the facility.

The construction work at Plesetsk proved far more difficult than anticipated. The winters were long and cold, thus preventing any serious construction work for nearly half the year. Local soil conditions were also atrocious. Much of the land was covered with swamps that froze in the winter and thawed in the summer, oozing mud and belching natural gas. To gain firm foundations for the massive missile structures, it was necessary to scrape the soil down to the underlying bedrock. But nature resisted these assaults, flooding the excavated roadways and construction sites with mud during the spring thaws and after heavy rains. To cut costs, several of the launcher sites were built on special extensions on a bluff over the Yemtsa River. The construction proved far more expensive than anticipated and was far behind schedule. In a special Kremlin meeting in 1958 to review the program, Khrushchev's temper exploded. He denounced the delays and the massive cost overruns and ordered the Plesetsk project cancelled. Barmin, who was in charge of the construction program, managed to calm him down. The engineer pointed out that 70 percent of the work was already completed and that alternative locations in northern Russia were just as bad. Khrushchev relented, but the scale of the R-7 deployment program was scaled back.[25]

The first launch pad was ready after two years' work, and on 15 December 1959 the first R-7 was test fired there. Two days later Nikita Khrushchev announced the formation of a new branch of the armed forces, the RVSN (*Raketniye Voyska Strategicheskogo Naznacheniya*) or Strategic Missile Forces. The new force was to take precedence over the army, navy, and air force. The formation of the RVSN was the culmination of the "revolution in military affairs" that started with the development of the A-bomb. Its creation recognized that the Soviet Union not only had nuclear weapons, but had the means to deliver them to nearly any point on the globe.

Gnawing Doubts

Missile base or not, the formation of the RVSN did not mark the end of the nuclear arms race, only the beginning of a new phase. The technology of war is dynamic, with one side actively pursuing the means to negate the other side's technological advances. The arrival of the R-7 and its American counterpart, the Atlas, marked the beginning of the missile race.

Twelve of the massive Tyulpan launchers were planned for the missile base at Leningrad-300. But in the end, only four were built (plus the three test launch pads at Baikonur). The reason for the cutback was the R-7's serious shortcomings as a weapons system, which were only beginning to be recognized.

The problem was quite simple. When the Soviets initiated their ICBM program in 1954, they presumed that the R-7 would be launched from secret bases. The fact that it took nearly twenty hours to assemble, erect, fuel, and launch an R-7 made little difference if secrecy was maintained. The Americans wouldn't know where the R-7s were based, so they couldn't attack before the missiles were launched. The Soviet Union was still a very closed society. American attempts to spy inside the Soviet Union had proven amateurish and were easily foiled by the omnipresent KGB. But the presumption of secrecy underestimated American talents for technological espionage.

The United States had erected a series of listening posts, mainly in Turkey, to monitor flight testing from the Poligon at Tyuratam. To supplement these ground stations, the U.S. Air Force began conducting signals intelligence flights near the Soviet border to listen in on Soviet military communications, as well as the telemetry transmissions from Soviet missile trials. This might not pinpoint a base, but it narrowed down its probable locations. The American effort was not without its failures. The CIA mounted a program, exploiting the jet streams in the atmosphere flowing over the Soviet heartland, to launch spy balloons to track down the missile sites. Code-named Moby Dick, the balloons were fitted with photographic cameras. Launched from bases to the west of the USSR, they would drift across the country and drop their camera film packages into international waters in the Pacific, where they could then be retrieved.[26]

The Rube Goldberg nature of this program is the clearest evidence of the U.S. intelligence community's desperation to learn more about Korolev's enigmatic missiles and other secret Soviet programs. Even this half-baked scheme gravely worried the Soviet high command. The appearance of the balloons over Russia led the KGB to issue a contract to the Myasishchev design bureau to develop a high-altitude aircraft capable of shooting down the balloons. The resulting aircraft, the M-17 *Stratosfera,* appeared too late to battle the balloons.[27] The shortcomings of the Moby Dick balloons eventually resulted in a far more successful idea.

The CIA sponsored an effort by Lockheed Aircraft's "Skunk Works" to develop a powered sailplane under Project Aquataine. A conventional aircraft would not have the range to traverse the Soviet Union, but a sailplane, relying as much on its gliding ability as its engine, offered more hope. The resulting design was given the cover name U-2, for Utility-2. Not only was the U-2 extremely long-legged, but it could cruise at altitudes far in excess of typical Soviet interceptors—over 70,000 feet—making it nearly invulnerable to interception. The U-2 began operational flights over the USSR in July 1956.[28] Among the first targets for the U-2's cameras was the R-7 launch pad at Tyuratam.

Although the U-2 had not yet found the new Plesetsk base, by 1958 Marshal Nedelin and the other leaders of the infant Soviet missile force had to prepare for the likelihood that it soon would. Repeated attempts to shoot down the U-2 had failed. The earliest Soviet air defense missile, the R-113 (SA-1 Guild), simply couldn't reach the U-2. Jet fighter aircraft had a very hard time reaching the upper altitudes where the U-2 traveled and, in the thin air,

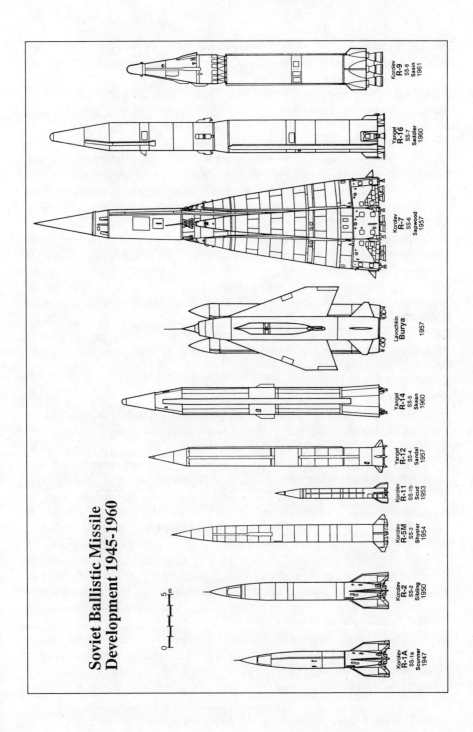

Soviet Ballistic Missile Development 1945-1960

Korolev R-9 SS-8 Sasin 1961

Yangel R-16 SS-7 Saddler 1960

Korolev R-7 SS-6 Sapwood 1957

Lavochkin Burya 1957

Yangel R-14 SS-5 Skean 1960

Yangel R-12 SS-4 Sandal 1957

Korolev R-11 SS-1b Scud 1953

Korolev R-5M SS-3 Shyster 1954

Korolev R-2 SS-2 Sibling 1950

Korolev R-1A SS-1a Scunner 1947

found it nearly impossible to maneuver into position to fire on the spy-planes. Early air-to-air missiles like the K-5 were equally unmaneuverable in the thin upper atmosphere, and went out of control. A crash program, the S-75 *Volkhov* (SA-2 Guideline) missile, was underway to replace the old R-113. But even when it became available in quantity in 1958, it was difficult to position the new batteries on the U-2s' flight path. The CIA kept track of the new S-75 batteries and instructed its pilots which areas to avoid.

The ungainly spy-planes crisscrossed the Soviet skies with impunity. Plesetsk was bound to be discovered eventually because it sat astride a main rail line. The CIA's flight plans had the U-2 cover all major rail lines, as large ICBMs would invariably have to be transported from their factories to the launch sites by train.

In the event of war, Nedelin realized that the R-7's slow launch time would make it very vulnerable to preemptive strike by American weapons. United States Air Force Atlas missiles could reach the R-7 launch pads in less than an hour, and even the B-52 bomber could strike Plesetsk before the missile was fully ready for launch. The massive Tyulpan launchers, although impressive engineering feats, were too fragile to offer any protection from a nuclear blast. What was needed at the very least was a fast-reaction missile, one which could be prepared for launch and sent on its way before the Americans could strike it with their own missiles.

Competition

Development of such a weapon had begun even before the R-7 was operational. But, for the first time, Korolev had a serious competitor: one of his former protégés, Mikhail Yangel.

Yangel was one of a crop of young engineers who had received his start in Kaliningrad, studying the art of missile construction under Korolev. He was, in many ways, Korolev's most talented pupil, and had led work on the R-5 intermediate range missile while Korolev was devoting his attention to the R-7 Semyorka. Korolev was not the easiest of men to work for. Although his former subordinates remember him as loyal and fair, he would also run roughshod over younger engineers, expecting as much from them as he did from himself. Korolev was often screaming and abusive. His staff recalled that he would often apologize once he calmed down, a trait which separated him from other general designers of the times, who accepted such behavior as one of their prerogatives. Another trait that set him apart from his contemporaries was his generosity. Korolev would allow younger designers on his team to receive credit and state awards for their accomplishments. As was the case with the Tupolev bureau before the war, the Korolev bureau served as the training ground for many future Soviet aerospace designers.

One of the technical issues that led to clashes between Korolev and other designers was the question of which storable liquid fuels to use. Korolev had a passion for simple fuels, particularly liquid oxygen, as the primary oxidizer. Although he considered other fuels for his missiles, even novel oxidizers such as fluorine, he kept coming back to LOX. Liquid oxygen had its merits, but from a military standpoint it had a major failing: it could not be left in the missile indefinitely. The natural heat of the sun and the local environment inevitably caused the super-cold LOX to begin to change back to its natural gaseous state. What the military wanted was an oxidizer that could be left in the missile for prolonged periods of time at normal temperatures. This would allow them to field missiles that could be fueled well in advance of a mission, then left on the pad waiting for the decision to launch or not.

Such an oxidizer had been found. It was red fuming nitric acid (RFNA). RFNA had been developed by the Germans for the very same reasons it was sought by the Soviet generals. The Germans, like Korolev, had preferred LOX for their ballistic missiles. But besides ballistic missiles, they were also developing antiaircraft missiles, such as the Wasserfall. The Wasserfall would have to be left fueled and ready to launch for hours at a time because it was impossible to predict when an Allied bomber formation would appear.

RFNA was first used by the Soviets in Korolev's R-11 tactical ballistic missile. Korolev was not happy with the use of nitric acid because it is extremely dangerous to handle. The chemical reacts violently with hydrocarbon fuels such as kerosene, which is why it is so useful as an oxidizer. For the very same reason, it reacts violently with other forms of hydrocarbon, including human flesh. Inhalation of small amounts of nitric acid can destroy the lungs, and a small splash of nitric acid on the skin can create horrible burns. Care needs to be taken when handling LOX, but it is more safe because trace amounts harmlessly evaporate.

In contrast, nitric acid was both a menace and a nuisance. If, for example, a launch failed, the nitric acid in the storage tanks posed real problems. It could be left in the tanks longer than LOX—for about two days—but not indefinitely. It is intensely corrosive and will eventually eat its way through metal joints. Because of this, the tanks had to be carefully cleaned between refuelings. Crews working with such a noxious material had to wear "slime suits," the rubber coveralls used to protect soldiers from chemical weapons. This might be acceptable in cool northern climes, but in the hot desert near the Tyuratam launch center, such suits were almost as hazardous as the chemicals. But the generals wanted storable liquid propellants, and they didn't care about such complications.

Korolev's abrasive personality led to problems with Yangel, and in 1954

Korolev further alienated himself from the generals with his sudden scheme to dump the R-3 intermediate range missile in favor of the R-7. This was not appreciated by military men like Nedelin, who preferred that such orders come from themselves, not the engineers. Furthermore, Nedelin and the artillery branch still wanted intermediate range missiles—in addition to intercontinental missiles—for possible use against targets in Europe. The British had developed nuclear weapons of their own after the war, so targets in England were of considerable concern. In addition, the U.S. Air Force's Strategic Air Command had equipped a sizeable portion of its bomber force with medium-range B-47 jet bombers and planned to fly them from European and Libyan bases in the event of hostilities, targets that could be hit with shorter-ranged missiles than the R-7. Nedelin, wishing to broaden the base of missile designers, was disinclined to give the intermediate range missile program to Korolev. Supporting this decision was an up-and-coming member of the Central Committee, Leonid Brezhnev, who was responsible for monitoring the progress of the missile programs for the Communist party.

As a result of these factors, in 1954 the Party and military authorities gave Yangel, forty-three years old at the time, the opportunity to head his own design bureau. Yangel was assigned to start a design bureau, code-named SKB-586, at the Dnepropetrovsk plant, where Korolev's R-7 missiles were under construction. It was probably more than coincidence that Dnepropetrovsk was Brezhnev's hometown.

Yangel's first project was the R-12 missile, a direct follow-on to the R-5 but with greater range. Initial design studies of the R-12 can be traced back as far as 1948, but serious work didn't begin until 1954. Compared to the complicated R-7 Semyorka, the R-12 was remarkably simple. It used a single engine cluster, and a very uncomplicated single-stage design. The first testing of the missile began in 1957. Development of a true successor to the ill-fated R-3, called the R-14, began shortly afterwards. The R-14 was Yangel's first missile to have a range of over 4,000 km. The first static firings of its engines began in 1958, and test launches commenced in 1960. Neither design was particularly challenging when compared to the R-7, but Yangel managed their development without any major snags and within a reasonable timetable. This gave Nedelin confidence that Yangel could embark on a far more complicated missile design in competition with Korolev.

The new requirement called for an ICBM with a range of over 8,000 km. Unlike the earlier R-7 design, the emphasis was no longer simply on getting the nuclear payload to the target. That was no longer enough. The missile also had to be easy to assemble and easy to fuel. It was now presumed that its base might come under attack, so it would be necessary to fire the missile before it could be destroyed on the ground. In the event it could not get off in time, the missile would be placed in a hardened underground silo. This meant that a bulky and awkward design like that of the R-7 was out of the question as it would be impractical to build a protected silo large enough to house it. It inevitably meant that a more conventional two-stage design would be needed.

Korolev's OKB-1 design bureau at Kaliningrad, and Yangel's new SKB-586 bureau at Dnepropetrovsk, were both given state authorization to begin conceptual work on the new missile. Korolev, much to Nedelin's consternation, insisted on using cryogenic fuel—LOX and kerosene. Korolev argued that the demand for rapid reaction before launch could be met by new high-speed fuel pumps. Yangel, more sensitive to the generals' demands, offered a design based on hypergolic-fueled rocket engines, with nitric acid as the oxidizer. Korolev hoped that the combination of high-speed fuel pumps and a simpler design would make his missile suitable for the new role. Yangel felt that his missile had an automatic lead over Korolev's since his missile could sit in its silo for two days fully fueled, while Korolev's could sit for only a few hours.

The need for a new missile was absolutely critical. Instead of turning out "missiles like sausages," as Khrushchev had boasted, the Soviet Union was quickly slipping behind the United States. This is all the more ironic since a major issue in the 1960 presidential race between John F. Kennedy and Richard Nixon was the so-called missile gap. The U.S. government knew that the Soviet Union was capable of building an ICBM, it just didn't know how many. The U-2 spy-planes were just beginning to find out when fate caught up with them.

On 1 May 1960, a U-2 piloted by Francis Gary Powers took off from Pakistan heading for a missile production facility in Sverdlovsk and the new Soviet missile base at Plesetsk. The CIA already had evidence that the Soviets were building a missile complex at Plesetsk but needed a firmer idea of the number of launchers. The absence of photos of possible launch sites had led to wild speculation about the number of missiles in service. The air force, seeking support for its own ambitious missile program, leaned in the direction of large numbers of purported Soviet missiles. The CIA leaned in the direction of smaller numbers, but a substantial force nonetheless. As in many of these turf fights, news of the estimates leaked to the press.

Kennedy, the Democratic candidate, blamed Vice-President Nixon and the Eisenhower administration for the precarious state of America's defenses. It was during their tenure in office that the Soviets had shocked the public with their *Sputnik*. And, in the wake of *Sputnik,* it seemed obvious that the Soviets were racing ahead in nuclear missile technology as well. Obviously, said Kennedy, the Republicans were to blame.

The earlier "bomber gap" of the mid-1950s should have provided some perspective on the controversy, but the intelligence sources were still too secret to permit widespread public education on the matter. The bomber gap had been largely illusory due to the absence of adequate intelligence. When U-2 photos became available in the 1956–57 period, it was quickly obvious that the Soviet bomber fleet was minuscule. Eisenhower reluctantly authorized Powers's flight, fearing that sooner or later one of the U-2s would be shot down or forced to land. With a critical summit meeting with Khrushchev coming up, he had no need for an international incident. Still, the president hoped evidence gathered during Powers's flight would settle the missile gap controversy, just as it had the bomber gap flap.

Eisenhower was concerned with the direction he saw the United States going in as a result of the missile gap controversy. Although no dove, he did not believe that a hasty buildup of America's strategic forces should be based on guesswork or the urgings of newspaper pundits. Programs were already underway to substantially increase America's nuclear might, and the presidential campaign was unlikely to do much more than politicize the matter.

Powers's flight was ill-fated from the start. The aircraft selected for the mission had a bad reputation among the U-2 pilots, who called it a "hangar queen," a plane in chronic need of repairs. Nor had the Soviets remained idle. Infuriated by the impudence of the CIA, Khrushchev had insisted that new S-75 antiaircraft missiles be rushed into service. By 1960, city after city, military base after military base, was receiving the new missile. The S-75 was a poor match for the U-2. The problem was quite simple. By the time the missile could reach the U-2's cruising altitude it would be out of fuel and basically coasting. To make matters worse, the air at 75,000 feet is so thin that the S-75's control surfaces had little to bite into to maneuver the missile. This was not a problem for the U-2 with its oversized wings. But the tiny fins on the S-75 missile were more effective in the denser air below than in the upper atmosphere where the U-2 operated.

As Francis Gary Powers's spy-plane approached Sverdlovsk, it was tracked by Soviet radars. PVO air defense force radars had monitored the flight past the border area, and an attempt was made to shoot it down. The PVO interceptor regiment on the approaches to Sverdlovsk was equipped with the new MiG-19PF fighter, and few pilots were entirely conversant with its advanced radar and missile systems. As it happened, a pilot from a neighboring unit ferrying a new Su-9 interceptor to another unit landed at the base. The Su-9 had a higher operational ceiling than the MiG-19, so the aircraft was ordered aloft to carry out the interception even though the pilot, a Captain Mityagin, didn't have a pressure suit or oxygen mask. As he approached Powers's U-2, Mityagin received an order from ground control to destroy the intruder by ramming it. The order came from Dragon, the code name for Gen. Yevgeniy

Savitsky, commander of the interceptor command of the PVO air defense forces. The intercept was fumbled by the ground controller and, much to his relief, the pilot was ordered to return to base.[29]

Powers's spy-plane was having problems of its own. Whether it was due to instrument failure or problems with the aircraft itself, Powers's aircraft was operating far below its optimal altitude of 75,000 feet. There have been rumors that Powers fell asleep at the controls, not altogether unbelievable given the duration of the flights.

It was now up to the S-75 Volkhov missile crews to deal with the U-2. The battery commander that morning, Maj. Mikhail Voronov, locked on the radar and began tracking the aircraft as it approached. He ordered missile after missile salvoed in hopes of scoring a hit, although the practice violated Soviet tactical doctrine. One of the missiles came close enough to the tail of Powers's U-2 for the proximity fuze to detonate its warhead. The shock wave from the explosion crushed the U-2's tail surfaces and Powers was forced to bail out.

The spy-plane shootdown had important repercussions in both the United States and the Soviet Union. Eisenhower put an end to any further overflights, even though this meant cutting off the most productive source of U.S. intelligence and leaving the missile gap argument unsettled for the time being. This added impetus to the air force missile program, which pushed ahead at full steam.[30]

Meanwhile Khrushchev, with a live spy-plane pilot in his custody, decided to take advantage of the propaganda value of the incident, even if it meant an abrupt end to his proposed summit with Eisenhower. The dozens of U-2 flights over the past four years had infuriated the Kremlin and Soviet military leaders. For those of the wartime generation, it was all too reminiscent of the embarrassing months before the outbreak of World War II, when German aircraft probed Soviet defenses with impunity. No such activities would be tolerated by Khrushchev in spite of any ill effects on international diplomacy.[31]

The Powers shootdown had another effect on the Soviet missile program: it further reinforced Khrushchev's infatuation with missiles. The success of the PVO missiles in shooting down the U-2 contrasted sharply with the fumbled attempts of fighter planes to bring it down. The U-2 incident came to a grotesque climax some thirty minutes after Powers had been shot down when Soviet missile batteries, not informed that the U-2 was already destroyed, shot down one of their own fighter planes.[32] This was too much for Khrushchev.

Khrushchev was faced with much the same dilemma that would confront Mikhail Gorbachev some thirty years later. He was insistent on reviving the Soviet economy, and one of the main stumbling blocks appeared to be the bloated Soviet military. Everywhere Khrushchev looked he saw inefficiency:

air force squadrons with thousands of obsolete fighter aircraft, navy flotillas equipped with outdated warships, army units using World War II tanks. Khrushchev became convinced that radical steps were needed to alleviate the situation. Missiles were his panacea. He decided to drastically cut back the size of the armed forces, as well as the number of its weapons. In their place he would substitute missiles—antiaircraft missiles for fighter planes, antiship missiles for big-gun cruisers, and antitank missiles for outdated artillery. Missiles seemed like a more efficient, cost-effective, and successful alternative than a World War II–style army.

Khrushchev ran roughshod over the armed forces and the Soviet defense industry. Soviet warship programs were slashed and many ships already laid down were broken up for scrap. The Soviet Navy's plan for aircraft carriers was terminated. In their place, Khrushchev insisted on small, missile-armed warships. Soviet heavy tank production was stopped; Khrushchev wanted missile-armed tank destroyers instead. Heavy artillery projects were terminated, to be replaced by ballistic missile programs. Bombers, too, were cancelled in favor of ballistic missiles. Even some high-tech programs were trashed because of the indiscriminate nature of Khrushchev's plan. P. V. Tsybin's RSR spy-plane and the Lapotok space-plane were both cancelled as part of a general consolidation of aircraft design bureaus in favor of new missile bureaus.

Khrushchev's first step had been the addition of the Strategic Missile Forces. Not only did he add the new organization, but he began to speak of it as the primary branch of the Soviet armed forces, receiving higher priority than even the long-favored Ground Forces.

Unfortunately, the new force was virtually unarmed. In 1960 it had four R-7 launchers at Plesetsk and a few hundred short-range missiles suitable for bombarding Poland. The RVSN was little more than a hollow boast—and a serious provocation to the Americans. A new generation of missiles beyond the R-7 was needed if the RVSN was to pose any real threat to the American heartland.

Chapter 7

The Missile Carrier

WITH THE SUCCESS of Korolev's missile program in 1957, the Kremlin began to take a more jaundiced view of the Soviet bomber program. Progress to 1957 in bomber design had been disappointing—the Myasishchev M-4A Molot was barely capable of the range needed to carry out its intercontinental mission, and Tupolev's Tu-95 was too slow to evade the expanding American air defenses. Both bureaus realized that if improvements were not soon forthcoming, the Soviet strategic bomber force would fade from the scene.

In 1954 Myasishchev's OKB-23 design bureau at Fili had embarked on a crash program to retrieve its bomber design from complete failure. The key change necessary was the substitution of a more efficient set of jet engines. In place of the Mikulin AM-3 turbojets on the initial production model, the new 3M Molot variant was fitted with Dobrynin VD-7 jet engines. The wingspan was increased, while weight-saving measures allowed for greater fuel and payload.[1] The new variant was available for test flights in March 1956 and it was soon found that the improvements boosted the 3M's maximum range from 6,000 miles to 8,000 miles.[2] This meant that it could finally reach most targets in the United States.

The 3M version of the Molot bomber became available for production in 1957, a time when the rationale for strategic bombers was under critical scrutiny by the Kremlin. With the R-7 strategic missile on the verge of entering service, there was real question whether a bomber like the 3M was really needed. Production was allowed to go ahead at Fili, but neither the 3M Molot nor Tupolev's Tu-95M bomber was manufactured in large numbers. By 1960 there were only 56 Molot bombers and 48 Tu-95Ms in service.[3] Nikita Khrushchev's growing infatuation with missile weapons was a major factor in the curtailment of Soviet bomber programs. Khrushchev was deeply skeptical of weapons programs initiated during Stalin's final years. Wishing to trim defense expenditures, Khrushchev sought new technologies that promised to perform the same combat function at a lower cost. Strategic missiles were extremely attractive in this respect, not requiring the large peacetime operation and maintenance budgets of the bomber force.

In addition, the Long-Range Aviation branch of the air force could not provide a convincing case for the new bombers in light of the extensive buildup of American defensive forces. The new bombers were substantially slower than new American jet interceptors and the bombers would have to run the gauntlet of Canadian and American air defense forces for more than three hours before reaching their targets. This was more than adequate time for the new radar networks in Canada and Alaska to find, track, and identify the incoming Soviet bombers and vector supersonic interceptors against them. There was no reason to believe the Molot and Tu-95M bomber regiments could successfully penetrate the American defenses and then find and attack their targets.

The American bomber force, the Strategic Air Command (SAC) under Gen. Curtis E. LeMay, was far more confident. Its leaders believed that their experience in electronic warfare technology and penetration tactics could overcome modern Soviet air defenses with minimal casualties. General LeMay later boasted that SAC could have carried out a nuclear strike against the USSR with losses not much greater than peacetime accident rates.[4] This confidence was the result of combat experience in long-range bombing against Germany and Japan in World War II, extensive peacetime training, combat experiences over Korea, and skepticism about the quality of Soviet air defenses in the mid-1950s. SAC was very familiar with the difficult art of celestial navigation, having developed these skills in combat during World War II, and its crews regularly practiced them in peacetime with long-range flights. LeMay, in particular, knew how easily these skills could be lost—or, as in the Soviet case, never learned—from his experience in rebuilding SAC after the demoralizing demobilization in 1945–46.[5]

LeMay also had confidence in SAC's technological superiority over the Soviet Long-Range Aviation force. The U.S. Air Force had been one of the pioneers of electronic warfare in World War II, and its ability to jam or elude enemy air defense radars was a major reason for its confidence in carrying out its postwar mission against the Soviet Union. In contrast, the Soviet Air Force had virtually no practical experience or serious technology development effort in the electronic warfare area during World War II. The solution wasn't simply a matter of technology; SAC had carefully built up an organizational infrastructure to support these critical warfighting skills. The Soviet

Long-Range Aviation branch had no comparable wartime experience, and it was only beginning to create an organization capable of learning such skills in the late 1950s. The head of the Long-Range Aviation branch, Marshal Vladimir Sudets, had been a decorated bomber commander during World War II, but his experience was limited to tactical bombers, not long-range strategic bombers like LeMay.

Retrieving the Bear

Andrey Tupolev had gradually become a trusted confidant of Nikita Khrushchev and had greater influence on the future course of strategic bomber development than did Myasishchev. Tupolev's personal friendship with Khrushchev in some ways parallels the relationship the Soviet premier built up with Korolev, the missile designer. Just as Korolev's personal vision of the glories of Soviet spaceflight was taken up with enthusiasm by Khrushchev, so too did Tupolev's infatuation with commercial passenger aviation gain Khrushchev's enthusiastic attention. Tupolev had been working on long-range passenger aircraft since the end of World War II, and on his own initiative had built such an aircraft on the basis of the Tu-4 bomber. Likewise, Tupolev had managed to win acceptance of the idea of creating a jet transport out of his Tu-16 Badger medium bomber. This aircraft, called the Tu-104, was comparable to Western jet transports of the time, such as the DeHavilland Comet. In April 1956, during Khrushchev's visit to London, the Soviet delegation flew to Heathrow in a Tu-104. The Western aviation press was surprised at the quality of the aircraft. Khrushchev boasted, "Russians, when compelled to do so, could make any kind of machine!"[6] Khrushchev took great delight in the success of the Tu-104 in London and enthusiastically supported Tupolev's plan to build a passenger version of the even longer range Tu-95M bomber, the Tu-114 airliner. A similar plan by the Myasishchev bureau, based on the Molot bomber and called Project 29, was rejected.

Tupolev gained a clear sense of Khrushchev's goals for strategic programs from their frequent friendly meetings. Tupolev's bureau was in no particular need of further strategic bomber programs; it was already quite busy with new transport aircraft, as well as a new strategic reconnaissance aircraft for the KGB, the Yu-R.[7] But his designers had come up with a new idea for the Tu-95 that would make it a more viable strategic bomber in the face of the American air defense system.

The Tupolev design bureau had been working on the idea of a *raketanosets* (missile carrier) for a number of years. The first example of this type of aircraft was the Tu-16K bomber, armed with the new Mikoyan KS-1 *Sopka* antiship missile. The Tu-16 was modified with a new radar to guide the missile to its target, and two missiles could be suspended under the wing of the aircraft. Testing of the new system had begun in 1951, and by 1954 the new bomber was in air force and navy service.[8]

What Tupolev proposed was a strategic missile carrier: a Tu-95M with larger, nuclear-armed missiles slung under its wings. The advantage of the missiles over nuclear bombs was twofold. From a tactical standpoint, the missiles made the penetration mission more likely to succeed. The missiles could be launched several hundred miles from the target, thus shortening the time the bomber would be exposed to American air defenses. Furthermore, the missiles would be supersonic and therefore more difficult to intercept than the bomber. This would help allay criticism of the Tu-95's slow speed. The second attraction of the bomber-fired missile was that it pandered to Khrushchev's infatuation with new missile technology. This increased the likelihood that the program would be approved by the Kremlin.

Development of this strategic standoff missile was turned over to P. N. Kuksenko, head of the SB-1 missile office at the MiG fighter design bureau. The Mikoyan bureau, not surprisingly, used an existing fighter aircraft, the Ye-2, to form the basis of the new missile, called the Kh-20. The Kh-20 was designed to fit under the belly of a modified Tu-95M bomber, called the Tu-95K-20 or Tu-20. The missile was armed with a large thermonuclear warhead and was initially guided by radio commands from the bomber, followed by inertial navigation for the final leg of its flight. The missile could be released from the bomber at a range of about four hundred miles from the target.

On release from the bomber, the large Kh-20 gradually accelerated from a high subsonic speed, reaching a maximum speed of Mach 1.8 about fifty miles from the release point. At this stage the missile made an abrupt climb, rising from the bomber's cruising altitude of 35,000 feet to a maximum altitude of 57,000 feet. This high cruising altitude was intended to take the missile out of range of American fighters. At such a high altitude, American fighter aircraft would find it nearly impossible to hit the incoming missile. The Kh-20 could cruise for twenty-two minutes from its release point. When it was within ten miles of its target, it executed a sharp dive, coming down at a very steep angle. This was intended to make it nearly impossible to shoot down the Kh-20 using the surface-to-air missiles of the time.[9]

In all, some fifteen Tu-95K-20 cruise-missile bombers were built, about one-third of the Soviet strategic bomber force in 1960.[10] The advent of the Kh-20 missile did not entirely solve the problems posed by the American air defense network, since the Tu-95 bomber still had to fly over Canadian and American airspace for more than two hours before releasing the missile. Tupolev's missile-carrying idea was a mere palliative, and didn't succeed in overcoming the more substantial impediments to the development of a large strategic bomber force.

The Soviet Long-Range Aviation branch looked with interest on American approaches to the penetration problem, especially the B-58 Hustler supersonic bomber. Although the Soviets have long been loath to admit it, American aircraft design played a considerable role in justifying Soviet aircraft programs. It was often easier to get a program approved by citing the existence of a similar American aircraft than by offering a new design without an American counterpart.

The Myasishchev design bureau was in a sorry state by the late 1950s. Its main program, the M-4 Molot bomber, was barely adequate to do the job. Its Project 40 strategic cruise missile was sopping up an enormous amount of talent and resources, and was being overtaken by the competitive Lavochkin design. Its plans for civil transport aircraft had been killed thanks to Tupolev's political contacts with Khrushchev. The bureau's only hope seemed to be the creation of a new supersonic bomber design that could survive in American airspace.

The new project was designated M-50, and serious work began in 1956, about the time the B-58 made its first flight. The M-50 was an adventurous design with many of the virtues and vices that had become trademarks of the Myasishchev bureau. On the one hand, the design took advantage of all the latest advances in aviation technology. Computers, a novelty in aircraft design in 1956, were used to simulate the flight characteristics of the new design and to plan the flight control system. Plans were made to use a remote-controlled, electrically actuated flight control system, a forerunner of today's fly-by-wire system. With the help of the TsAGI research center, advanced wing and tail designs were developed that minimized the weight of the airframe while increasing its structural strength.

On the debit side, the M-50 was based on the premise that extremely powerful and economical engines would be available. This was the same wishful thinking that had caused so many problems with the earlier Molot design. The new engines were being undertaken by a team under P. F. Zubets at the TsIAM (Central Aviation Propulsion Institute). As in the case of the Molot, the engines proved to be one of the key shortcomings of the new design. By 1959 it was clear that the Zubets engines would not be available. In their place, Myasishchev was forced to substitute Dobrynin ND-7 engines, which did not have the power or fuel economy of the planned jet engines.

The program was further undermined by problems in the fuselage configuration. By the mid-1950s, aeronautical engineers were confronting serious problems when designing aircraft capable of flying at supersonic and transsonic speeds. In spite of the use of sleek fuselages, new aircraft designs were demonstrating far higher levels of aerodynamic drag than were predicted using available mathematical models. In the mid-1950s these problems were finally overcome with a design procedure referred to as "area rule." One of the most obvious outcomes of this new modeling technique was the "waisting" of fuselages, as it was called in Britain, or the famous "Coke bottle" fuselage shape, as it was referred to in the United States. The clearest example of the impact of the new area rule design was the American Convair F-102 interceptor, which failed to meet its specifications due to the drag problem, and its successor, the F-106, which succeeded due to incorporation of area rule into its design.[11]

The Myasishchev M-50's fuselage design and wing configuration was not ideal for efficient transsonic flight. Combined with its inefficient engines, its performance was seriously below the expected goals. Nor was the program helped by political infighting among the aviation designers.

In the autumn of 1959, when the M-50 was sent to Ramenskoye test field for trials, Andrey Tupolev made it a point to be present on the day of its scheduled demonstration for Nikita Khrushchev. Tupolev had his chauffeur fake car trouble. When Khrushchev's limousine passed by, Khrushchev offered Tupolev a ride. Tupolev made use of the opportunity to belittle the new Myasishchev design. Tupolev was familiar with the area rule design problem, as his own Tu-22 design was one of the first large Soviet aircraft to take advantage of the innovation. Tupolev also told Khrushchev that the day's test flight had been cancelled due to mechanical problems, an underhanded move to further besmirch the troubled project's reputation. Khrushchev returned to Moscow, fuming over the waste of his time driving all the way out to Ramenskoye.

Tupolev's influence with Khrushchev, the unimpressive performance of the M-50, and Khrushchev's growing infatuation with intercontinental missiles doomed the new bomber. Myasishchev's fate was further sealed by more behind-the-scenes politicking. Khrushchev had authorized the opening of a third new strategic missile design bureau, to be headed by Vladimir Chelomey, who had headed the early cruise missile program in the late 1940s and the later naval antiship missile program. Talented and ambitious, Chelomey realized that strategic missiles and spacecraft represented the future of the aerospace business. His success with the naval cruise missile projects and his plans for future missile designs won him bureaucratic support within the military. Frustrated by Myasishchev's repeated failures, Khrushchev authorized the closing of Myasishchev's design bureau at Fili. Chelomey was allotted the Fili plant for his new design bureau, along with many of the talented aviation engineers located there.

Khrushchev's growing disenchantment with the numerous schemes to develop strategic weapons pushed him farther and farther in the direction of strategic missiles. The success of *Sputnik,* the successful test flights of the R-7 missile, and the obvious shortcomings of the bombers prompted him to concentrate state resources on one single technology. The December 1959 announcement of the formation of the RVSN Strategic Missile Forces was the final nail in the coffin of the strategic bomber force. Further production of the Tu-95M and M-4A bombers was halted, and the inventory remained at hardly a hundred aircraft for the rest of the decade. The air force was gradually nudged out of the strategic mission. To add insult to injury, efforts were underway to turn over some of its heavy bombers to the navy to carry out long-range patrol missions.

Chapter 8

Attack from the Sea

ON AN OVERCAST autumn day in September 1955, the choppy arctic waters off the Russian port of Severodvinsk on the White Sea were cordoned off from fishermen by KGB patrol craft. Hidden from onlookers, a Soviet submarine lay on the surface, its decks swarming with technicians. From within the conning tower, mechanical sounds became audible. Moments later the pointed shape of a ballistic missile could be seen slowly rising out of the submarine, finally coming to rest at the top of the sail. After a diligent check by the technicians, the deck was cleared of personnel. Small craft wallowing in the waters nearby were cleared away. Sergey Korolev gave the order and the submarine's crew triggered the missile engine. A blast of flame erupted from its base and the R-P ballistic missile gradually lifted off from its shipborne platform. The world's first submarine-launched ballistic missile (SLBM) had been successfully fired.

In 1950 the U.S. Navy's Office of Naval Intelligence concluded that it would take the Soviet Navy at least ten years to adapt ballistic missiles to submarines. In fact, it took less than half that time. The U.S. Navy's intelligence experts had more accurately forecast their own SLBM program. But, as in the case of the R-7 land-based missile, the Soviets were quickly overtaken by their more technologically sophisticated counterparts in the United States. The Soviet Navy's inability to sustain the momentum of its SLBM program was in part technological and in part political.

The priority afforded the Soviet naval missile program reflected the structure of the Soviet armed forces. Unlike the United States, where the navy's influence was equal to that of the army, in the Soviet Union the navy had long been a very junior partner to the Red Army. The reasons were geographic. The Soviet Union has an enormous coastline, but nearly all of it is in the

169

frozen arctic north. Its warm-water ports—on the Baltic, near Leningrad, and on the Black Sea—do not offer easy access to the high seas. Its Pacific ports, like Vladivostok, are likewise confined, with access to the Pacific being restrained by the string of islands of the Kurile chain off Japan's northern coast.

The marginal role of the Soviet Navy was nowhere more evident than in the Second World War. In spite of a massive building program in the 1930s, the navy's World War II performance was disappointing.[1] The Soviet Union started the war with the world's largest submarine fleet, greater in number than even the vaunted German U-boats. Other combatants' submarine forces played major roles in the naval campaigns of the war, especially the U-boats in the Atlantic and the American submarine fleet in the Pacific. In spite of its size, the Soviet submarine force had little impact on the naval war, hampered as it was by geography. It spent much of the war bottled up in its Baltic seaports, hindered as much by the narrow choke points in the northern Baltic as by German naval actions. In the Black Sea, German air and naval supremacy limited Soviet activities. The only theater where the Soviet submarine fleet had some freedom of action was in the northern arctic waters. But there were slim pickings in so remote an area. The Soviet surface fleet had little more success. The Soviet Navy finally came alive in 1944 as the Red Army swept along the Baltic coast, freeing the Soviet Navy from the depredations of the German Navy. But by then, the outcome of the war was a foregone conclusion.[2] Stalin remained a firm advocate of a strong Soviet fleet, able to extend Soviet power beyond its geographic limits. But the Soviet Navy remained in the shadows of the real victor of the war—the Red Army.

The navy's modest influence in Soviet war planning affected the role it would play in the development of Soviet strategic forces after the war. A country like the United States might seem naturally vulnerable to sea attack. Its coastlines are long and many of its major cities and industrial centers are located along the Atlantic and Pacific coasts. But few Soviet leaders were confident that the navy's warships, especially submarines, could carry out such long-range missions. The Soviet submarine fleet was primarily a coastal defense force. The majority of its submarines were small, short-range boats intended to operate only modest distances from their bases. Nor was the Soviet fleet equipped or trained to carry out missions so far from its home ports. It would take over a decade for these skills to be learned. Gradually, Soviet engineers began to look at ways to deliver attacks against strategic targets in Britain and the United States using the new weapons of war: the missile and the atomic bomb.

Baltic Booty

The vulnerability of the United States to coastal missile attack had not escaped the attention of the Germans, whose U-boats had operated off the coast of the United States since the outbreak of the war. But with the advent of new tactics such as convoys, and new antisubmarine technologies, by 1944 these missions near America had become almost suicidal. Once able to roam off the Atlantic coast with hardly any opposition, by the final year of the war the U-boats had become the hunted. Anglo-American antisubmarine warfare technology and tactics were reaching the peak of their efficiency, taking a bloody toll on the once dangerous U-boats. In spite of the dangers of submarine operations off the coast of America, the lack of intercontinental bombers or missiles persuaded Hitler and other German leaders to authorize one of the least-known secret weapons of World War II: a submarine-launched version of the V-2 ballistic missile.

The German Navy had begun small-scale tests of the feasibility of launching rockets from submarines in the summer of 1942, but the matter was quickly forgotten in the face of more pressing problems. The issue was revived in 1944 by Dr. Ernest Steinhoff, one of the Peenemünde engineers working on the V-2 ballistic missile, whose brother Fritz happened to be a U-boat officer.[3] Submarines of the time were much too small to enclose a V-2 missile, so Steinhoff developed the idea of placing a V-2 and its associated launch equipment inside a submersible barge resembling a miniature submarine hull in shape. The barge could be towed by the submarine to the American coast. There its ballast tanks would be flooded, elevating the missile to its vertical launch position. The missile could then be prepared and fired. The submarine missile launcher was given the code name Test Stand XII, although it was also called the Laffrentz Project. Work was begun at the Wolfsburg Volkswagen factory. The idea was eventually modified to permit a single submarine to tow three missile containers. Towing tests were conducted in the Baltic in 1945, and several different versions of the submarine missile container were under construction when the war ended.[4]

When Soviet troops occupied Peenemünde in 1945, they found some of the documentation relating to Test Stand XII. Also located were some of the uncompleted launch capsules. According to intelligence reports, the Soviets continued to pursue this effort in the later 1940s under the code name *Golem*. However, the system did not prove practical and, so far as is known, no test firings ever took place.[5]

The Super Torpedo

Difficulties in launching missiles from submarines led Stalin to authorize one of the most bizarre weapons of the Cold War, a nuclear-armed "super torpedo." Such a weapon could be launched from a submarine and targeted at major U.S. port cities such as New York, Boston, San Francisco, or San Diego; major navy bases, such as Norfolk; or other strategic targets, such as the Panama Canal. The navy could attack coastal cities by submarine, while the army and air force would attack inland cities and bases with missiles and bombers. The atomic torpedo program began in 1949 or 1950. There is no information regarding who came up with the idea, although Soviet accounts indicate the idea did not come from the Soviet Navy.

Because of the sheer size of the early atomic bombs, some 5 tons, no ordinary torpedo would be suitable. The super torpedo was enormous, measuring about 2 meters (over 6 feet) in diameter. It weighed 400 tons and had a top under-sea speed of 19 knots. It was powered by a diesel engine, much like a conventional submarine.[6] The plans called for a sophisticated guidance system using acoustic signals emitted by the submarine that launched it. Because of its huge size, it could not be carried by any existing submarine. A whole new type of submarine would have to be developed to carry it.

Nor was an ordinary diesel-powered submarine deemed suitable. The Soviet Navy had studied the most advanced submarine of the time, the German Type XXI, and found it insufficient for the task.[7] The problem was the vulnerability of submarines to aircraft detection. A submarine carrying a super torpedo would have to traverse thousands of miles of open ocean from Soviet bases to its American target. If detected by American aircraft or warships, the submarine could be hunted down and destroyed. As the preeminent Soviet submarine designer of the day, Boris Malinin, said, "Aircraft radar is a steel broom which just brushes conventional submarines away."[8]

Conventional diesel-powered submarines were vulnerable to detection by American antisubmarine planes because, no matter how sophisticated, they all required air for their engines. To reduce their visibility to aircraft, the Germans developed snorkels for their U-boats in the final years of World War II. The snorkel allowed the submarine to remain completely submerged. All that remained on the surface was the small upper portion of the snorkel. But British and American antisubmarine aircraft were able to find even the small snorkel tip using new radars. What was needed was a submarine that could travel all the way to the U.S. coast completely underwater for the whole voyage. The solution was a nuclear reactor, because a nuclear powerplant does not consume air during operation. This meant that submarines could remain underwater indefinitely, greatly reducing their vulnerability to detection. An atomic powerplant seemed to be an essential ingredient in developing a submarine capable of launching missile strikes from off the American coast.

The idea of powering a ship with a nuclear reactor had been suggested by Petr L. Kapitsa in 1946. At the time, Kapitsa headed the Institute of Physics Problems, which was not heavily involved in defense work thanks to Kapitsa's long-running feud with Lavrentiy Beria's special police. When Beria learned of Kapitsa's unauthorized work on the nuclear powerplant idea, he ordered it closed down. Beria argued that all attention must be concentrated on developing the atomic bomb and that no diversions would be tolerated. Beria ordered Kapitsa to turn his attention to nuclear fuel processing. After further disagreements, Kapitsa was removed from his position and replaced by Anatoliy Aleksandrov, one of the original members of Kurchatov's nuclear program. Aleksandrov reexamined the matter of nuclear submarine propulsion in 1948, only to have Beria again terminate the program as a needless distraction from the primary goal of developing nuclear weapons.

Attitudes changed. In 1952 Beria ordered Aleksandrov to reopen the nuclear powerplant idea. By then the first atomic bomb had been detonated, the first series production of atomic bombs completed, and work was well underway on the development of thermonuclear bombs. Diversification of Soviet nuclear technology was now permitted.

The program to develop a nuclear-powered submarine capable of attacking U.S. port cities with the super torpedo was code-named Project 627. The submarine itself was designed by Central Design Bureau 143 in Leningrad.[9] Like many of the atomic programs of the time, Project 627 was kept secret even from military leaders. The head of the Soviet Navy, Admiral N. G. Kuznetsov, was aware that a nuclear-powered submarine was under development, but he was kept in the dark about its most secret component, the super torpedo. It was not until the design had almost been completed that Admiral Kuznetsov was finally shown the plans.

Kuznetsov took one look at the blueprints and stated quite bluntly, "I don't need that kind of boat."[10] Kuznetsov had a far more practical appreciation for the difficulties in using such a weapon than did Beria and Stalin. A super torpedo was nothing more than a miniature submarine. It had the slow speed of a submarine, not the high speed of a conventional torpedo. Its slow speed would doom the crew of the submarine that launched it, since the submarine could not escape fast enough from the blast waves. It was a completely impractical idea. Because of Kuznetsov's stubborn resistance, the super torpedo project was eventually cancelled and the Project 627 nuclear submarine was redesigned to fire conventional torpedoes, thus delaying its entry into service.

The Missile Option

With the torpedo idea ruled out, Beria ordered the head of the Second Chief Directorate, Dmitriy Ustinov, to examine other possible ways of firing nuclear weapons at American targets from submarines. The most obvious alternative was to employ missiles. Even though the German submersible launch capsule idea had proven impractical, new missiles, of a smaller size more suitable for submarines, might be feasible. The new project was given the code name R-P.[11]

Until the death of Stalin and the removal of Beria in 1953, open discussion of nuclear weapons in the navy was strictly forbidden, part of Stalin's ruse to minimize the significance of America's nuclear advantage. Secrecy about the Soviet nuclear program began to loosen after the successful test of the first atomic bomb in 1949, but it was not until after Stalin's death that the navy began to seriously participate in nuclear weapons planning. The first published discussion of the potential role of submarine-launched ballistic missiles in nuclear strikes against strategic targets came in 1955.[12] This marked the beginning of a heated debate within the Soviet military over the shape of future strategic forces. Nevertheless, the development of doctrine governing the use of such weapons was still in its embryonic stages, given the early stage of development of such missile technology.[13]

Development of submarine missiles was added to the long list of projects already underway at Sergey Korolev's OKB-1 design bureau in Kaliningrad. Korolev took his first trip to sea in a submarine in 1953 to acquaint himself with the problems of a submarine-launched missile. He envisioned two approaches to the R-P program: use an existing missile and adapt it to naval launch, or develop an entirely new missile. Due to the pervasive sense of urgency in those Cold War days, it was decided to begin with an existing missile. Even if such a missile might not be entirely satisfactory, it would give the Soviet Navy important experience in the design and handling of naval ballistic missiles.

This approach was typical of Korolev's design style. It can best be summed up by a popular engineering slogan of the day, "Build it, break it, build it better." Korolev preferred to take a series of incremental leaps forward rather than a single revolutionary leap. The technological challenge posed by the submarine missiles was not the missiles themselves, but rather the launcher technology. The early Soviet SLBMs were very simple designs compared to their contemporary land-based counterparts.

Korolev's approach was very different from that adopted by the U.S. Navy. Although the original plan had been to adapt an army missile for submarine launch, the U.S. Navy decided to forgo such a program and leap forward to a far more revolutionary design using advanced solid-fuel engines and a launch system that enabled the missile to be fired underwater.[14] The Americans realized that such a system would take longer to develop, but their underestimation of Soviet missile capabilities left them in no particular rush to push such a missile into service.

Submarine Missiles

The only Soviet missile small enough for submarine launch was the new R-11. The existing R-2 and the new R-5 were simply too large to fit into a submarine. The R-11, better known in the West as the Scud, was compact enough to fit inside the sail of an existing submarine. Having selected a missile, the next issue to be resolved was the launch method. Ideally, the missile should be launched from a submerged position, so that the submarine could not be detected by antisubmarine aircraft. But this posed an enormous technological challenge.

It was not clear what the interaction of the missile and an undersea environment would entail. Would the water pressure crush the thin outer skin of the missile? Would the seawater impede the ignition of the rocket engine? Would the water rushing into the missile tube at launch form strong eddies that would deflect the path of the missile's ascent? Korolev's bureau, already burdened with the higher priority R-7 ICBM program, opted for a less risky and more predictable approach. The missile would be much easier to fire with the submarine resting on the surface.

But wave motion proved to be a major technical difficulty. Unfortunately, because the R-11 had been developed from the outset as a land-based missile, its accuracy was entirely dependent upon the missile being steady and completely vertical. Should it be tilted even a fraction of a degree at the moment of launch, it would miss its intended target by miles because its simple inertial navigation system could not be adjusted in flight.

The solution to this problem was suggested by Anatoliy Abramov of Korolev's team: a stabilized launch platform. Such a platform was controlled by a set of gyroscopes that monitored the submarine's motion in all three axes. Two axes could be controlled by rotating and tilting the platform. Motion in the third axis could be controlled by monitoring platform movement. The missile would only be released at the precise moment when it was in a true vertical position. The idea of a stabilized platform was not particularly worrisome to naval engineers, resembling in many respects the problems of aiming large guns on battleships. In fact, Viktor Kuznetsov, one of the chief designers collaborating with Korolev on the ballistic missile program, had been one of the foremost naval armament engineers before his switch to missile work. Kuznetsov was able to outline the requirement for the platform, which was much like the gyro-stabilized systems he had designed for Soviet warship gun turrets. Work on the launch system, nicknamed the "Horn and Hoof," was entrusted to E. G. Rudnyak, head of the TsKB-34 naval artillery design bureau in Leningrad. The "Horn" was the four vertical supports that held the missile erect on the launcher, the "Hoof" was the specially designed attachment points on the launcher; which kept the missile from lifting off the pad until the precise moment the system's gyroscopes determined the missile was vertical.

Korolev had played a very minor role in designing the army version of the R-11 missile, leaving the project to his aide, Vasiliy Mishin. But Korolev took a more active interest in the naval version, if only because of the unique challenges that it posed for his design team.

The army's R-11 missile had begun its test flights in the spring and summer of 1953. During the ten test flights, serious flaws were found in the Isayev engine. After corrections were made, a second series of test flights was conducted at Kapustin Yar in April and May 1954. The missile proved successful and was officially accepted for Soviet Army use in July 1955 after it had been tested with a nuclear warhead.

The naval version of the missile, the R-11FM, was ready for testing in late 1954. A special platform was erected at the Kapustin Yar test range to simulate the natural motion of a submarine at sea. On top of this platform, the Horn and Hoof launcher was fastened. The launcher consisted of a canister that completely enclosed the missile, preventing water from entering it while the submarine was submerged. Once on the surface, the missile tube would be opened. Abramov considered launching the missile directly from the tube. However, this proved impossible because the hot exhaust gases from the rocket engine would flow around the missile while in the tube, possibly igniting the remainder of the fuel in the missile. Instead, the missile would be pushed out of the tube on its stabilized platform, resting precariously on the top of the sail moments before firing. The stabilizing gyroscopes determined when the rocket motor would be ignited and the missile released. The system required that the launch wait until the sea motion was reduced, but the high launch position of the missile exacerbated the submarine's natural rolling motion by raising the submarine's center of gravity.

A series of eight test flights was conducted from ground launchers at Kapustin Yar between 26 September and 20 October 1954 to examine the functioning of the missile launcher. Tests were also conducted to determine the effect of the rocket exhaust on periscopes and other elements in the submarine's sail to make certain that no permanent damage was caused. The tests proved successful. The next step was to fit the launch system to the submarine itself.

The R-P project was turned over to a prominent Soviet submarine designer, Nikolay Isanin, after Korolev's bureau had completed work on the missile and its launch system. Although it was hoped that such a system would be mounted on a nuclear-powered submarine, the Project 627 nuclear submarines were not yet in service. Isanin chose to mount the first test system on an existing diesel submarine, a Project 611 class submarine with the hull number B-67.[15] The B-67, commanded by Capt. 2d Rank S. Kozlov, was sent to Shipyard 402 in Severodvinsk for rebuilding. The aft portion of the sail was enlarged to accommodate a single Horn and Hoof launch system. This was a test submarine only, not intended for actual service use.

As mentioned earlier, the first successful test of this missile took place on 16 September 1955. In December B-67 was transferred to the Central Scientific Research Test Range at Severodvinsk in the Russian arctic. The White Sea proved to be a very poor location for the tests. As the winter weather closed in, the seas became more and more turbulent. B-67 was eventually transferred to Severomorsk on the Barents Sea, which does not freeze during the winter months.

The testing was prolonged and troubled. The R-11FM was loaded into the submarine with its fuel tanks already filled. A new form of nitric acid oxidant had been developed, the so-called inhibited red fuming nitric acid, which had agents added to reduce its corrosive effects on the storage tank. In addition, a special coating was used on the fuel tanks to prevent the oxidant from eating through the metal. This was supposed to be durable enough for three months of storage inside the submarine. But it often proved inadequate, and the nitric acid ate its way through joints and piping. Poor quality control of other components also led to a string of launch failures.

Only one test was a complete failure. More often than not, the missile would safely lift off its launcher and then go out of control some distance from the submarine. But on one occasion the missile engine failed to ignite and could not be retracted into the launch tube because the nitric acid oxidant was leaking. The oxidant could have eaten through the metal parts and contaminated the submarine's interior with poisonous fumes. Luckily for the crew, Sergey Korolev was present and ordered the missile ejected over the side. The navy personnel were flabbergasted that Korolev dared to take this initiative on his own without permission from Moscow. Missiles were expensive and Beria's legacy still lingered, but Korolev grasped the new freedoms possible under the more rational leadership of the new Kremlin bosses.

At the completion of the second test series, a conference was held, chaired by the new head of the Soviet Navy, Admiral Sergey G. Gorshkov, and including the representatives of the design bureaus responsible for the R-P project: Korolev (missiles), Isanin (submarine), Slavskiy (nuclear warhead), and the naval officers involved in the test. The presentation of the test results was handled by Capt. Ivan Gulyayev, the new skipper who commanded B-67 during the second launch series. Gulyayev was questioned harshly by the admiral, who appeared to be no friend of the missile submarine idea. But supported by industry representatives and the minister of the defense industries, Dmitriy Ustinov, the R-P project was approved for further development.

Although Soviet accounts of the R-P program remain vague, some of the problems encountered can be deduced from similar programs undertaken in the United States, Britain, and France.[16] One of the central technological hurdles in all SLBMs is accuracy. The R-11 missile in its land-based version had a CEP (circular error probability) of about 4 kilometers (about 3 miles) at a range of 180 km, meaning that half of all R-11 missiles fired at a given target would strike within 4 kilometers of the target.[17] This meant that the R-11FM could expect no better accuracy than that.

But the naval missile's accuracy was further impeded by two other serious problems: the submarine's motion and the uncertainties of the launch point. The Horn and Hoof launcher could not offer the stability of its land-based counterpart. These early ballistic missiles did not leap off the pad instantly, but gradually accelerated. Disturbances to the naval missiles during the first few seconds of flight introduced accuracy problems not suffered by the land-based versions.

The second problem was the uncertainty of the submarine's location. Submarines during the 1950s lacked a sophisticated inertial guidance system. Traditional methods of navigation, such as celestial navigation, could place a submarine within a few dozen miles of its intended location. In the open ocean, a submariner would feel lucky to be within ten miles of his intended destination. Such an inaccuracy was completely unacceptable for a missile submarine, since it would add to the already considerable inaccuracies of the missile and its launch system. There were a variety of ways around this problem.

The American approach was inertial navigation.[18] These systems operated much like the inertial platforms in the missiles themselves, monitoring the change in course of a submarine in three axes by monitoring a set of gyroscopes. Little is known of the Soviet gyroscope technology of this period, but there is little reason to believe it was comparable to American inertial navigation technology.

An alternative to the inertial platform was some external form of guidance. Bombers had used radio guidance systems since the Second World War. These worked by transmitting two radio beams from widely spaced transmitters and determining location from the relationship of the ship or aircraft to the beams. The American Loran-C system of the late 1950s could place a ship within about 1,500 feet of its intended location. The Soviets faced substantial difficulties in implementing such a system for submarine missions off the American coast, since the likely missile launch locations were too far from any land-based radio navigation sites accessible to the USSR.[19]

Other types of systems appear to have been considered, such as imbedding navigation transmitters off the American coast. But such a venture would have been extremely risky from many standpoints, not the least of which was the possibility the transmitters might be discovered and moved. Another alternative would have been cooperative target location with another ship, such

as a freighter or other disguised vessel. While possible under extreme conditions, such an arrangement would have been exceedingly difficult to carry
out on a routine basis.

The Soviets apparently chose the beacon method. In the late 1950s, Soviet ships began conducting detailed bottom-surveys off the American coast.
It is not clear how the beacon system would have been deployed, whether a
short time before an anticipated strike or a long time ahead, using some form
of submarine-controlled trigger to activate the beacon signal.

Even had the Soviet Navy managed to improve submarine navigation accuracy,
another problem arose. The inertial navigation system in early Soviet missiles was "hard-wired." That is, it was configured to guide the missile to a
specific target using one, and only one, trajectory. Unlike later missile guidance systems, there was no possibility for the missile launch crew to alter
the missile's trajectory, short of reconfiguring the guidance package. Such a
limitation posed no insurmountable problem to land-based systems under most
scenarios.[20] But at sea, such a system implied that the submarine would have
to launch its missile from a preplanned location. Because of this limitation,
the submarine lost its main advantage: its flexibility of operation.

Imagine for a moment that a Soviet submarine had been given the mission of attacking the U.S. Navy base at Norfolk, Virginia. The R-11FM missiles
in its sail have a maximum range of 180 km (110 miles). The submarine
commander might be given three alternative locations from which to conduct his missile strike on the target. In each case, the missiles would have to
be launched from a single precise point, with the Horn and Hoof launcher
traversed in such a way as to be accurately pointed within a fraction of a
degree of the impact point over a hundred miles away. The commander would
face the daunting task of steering his submarine to this precise point, while
at the same time the crew was involved in the laborious task of surfacing,
erecting the missile, and preparing it to fire. During this preparation phase,
which would probably last about a half an hour, the submarine would be exposed
to any antisubmarine defenses in the area: radar-equipped aircraft, American submarines, or surface antisubmarine ships, such as destroyers or frig-
ates. Surprise would be difficult if not impossible. The Soviet submarine
commander would have a hellish time trying to evade any antisubmarine forces
appearing on the scene. Not only was the missile awkwardly erected over
the sail, it was virtually impossible to retract.[21] But even if it could be retracted
and the launch sequence restarted, the submarine commander would encounter
the same difficult tactical problems at his alternative launch positions.

In short, the early submarines did not represent a mature strategic weapon.
Their limited accuracy raised real questions about their actual military util-

ity. As a Soviet officer connected with the test program concluded, the early missiles were adopted as much to gain experience as to form an element of the Soviet Union's growing strategic arsenal.[22]

The service version of the R-P missile submarine, designated Project 611AB (Zulu V) had two launchers, rather than the single launcher mounted on the B-67. A total of five Project 611AB submarines were modified to fire the R-11FM missile. The problems with the missile and its launch system made the R-P program one of the most protracted development efforts of this era, taking almost four years, until early in 1959, before official acceptance by the Soviet Navy.[23]

Even with the delays, the Soviets had managed to beat the U.S. Navy by launching the first submarine ballistic missile and putting the first missile submarines into service. There were several reasons for this success. The U.S. Navy had, in fact, launched missiles at sea before the Soviets. The Americans had test fired copies of the German V-1, called Loons, from submarines and other warships since 1947 and had also fired ballistic missiles from surface warships. But the U.S. Navy favored winged cruise missiles, rather than ballistic missiles, for the short-range bombardment role from submarines. It deployed a submarine-launched cruise missile, the Regulus, in 1954, before the Soviets adopted the R-11FM submarine ballistic missile. Furthermore, the U.S. Navy had other systems with which to deliver nuclear weapons to targets farther inland, especially aircraft. It had been operating nuclear-capable carrier-launched P2V bombers since 1949, and had been developing jet-powered, nuclear-capable carrier aircraft since the early 1950s. Finally, the U.S. Navy was very wary of liquid-fueled ballistic missiles after a near disaster aboard the aircraft carrier *Midway* while test launching V-2 missiles.

The different approaches taken by the U.S. Navy meant that work on an American submarine-launched ballistic missile did not begin until 1955, by which time the Soviets were already test firing missiles from submarines. At this point, the U.S. Navy was studying plans to adapt the U.S. Army's Jupiter missile to submarines. This program had been pressed on the navy by the Department of Defense. The program was finally postponed in 1957 because the navy preferred to wait for the development of a solid-fuel missile. American submariners were reluctant to use a liquid-fueled missile like that developed by the Soviets, fearing that it would pose unacceptable safety problems in the close confines of their craft.[24] The U.S. Navy was also awaiting the development of satisfactory navigation systems for submarines, to avoid the problems endemic in the rushed Soviet R-P program. Even though the American Polaris submarine missile system came nearly five years after its Soviet counterpart, it was a far more mature system in both a technical and tactical sense. Its true Soviet counterpart, the Project 667 *Navaga* (Yankee I) did not appear in active service until 1968, more than eight years after the first Polaris submarines, and over a decade after the launch of the first Soviet SLBM.

Missiles at Sea

The new Soviet missile submarines were identified by the U.S. Navy for the first time in 1956 when B-67 was spotted in Rosta naval shipyard in the Kola inlet by a U.S. submarine. American submarines made frequent visits to the Soviet coast, lying in wait offshore to monitor Soviet naval activity. There are reports that their snooping took more dramatic forms, including clandestine incursions into Soviet waters.

At first, the U.S. Navy was not certain what the enlarged sail of the B-67 contained. In 1958, three of the new Project 611AB Zulu V submarines were spotted in the Northern Fleet's operating area, and the first tentative glimpses were seen of the circular hatch covers over the Horn and Hoof launcher. At first, there was some speculation that the covers concealed a radar or sonar device. It was only in 1959 that the U.S. Navy began to appreciate that it might be a ballistic missile launcher. This assessment was finally confirmed in May 1959. A U.S. Navy task force operating off the coast of Iceland located and tracked a Project 611AB submarine, the PL-82. There was a drawn-out pursuit of PL-82 by an American diesel-powered attack submarine, the *Grenadier,* which at one point nearly collided underwater with the Soviet boat. The PL-82 was finally forced to the surface where U.S. naval surveillance aircraft were able to take detailed photos of the launch canisters. It was apparent from the photos that it was carrying ballistic missiles.[25]

Early patrols by Zulu V missile submarines in 1959 marked only the first phase of the Soviet SLBM program. The R-11FM and the modified Zulu V submarine were viewed as an interim measure. Work on a new missile, specifically designed for submarines, and a new submarine, designed from the outset for missile launching, had been underway since the mid-1950s.

Korolev had gradually withdrawn from the naval ballistic missile program, letting his junior designers take over the work. Viktor Makayev, a thirty-year-old engineer, was responsible for putting the army version of the R-11 into production at a new facility at Chelyabinsk in the Ural industrial region. Korolev offered him the position of deputy chief designer at the new facility, to be in charge of naval ballistic missiles. To Korolev's complete surprise, Makayev said he would take the job, but only as chief designer! Korolev admired his audacity, but was unwilling to place so junior an engineer in charge of the project. However, Makayev's success in preparing the R-11FM for navy service encouraged Korolev to entrust him with the design of the R-11FM's successor, the R-13. A draft design of the R-13 was given to Makayev in early 1956.

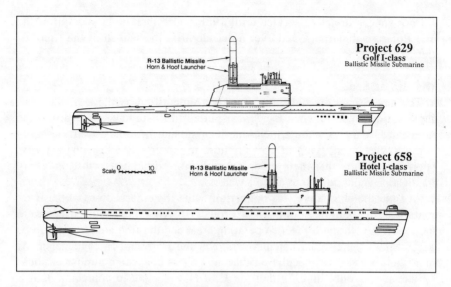

This missile was designed to be fired from the Horn and Hoof launcher used on the modified Project 611 submarines. One of the few changes was the decision to leave the missile unfueled in the launch tube until launch time. The limitations of the nitric acid oxidant forced the designers to store the fuel and oxidant separately. It would have to be pumped into the missile prior to the scheduled launch.

The R-13 missile, known in the West as the SS-N-4, was intended for the new Project 629 and Project 658 submarines.[26] The Project 629 class, like the modified Project 611 Zulu V before it, was designed by N. N. Isanin's design bureau in Leningrad. The Project 629 was conventionally powered, with all the tactical limitations that implied when used in the strategic strike role. At the same time, a more ambitious nuclear-powered missile submarine, also carrying Makayev's R-13 missile, was under development. Called the Project 658, this class of submarine was based on a modified version of the first class of Soviet nuclear-powered submarines, the Project 627 (November) class. This effort was undertaken by V. N. Peregudov's design bureau in Leningrad. The decision to build both nuclear- and conventional-powered missile submarines was due as much to economy as any other factor. The conventionally powered Project 629 submarines were considerably less expensive to manufacture than the nuclear Project 658 submarines. Even though the nuclear-powered designs had distinctive tactical advantages, the high cost of such weapons could not be ignored. In the end, some eight nuclear-powered Project 658 Hotel submarines were built, compared to three times as many conventional Project 629 Golf submarines.

The first of the Project 658 nuclear missile submarines was completed in 1960 and went to sea for trials. Identified by hull number K-19, its first mission was a patrol off Canada and the United States.[27] Unfortunately, as will be seen, the new submarine was plagued with problems.

The Soviet Buzz Bomb

Ballistic missiles, as the Americans showed with their cruise missiles, were not the only alternative for submarine-launched weapons. Not surprisingly, U.S. intelligence agencies expected the Soviets likewise to begin with cruise missiles on submarines. American intelligence officers questioning German missile engineers returning from the Soviet Union in the mid-1950s were frequently told tales of Soviet experiments with V-1 buzz bombs and other missiles on submarines. Yet no Soviet submarines were seen on patrol carrying such weapons. This puzzled U.S. Navy intelligence officers, who had long presumed that the Soviets would follow the same path their own service had. The Soviet side of the story is somewhat more complicated and, even now, not entirely clear.

As described earlier, the Soviet Air Force had sponsored an effort to develop a cruise missile in 1944, spurred on by the first reports of the German V-1 buzz bomb. Designed by Vladimir Chelomey, the 10X missile was fired from ground launchers and from aircraft in 1945. But the 10X never went into series production.

One of the reasons that 10X production had been put off was the availability of captured German missiles. Following Germany's defeat in the spring of 1945, Chelomey, like many other young missile designers, was sent to occupied Germany to study captured missile technology. This led to a series of improvements in the 10X design. The next derivative, the 14X, used two pulse-jet engines mounted in tandem over the tail. The 14X went through a number of test flights but was never placed in quantity production. From a military standpoint, the problem was accuracy.

The German V-1 buzz bomb had been designed as an inexpensive alternative to the high-tech V-2 ballistic missile. The V-1's guidance system was elementary. A simple inertial guidance set steered the missile on its flight path and, at a predetermined distance, cut off the engine. The V-1 then glided downward until impact. This method of guidance was not very accurate, and made the missile suitable only for bombarding large cities. Part of the accuracy problem was due to the nature of cruise missiles. They rely on their wings for lift and range. But their large aerodynamic surfaces are also a curse so far as accuracy is concerned. They are more subject to the vagaries of the wind than ballistic missiles, particularly when using as elementary a guidance system as the V-1's. When launched from a bomber, accuracy was even worse because of uncertainty about the bomber's precise location at the moment of launch. Even with advanced radio navigation aids, the V-1s launched from German bombers were one-fourth as accurate as their land-launched counterparts.

The 14X might have been adopted by the Soviet Air Force as an anti-city weapon, but there were growing doubts about its utility even in this role. When first employed against London, the V-1 proved reasonably successful. But the British, with help from the Americans, quickly developed methods to limit its damage. The V-1 could be shot down by fighters vectored by radar or blocked from reaching its target by barrage balloons. It also fell prey to U.S.-designed antiaircraft artillery projectiles employing the proximity fuze, which detonated when they came near an aircraft. This innovation drastically improved the effects of large-caliber antiaircraft weapons and was first used against the buzz bombs in 1944.

Antimissile defenses reached their peak during the battle for Antwerp. The Germans tried to close the Belgian port city in the winter of 1944–45, since it was the main conduit for Allied supplies coming from England to the Continent. Antwerp was subjected to a punishing barrage of V-2 ballistic missiles and V-1 cruise missiles. The Allies could do little to stop the V-2, but they had great success against the buzz bombs, downing 97 percent by the end of the campaign.[28]

Chelomey came to realize that simple jet-powered cruise missiles like the V-1 or his 14X needed a new military role. But their inertial guidance system limited their usefulness. What was clearly needed was a new form of guidance. Chelomey began investigating radio command guidance. Radio guidance can work in a variety of ways. The Germans had already developed a successful system for their Hs-293 antiship missiles. The command radio was located in the bomber carrying the missile to the target area. When the target was spotted, the missile was released. The bombardier in the parent aircraft then used the radio command system to steer the missile into the target. The radio emitted a coded signal that was received on the missile and converted into guidance corrections for the flight controls. In most cases, the bombardier in the parent aircraft used a simple joystick to control the missile's flight path.

The pinpoint accuracy of radio guidance opened up a variety of new uses for the cruise missile. They could be fired from aircraft to attack ships or vital land targets, such as bridges. They could also be fired from ground launchers located along the coastline to attack ships on the horizon. Chelomey began exploring these options with improved versions of his missile, such as the 16X. But work on the Soviet buzz bomb came to an abrupt halt in 1953. By order of Stalin, Chelomey's design bureau was shut down and its engineers parceled out among the other bureaus. The reasons for the abrupt termination of the program have never been made clear. Chelomey's biographers mention only that it was due to "intrigues and machinations."[29] The bulk of the design bureau was absorbed into the Mikoyan fighter design bureau, which was itself beginning to work on aircraft-launched cruise missiles.

Chelomey was out of a job, but he was not subject to the type of political persecution that had been common in the late 1930s. He finally found a position with a research institute headed by Admiral Kotov.[30] His employment by a naval weapons institute instead of an aircraft ministry design bureau shifted his attention to possible navy uses for cruise missiles.

Chelomey's work on the 14X and 16X was a critical underpinning for the most ambitious navy cruise missile program attempted in the early 1950s, the P-5, the first nuclear-armed naval missile. The P-5 was intended to be a counterpart to the U.S. Navy's Regulus strategic cruise missile. Like the Regulus, it was submarine launched from a container on the deck. It was propelled out of its launch canister by a pair of solid-propellant rocket boosters and then a jet engine kicked in. It had a range of 600 kilometers (about 400 miles), and could carry the same nuclear warhead as the R-11 ballistic missile.

A single Project 613 (Whiskey class) submarine was configured with a missile launcher for trials in 1956. In 1957 two more Project 613 submarines were converted, but with two missile launchers instead of one. These were called Project 644 by the Soviet Navy, and Whiskey Twin Cylinders by NATO. The navy's cruise missile test program was prolonged and marred by tragedy. The missile was cumbersome to prepare for launch, taking over forty minutes. Additionally, the launch tubes required precise aiming and the added containers greatly degraded the submarine's performance at sea. Finally, the missile's accuracy was poor and its simple barometric altitude reference system was unreliable, causing it to crash on occasion. Although only one year behind the R-11FM ballistic missile program, the lack of success with the P-5 caused it to lag farther and farther behind.

The last straw came in February 1961 when one of the Project 644 submarines with twin cylinders, commanded by Capt. Sitarchik, went into the Barents Sea and disappeared. The Soviet Navy searched for it for two years without result. It was finally discovered and raised in June 1969. The canisters apparently made the submarine top-heavy and the boat capsized with the loss of its entire crew.[31]

The failure of the P-5 program led to the development of improved variants, the P-6 and P-7. By the time these missiles were ready for service use, ballistic missiles like the R-11FM and R-13 were already firmly ensconced in the Soviet Navy's arsenal. To compete with ballistic missiles, a new intercontinental cruise missile program was started in 1960 by the Ilyushin aircraft design bureau. Khrushchev's obsession with missile weapons convinced many design bureaus that the only way to ensure their future was to become involved in missile design. Ilyushin's bureau, best known for light jet bombers, was particularly vulnerable. The bureau's engineers selected cruise missiles because of their similarity to aircraft in construction. They proposed a massive missile, some 25 meters long, which would be propelled out of a tube on the submarine's deck by two big rocket boosters. The missile was projected to have a range of several thousand kilometers, rather than the piddly few hundred kilometers of Chelomey's missiles. Work on the associated submarine, code-named Project 653, began in 1960.

Chelomey's success with the submarine cruise missiles, as well as Khrushchev's missile obsession, led the Kremlin to approve Chelomey's requests to reopen his old design bureau. In 1959 he was allowed to take over the Myasishchev OKB-23 facilities at Fili. Myasishchev had fallen victim to Khrushchev's prejudices against traditional weapons, such as bombers, as well as to his own flawed bomber designs. The new Chelomey bureau, code-named OKB-52, continued to work on the submarine cruise missiles. But Chelomey appreciated that the real prestige was in the field of ballistic missiles. He thus focused his attention on ballistic missiles—ICBMs in competition with Yangel, SLBMs in competition with Makayev's design bureau, and spy satellites in competition with Korolev.[32]

The Soviet Navy also considered the possibility of using cruise missiles fired from surface warships to attack strategic land targets in the United States, Europe, and Japan. Versions of Chelomey's cruise missiles were fitted to the Type 58 Kynda class cruisers for the strike role. But the navy was soon to lose its strategic strike role for bureaucratic rather than technological reasons.

Submarine Missiles in Limbo

In spite of the impressive technological accomplishments of the Soviet naval engineers, their efforts were frittered away by bureaucratic struggles going on within the Soviet Defense Ministry. Ever since Korolev's successful launch of *Sputnik I* in 1957, Nikita Khrushchev had grown increasingly preoccupied with missile weapons, seeing them both as a vanguard of future warfare and as an alternative to the USSR's bloated conventional forces.

The navy was particularly vulnerable to Khrushchev's changes. The army had long dominated Soviet defense decision making. The brains of the armed forces, the General Staff, was manned almost entirely by army officers. There were compelling reasons for this bias. As mentioned earlier, the navy had not played a significant role in the World War II victory, so its influence was accordingly small.

When it came to reducing the armed forces, the navy took some of the worst cuts. Prized navy programs, including the new Type 68-bis Sverdlov cruiser class, were halted. Ships already under construction were simply cut up for scrap. The navy had also been pressing for an aircraft carrier program, an effort that was squashed before the first keel was laid down.[33]

The culmination of Khrushchev's reforms came in December 1959 when he announced the formation of the Strategic Missile Forces, trumpeted as the primary element of the Soviet armed forces and receiving the highest priority in men and materiel. And, as we have seen, the missile force was basically an army operation, run by its artillery branch and manned by army troops.

The Soviet naval missile force was downgraded in its role, according to most Western analyses. The strategic nuclear strike role of the missile submarine force, built up at such cost, was abandoned—at least during the early 1960s.[34] The Soviet Navy was thus forced to dream up a new role for its ballistic missile submarines. It fastened onto the idea of using them to attack American aircraft carrier battle groups. While the American carriers posed a real threat, the notion of using the early SLBMs to attack them seems more an act of desperation than a prudent tactic.

Detailed Soviet accounts of this period are still scarce and what writing does exist is often tendentious and unconvincing. Two suppositions can be suggested for the abrupt shift in Soviet naval missile efforts. In all likelihood, it was not only bureaucratic infighting that caused Khrushchev to limit the navy's part in the strategic strike role. Khrushchev was so desperate to attain strategic parity with the United States that it is unlikely he would have given up the use of submarines in this contest simply because of army pressure. Indeed, there is evidence that Soviet ballistic missile submarines were carrying out missile patrols off the U.S. coast in 1961, more than a year after the formation of the Strategic Missile Forces.[35]

But the primitive state of the early Soviet missile submarines could hardly have given Khrushchev much confidence in their ability to carry out strategic missions. The Soviet Navy's decision to deploy immature technologies, especially the liquid-fueled, surface-launched missiles, ultimately may have backfired on it. There were a string of missile submarine accidents in 1961, including the loss of a Project 644 P-5 cruise missile submarine in February 1961, and a serious reactor failure on a Project 658 ballistic missile submarine in July 1961. It is unclear if either ship had nuclear weapons aboard, although it is somewhat doubtful. The early Soviet nuclear submarines had an appalling reliability record. The thought of the loss of nuclear weapons on a submarine operating close to the U.S. coast must have caused the Kremlin great anxiety. American naval analysts have long presumed that the early Soviet ballistic missile submarines went to sea with conventionally armed missiles or unarmed test missiles because of these concerns.

Soviet naval leaders, appreciating the limitations of 1960-era submarine technology, were aware both of American programs of the period and the possibilities of future Soviet developments in this area. On the surface, Admiral Gorshkov accepted the Kremlin's decision to exclude the navy from the strategic strike role. Yet the navy continued to pursue weapons suitable for nuclear strikes under the guise of the anticarrier strike role.

A good example of this was the *Navaga* program. The navy contracted a new submarine design bureau under Sergey Kovalev to develop a submarine patterned on the American Polaris submarines. Called Project 667 Navaga (NATO code name Yankee), the new submarine would be armed with Makayev's new RSM-25 Zyb (SS-N-6 Serb) missile. Ostensibly, the RSM-25 Zyb was developed as an anticarrier weapon, a barely plausible cover for what was clearly a strategic weapons system.[36] In view of its active pursuit of missile and submarine programs clearly configured for the strategic mission, the navy viewed the suspension from its role in nuclear strike missions as temporary. By the time the Navaga and its new missile were ready for service in 1968, Khrushchev had left the scene. Fortunately for the Soviet Navy, Admiral Gorshkov had belatedly appreciated the importance of submarine ballistic missiles and continued their development against the wishes of the Soviet Union's political leaders.

The mission of a strategic strike against the continental United States became the most prestigious role of the Soviet armed forces in the 1960s. After Stalin's death, the Soviet armed forces sought an active role in the nuclear debate. Khrushchev's decision to give top priority to the new Strategic Missile Forces may have submerged the debate for a time, but the navy was intent on reclaiming its share. Admiral Gorshkov managed to keep the designers focused on that task, even if the eventual role of such weapons was disguised.

Navaga was not the only such program. In the late 1950s and early 1960s, the missile design bureaus run by Yangel, Makayev, and Chelomey, and the submarine designers, Isanin, Peregudov, and Kovalev, were all assigned the task of developing a new generation of strategic nuclear missile systems. These missiles, and their submarine launchers, would outlast Khrushchev and find their way into Soviet Navy service by the end of the decade.

Chapter 9

Losing the Race

THE SHOCK OF *Sputnik* in 1957 and exaggerated assessments of the Soviet Strategic Missile Forces in the mid-1950s gave the American missile program considerable impetus. The sense of urgency created by *Sputnik* led to a feverish rush to field any missile systems that would help overcome the imagined imbalance.[1] The American aerospace industry, immensely richer than the Soviet industry, quickly sprinted ahead in the development of intercontinental missiles.

But the American program, like the Soviets', was plagued by the problems common to all novel technologies. Like the Lavochkin Burya, some of the programs were based on superficially attractive ideas that proved impossible to realize in the real world of mid-1950s technology. No better example can be found than the Snark. The U.S. Air Force first developed the idea of a rocket-boosted cruise missile right after the Second World War. The Navaho program had proven beyond American technological capability, however. This did not discourage air force interest in cruise missiles—far from it. A parallel program using more conventional jet-propulsion, the SM-62 Snark, continued after Navaho's cancellation. Snark's prodigious range made it capable of flying to the Soviet Union from bases in the United States. But the program was plagued by guidance glitches and other problems. During testing, one Snark went haywire and was last seen flying south over the Caribbean. It was discovered in the 1980s in the jungles of Brazil. There were so many offshore crashes during the test program that the development team ruefully referred to the area off the Florida coast as "Snark-infested waters." That such a dubious weapon was actually put into service is ample evidence of the sense of urgency *Sputnik*'s success created in the Pentagon.

Of equally questionable value were the intermediate-range missiles installed in Europe. Lacking intercontinental missiles, the United States convinced its NATO allies to allow the installation of the new Jupiter and Thor missiles at bases in the United Kingdom, Italy, and Turkey.[2] The missiles were intended to counter Soviet intermediate-range missiles, namely the R-5M, which were viewed as posing a threat to American strategic bomber bases in Europe. It was an exaggerated threat, as later became apparent: only about forty-eight R-5Ms were ever deployed. Such missiles also served as a stopgap until more-advanced ballistic missiles could be deployed.

The NATO missiles were nuclear-armed, with American crews responsible for the warheads and host-nation crews responsible for the missiles. The positioning of nuclear-armed missiles so close to the Soviet frontier seemed like a prudent antidote to the perceived Soviet missile superiority at the time. This was not the case from the Soviet perspective. The Kremlin saw the NATO deployment as being extremely provocative and, as we shall see, it had unintended consequences that brought the United States and the Soviet Union to the brink of nuclear war.

These marginally useful missile systems aside, the U.S. Air Force Strategic Air Command's real accomplishments were made with intercontinental missiles. The first of these, the Atlas, entered testing shortly after Korolev's R-7, although it entered service much sooner and was deployed more rapidly and in much greater numbers that its Soviet counterpart. The first Atlas base, with nine missiles, was activated on 1 April 1958.[3]

The Atlas shared some similarities with the R-7. Like the R-7, it was a stage-and-a-half design. It also used a pair of supplementary thrusters that were jettisoned after lift-off. Unlike the R-7, it was much smaller and lighter. This possible due to two factors. First, the R-7 was designed around the need to carry a massive boosted-fission bomb, while in contrast, the Atlas was to carry a more compact and advanced thermonuclear warhead. Second, the Atlas took advantage of every conceivable advance in aerospace design, using a remarkably light fuselage. The R-7's design was more reminiscent of the "Iron Age" of aerospace design: sturdy, robust, and extremely heavy. Soviet space design was Romanesque; the American style more Gothic.

The Atlas shared another important similarity with the R-7: it eventually proved unsuitable as a weapon system. Like the R-7, the Atlas took an inordinate amount of time to prepare and fuel. And its basing mode was equally vulnerable to missile attack. Also like the R-7, the Atlas served as the basis for the early space program, serving as the booster for the first American manned space flights. But as a weapon system, Atlas was soon overshadowed by its successors, the Titan and the Minuteman.

The next generation of American missile weapons was fast in coming, a tribute to the latent powers of the American aerospace industry and to the urgency spawned by the perceived missile gap. Two land-based missiles were on the drawing board. Titan, as its name implied, was a monster of a missile, similar in weight to the massive Soviet R-7 Semyorka, but with superior range and accuracy. The first Titan I squadrons were activated in February 1960. Minuteman, in contrast, was a small, solid-fuel missile—the first of its kind ever developed. It was in service by 1962.

By the end of 1960 there were 30 Snark cruise missiles and 12 Atlas ballistic missiles operational, but, in just a little more than a year, there were 224 ballistic missiles operational: 142 Atlases, 62 Titan Is, and 20 Minutemen.[4] During this entire period of time, Soviet intercontinental missile strength was limited to the four R-7 Semyorkas sitting at Plesetsk.

Nor were numbers the only American advantage. The early Titan I was not much superior to the R-7 in terms of throw weight or reaction time, but it was superior in range and accuracy. Furthermore, the subsequent Titan II used hypergolic fuel for rapid reaction, had more-powerful engines, employed a new guidance system, and carried a more potent warhead. Still more impressive was the new Minuteman missile. Relatively small, the Minuteman design stressed the war-fighting features only then becoming apparent as the missiles were actually entering service.

The Minuteman was the first ICBM developed with a solid-fuel rocket motor. Solid-fuel motors were an important innovation since it meant there was no fuel to be pumped into the missile before launch. The fuel was permanently stored in the missile, thereby greatly shortening launch time. The U.S. Air Force was also in the process of building hardened launch silos for its new Minuteman and Titan missiles. The Minuteman design was so successful that it has remained in service, in modernized form, to this day.

Research on solid-fuel missiles allowed the U.S. Navy to enter the missile race. The Soviet fleet, as we have seen, had significant technical problems with its early strategic missile submarines due to their awkward liquid-fueled configuration. The American solid-fuel program permitted the development of the U.S. Navy's first submarine-launched ballistic missile, the Polaris.[5] The Polaris submarine avoided nearly all of the problems that had plagued the Soviet missile subs. It could fire its missiles from underwater, thereby reducing its vulnerability. An inertial navigation system on board the submarine made it far more accurate. The solid-fuel Polaris missile was much more reliable and safer to handle than the Soviet liquid-fueled missiles. The first Polaris submarines became operational in November 1960 and, unlike Soviet submarines which had proven to be a weak alternative to land-based missiles, quickly proved to be as viable a weapon system as their land-based cousins.

The central problem facing the Soviet Union's strategic weapons program was its failure to develop intercontinental delivery systems. Central Intelligence Agency estimates from this period concluded that the Soviet Union possessed several hundred large-yield (500 kiloton to 10 megaton) thermonuclear warheads and probably over 500 medium yield (5 to 500 kiloton) nuclear devices. Yet only a small fraction of these could be mounted on delivery systems with reasonable prospects of successful delivery to targets in the United States.

The Soviet Response

Having provoked a vigorous riposte from America's aerospace industry, the much weaker Soviet industry was hard pressed to keep pace. A second generation of ICBMs was already on the drawing board at Korolev's OKB-1 and Yangel's SKB-586 design bureaus. Even before these were completed, initial design of a third generation of missiles was underway, intended for service in the late 1960s. A third design bureau, OKB-52 headed by Vladimir Chelomey, was opened in 1959 to take part in the third stage of the race.

The main problem with the existing R-7 missile base at Plesetsk was its vulnerability to a preemptive strike. The missile took too long to assemble and fuel. The next generation had to be ready to launch on short warning in order to avoid being destroyed in a surprise attack. A new network of early-warning radars was under development, which would alert the missile sites of an American bomber or missile attack.[6] But the alert would do no good if the missiles could not be launched before the impact of the first nuclear bombs and missiles. The objective was to design a missile capable of being launched within thirty minutes of warning.

The program to deploy a rapid-reaction missile was undertaken by Korolev's OKB-1 design bureau in competition with Yangel's SKB-586 design bureau. The new generation of ICBMs would take advantage of two technological breakthroughs. New thermonuclear warhead designs were much lighter and more compact than the bulky boosted-fission bomb on the R-7. This meant that the new missiles could be made far more destructive with the same throw-weight. In addition, the success of two-staged designs like the Vostok booster and the new intermediate-range ballistic missiles meant that a more efficient and compact configuration could be used than Korolev's original "packet" design.

Korolev's new design was called the R-9. It employed a very conservative approach, sticking with Korolev's preferred cryogenic LOX and kerosene fuel mix. Korolev got around the rapid-reaction requirement by using rapid fuel-pumping equipment, rather than a more versatile storable fuel. In fact, the design seemed very half-hearted. Although it did use a new multi-stage configuration, it didn't reflect the ambitious, imaginative approach that had been the hallmark of previous Korolev designs.

Korolev's heart was not in ICBM design—it never had been. Space was his objective, and designing ICBMs was his only means of securing government funding to accomplish his goal. An ICBM makes a perfectly usable space booster, and the R-7 was better suited than most for the task. Because of the heavy payload requirement of the early Soviet thermonuclear bombs, the R-7 had a massive throw-weight capability, some five tons in all. This made it suitable not only for tiny *Sputniks*, but for large satellites, including manned spacecraft.

Korolev had won a critical battle in his space campaign by making Khrushchev excited about the potential of spaceflight. Khrushchev was no romantic space-travel enthusiast like Korolev. But Khrushchev was very much taken by the worldwide reaction to *Sputnik* and the later space launches. Korolev's space successes were the most stunning achievements in Soviet technology since World War II. They were a symbol for a Soviet Union that had recovered from the horrible losses of the war and which was now on its way to surpassing the West in science and industry. Even if Korolev showed little enthusiasm for ICBMs, as his critics claimed, Khrushchev was not about to pressure him. Pressure for more space spectaculars, certainly. But there were enough new design bureaus to take over the burden of the ICBM race. Besides, Khrushchev had approved Korolev's plan to beat the Americans to the next important space milestone: a manned space mission. This project was receiving far more of Korolev's attention than was the new ICBM.

Korolev's former student, Mikhail Yangel, was already well along with a competing design of his own, the R-16. Yangel's new bureau had already chalked up two successes with intermediate-range missiles, the R-12 and the R-14, intended to fill the gap created by Korolev's abrupt cancellation of the R-3 missile. Yangel's new R-14 was an efficient intermediate-range delivery system that could reach key targets in Europe and Japan.

Yangel, with the enthusiastic approval of Nedelin and the military, was taking a more adventurous course with his R-16 missile than Korolev was with the R-9. Neither the Yangel nor Korolev bureaus seriously contemplated solid-fuel rockets like the American Minuteman, as it was outside the technological capability of the Soviet Union at the time. Yangel's missile would be powered by a liquid-fueled rocket using hypergolic fuel: nitric acid as the oxidant and an improved kerosene derivative. Korolev, as noted previously, had a long-standing aversion to hypergolic-fueled rockets, and called nitric acid "the devil's venom."

But hypergolic rocket engines allowed the missile to be fueled long before its intended launch time. In practice, the R-9—with its cryogenic-fueled engines—could sit on the pad for only a few hours before launch, while Yangel's missiles could sit on the pad for up to two days. In the event of an international crisis, Yangel's missiles could be fueled and prepared for launch without worry that they would have to be launched almost immediately. Korolev's missiles were less flexible, having to be left unfueled until their launch seemed imminent. Moreover, there was the promise that the nitric acid storage problem could be tamed by corrosion inhibitors. This meant that missiles like Yangel's could sit in their silos for six months or more, ready for action.

A popular joke among the engineers around the missile launch sites that summer was, "Korolev is working for TASS, Yangel is working for the rest of us!" While it may seem strange that many young engineers viewed Korolev's historic successes as little more than publicity stunts, it should be remembered that most of them had gone through the war years, and military projects aimed at catching up with the United States were sincerely and enthusiastically supported by nearly all.

Victim of the Devil's Venom

Both Korolev's R-9 and Yangel's R-16 programs were rushed. Given the rapid pace of American missile deployments, Khrushchev placed great pressure on the military and the engineers to field more missile units. Nevertheless, the Soviet missile program lagged behind the American program in all respects.

Engine tests for Yangel's R-16 began in late 1959 and the first missiles began to move off the assembly lines at Dnepropetrovsk in 1960 for shipment by rail to the Tyuratam test range. Initial efforts to set up an R-16 for test launch began in the summer of 1960 on Pad 41.[7] It was some 20 kilometers from the legendary Pad 2, which was used for many of the early Korolev space missions and was then being prepared for the first manned spaceflight. Work during the summer concentrated on the construction of two R-16 launch platforms.

On 14 October 1960, Nikita Khrushchev returned from his visit to the fifteenth U.N. General Assembly meeting in the United States. His speeches in New York, a mixture of boasts and threats, punctuated by the legendary shoe-banging on the podium, further colored American perceptions of Soviet aggressive intent. Nor did Khrushchev let up on the extravagant rhetoric. Several days after his return, he made another speech:

> You [the United States] don't scare the people of the socialist world! Our economy is flourishing, our technology is on the rise, and the people are united. You want to embroil us in an arms race competition? We do not want this, but we are not afraid! We will beat you! We have put

missile manufacturing on a production line basis. Recently, I was at one plant and saw that missiles were being churned out like sausages from a machine. Missile after missile is being produced on our production lines.

It was all bluff and bluster. Soviet production was limited to the manufacture of short-range missiles like the R-11 and the R-14, which could only hit targets in Europe. The R-7 continued in production mainly for space spectaculars, and the new Yangel R-16 was years away from series production. Khrushchev and his representative to the missile industry, Leonid Brezhnev, placed even more pressure on Yangel to push his ICBM program along.

The rush to deploy the new weapons resulted in a tragedy that nearly derailed the entire Soviet missile program. The test launch of the first R-16 was originally scheduled for early in October, but it was postponed until 23 October due to many small problems. Fueling the missile with the volatile nitric acid and propellant was completed in the morning. In the afternoon, problems were detected in the automatic equipment controlling the first-stage engine. The control equipment had accidentally allowed fuel to prematurely flow into the first-stage turbopump. This assembly fed fuel into the main combustion chambers, but had a separate source of fuel for power. The accident caused a 24-hour delay. Crews removed paneling from the lower structure and, contrary to safety regulations and common sense, began to resolder several fuel pipes in the lower structure. The crews worked through the night to rectify the problem. Pressure was on to launch the missile, since the nitric acid could sit in the tanks for only two days before it had to be flushed—a complex and risky business that would delay the first flight test at least a week.[8]

Monday morning, 24 October 1960, proved equally frustrating. A small fuel leak was detected. The state commission for the test launch, headed by Marshal Nedelin, insisted that the matter be rectified. Crews from Nedelin's team concluded that the leak was minor and would not affect the launch. Much to the relief of all concerned, there would be no need to top off the fuel tanks. The correction of the problem with the first-stage fuel pump was overcome in the late afternoon and the launch was set for 7:15 P.M.

Due to the string of problems plaguing the missile, the launch pad area was crowded with personnel, not only the test crew, but Nedelin, Yangel, and many of their assistants. At 6:45 a readiness-to-launch alarm was sounded, indicating that lift-off would occur in a half hour. Technicians scurried about making last-minute checks on systems before leaving the pad area. Major General Aleksandr Mrykin, deputy chief of the test range, was a smoker whose habit had gotten worse because of job stress. He walked over to Yangel. "This is it, Mikhail Kuzmich. I'm quitting smoking. But let's go over and have a last smoke."

Yangel, himself a chain-smoker, agreed. It was forbidden to smoke near the fueled missile. Their presence wasn't really required anymore, as the missile was undergoing final prelaunch guidance checks. They retired to the KPP command bunker for a cigarette. The chief of the test range, Colonel General Gerchik, in a foul mood after all the delays, ordered several teams of technicians to the neighboring hill where an observation post was located. They were the lucky few.

Marshal Nedelin, ordered by Moscow to get the program working, stayed with his crews. Nedelin had the reputation for being inordinately careful. His subordinates recalled that he was the sort of person who would show up at a train station an hour early to make certain he didn't miss the train. The lack of care taken at the launch site that day suggests the terrible pressure he was under to carry out a successful launch. He had found a stool and placed it less than twenty yards from the missile. He was sitting there, barking out orders, when the accident occurred.

Shortly after Yangel and Mrykin entered the observation bunker, a technician in the command post cabled a signal to the missile intended to test the system and set it up for the initial launch command. Instead, the cable's distribution system malfunctioned and sent the ignition command to the second-stage rocket engine. A spectacular explosion ensued.

The second-stage engine was located immediately above the fuel and oxidizer tanks in the first stage. When it ignited, the enormous thrust crushed the fuel cells below, igniting a cataclysmic blaze. A technician near the site later recalled:

> At the moment of the explosion, I was approximately 30 meters from the base of the missile. A thick plume of flame suddenly erupted, covering everything around it. A portion of the team instinctively attempted to run away from the danger zone. People were running to the side of the right launch pad and towards a special overhang where various equipment like fire engines, refueling trucks and mobile cranes were shielded. But in their path was a strip of freshly laid asphalt. It immediately burst into flames, trapping many in the hot, sticky mess. They became prey of the fire. Later, outlines of men and noncombustible items like metal coins, bunches of keys, pins, belt buckles and gas mask filters could still be seen at this site. For some reason, the heels and soles of their shoes also were not consumed by the fire. The most terrible fate fell upon those who were on the upper levels of the servicing gantry. People were enveloped by the fire and burst into flames like intense flares. The temperature in the fire's center was about 3,000 degrees.[9]

There was little anyone could do. The suddenness and severity of the fire was beyond the capabilities of normal fire-fighting equipment. Yangel rushed out of the bunker towards the accident site and had to be restrained by survivors. Even after the flames died out, few were allowed near the site as it was feared the area remained contaminated with the devil's venom—nitric acid. Several large tanker trucks filled with milk were brought in from neighboring settlements in an attempt to neutralize the remaining propellants.

More than two hundred men were killed. Most were totally consumed by the flames. Only a few dozen carbonized husks were identifiable as human remains. A common grave was prepared at Tyuratam.

Nedelin was killed almost instantly. General Gerchik, the range chief, survived but was badly burned. Nearly the entire leadership of Yangel's design team, including his deputy, L. A. Berlin, were killed. It was a horrible setback for the program.

The Race Continues

In spite of the losses, the program had to go on. There was no other program mature enough to replace it. Korolev's R-9 missile did not enter flight tests until 1961 and, predictably, could not compare to Yangel's more polished design. Yangel's missile, in spite of the freak accident, had the features that the Strategic Missile Forces were most anxious to obtain.

Tests of the R-16 did not resume until 1961. According to recent U.S. intelligence estimates, some twenty-three R-16 launchers were ready for operation by the end of 1960.[10] In retrospect, this seems extremely unlikely. The Soviets may have begun constructing the R-16 launch pads, but the missiles were not ready in any significant numbers until 1962. Even then, there were fewer than two dozen missiles deployed. Korolev's R-9 missile was even slower in being deployed. Preoccupied with the manned space program, and later with an abortive lunar-landing program, Korolev didn't have the missile ready for testing until 1961, a year later than Yangel. In October 1961, one of the test missiles blew up in its silo. The R-9 finally began to enter service in 1963, when the first thirteen launchers became operational.

Not only were the new ballistic missile programs delayed, but the basing systems were more complicated than originally expected. Originally, the R-16 was planned to be launched from above-ground launchers since it was felt that its rapid launch capability would afford it sufficient protection from bomber attack. However, as the American strategic force began to turn more and more to missiles, the surface-basing mode was viewed as a mistake. As in the American case, silo basing was finally selected.

The Strategic Missile Forces had come to appreciate that rapid reaction alone was not enough to protect the missiles. Radar detection was proving to be enormously difficult, particularly early-warning, over-the-horizon radars. There might not be enough time between the warning of incoming missiles and their impact for Soviet missiles, even those of a new generation, to be launched. An exposed surface launcher like the Tyulpan was vulnerable to any near miss, and the new above-ground concrete launchers planned for the R-16 were not much better. So the missiles had to be protected from American nuclear missiles. This was not as impossible as it might sound. Even with the enormous destructive power of the thermonuclear bomb, the weapon had to land somewhere close to its target to do real damage. But the early strategic missiles, both Soviet and American, were not particularly accurate.

The idea of burying the missile launchers in underground silos was suggested. In his memoirs, Khrushchev claimed that he had come up with the idea. In fact, the idea of missile silos had been around for a number of years. The Germans had developed a primitive underground antecedent of ICBM silos and began construction of two sites in France in 1944.[11] However, they underestimated the striking power of Allied bombers, which destroyed the facility before it was completed, using massive concrete-penetrating bombs. In the case of ICBM silos, the sites need only be hard enough to protect the missile from near misses by inaccurate missiles. The presumption, at least in the first generation of silos, was that the missiles would be launched before the more accurate bombers arrived. The Soviet objectives were similar to those already being undertaken in the United States.

The first R-16 regiments deployed in 1962 used above-ground launch systems designed by Barmin's design bureau. Each site consisted of two launchers sharing common fueling equipment. Even though basing two launchers so near one another made them more vulnerable to being knocked out by a single attack, the cost of the pumping equipment and other support machinery was so great that economies had to be taken. The missiles rested in "coffin" shelters, and were erected prior to fueling and launch. The coffin shelters, so named for their shape, gave little protection to the missile from nuclear attack. But they were only an interim measure until the new silos could be made ready.

In early 1960 a Leningrad design bureau, TsKB-34, was given the task of developing a launch silo for the new missiles. TsKB-34 was involved in the design of launch tubes for submarine-launched missiles, and so was thought to be the firm most suited to develop a land-based complex. To help accelerate the program, another design group, OKB-172, was merged with it, forming the much larger KBSM (Mechanization Device Design Bureau).[12] KBSM studied a number of different approaches to missile silos. To start off, it considered adapting the design already in use on submarines. The missile would be mounted on an elevator inside the silo. When the launch order came, the overhead door would open and the missile would be lifted to the surface. It could then be launched.

This approach had been used with early versions of the American Titan missile. It was not an ideal solution because the elevation mechanism was complex and expensive, and the missile would be vulnerable as it rose to the surface. The KBSM designers were wary of placing a launcher within the silo tube, due to their experiences with the concept when designing the submarine launch tubes. But they reconsidered this alternative after realizing that the land-based silo did not have the space constraints of a submarine launch tube. By widening the silo and placing the missile in a simple inner tube, the hot exhaust gases could be driven away from the missile body through the outer perimeter of the launch silo. This configuration was adopted for the new silo system.

The silo program was code-named *Sheksna,* after a river. Unlike American silos of the time, the Sheksna silo launch center was based around three missile launch tubes. American launch silos were stationed some distance from one another, which reduced the possibility that a single enemy missile could knock out more than one silo complex.

Once again, cost constraints drove the Soviet design. Although it would have been safer to base the three missile launch tubes some distance from one another, the Sheksna launch complex bunched them together to save money. The most costly element of the launch complexes at this time was the fueling system. In order to fuel the missile in under thirty minutes, a sophisticated high-speed fuel pump network had to be designed. By placing three missiles together, one set of fueling pumps could service all three. The first of the Sheksna complexes was ready in 1964. But the majority of R-16 missiles were based in the unprotected coffin launchers.

The Cuban Gamble

In spite of Nikita Khrushchev's extravagant rhetoric about Soviet missile superiority, the Soviet Union was still woefully behind the United States in 1962. As already noted, the shock of *Sputnik* in 1957 stirred the United States out of its complacency and triggered one of the greatest arms races in history—a race in which America, after a slow start, was clearly ahead.

In the early spring of 1962, Khrushchev and Marshal Rodion Malinovskiy, the defense minister, met at Khrushchev's dacha in the Crimea. Malinovskiy complained to Khrushchev about the positioning of fifteen American SM-78 Jupiter intermediate-range ballistic missiles on the opposite shores of the Black Sea in Turkey only a few hundred miles away.[13] The missiles had been operational for about a year and, while nominally in Turkish hands, they were supported by U.S. troops who had control over the nuclear warheads. The Soviet Army had responded to the American missiles in Turkey by deploying their own medium-range ballistic missiles to sites in Krasnovodsk and Kirovabad.[14]

Khrushchev's conversations with Malinovskiy led him to consider a bold gamble. If it were permissible for the Americans to base *their* nuclear missiles on the Soviet frontier, why not position Soviet nuclear missiles on the American frontier? Intercontinental missiles were in short supply, but the Soviet forces had an ample supply of intermediate-range missiles like Yangel's R-12 and R-14. By basing them near the United States, their strategic value would be the equivalent of far more expensive ICBMs at a far lower cost. This would help relieve the gross imbalance in strategic arms between the United States and the Soviet Union until the new R-16 missiles and their Sheksna launch silos were ready. The best location for the missiles was obvious: Cuba.

Chapter 10

Operation Anadyr

AFTER HAVING ENJOYED a string of missile successes in the mid-1950s, including the first intercontinental missile and the first submarine-launched ballistic missile, by the early 1960s the Soviet Union had begun to fall behind the United States in the nuclear arms race. Khrushchev's blustering talk of missiles being produced like sausages was made more plausible by Soviet secrecy and the inadequacy of American strategic intelligence. Spurred on by fear of a "missile gap," the United States had committed its substantial technological and industrial resources to the missile race. The program received an added boost in 1960 when the Democratic presidential candidate, John F. Kennedy, used the missile controversy as a campaign issue against his opponent, Vice President Richard M. Nixon. By 1962 it was the United States, not the Soviet Union, that was turning out missiles like sausages. The Soviet missile program was floundering due to disasters like the 1960 Nedelin catastrophe, and to the technological limits in its aerospace industry.

In 1960 the Soviet Union's vaunted Strategic Missile Forces had only four ballistic missile launcher systems capable of reaching the United States. In 1961 it still had only four. By the beginning of 1962 the number had not changed. The Soviets had only a hundred bombers that could reach the United States, and their probability of successfully bombing American targets was low.[1] The Soviets also had more than two dozen submarines with nuclear missiles, but their probability of surviving a long sea voyage and launching their missiles off the American coast with any degree of accuracy was equally low.

Nikita Khrushchev became increasingly frustrated. Not only was his plan to revolutionize the Soviet armed forces not materializing, but the Americans were ringing the Soviet Union with nuclear-armed missiles. In June 1959 the first Thor ballistic missiles, jointly operated by British and American crews, arrived in Britain. Charles de Gaulle refused to allow the new American missiles to be based in France, but Italy and Turkey agreed. In 1961, fifteen nuclear-armed Jupiter ballistic missiles, as part of the NATO II Squadron, became operational at Cigli, Turkey, only a few hundred miles away from the Soviet Union.

The spring 1962 meeting between Marshal Rodion Malinovskiy and Khrushchev at the premier's Crimean dacha sparked the notion of placing missiles in Cuba.[2] The idea had not come out of the blue. Khrushchev began castigating American ambassadors about their bases in 1958 and, in a 1959 meeting with Ambassador Averell Harriman, complained the American missile basing in Europe was as provocative as if the Soviets had placed missiles in Mexico or somewhere else nearby. The Cuban revolution and Castro's growing alignment with the Soviet Union made such a threat practical for the first time.

The Cuban deployment was a compelling idea to Khrushchev for several reasons. On the one hand, such missiles would act as a deterrent to any further American attacks on Cuba.[3] This was the explanation that he put forward in his memoirs. But the rationale is not entirely plausible. The deployment of a significant Soviet conventional force of a division or more in Cuba would have been a far less provocative move. The presence of a large Soviet force in Cuba would have given the United States serious pause in the event it planned an invasion of Cuba.

What was especially attractive about the Cuban missile deployment was that it would greatly expand the size of the Soviet arsenal capable of striking targets in the continental United States. Missile bases in Cuba would give the Soviet Union near parity with the United States until a new generation of Soviet missiles could be fielded in the USSR.

Underlying Khrushchev's decision to place missiles in Cuba were his own setbacks from the year before. The Berlin crisis of 1961 had proved an embarrassment, with the Soviet Union unable to extract any concessions from the United States despite Khrushchev's saber-rattling. After years of Khrushchev's blustering about Soviet strategic strength, the Americans had learned from their spy satellites that while a missile gap did exist, the Soviet Union was on the short end of the stick. Kennedy and his defense secretary, Robert S. McNamara, had made public statements clearly stating as much. Khrushchev had to worry about how his Kremlin rivals would respond to his continuing failure to bring about an oft-stated strategic superiority over the United States in light of new-found American confidence in their own strategic position.[4]

Khrushchev's Cuban missile idea was not well received by all military leaders. When, in April, the head of the Strategic Missile Forces, Marshal

Kirill Moskalenko, and Gen. Filip Golikov, head of the Main Political Directorate of the armed forces—the Communist party's watchdog in the military—criticized the plan, they were removed from their posts and exiled to the military inspectorate.[5]

Khrushchev appointed a new head of the Strategic Missile Forces, Marshal Sergey Biryuzov, who previously commanded the *PVO-Strany* (National Air Defense Forces). Golikov was replaced by Gen. A. A. Yepishev, a KGB security police officer close to Khrushchev. It is still unclear why Moskalenko and Golikov were critical of the Cuban deployment. It is likely that they had a greater appreciation of its difficulties, especially if it had to be kept secret from the Americans. But Khrushchev was impulsive and stubborn. The objections of the more cautious military leaders were brushed aside. Marshal Biryuzov enthusiastically supported the basing plan, and Yepishev was able to keep a lid on officers who might have objected.

Khrushchev's conviction to deploy missiles to Cuba was further reinforced by a visit to Bulgaria in May 1962. Staying at the Black Sea dacha of Bulgarian premier T. Zhivkov, he was again reminded of the Turkish missiles. The Bulgarians, whose country had been occupied by the Turks less than a century before, were especially sensitive to nuclear weapons in the hands of traditional enemies. Zhivkov and his wife also spoke to Khrushchev of their recent visit to Castro's Cuba, and their alarm at the prospect of American missiles aimed at the tiny "Island of Freedom."[6]

Following his Bulgarian visit, Khrushchev called a meeting of the Presidium of the Central Committee, limiting attendance to a narrow group of trusted supporters. After his political allies rubber-stamped the decision, a meeting of the Defense Council was called. Khrushchev, supported by several of the Central Committee members, sought firmer backing from the military than he had received in April. The meeting was chaired by Marshal Malinovskiy. Not surprisingly, this time Khrushchev got the desired support.[7] A commission under Marshal Biryuzov was set up to determine whether the missiles could be deployed secretly, without American knowledge, and thus assuage any lingering military concerns.

There can be little doubt that Marshal Malinovskiy and the new head of the Strategic Missile Forces, General Biryuzov, accepted Khrushchev's argument that such a deployment would serve as a deterrent to further American aggression against socialist Cuba. The military leaders were also very much aware of the failure of Khrushchev's ambitious strategic programs up to that point, and the growing disparity in nuclear strength between the Soviet Union and the United States. The Cuban deployment promised to help redress this imbalance in favor of the Soviet Union. In the summer of 1962, the first R-16 missiles were finally being deployed. But by the fall of 1962, the Soviet Union still had only twenty missiles capable of hitting the United States from bases in the USSR.[8]

Missiles deployed in Cuba would considerably enhance Soviet strategic capability. In the spring of 1962, the Soviet RVSN had three nuclear-capable missile systems that could be easily shipped to Cuba. Sergey Korolev's R-5 *Pobeda* (SS-3 Shyster), with a range of 1,200 km, could threaten the southeastern United States. However, the R-5 was never manufactured in large numbers, with only four regiments in service by 1960 employing just forty-eight launchers.[9] The R-5's range was shorter than desirable and, since it had been supplanted by more effective systems, apparently led to its exclusion from the Cuban deployment program. This left only two other of Yangel's missile systems with the characteristics desired for a Cuban-based nuclear force: the R-12 (SS-4 Sandal) and the R-14 (SS-5 Skean). The Soviet plan called for deploying twenty-four R-12 medium-range ballistic missiles and sixteen R-14 intermediate-range ballistic missiles, effectively tripling the Soviet nuclear missile force capable of reaching the United States. Futhermore, the cost of deploying ballistic missiles in Cuba was only about half that of deploying missiles with comparable payloads and targeting ability in the USSR.[10]

The Deployment Begins

Having won support of the missile deployment from both the Communist party leadership and the military, Khrushchev turned his attention to the Cubans. He was by no means certain that his mercurial young ally, Fidel Castro, would permit the construction of Soviet missile bases on Cuban soil. There was never any question that the missiles would be manned and controlled by Soviet troops and Soviet troops alone. Khrushchev never contemplated a relationship similar to the American-Turkish Jupiter program, with Cuban missile crews and Soviet nuclear warhead officers.

On 30 May 1962, a delegation headed by Presidium member Sharif Rashidov visited Cuba in the guise of an agricultural exchange. Present, in civilian dress, was the head of the Strategic Missile Forces, Marshal Biryuzov, called "Engineer Petrov" by his fellow passengers. Two other high-ranking missile forces officers accompanied him, Lt. Gen. Sergey F. Ushakov and Gen. N. G. Ageyev. On arrival in Cuba, Rashidov presented a letter to Fidel Castro, requesting permission to base the missiles in Cuba. Much to Khrushchev's relief, Castro enthusiastically consented, citing it as his "socialist duty."

Biryuzov and his team spent the next week examining possible missile basing options. The plan required that the missiles be kept secret from the Americans, so the bases would have to be placed in remote locations. The Soviets eventually settled on the hilly region near San Cristobal in western

Cuba, and the area near Segua la Grande in central Cuba. The San Cristobal deployments were especially attractive since there were large numbers of natural caves nearby that could be used for hidden storage if necessary. The missile leaders returned to the Soviet Union, followed on 2 July 1962 by Cuban Defense Minister Raul Castro, Fidel Castro's brother, who was dispatched to coordinate the Soviet efforts with the Cuban armed forces and to assist in planning.

The missile deployment, code-named Operation *Anadyr,* would be conducted in phases. First, Soviet military construction units would be dispatched to Cuba to begin work on the facilities needed by the missile units. These engineer troops would also build launch sites for air defense missiles and coastal defense missiles that would be used to defend the ballistic missile sites from conventional attack. In addition, barracks and other facilities would have to be provided for the nearly forty thousand Soviet troops and missile personnel who would be deployed to Cuba. Besides the missile sites, Khrushchev had also ordered the deployment of a Soviet motor rifle division to bolster the existing Cuban army units, as well as a regiment of MiG-21 interceptors and a regiment of Il-28 jet bombers. The additional troops were provided so that if the Americans decided to attack the missile sites, they would be resisted by both Soviet and Cuban troops. While Soviet accounts have not said so, it is likely that the Soviet planners were not entirely confident about the professionalism of the new Cuban army.

The Soviet contingent began to arrive in Cuba in late July. Extensive efforts were made to keep the military deployment a secret. Soviet troops wore civilian clothes and it was reported that they were agricultural specialists. Fake meetings were held with Cuban peasants to make the cover story more plausible. Weapons shipments and heavy equipment were off-loaded at the docks at night—with no Cubans present.

The Soviet contingent in Cuba was nominally commanded by General of the Army Issa Pliyev, a stodgy old horse-soldier best known for his command of cavalry units in the 1945 Manchurian campaign. This strange selection was intended to mislead American intelligence in the likely event that elements of the Soviet forces were spotted in Cuba.[11] Should this occur, Pliyev's position would suggest that the troops were simply conventional forces, and thus give no hint that missile units were present. In fact, it was his chief of staff, Gen. Igor D. Statsenko, who was in effective charge of the Soviet Anadyr contingent in Cuba.[12] Statsenko was a young artillery officer with useful experience in the new Strategic Missile Forces.

The first step in installing the missile sites was to erect a defensive barrier against possible American air attack. Beginning in July 1962, Soviet construction battalions began deploying a total of eight air defense missile regiments with twenty-four V-75 Volkhov (SA-2 Guideline) battalions totalling some 144 missile launchers.[13] The battalions were deployed first in the San Cristobal region and in western Cuba where the ballistic missiles were to be installed. The first site was completed near San Cristobal by the end of August. The air defense troops and their equipment followed in September. The sites were constructed in a standard pattern: a central enclosure for the engagement radar and command vans protected behind earthen berms, with six missile launcher emplacements positioned around the central enclosure in a star shape. Little thought had been given to deploying the missiles in a less predictable fashion. This seemingly minor oversight proved to be a fatal flaw in the Operation Anadyr plan.

The Soviet troops deployed to Cuba were kept in the dark about their destination. Leaving from the Black Sea port of Nikolayev, they were issued the usual winter coats and fur-lined boots. Rumors spread that they were going to Bulgaria for joint Warsaw Pact exercises. It was only when their ships had passed Gibraltar that the officers opened their sealed instructions.

The first surface-to-surface missiles in Cuba were not the longer-ranged strategic missiles, but six Luna-2 tactical artillery rockets, along with nine of their nuclear warheads. These are better known in the West by their NATO code name, FROG (Free-Rocket-Over-Ground). The Luna-2 was a short-range (35 km) artillery rocket, and there was a battalion with three launchers each in two of the Soviet divisions moved into Cuba. The missiles were intended for use in the event of an American invasion of Cuba, and local commanders were given the authority to employ nuclear warheads without Kremlin approval beforehand.[14]

The marked increase in Soviet merchant marine traffic into Cuba in the summer of 1962 led to increased CIA attention to Cuban developments.[15] The CIA had halted its spy missions over the USSR after Francis Gary Powers was shot down two years earlier. But Cuba was another matter. Spy missions were routinely flown over the island when weather permitted, as the Cubans lacked the weaponry to contest them. But the late summer and early fall were difficult times for U-2 spy flights. Hurricane season brought with it frequent rain storms and cloud cover, which made it impossible to photograph the ground below. The CIA first noticed the Soviet preparations on 29 August 1962 when a U-2 spy-plane brought back photographs of curious ring-shaped construction sites in western Cuba.[16]

For CIA photo analysts, the ring sites meant only one thing: Soviet V-75 Volkhov/SA-2 Guideline antiaircraft missiles. This was of considerable concern to the CIA, since it was an SA-2 missile which had brought down the U-2 over the Soviet Union in 1960. But why were such advanced weapons showing up in Cuba? The V-75 system had never been deployed outside the Warsaw

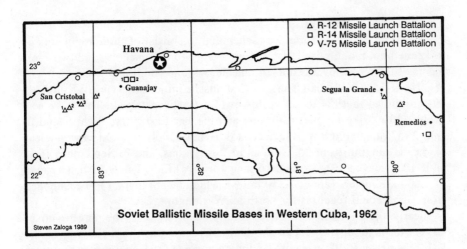

Soviet Ballistic Missile Bases in Western Cuba, 1962

Pact or China before. It was a very advanced weapon for its day. Not only was it expensive, but it required extensive crew training. Peculiar details of its deployment in Cuba suggested to some air force and CIA analysts that it might be intended to protect something of a very sensitive nature. Some CIA analysts suspected the "something" was ballistic missiles, but there was no consensus.

The SA-2 deployment in Cuba was unusually rapid. The previous Soviet pattern in the Warsaw Pact countries had been to bring a cadre of officers and technicians to the USSR for initial missile training. This cadre then returned to its home country, along with a group of Soviet specialists, to establish a training facility for the remaining air defense troops. Only after the basic infrastructure of trained personnel was available were the first SA-2 launchers deployed. This process usually took two years. In the Cuban case, there was no evidence of any Cuban air defense cadre, nor any evidence of a training facility. This would have been obvious from the associated radar transmissions.[17]

For Operation Anadyr, the premature erection of the SA-2 missile bases was a fatal mistake. Their presence alerted the CIA to the possibility that the Soviets were attempting to surreptitiously move some type of undisclosed military force into Cuba. From late August 1962 the CIA, as well as the U.S. armed forces, began to pay more and more attention to activities in Cuba. Soviet ships took nearly two weeks to reach Cuba from ports in the Black Sea. They now began to receive the special attention of American reconnaissance aircraft. The stage was being set for a confrontation that would bring the United States and the USSR close to the brink of nuclear war.

The Missiles of Anadyr

The Anadyr missile force was scheduled to consist of three regiments of R-12 medium range missiles, totalling twenty-four launchers, and two regiments of the more advanced R-14 missile, with an additional twelve launchers. The R-12 was Mikhail Yangel's first missile project after he left Korolev's design bureau in 1954 to set up his own at Dnepropetrovsk. The R-12 was designed to strike targets in Europe and the Far East. First flight tested in June 1957, it entered Soviet service at the end of 1960. It could carry nuclear warheads ranging from 25 kilotons to 2 megatons, and in September 1961 an R-12 was even tested with a 16-megaton city killer. The R-12 had a range of 2,000 kilometers (about 1,250 miles), which meant that an R-12 launched from Cuba could reach as far north as Washington, D.C.[18]

Ideally, the Soviets would have preferred a missile with the range to cover targets throughout the rest of the United States. But the follow-on to the R-12, the newer R-14, was only beginning to come off Soviet production lines in the summer of 1962. The first R-14 flight tests took place in 1960 and the missile had not had all its bugs ironed out in time for the Cuban deployment, due to the loss of so many of the bureau's engineers in the 1960 Baikonur pad explosion. The R-14 was a far more suitable choice for Cuba, able to cover nearly the entire United States from Cuba—except for a small portion of the Pacific Northwest. It could carry a 3 to 5 megaton warhead 4,075 kilometers (about 2,500 miles). For example, if American B-52 bomber bases were the target, the R-12 could strike only 38 percent of them, while the R-14 could cover 98 percent.[19]

The R-12, although lacking in range, did have some advantages. Its launch system was very simple, consisting of a launch platform not much different from that used by the German V-2 during World War II. This meant that such bases could be very elementary and not take very long for Soviet engineers to erect. In contrast, the R-14 used a more elaborate launcher complex, including a concrete shelter for protection against attack. This complicated structure took longer to erect and would be more visible to American spy-planes.

Soviet missile survey teams arrived in Cuba in the summer and began preparations for the ballistic missile sites. Missile base construction began in August. Soviet construction units used special prefabricated materials to speed up the process.[20]

The first shipment of R-12 ballistic missiles left the Soviet Union in late August aboard the merchant ship *Omsk*. It arrived in Cuba on 8 September, followed by the *Poltava* on 15 September. The ships' cargo was unloaded in secret at night, but Cuban informants reported the unusual convoy to U.S. intelligence. The CIA had numerous spies on the island, and the main prob-

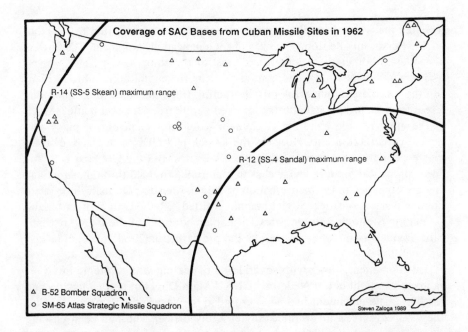

Coverage of SAC Bases from Cuban Missile Sites in 1962

R-14 (SS-5 Skean) maximum range

R-12 (SS-4 Sandal) maximum range

△ B-52 Bomber Squadron
○ SM-65 Atlas Strategic Missile Squadron

Steven Zaloga 1989

lem was sorting out reliable from unreliable reports. Some of the Cuban reports were judged to be related to the SA-2 Guideline antiaircraft missiles. Further evidence was needed to determine whether any of these weapons were the much larger ballistic missiles. The CIA became suspicious of the San Cristobal area due to repeated reports from Cuban agents.

The R-12 regiments were the first dispatched to Cuba. Deployed in two areas, near San Cristobal in western Cuba and Segua la Grande in central Cuba, each regiment was broken down into two launch battalions located some distance from one another. The San Cristobal base had two regiments at four sites, with a total of sixteen launchers. In the third week of October 1962 the base became fully operational and the troops there began exercises with their launching equipment. The third regiment was assigned to Segua la Grande. One of its sites became operational on 25 October 1962 and the other around 28 October 1962.

Due to persistent cloud cover through most of September, the first U-2 flyovers of the San Cristobal area did not take place until 14 October. When the photos were processed, CIA and air force analysts were shocked by what they saw. Since the first photos taken in August, when there had been no real evidence of ballistic missiles, the Soviets had managed to lay the foundations for nearly two full regiments of R-12s. Careful inspection of the photos revealed the whole panoply of missile equipment: erectors, fuel trucks, theodolite stands, missile storage tents, and communication equipment. The Soviets hadn't even bothered to camouflage most of the equipment.

The Soviets may have counted on the Americans not being able to identify the missile equipment. A missile fueling truck does not look much different from an ordinary fuel truck, or even a milk truck for that matter. Much of the other missile handling equipment would not seem out of place at a typical construction site. Nor was the launch pad area particularly distinctive, especially when compared to the SA-2 sites. But the CIA and U.S. Air Force photo interpreters had access to materials provided through espionage that greatly aided in the identification of the missile sites. On their desks were English translations of a Soviet manual entitled "Methods of Protecting and Defending Strategic Missile Sites." It explained in detail the layout of standard Soviet missile sites, as well as the prescribed methods for camouflaging such bases.

This document, along with several others dealing with strategic missiles, had come straight out of Nedelin's GRAU Main Directorate for Missiles and Artillery. The document had been provided to Western intelligence by Col. Oleg Penkovskiy, a disgruntled Soviet Army officer who had been passing along secret material since the spring of 1960.[21] It was a rare example of clandestine human intelligence in an era better known for the dominance of spy-planes and other technological espionage methods.

The credit for exposing the sites went not only to Penkovskiy. Soviet attempts at camouflaging the Cuban missile sites were half-hearted at best. Some equipment had camouflage nets erected over it, but much of the support equipment was in the open. Even without the help of the manuals, the sites would have looked extremely suspicious. Camouflage nets immediately hint of military construction. Large fuel trucks suggest the presence of aircraft at the very least. But without runways nearby the fuel trucks could only mean missiles. The manuals helped to confirm the exact type of site and provided a rough idea of the time needed to put it into working order.

The Cuban launch sites differed in a number of respects from launch sites for R-12 and R-14 missiles in the USSR. Due to the haste in deploying the missiles, the sites were of a more improvised nature. In the Soviet Union missile checkout facilities were located in hardened bunkers, while in Cuba they were contained in long tents. The Soviets may have planned to use nearby caverns to shelter the missiles.[22] Soviet sites usually had a significant portion of the road net and launch pad areas protected by berms or otherwise hardened, a feature lacking in the Cuban sites because it cut construction time. However, other characteristic features were present. The launch pads were made of reinforced concrete to help ensure level platforms for the launch table.

Nearby were stations for theodolites, devices used to prepare and track the missiles. The most extensive single structure was the reinforced concrete control bunker near each battalion site.

Photo interpreters were especially anxious to determine whether the sites were being prepared to handle nuclear warheads. The Soviet practice was to erect a special hardened shelter for the nuclear warheads, since these warheads were not regularly fitted to the missiles until they were ready for launch. They were kept under guard by special KGB warhead security teams, called OSNAZ teams.

Low-altitude air force RF-101 reconnaissance aircraft were sent in under the cloud cover. The RF-101s could provide more detailed photos than those from the high-flying U-2s. As these photographs came in, the first traces of the special 18m x 35m earth-reinforced concrete bunkers were spotted.[23] A complete nuclear warhead bunker was spotted near the Guanajay R-14 site, and another at the Punta Gerardo port facility.[24] Later searches indicated that steps were under way to provide each regiment with a warhead shelter, although few had been completed by the time of the crisis.[25] In fact, the first twenty nuclear warheads to arrive were temporarily stored in caves about a kilometer from the launch pads. Twenty more were on ships in transit to Cuba in late October.[26]

By the third week of October 1962 final preparations were made at the missile sites, including deployment of entrenched antiaircraft guns for site defense, the construction of bomb shelters and defensive trenches for support personnel, and the erection of microwave and high-frequency radio antennas for command and control purposes. Besides the launch sites themselves, the Soviet engineer troops also constructed a missile handling facility 50 miles west of Punta Gerardo near Bahia Honda capable of off-loading missile propellant chemicals and preparing them for transshipping.

Construction of the longer-ranged R-14 missile launchers began about the same time as the R-12 sites, but they were far more complicated to erect. Central Intelligence Agency analysts concluded that the first R-14 battalion at Guanajay would not be operational until 1 December 1962, and another two battalions at Guanajay and Remedios would be ready by 15 December. The fourth battalion site was not started until the middle of October at Remedios, and probably would not have been operational until 1963.

The original Soviet shipments to Cuba included launch equipment sufficient for twenty-four R-12 missile pads, twenty nuclear warheads, and a total of forty-two (of a planned forty-eight) R-12 missiles. This followed the usual Soviet practice of two missiles per launch system. The launchers were capable of at least two launches, and possibly a third if exhaust damage from the second launch was not excessive. The Soviet R-12 missile regiments in

Cuba were still expecting six additional R-12 missiles, twenty more nuclear warheads, and the first R-14 missile components in late October, already on board ships heading for Cuba. These never arrived.

The Cuban Missile Crisis

With photographic evidence in hand, President Kennedy ordered a quarantine of Cuba to prevent the missile sites from being completed. So started the tense days of the Cuban missile crisis. American forces, including the new strategic missile units and strategic bombers, were alerted. Naval forces were moved into the Caribbean in preparation for an amphibious invasion of the island if need be. The North American Air Defense Command prepared its interceptors to deal with any Soviet strategic bombers that might attack the United States from the direction of the North Pole or Alaska. Moscow responded by bringing strategic missile units in the USSR to full alert. The missiles were fueled and readied for launch.[27] The United States and the Soviet Union were as close as they would ever come to thermonuclear war.

Khrushchev failed to appreciate the intensity of the American reaction because of his disdain for the young president and his failure to recognize the impact such a move would have on the United States. Khrushchev's contacts with Kennedy had not left him impressed with his backbone or savvy. The bungled Bay of Pigs invasion the previous year had convinced the Soviets that the new American president was inept and feckless, lacking the conviction to press forward with his objectives. This underestimation of Kennedy was compounded by Khrushchev's lack of understanding of traditional American attitudes towards foreign military intervention in the Caribbean. Khrushchev's own experience with international politics was mostly with neighboring regimes in Europe and Asia. He did not understand that the Americans might react very differently to military activities in their own backyard. Finally, Khrushchev had been assured by General Biryuzov's commission that the deployment could be conducted secretly. He expected that he could hand the Americans a fait accompli sometime after the November 1962 congressional elections. Khrushchev expected Kennedy to react as Khrushchev had reacted to the Turkish missiles: with diplomatic protests, not military action.[28] "The Americans will have to swallow our missiles, as we have had to swallow their missiles," he said.[29]

But Kennedy refused. He decided that the Soviet actions in Cuba were completely unacceptable. Given the American preponderance in strategic weapons, he could afford to act forcefully.[30] Publicly, the Soviets denied that they had placed missiles in Cuba. Privately, they compared their missile deployment to earlier American actions in Turkey and Italy. Whether the actions were parallel or not, the U.S. government was determined not to allow the Soviets to place nuclear weapons so close to the American heartland.

Not only did the Cuban deployment considerably enhance the Soviet nuclear strike force, it opened the door for future expansion. Instead of basing expensive strategic weapons on Russian soil, Cuba could become a major base for strategic bombers, submarines, and more missile launch sites. Such intermediate-range weapons would cost only a fraction of the intercontinental weapons based in the USSR.

Kennedy's strongly worded television address on Monday evening, 22 October, initiated the crisis and forced Khrushchev to consider his own weak position.

The Strategic Balance in October

Soviet strategic forces amounted to about twenty operational missile launchers: the four Tyulpan launchers at Plesetsk, several training launchers at Baikonur, and a handful of new and untested R-16 missile launchers being installed at Yurya. The Soviet missile submarine fleet, disparaged by the army officers two years earlier, was mostly in port. The lead ship of the new nuclear missile submarine class had suffered a major reactor failure in 1961, which limited further forward deployments of the class until the problem was solved. Even if dispatched to the American coast, the submarines were likely to find their paths blocked by American antisubmarine forces. Of dubious utility even in a surprise attack, under the crisis conditions of October 1962 such a mission had a negligible chance of success. About a hundred Soviet bombers of the Long-Range Aviation force could reach targets in the United States, but, given the heightened level of American security, it was questionable whether the Tu-95 Bear and M-4 Bison bombers could run the gauntlet of American air defenses.

In contrast, the American nuclear strike force was formidable. American missile strength at the time of the crisis was 179 ICBM launchers. Added to this was a further 112 SLBMs, which could be reinforced by 32 more if all submarines put to sea. The main American strike force, the strategic bombers, numbered 1,450. In all, the United States could strike the USSR with about 4,000 nuclear warheads, most of which had a high probability of penetrating Soviet defenses. The Soviets, in contrast, could deliver only about 220 warheads—with little probability of success.[31]

American forces began to erect a naval barricade to prevent any more Soviet ships from reaching Cuba. Soviet submarine forces in the area were harassed by American antisubmarine forces to ensure that none of them were carrying ballistic missiles. This was done by concerted and prolonged search tactics, which eventually forced the conventionally powered submarines to the surface to recharge their batteries.

By the time the crisis reached its peak on Saturday, 27 October 1962, the CIA estimated that half of the twenty-four R-12 launchers were operational, or three of six battalion sites. It was anticipated that all six battalion sites would be operational the following day.[32] At the time, the CIA estimated that in an attack launched from Cuba, about 70–75 percent of the missiles would prove functional.[33]

The Crisis Peaks

American reconnaissance aircraft continued their flights over Cuba to monitor the progress of the Soviet missile teams. The few combat actions that took place during the crisis occurred on Saturday, 27 October. In the early morning, Cuban antiaircraft gun sites fired without effect on two low-flying RF-101Cs of the 363d Tactical Reconnaissance Wing. The Soviet V-75 air defense missile batteries were not entirely ready, but Soviet PVO air defense crews were rushing to complete their preparations.

At a higher altitude, a U-2 reconnaissance aircraft flown by Maj. Rudolph Anderson of the U.S. Air Force's 4080th Strategic Reconnaissance Wing flew over Cuba taking photographs of the missile sites. The aircraft passed harmlessly over six V-75 sites before being picked up on Soviet radar at about 9:30 A.M. near Banes in eastern Cuba. The nearby missile site at Los Angeles, commanded by Ivan Gerchenov, contacted the air defense command center and requested permission to fire. At the command center was Lt. Gen. Stepan N. Grechko. Grechko attempted to contact the commander of Operation Anadyr, General Statsenko, but was unable to do so. Authority to engage American aircraft had already been provided days earlier, so Grechko decided to act. He ordered Gerchenov's battery to engage and destroy the U-2.

The Los Angeles V-75 battery fired a salvo of missiles at the U-2 and the missiles arced high into the stratosphere. The U-2's usual flight altitude was in excess of 60,000 feet. If a pilot saw the missiles coming upward, he could begin maneuvers to reduce his vulnerability. Perhaps Anderson never saw the missiles coming; the first salvo detonated near enough to the U-2 to destroy it and kill him.

When Khrushchev learned of the action, he became quite upset and called it a big mistake.[34] He quickly appreciated that the situation was getting out of hand. The same understanding gripped the Kennedy White House, and steps were taken to defuse the situation diplomatically rather than militarily.

After intense negotiations, Khrushchev agreed to withdraw the missiles from Cuba. Kennedy agreed to refrain from an American invasion of Cuba, and there was a tacit understanding that the missile bases in Turkey would be withdrawn. The latter agreement posed no problem for Kennedy as the missiles were no longer of much value to the American ICBM program.

Orders from Moscow to begin withdrawing the missiles came on Sunday, 28 October 1962, ending the crisis. The missiles had never been armed with their nuclear warheads.

The Cuban missile deployment was both a colossal diplomatic blunder for Khrushchev and a badly bungled military operation. The plans for the missile deployment were not skillfully executed. Coordination of the construction of the V-75 air defense sites and R-12 ballistic missile sites was lacking and the plan to conceal the effort was very poorly developed. The characteristic star-shaped SA-2 Guideline sites became evident to U.S. reconnaissance aircraft as early as 29 August, even though the sites were not operational until 27 October. The use of stereotypical deployment configurations made their early discovery a near certainty. The Soviets may have been overconfident that the simple configuration of the R-12 site would prevent positive identification. Yet American and British photo interpreters regarded the discovery of German missile sites in World War II as one of their crowning glories, and they had been obsessed with Soviet strategic missile site identification since the late 1950s. With or without Penkovskiy's timely help, the sites would have been identified. Even the Cubans were surprised by the lack of adequate camouflage precautions.[35]

Khrushchev did not appreciate the fragility of the early missile technology. Even had the missiles reached operational status before being discovered, they still would have been vulnerable to American air attack. Unless used in a surprise first strike, the long preparation time for missile launch and the short time that the missiles could be left fueled and erected meant that the force could be easily destroyed on the ground. The R-12 missiles could not be left on the launch pad for more than five hours due to their design, so the force's readiness for launch at any given time was extremely low. The Soviets might have considered keeping a portion of the force on standby through an alternating cycle of missile erection and unloading. However, this is very doubtful. A repeated cycle of fuel removal from the missiles would have probably worn out both the missiles and support equipment, and would have been extremely dangerous, given the use of nitric acid oxidant in the R-12 missile.

Furthermore, the missile sites were very soft targets. Their passive and active defenses were inadequate. The sites were not protected by earth berms, the normal practice in the USSR, making them particularly vulnerable. Bomb strikes were likely to cause significant collateral damage to unprotected support equipment. The sites also had little redundancy, so the elimination of single key pieces of support equipment would have made preparation and fueling of the missiles impossible. Active defenses, such as the air defense missile and gun sites, were too thin to seriously challenge a concerted air attack.

The V-75 Dvina missile system was intended for strategic air defense against high-altitude bombers, not site defense against smaller, more agile strike fighters. When used against strike fighters, such as in initial encounters in Vietnam in 1965, the V-75 successfully engaged targets less than 20 percent of the time. Furthermore, U.S. attrition rates soon dropped as the few sites were easily avoided. In the Cuban case, the San Cristobal missile sites were covered by only four V-75 battalions, meaning that only four intruding aircraft could be engaged at a single time, with a relatively low probability of kill.[36] Cuban antiaircraft artillery deployment was neither dense enough nor of adequate quality to expect even modest rates of attrition against high-speed strike aircraft.

The American political and military leaders would have been reluctant to attack fully operational sites, knowing that no air strike could guarantee that every launcher would be eliminated before it could fire. There was a significant risk that one or two nuclear-armed missiles might be launched during the course of such an attack. But American military leaders also knew that they enjoyed a substantial superiority over the Soviet Union in strategic weapons. It is doubtful that local commanders in Cuba had the authority to launch the missiles without the Kremlin's permission, and Khrushchev, knowing the consequences, would probably have been very reluctant to give the order.

The Lessons of Anadyr

The Cuban crisis was an acute embarrassment for the Soviet Union. Kennedy's success in forcing Khrushchev to remove the missiles was a tacit acknowledgement of the weakness of the vaunted Soviet strategic forces. Operation Anadyr's failure convinced most of the Soviet leadership that the modernization of Soviet strategic forces required the highest possible priority. The Soviet Union embarked on a massive missile-building program that did not relent even in the face of arms control agreements. It was the humiliation of the Cuban missile crisis, more than any other factor, which motivated the Soviet missile-building programs of the 1960s and 1970s.

Khrushchev's impetuous and emotional conduct during the crisis aggravated many other party and army leaders. It was the beginning of the end of his leadership of the USSR. Within two years Khrushchev was ousted as the Soviet leader by a coalition of Party and KGB leaders, with tacit military support. Leonid Brezhnev took his place.

The upper ranks of the Soviet military were deeply disgruntled by Khrushchev's leadership. His attempts to shrink the conventional forces were strongly resented. Tens of thousands of officers were thrown out of the armed forces, with no program to help assimilate them back into Soviet society. Khrushchev also meddled in every detail of military affairs, no matter how trivial. For example, the adoption of a new scout tank was delayed almost a year because he had simply forgotten to give his approval. While few leaders disagreed with Khrushchev over the need to adopt the new strategic missile weapons, his missile obsession led to the cancellation of a wide range of conventional weapons programs, closed many design bureaus, and created turmoil in the defense industries.

Operation Anadyr was as much the military's fault as it was Khrushchev's. Senior officers, such as Malinovskiy and Biryuzov, had given him bad advice. But it was Khrushchev who paid for their mistakes. Although the armed forces do not appear to have played a major role in the 1964 coup to overthrow Khrushchev, it is quite likely that the KGB and Party conspirators knew that the armed forces would no longer support him as they had in 1953.

Brezhnev, who had served as the Communist party's administrator of strategic military programs in the late 1950s, was personally known to the Strategic Missile Forces leaders and the missile designers. The decision to build the largest missile plant in Dnepropetrovsk was probably due to the fact that it was Brezhnev's old political home. Brezhnev, the polar opposite of Khrushchev in temperament—bland, uninspired, anxious to please—was a follower who was suddenly thrust into the role of leader. After a decade of Khrushchev's rough-and-tumble direction, the military leaders looked forward to reasserting their power.

Chapter 11

The Nuclear Toll

AT 4:20 P.M. ON 29 September 1957, Dr. Lev Buldakov was driving back to his medical lab near Kasli in the Urals industrial region. Buldakov, a surgeon, had been assigned to the nuclear complex in the Chelyabinsk area in 1950 at the height of the atomic program's expansion. After treating the nuclear workers for five years, he eventually became associated with a research group under Nikolai V. Timofeyev-Resovskiy, which was studying the influence of radiation on humans, animals, and plants. ·

Buldakov was late for a meeting. He stepped on the gas and his *Pobeda* automobile accelerated ahead. There were few private cars in Russia at the time, but the staff of the nuclear program in the Urals received special attention. As he was driving near the town of Kyshtym, his car suddenly lurched sideways, slammed by the invisible hand of a massive explosion. Buldakov hit the brakes, stopped, and got out. Looking toward the explosion's source, the top-secret "chemical combine," he saw an enormous column of smoke rising. The cloud eventually rose nearly a kilometer in the sky. Soon, winds blew the cloud over neighboring villages. Little did Buldakov know that his theoretical work on the effect of radiation on humans and plants would soon take a very practical turn. The cloud was no mere pillar of smoke. It contained massive amounts of deadly radioactive particles, slowly falling to the ground and contaminating vast areas.[1]

The explosion that Buldakov had witnessed near Kyshtym was, until the Chernobyl disaster in 1986, the largest nuclear accident to occur since the invention of the atomic bomb. Unlike Chernobyl, which occurred at a civilian power station, the Kyshtym explosion occurred in the center of the top-secret nuclear weapons production facilities. The story of the Kyshtym explosion remained a secret in the Soviet Union until 1989, even though an émigré Soviet scientist had deduced the extent of the accident from obscure Soviet medical writings nearly a decade before.[2] The Kyshtym disaster was only one of a number of accidents that plagued the Soviet strategic weapons program in the first two decades of its existence. Only in the past few years have details of these disasters begun to emerge.

The Kyshtym disaster took place at a facility known as the Intermediate Storage Facility. The storage site contained radioactive by-products from the Mayak chemical plant, which was processing plutonium for Soviet nuclear bombs. Given the urgency of the bomb program, the Soviets had paid little attention to environmental concerns when handling radioactive materials at the Chelyabinsk-65 complex.

At first radioactive waste was simply dumped into the nearby Techa River. From 1948 to 1951, enormous amounts of radioactive water and contaminated chemicals were drained directly into the local water system.[3] In the rush to build the first bomb, elementary safety precautions were simply ignored. But in September 1951 Soviet scientists discovered radioactive traces from Chelyabinsk-65 as far away as the Arctic Ocean.[4] Program leaders became concerned that American intelligence agencies could trace the contamination back to its source and thus locate the top-secret bomb manufacturing facilities. The contamination had to stop.

A team of scientists was dispatched from Moscow to investigate the extent of the damage. They discovered that the Techa River was intensely contaminated to a range of some 35 kilometers from the plant. The contamination had spread into the neighboring water table, and some 124,000 local inhabitants had been exposed to varying amounts of radiation. Nearby farmers who fished in the river or who allowed their cattle to use the river, were the most severely contaminated, with doses as high as 170 rems recorded.[5] The river was cordoned off by double rows of barbed wire, and the villagers closest to the river were given the token sum of 600 rubles and ordered to move away from the site.[6]

To isolate the chemical and radioactive discharge, the plants at Chelyabinsk-65 began dumping the material into nearby Lake Karachay. This lake was selected because it did not drain into the neighboring river system. Over a span of a few years an enormous amount of radioactive material was dumped into the lake, causing scientists to worry about the long-term consequences for the area. In 1953 an intermediate storage facility was built near Kyshtym to process the radioactive waste.

The storage facility was an enormous underground reservoir, lined with stainless steel, which had concrete walls one-and-a-half yards thick. Inside this reservoir were twenty gigantic stainless steel tanks, each with a capacity of 80,000 gallons of liquid. The tanks' exteriors were water cooled because the chemical waste continued to generate heat due to continuing chemical reactions. Untreated chemical wastes were first placed in one of the facility's temporary storage tanks to cool down. The chemical solution was then returned to the processing plant where recoverable traces of uranium or plutonium that could be extracted from the solution were removed. Less radioactive or chemically active material was then dumped into Lake Karachay and the most hazardous residue was returned to Kyshtym and placed in permanent storage.

Compounding the problem was the Chelyabinsk-65 plutonium production plant's use of an "all-acetate" precipitation method to dissolve the nuclear fuel elements. The by-products of this process included potentially explosive organic nitrate compounds, and the radioactive waste solution typically contained 100 grams of sodium nitrate and 80 grams of sodium acetate per liter of solution.

The solution in Kyshtym's storage tanks continued to chemically react even after the first reprocessing stage. Heat monitors were placed in the water near the tanks to make certain that the solution did not reach dangerous temperatures. But there were serious design flaws in the storage facility. The high levels of heat in the permanent storage tanks led to evaporation of the water and chemicals inside them. The tanks gradually rose, and broke the seals of pipes feeding into the tanks. This contaminated the cooling water outside the tanks. Several heat monitors eventually failed, but could not be replaced due to the radioactive contamination of the cooling water surrounding them. Furthermore, because the cooling water was contaminated, it too had to be reprocessed as it could no longer be dumped straight into the local water system. The volume of contaminated water exceeded the capacity of the reprocessing facility, which forced the waste facility operators to reduce the volume of cooling water used around the permanent storage tanks. To make matters worse, there was no clear understanding of the chemical interactions taking place inside the tanks. In the autumn of 1957, the water cooling system of one of the tanks at the facility failed. This went unnoticed by the staff due to the earlier failure of the heat monitors on this tank.

On the afternoon of 29 September the heat buildup in the tank dried up the solution and the chemical waste's temperature soared to 660° F. The resulting interaction of the nitrate and acetate wastes led to a massive explosion estimated to be equivalent to as much as 100 tons of TNT.[7] The explosion blew the yard-thick concrete lid completely off the tank. It landed more than twenty-five yards away. About 70 to 80 tons of radioactive waste were blown outwards and the two neighboring storage tanks were damaged as well. The radioactive material included about 2.1 million Curies of radioactivity. (The Chernobyl accident ejected about 50 million Curies). The enormous plume from the explosion spread over the neighboring cities of Chelyabinsk and Sverdlovsk, and into the farmland of neighboring Tyumen County. In all, about 23,000 square kilometers, an area roughly the size of the state of Rhode Island, were contaminated by the blast. About 270,000 people lived in areas contaminated by the explosion.[8]

The blast was seen by a large number of people in neighboring towns and cities, yet the ministry of defense was adamant that it be kept secret. Local papers carried a preposterous story that said the explosion was an unusually bright manifestation of the aurora borealis, the northern lights.

Those most severely affected by the blast were the guards at the waste storage facility where the blast occurred. No one was near the tanks at the time of the explosion, so no one died immediately. But the guards received about 100 rads of radiation, the threshold at which radiation sickness begins. It took ten days to evacuate the 1,500 villagers nearest the storage facilities. Had they remained, they would have received a fatal dose within about a month. They took away every last chicken, every last scrap of firewood. The frightened villagers were given a red-banded paper and hustled off to nearby railroad stations for evacuation. The villages were then burned to the ground to prevent their return. A participant in the evacuation recalled, "The glow on the horizon was that of a terrible foreboding."[9]

The blast contaminated farms in the region and created immediate problems with local food supplies. Several days after the explosion, meat and dairy products were removed from store shelves without explanation, and it took days to truck in new supplies from outside the region. Long lines formed outside the shops. These bizarre activities and the lack of any official explanations led to a near panic in some areas. Rumors of unusual diseases spread, deepening the fear. Some senior government officials were given small personal radiation counters to measure their own exposure, but there were not enough for general distribution. All of this did little to alleviate popular anxieties.

During the next eleven months 6,500 more people were evacuated. Most moved into hasty houses, the slapdash construction of which made them eventually uninhabitable.[10] The authorities were reluctant to publicly warn the village population about radiation poisoning of the local crops for fear the announcement might be noticed by American or British intelligence agencies. This increased the amount of radioactive contamination endured by the villagers nearest the explosion site, since they continued to eat local crops, pick contaminated mushrooms, and fish in contaminated rivers and lakes.

Large areas remained cordoned off for years to prevent villagers from fishing, farming, or mushrooming. The area became known as "the vast nothing" for its desolation. It took nearly twenty years of careful effort, until 1978, before Chelyabinsk County had all of its farmland returned to use. Layers of topsoil were plowed under in the less contaminated areas; in other areas, the topsoil was completely removed. Even today, fish in parts of the region are a hundred times more radioactive than normal.

The toll of the Kyshtym explosion has never been accurately determined. Although CIA records include émigré accounts of hundreds dying in local hospitals due to radiation poisoning, official Soviet sources long denied any immediate radiation deaths. Slapdash efforts were made to monitor the health of workers and villagers in the areas closest to the explosion. Some villages were subjected to intense scrutiny, others were ignored. Evidence was found that the radiation exposure had reduced the number of white blood cells in the bloodstream of nearly ten thousand people, but rates of blood disease and cancer were not significantly different than in the rest of the population, according to official Soviet sources. Surveys were conducted every three years after the accident, and are still conducted today, but at ten-year intervals.[11]

Some Soviet scientists believe that the official pronouncements, even under *glasnost,* did not adequately reveal the full magnitude of the disaster. In the wake of the failed August 1991 coup, previously suppressed reports began to surface. According to a medical commission studying nuclear contamination in the region, records indicate at least 935 cases of radiation poisoning and a regional leukemia incidence 40 percent higher than normal. Moreover, the soldiers who fought the fire at the Kyshtym plant were never adequately monitored and their medical records are unknown.[12] The ecological effects of the disaster were far more severe. To this day, 20 percent of "the vast nothing" remains too heavily contaminated to permit humans to enter.

Recent revelations about the Kyshtym accident are closely connected to efforts by Moscow to establish additional nuclear power plants in the Chelyabinsk area in 1990. Residents of the area, frightened by the Chernobyl disaster, and aware of the rumors of accidents in their own region, firmly resisted these plans. The new power plants were needed because of a shortage of electrical power in the Chelyabinsk industrial region, so the government undertook a publicity campaign to quell fears. If anything, the publicity only underscored concerns in the region. It was disclosed that there are two hundred burial sites with over a half-million tons of solid waste and a half-billion cubic meters of contaminated water in the area. The radioactive waste remaining in the area amounts to 1.2 billion Curies, the most concentrated mass of radioactive waste material in the world today.

The impact of radioactive contamination from the bomb plants has never been accurately tallied. Recent studies near the Chelyabinsk-40 and Chelyabinsk-65 bomb production facilities, now known by their corporate name as the *Mayak* (Lighthouse) plant, indicate that some 437,000 local residents have been subjected to increased radiation dosages. Some of this has been due to accidents such as the 1957 blast and later events, but the worst is due to the large amount of radioactive waste dumped into the local water system, amounting to 150 million Curies from 1949 to 1991.[13] (Chernobyl, as noted earlier, released 50 million Curies). Health conditions in the region have suffered accordingly, including high rates of asthmatic diseases, increased cases of blood diseases such as leukemia, and a higher mortality rate than in surrounding areas. The rates of some radiation-induced blood diseases found in the Chelyabinsk area are equalled only in the Hiroshima and Nagasaki areas. The most serious cases are found among the Mayak plant workers. Recent estimates indicate that 4,000 workers died from acute radiation poisoning, while 10,000 workers, mainly from the early days of the plant, suffered from chronic radiation poisoning.[14]

Human Guinea Pigs

The Kyshtym disaster resulted in the accidental radiation poisoning of thousands of Soviets. Far less well known were a number of small-scale programs in the early 1950s designed to gauge the effects of radiation on humans by *deliberately* exposing them to the effects of nuclear weapons.

The second area of the Soviet Union to suffer from radiation problems was around the Semipalatinsk Poligon in Kazakhstan, where the first atomic bombs were tested. The early cases of radiation poisoning were caused by the haste and urgency of the program, and the willful ignorance of the consequences of fallout. The first bomb in 1949 caused severe fallout in the area, registering 200 rems in the nearby town of Dolon. As Kurchatov and his team began to appreciate the consequences of these tests, steps were taken to move villagers away from the test site. After Stalin's death in 1953, the army was first permitted to begin plans to employ atomic weapons under tactical battlefield conditions. This led to some curiosity about the psychological and medical impact of nuclear blasts on humans.

In the summer of 1953 the Soviet Army prepared to test its first thermonuclear device at the Poligon. As mentioned earlier, the bomb designers, including Andrey Sakharov, became concerned that the bomb might be so destructive that Kazakh villages on the periphery of the blast would be contaminated by heavy fallout. As a result of their pressure, the Soviet Army removed many of the villagers from their homes before the test explosion— but not all of them.

In the village of Karaul, all the inhabitants, as well as all of their cattle, were transported away—with the exception of forty villagers. They were instructed to stay, though no reason was given by the soldiers. At the village of Kainar, sixteen people were intentionally left behind during the test.

One of the forty Kazakhs from Karaul, Tugaj Rakiembiev, recalled the day of the bomb test:

We were left behind without any inkling of what would happen. The next morning, we experienced a powerful flash of light, far stronger than the rays of the sun. The horizon became red, and a large black mushroom cloud appeared. Shortly after the blast, a cloud of dust came toward us. An hour and a half later, soldiers appeared with gas masks and vehicles and drove us away. Our names were called and recorded. They walked around us and scanned us with a dosimeter. After that, we were told to drink 20 centiliters of vodka.[15]

The villagers from Karaul were driven away to another collective farm farther from the blast site. They remained there for more than two weeks, and were finally allowed to return to their homes with the rest of the displaced villagers. A year later, in August 1954, eight of the forty who had witnessed the blast were taken to a secret military facility in Semipalatinsk run by the KGB and code-named Dispensary No. 4. They were subjected to a variety of tests. The degree of contamination suffered by the forty has never been made public. But, as of 1990, only seven were still alive, most having died before reaching age fifty from leukemia or bone, stomach, or brain cancer. The results of the studies at Dispensary No. 4 have been kept secret for many years due to the KGB connection.

In 1954 the Soviet Army decided to explode a tactical nuclear bomb to test the reaction of troops fighting in a nuclear environment. Rather than locating the test at one of the usual proving grounds, the blast was to take place in the southern Ural Mountains area, in Totskoye County, Orenburg Province.

At the epicenter of the blast, a variety of buildings were constructed, including specially reinforced bunkers. Tanks and other armored vehicles were placed around the site to gauge the effect of the blast. Twenty old Lavochkin La-15 jet fighters were placed about a mile from ground zero, and twenty-two obsolete Il-10 Shturmovik ground attack planes were placed still farther away.

Troops from an army rifle division were moved into the area as well. A series of trenches was dug one and a half miles from the intended epicenter of the blast. Igor Kurchatov visited the trench line some days before the blast in the company of Marshal Georgiy Zhukov, the deputy defense minister, and other senior Soviet generals. Kurchatov warned the troops that wooden logs used to reinforce the front of the trenches should be smeared with clay to prevent them from being burned by the nuclear blast. The troops were issued special gas masks that had a piece of smoked plastic over the eyepieces which allowed them to look at the blast without being blinded. Near the trenches were bunkers that some of the troops would occupy during the test. The soldiers, curious to measure the effect of the blast themselves, moved a 700-pound boulder onto the roof of the bunker.

At 6:28 A.M. on 14 September 1954, a Tu-4 heavy bomber left its airbase some 425 miles from the test site. Although the crew had flown some thirteen test flights, the path to the target was marked with special corner reflectors to make it easier for them to confirm their course using their navigation radar. The Tu-4 was escorted by six MiG-17 fighters, as well as a pair of Il-28 jet bombers, which would conduct weather reconnaissance and photograph the bomb site. Kurchatov had instructed the crew on the maintenance of the bomb, reminding them that the bomb is like "a living being" and that constant monitoring of temperature, humidity, and other data was essential. The crewmen busied themselves with constant checks during the hour-and-a-half flight.

The Tu-4 bomber reached the target area at about 9:20 and received permission to execute the drop. The bomb was dropped and detonated at 9:33. A young soldier, Vladimir Bentsianov, who observed the blast from a bunker recalled his impressions:

> The ground seemed to start shaking. The deputy political officer said, "Comrade Bentsianov, why are you rocking the box?" Then suddenly, the shock wave. It was as though a pile had been driven into the ground, but with frightening force. And then immediately, the sound; like nothing you've ever heard. Terrible. None of the instructions had said anything about this, not a word. There was a cracking, a grinding. All the equipment readings shot off the dials.[16]

Five minutes after the blast, artillery began firing to simulate an attack into the blast zone. Troops located in distant trenches began to advance forward. Thirty minutes after the blast, regiments of jet fighter-bombers began making rocket and bomb attacks in the area around ground zero. The crews had been instructed to avoid flying through the mushroom cloud. On encountering other clouds of dust and debris, they maneuvered to avoid them, dropping their bombs some distance from the intended target.[17]

There were two concentrations of troops nearest the blast, one group in an advanced post, and the others, including Bentsianov and his regiment, about three miles from the epicenter. Bentsianov was one of the first soldiers to reach the advance post where a small group of troops were huddled. He shouted through the blast door, but the men were so terrified from their experience that they refused to budge. The bomber had missed the target by three hundred yards, and the bomb exploded closer to them than intended. Bentsianov and the other troops in his unit placed measuring instruments at the epicenter before they were carried by trucks to carry out "attacks" on simulated objectives elsewhere in the blast zone.

The troops taking part in the exercise had been given very little information on the effects of radiation or how to prevent contamination from fallout. By the time they returned to their base in the evening, some were suffering from the early symptoms of radiation poisoning. They were given showers and new uniforms, but kept their contaminated boots and original underwear. Other soldiers began to experience the long-term medical effects of radiation poisoning within a year. They were not given any special medical attention. All had sworn oaths that they would not reveal anything about the bomb tests for twenty-five years—on pain of death. This prevented them from telling their doctors about the event, which may have caused many of their medical problems. The Ministry of Defense refused to provide special medical care, and it wasn't until 1990 that a Committee of Special Risk veterans was finally established to treat the small number of surviving soldiers.[18]

The purpose of the southern Urals test appears to have been to determine the psychological effects of nuclear weapons on soldiers, not the medical effects. By 1954, the immediate medical consequences of nuclear blasts were fairly well known, even though long-term consequences may have been underestimated. But, following Stalin's death, the Soviet armed forces were no longer circumscribed from including nuclear weapons in their tactical doctrine. The southern Urals test allowed the generals to see if soldiers would be so terrified by the blast that they would be unable to function in a nuclear environment. The 1954 test demonstrated that soldiers would still fight in a contaminated area. Although many of the troops were obviously very anxious about what they experienced, only those in the forward bunkers absolutely refused to emerge from shelter. No further tests with troops were conducted.[19]

In the twelve years of above-ground testing at Semipalatinsk, almost a half-million people were exposed to varying degrees of radiation.[20] Not surprisingly, the environmental consequences of the blasts triggered one of the first activist environmental groups in the Soviet Union.

The Atom at Sea

If Soviet Army troops were largely spared the consequences of the new age of nuclear weapons, their naval counterparts did not enjoy the same relief. The sailors in the nuclear submarine fleet endured the worst consequences of the nuclear program because of safety problems endemic to the nuclear reactors aboard their submarines.

The submarine units of the Soviet Navy began receiving the new Project 627 class nuclear-powered attack submarines in 1958. The first of these, known as the November class in the West, was christened K-3 *Leninskiy Komsomol* and commanded by Captain L. G. Osipenko. *Leninskiy Komsomol* had a number of problems with the steam generators aboard, causing occasional leaks of radioactive water. But the worst accident aboard the submarine, a serious fire on 8 September 1967, was caused by a problem unconnected with the nuclear power plant. The accident occurred while the submarine was submerged. Thirty-nine crew members died.

The class as a whole was plagued by problems, brought about in no small measure by the haste in which they were launched. Several of the later submarines of the class were sent to sea only partly completed as the shipyard rushed to meet its contract obligations. The worst was the third of the class, K-5. It was quickly dubbed the "Automat" by its crew. The name stemmed from the fact that the submarine seldom lasted more than a day at sea before having to return to port with a serious mechanical malfunction. The second submarine of the class, K-8, was somewhat better. It later earned the nickname "Half-automat" since it could usually last a couple of days before returning. The November class submarines' severe teething pains forced the fleet to restrict their operations to no farther than 200 km from base.[21]

The first serious nuclear accident occurred aboard submarine K-19, lead ship of the Project 658 (Hotel I) submarine class, armed with nuclear-tipped R-13 missiles. In June 1961, the K-19 was cruising in the Norwegian Sea a hundred miles south of Jan Mayen Island, north of the Scottish coast. A test launch of one of its R-13 missiles was scheduled in the weeks to come, as well as a transit under the Arctic icepack and a surfacing from below the ice. On the early morning of 4 July 1961, an alarm bell sounded in the port nuclear reactor. The reactor's emergency shielding was being breached. The crew checked the reactor instruments, which indicated that the primary cooling loop was rapidly losing pressure. If the cooling system failed, the engine could suffer a melt-down. The main pump feeding the primary loop failed due to the pressure drop and the backup system failed shortly afterwards. The reactor's designers had not anticipated both pumps failing, so no additional backup systems were available.

The reactor crewmen knew they must keep the core cool or a catastrophe would ensue. Several reactor engineers decided to attempt rigging a set of pipes from the submarine's fresh water reserve into the reactor core. This meant that the reactor shielding would have to be opened, exposing the work crew to heavy radiation doses. In spite of the risk, the reactor crew, led by Lt. Boris Korchilov, began working. The fuel rods soon reached 800° C and were approaching melt-down. The enormous heat inside the reactor core caused combustible material in the reactor to ignite, filling the compartment with smoke and further hampering the repair effort. Water trapped under the reactor turned to pressurized steam, threatening to explode outward and scald the crew. Before this could occur, the crew managed to install the piping.

Korchilov's team had taken nearly two hours to install the improvised cooling system. But in doing so they had been poisoned by 5,000 to 6,000 rems. One of the crewmen, recalling the scene as they exited the reactor compartment, said, "I saw the boys right after they were brought out of the reactor compartment. They were unable to move. It was horrible, I must say. Their faces were changed beyond recognition, they were unable even to speak."[22]

The problems faced by K-19 were not yet over. Korchilov's men had been so weakened by their radiation exposure that they had been unable to rig a system to ensure that the cooling water was properly expelled. Soon the reactor compartment was awash in dangerously radioactive water. The ship's commander, Nikolay Zatayev, ordered all sailors except those involved in essential work to get outside of the submarine on the outer casing. Shortly after the heroic attempts by Korchilov and his men to save the ship, a valve to pump out the water and steam malfunctioned. Volunteers were called for and a senior petty officer, Ivan Kulakov, headed back into the reactor room to solve the problem. The valve was submerged in radioactive waste water, and the reactor room was scalding hot, 140° F, due to the steam. Two trips were needed to correct the problem, by which time Kulakov and others received doses of 500 rems or more.

As the submarine surfaced, it became obvious that the crew would be at nearly as much risk on the outside of the submarine as inside. In true North Atlantic fashion, the sea was stormy. Zatayev attempted to contact the fleet command center by radio, only to discover that the main antenna had been critically damaged during their earlier transit under the arctic ice. In desperation, Zatayev used his low-power emergency transmitter, hoping that other submarines taking part in the exercise might hear his distress call. Later in the day, two diesel-powered attack submarines appeared and took off much of the crew.

Using radios aboard the rescue submarines, intermittent contact was finally made with the fleet command. The situation with the reactor was explained. The command center radioed back that contaminated sailors should be fed fresh vegetables, fruits, and juices. It was a remarkably bizarre suggestion, little better than a folk prescription for a bad cold. It was of no consequence, however, since the submarines had exhausted their larder of fresh fruit and juices earlier on their mission.

Zatayev radioed for permission to abandon the submarine. Whether his request was ever received is not known. But no permission was granted. Zatayev took matters into his own hands. He ordered the second reactor shut down, and the submarine sealed up. One of the diesel submarines prepared to torpedo K-19 in the event any British or American warships turned up and attempted to interfere. Eventually a fleet salvage ship, the *Aldin,* appeared, and the damaged K-19 was nursed back to Soviet waters.

The public explanation for the accident was that a bit of metal spall from sloppy welding had jammed one of the coolant pipes. While this is possible, accounts of the operation of K-19 in the months before the accident suggest another factor that may have caused the accident or exacerbated the clogging of the pipe by the welding mistake. The tactic used by the K-19 to evade U.S. and Canadian antisubmarine warfare ships and aircraft was to allow the submarine to rest on the bottom of the ocean. This tactic is forbidden in most navies operating nuclear-powered submarines since it often leads to silt being stirred up as the submarine settles on the ocean floor. This silt is then drawn into the reactor's water-cooling system, which uses seawater to keep the reactor from overheating. This problem may not have been understood in 1961 when the K-19 first went to sea.

Of the crew, Lieutenant Korchilov and six others from the first repair team suffered excruciating pain and died a few days later while in transit back to port. Three more sailors, who had received far lower doses, died by the end of the month. Ivan Kulakov, who had received a dose of 500 rems, survived and was still alive at the time this book was written.

After refitting, the K-19 returned to navy service. It was nicknamed the "Hiroshima" after its 1961 accident. The K-19 proved to be a particularly unlucky ship. On 24 February 1972, off the coast of Newfoundland, a severe fire broke out in the berthing quarters, leading to the death of twenty-eight sailors. In spite of these tragedies, K-19 was again repaired and was still in service in 1991.

For their part in rescuing the K-19 after the 1961 nuclear accident, several of the surviving submariners were decorated. The navy was less than magnanimous in this regard. During the presentation ceremony, the Leningrad Naval Base commander, Adm. I. Baikov, remarked, "Why do you consider yourselves heroes? Accidents happen even on our streetcars in Leningrad."

Admiral Baikov's callous remark to the survivors of the K-19 was not untypical of official Soviet attitudes towards radiation hazards in the military. Nearly all senior officers had gone through the searing experience of the Second World War, in which more than 8 million Soviet servicemen died. Accidents like Kyshtym and the K-19 were simply viewed as the acceptable cost of an urgent, high-priority program. Kyshtym caused no immediate deaths, and, even if it had, they would have been accepted as part of the inevitable price for an essential defense program. From the end of World War II to the present, the Soviet armed forces have suffered a far higher accident rate than most other European armed forces, losing some 310,000 soldiers, sailors, and airmen.[23] The occasional nuclear accident seemed no different than other mishaps.

The official callousness towards radiation victims is nowhere more evident than in the lack of any comprehensive overview of nuclear accidents during the early days of the Soviet nuclear program. Although there are anecdotal accounts of the heavy toll paid by forced laborers in the mining and processing of radioactive material, there is very little historical material to gauge the extent of these problems. Only in recent years has the budding Russian environmental movement begun to explore this previously forbidden topic.

The public silence over the human and environmental consequences of the nuclear program was one of the underlying causes of the 1986 Chernobyl disaster. The complete absence of reporting on the hazards of naval nuclear powerplants, like that on K-19, or of the other accidents in the nuclear weapons industry, created an unjustified hubris in the Soviet nuclear power industry.[24] It was this underlying complacency that nothing could possibly go wrong which was a major contributing factor in the Chernobyl accident.

Chapter 12

Borodino's Legacy

THE HUMILIATING OUTCOME of the Cuban missile crisis convinced Soviet military and political leaders of the necessity of overcoming America's overwhelming nuclear weapons advantage. The area of greatest concern was in missile technology, since Soviet bomb designers had already matched American H-bomb designs in brute force.

With two nuclear design bureaus at work, the nuclear test site at Semipalatinsk and the new arctic test site at Novaya Zemlya had been very busy. Since the 1955 explosion of the first true thermonuclear bomb, successively more refined nuclear devices were exploded. The culmination of these tests came on 30 October 1961 when a 58-megaton bomb was detonated at the Novaya Zemlya test site. This was nearly four thousand times more powerful than the bomb dropped on Hiroshima in 1945. Aside from publicity extravaganzas of this sort, the bomb designers at Synezhinsk and Sarova had succeeded in developing smaller, more compact nuclear devices, not requiring the heavy throw weight of the R-7. Yangel's new R-16 ballistic missile had a throw weight only a third of the R-7's, but its new and more compact thermonuclear warhead could deliver as great a blast—up to 5 megatons, an explosion three hundred times as great as the Hiroshima blast. The years 1961 and 1962 marked the peak of Soviet nuclear weapons testing, with detonations totalling over 200 megatons in both years.[1] Indeed, Soviet leaders were confident enough with the progress in nuclear warhead design that in 1963 Khrushchev signed the first significant nuclear arms treaty with the United States, the Limited Test Ban Treaty.

The Limited Test Ban Treaty did not signify that the Soviet Union had given up its attempts to reach strategic parity with the United States. Indeed, the Cuban humiliation prompted an extensive new range of nuclear weapons

233

programs. In the early 1960s, Soviet physicists began working on one of the most bizarre programs of the Khrushchev years, an antimatter bomb. In 1903, a large blast had leveled an enormous area of forest in Siberia near the Tunguska River. The blast had not left an impact crater. Interest in the Tunguska blast revived in the 1950s. The source of the blast was a great mystery, leading to wild speculation by amateur scientists and cranks. Some believed it to have been the explosion of the nuclear powerplant of an alien spaceship. Some astronomers leaned towards the idea of a comet impact. But one idea particularly intrigued physicists—that the Tunguska event represented an impact by a meteorite made of antimatter.

The concept of antimatter was a relatively novel one. Antimatter atoms were believed to be identical in appearance, structure, and other features to normal atoms, but with electrical charges and magnetic properties reversed. From a military standpoint, the intriguing detail was that in contact between an antimatter atom with a normal atom, both particles would be annihilated, resulting in a tremendous release of energy. Antimatter seemed to offer the hope of greater destructive power than thermonuclear reactions.

While the idea of antimatter would eventually become generally accepted in the physics community, some Soviet physicists took the notion far beyond what the scientific evidence suggested. A team of scientists under Boris P. Konstantinov, director of the LFTI, was promoting the idea that not only the Tunguska visitor, but all meteors and comets, were, in fact, comprised of antimatter! It was difficult for Kremlin bureaucrats to dismiss the idea, as Konstantinov was a respected scientist and the LFTI was, of course, the research institute where Igor Kurchatov had undertaken his first nuclear research work. Konstantinov's antimatter program was approved and millions of rubles were allotted to it. The program survived for several years due to secrecy. It was not open to scrutiny by other scientists who might have noted obvious flaws in its basic premises. In December 1962 the program was discussed in a closed meeting at the Academy of Sciences in Moscow involving the nuclear bomb development scientists and a number of other scientists, including astronomer Iosif Shklovskiy. Under such scrutiny, the project was exposed as a wasteful delusion and it eventually petered out as funding dried up.[2]

Cyclone

Aside from diversions like the antimatter bomb, the heaviest funding in the strategic weapons budget was being concentrated on a crash program to field new intercontinental ballistic missiles (ICBMs). On the one hand, Yangel's new R-16 (SS-7 Saddler) and Korolev's new R-9 (SS-8 Sasin) missiles had finally passed their tests and were being rapidly installed in concrete launchers or, after 1964, in Sheksna silos. The combination of the R-16 and the new

Sheksna missile silo represented the first mature Soviet strategic weapons system. The R-16 had a reasonably short reaction time, increasing its survivability over slow-to-launch systems like the old R-7. And safely ensconced in its hardened concrete silo, it had a reasonable chance of surviving a surprise missile attack by the United States. A measure of the R-16's success can be gauged from the numbers deployed. By 1965, some 190 R-16 launch complexes were under construction. This compares to only 4 R-7 complexes and 19 of its Korolev contemporary, the R-9.

In the early 1960s the technology of thermonuclear war was still in its infancy. Soviet doctrine on the employment of strategic weapons was equally embryonic. Khrushchev's conception of strategic nuclear missiles as the basis of the Soviet armed forces was not entirely shared by Soviet military leaders, especially in the army. The leaders of the ground forces and air force continued to argue for the need for modern conventional forces as well. In spite of the lack of consensus between the political and military leadership, growing attention was inevitably being paid to actual employment of these weapons in the event of war. The formulation of nuclear doctrine was a difficult endeavor for Soviet theoreticians, as their own capabilities were rapidly changing and growing after 1962.

Khrushchev was not overly concerned about the fine points of nuclear doctrine. By 1964 he was content with the way the Strategic Missile Forces were shaping up, even though they were still numerically and technically inferior to the American SAC force. His son later recalled:

> In contrast to many contemporary military men, both Soviet and American, Khrushchev considered nuclear weapons so terrifying that the existence of even a small quantity of warheads and the means to deliver them made war unacceptable for both. He knew, he often said, that the United States surpassed us, but added that those who perished in nuclear war would not care whether they had been killed several times over.[3]

Khrushchev's view, sometimes labeled as a "minimal deterrence theory" by American analysts, was not necessarily shared by the military or the military-industrial sector. The military was anxious to develop a new generation of weapons, even beyond the R-16. This program was well underway in the final year of Khrushchev's regime.

The constellation of missile designers had changed greatly since the 1950s. Korolev's growing political influence allowed him to withdraw almost completely from the military sphere. The main attention of his bureau was devoted to an ambitious new program, the N-1 space booster, intended to put Soviet astronauts on the moon.[4] Korolev's bureau was obliged to submit a proposal for the new ICBM program, but the resulting design, the SS-10 Scrag, shared the same faults as the earlier SS-8 Sasin (R-9). It continued to employ a cryogenic fuel system, which gave it much slower reaction time than the hypergolic fuel systems on Yangel's missiles. It was not a serious contender for the new missile program.

The real competition involved the design bureaus headed by Yangel and Chelomey. Yangel's bureau was the obvious favorite in the competition. It was by far the more experienced of the two, having successfully fielded the first effective Soviet ICBM, the R-16. But Chelomey was not easily deterred.

Vladimir Chelomey had managed to push his bureau from its second-rate status as a naval cruise missile design team, into the big leagues of ballistic missile design. He was able to do this in no small measure by careful cultivation of political contacts, and an astute sense of future trends in missile design. On the political side, he hired Khrushchev's son, Sergey, to work as an engineer in the missile guidance group of his design bureau. His contact with the Khrushchev family allowed him to strike up a friendship with the premier that could not but help the fortunes of his growing enterprise. In 1959, Chelomey was given control over the Fili plant, where Myasishchev had been unsuccessfully developing strategic bombers. At the same time, a significant portion of the design teams of two smaller missile bureaus, those led by Lavochkin and Dzhaparidze, were absorbed into Chelomey's expanded OKB-52 design bureau at Fili.[5]

Nor was Chelomey any less astute in dealing with other key players in the technological community. Central to any new ICBM effort was the matter of propulsion. Until the early 1960s, the only successful ICBM propulsion design effort was led by Valentin Glushko and his GDL-OKB design group. Without Glushko's strong support, Chelomey's hopes of entering the world of ballistic missile design would simply evaporate. Glushko had begun to lose his enthusiasm for conventional rocket fuels and was beginning to explore more advanced fuel combinations, especially fluorine and nitrogen tetroxide oxidizers. Chelomey won Glushko's support, readily accepting the unproven approaches for several of his projects, such as the UR-500 Proton space booster and the UR-200 ICBM. Relations between Glushko and other designers had begun to turn acrimonious over this issue.

Chelomey represented a new breed of general designers who, unlike pioneers such as Korolev, were propelled more by personal ambition than infatuation with spaceflight. Had he been less ambitious, Chelomey could have been content with life as a naval cruise missile designer. But such a position had its limitations. Even the most successful cruise missile designer was unlikely to rub elbows with the Kremlin elite. Chelomey realized that ballistic missiles and space boosters, two closely related endeavors, were the most prestigious projects for a missile designer. He dreamed of establishing an enormous design center like Korolev's at Kaliningrad. Chelomey had chosen his own name for his design bureau, KB-2, to link it to other prestigious establishments—Beria's KB-1 of the 1940s and Korolev's OKB-1. Officially, though, it was known by the less impressive moniker OKB-52.

The clash of personalities among the general designers in the early 1960s has been described by participants as a "civil war." Glushko and his old colleague Korolev were at the center of one of these controversies. Korolev insisted on using liquid oxygen for the engines in his new N-1 moon rocket program. Glushko was equally adamant, refusing to design a new propulsion system for the N-1 unless it employed the new oxidizers. Glushko dismissed Korolev's experience in missile design, quipping that "with the right engine, you can make any old stick fly." Khrushchev tried to intervene in the dispute, but was unsuccessful due to the power and prestige of both men in the space engineering community. In the end, Korolev was obliged to turn to a less experienced engine design bureau to power his moon rocket, a situation which many Soviet space engineers believe doomed the Soviet moon program.[6]

Yangel managed to avoid much of the infighting taking place over the lunar program between Glushko, Chelomey, and Korolev, and concentrated on his own ICBM effort. His new ICBM, the R-36 (8U64) *Tsiklon* (Cyclone), was an evolutionary outgrowth of the successful R-16 missile, considerably larger in size. The rationale for so large a missile, with a massive 20-megaton warhead, has long been the subject of speculation in the West. Three notions have predominated. Some analysts think the Tsiklon was a typical reflection of Soviet engineering, opting for large size in order to give the missile future growth potential. In view of the fact that the Tsiklon played a key role in later years with new payloads, such as a fractional-orbiting bomb system and multiple reentry vehicles, this is entirely possible. Others have suggested that the Tsiklon was the first Soviet response to American antimissile defenses being considered in the early 1960s. The idea was that the Tsiklon's massive payload would include radar decoys that could be released outside the atmosphere as penetration aids, confusing any exoatmospheric antimissile that might be launched against it. Once inside the atmosphere, the Tsiklon's massive warhead could be detonated before short-range interceptors, like the American Sprint missile, could reach up and destroy it. A third theory is that the Tsiklon was, in fact, the first evidence of a Soviet desire to develop a first strike capability. The warhead was so massive that it might have been intended to destroy the command centers that controlled each field of ten Minuteman missiles.[7]

Glasnost still has its limits, however, and no inside stories of the reasons behind the Tsiklon's design have yet surfaced. Although the precise origins of its design remain obscure, Tsiklon clearly represented a missile design with objectives beyond simply delivering a nuclear warhead to targets in the United States. Its configuration implies a maturation in Soviet strategic warfare doctrine, and represents the first case where the missile design requirements were shaped by tactical considerations rather than being based on the limitations of existing technology. Until the Tsiklon, Soviet leaders were more or less forced by the existing levels of Soviet aerospace technology to take whatever could be developed by the designers. With the maturation of the missile technology, it was becoming possible for Soviet war planners to actually tailor missiles for specific missions against the United States. Nuclear warfighting doctrine was finally beginning to direct technology.

In addition to the important changes behind the design of the Tsiklon missile itself, other aspects of the program further reflect the growing maturity of Soviet missile technology. The R-36 was designed around a new generation of launch silo, which offered considerably greater survivability than the Sheksna type used with the R-16. This second-generation silo, called the OS for *Odinochnny Start* (Individual Launch), was developed by the KBSM design bureau in 1962. Like American silos, and unlike the earlier Sheksna, OS silos would be widely scattered in an effort to prevent a single incoming American missile from wiping out several silos with a single blast. This was made possible by changes in the Tsiklon's fuel system. By using a new oxidizer, nitric tetroxide instead of the nitric acid used in the R-16, the missile could be kept fully fueled for up to six months. This meant the OS silo needed no expensive high-speed fuel pumps, the main reason the old Sheksna silos had been clustered together in the first place. Instead, the missiles could be periodically refueled using mobile fueling systems mounted in trucks that could be driven from site to site as required. Instead of spending the money on fuel pumps, the designers turned their attention to increasing the silo's protection from attack. The Sheksna silo was designed to withstand a blast of about 28 psi. The OS silo was designed to withstand blasts of up to 280 psi against its cover, a substantial increase indeed. The complexity of the new silo design meant that it lagged behind development of the Tsiklon missile itself, and so was not ready until 1969, some three years after the Tsiklon was ready for deployment.

By October 1964, the competition for the new ICBM had been reduced to two missiles: Chelomey's UR-200 and Yangel's R-36 Tsiklon. The test firings favored the Yangel design. There were political factors to consider as well. Khrushchev had closer ties to Chelomey, though it is evident from his son's recollections that these political considerations did not interfere with his judgment as to which missile to accept for production. Yangel's design was the clear favorite of Dmitriy Ustinov, head of the Soviet nuclear weapons delivery program since the Stalin years. In the end, Khrushchev was not swayed by his ties to Chelomey. Yangel's design was the clear winner.

The Tsiklon represented a watershed in the strategic arms race, a point at which technology's importance in determining the shape of the competition was beginning to decline.

In October 1964, shortly after the first tests of the Tsiklon and UR-200 missiles, Khrushchev was overthrown by a clique of his closest associates, headed by Leonid Brezhnev. Brezhnev's coup marked the end of the acrimony between the Kremlin and the military, bringing to an end an era of turmoil and change in the Soviet armed forces. Brezhnev lacked Khrushchev's maverick vision of Soviet defense needs and was willing to follow the lead of the Soviet military and industrial leaders. The strategic missile program remained a high-priority element in Soviet defense planning after Khrushchev's fall, even after Brezhnev blessed the buildup of Soviet conventional forces. Soviet leaders vowed to never again permit so humiliating a rebuff as the Cuban missile affair. Parity with the United States in strategic weapons had not taken place in the Khrushchev years, but it would take place under Brezhnev.

The Nuclear Legacy

In two decades, from 1945 to 1964, the Soviet Union had gone from a second-rate technological power to a superpower rivalling the United States. The success of its strategic weapons program was at the center of this change. How had the Soviet Union managed to accomplish this? How could a country with only a third to a half of the national output of the United States match it in such a technological struggle? As this book has described, Soviet programs were able to keep pace with, and sometimes even race ahead of, American strategic programs. The United States was first with the atomic and hydrogen bombs, but the Soviet Union was first with intercontinental missiles and submarine-launched ballistic missiles.

The United States enjoyed substantial industrial and scientific advantages over the Soviet Union during this period. Its electrical output and crude oil production were nearly four times greater than the USSR's, its aluminum production three times greater, and cement production twice as large. America's aviation and aerospace industry was the largest and most sophisticated in the world. Its wartime successes were followed by equally impressive postwar triumphs, such as the first supersonic and multi-Mach aircraft and the first jet-powered strategic bomber. The American aviation industry was equally dominant in civil aviation, breaking new ground with its passenger aircraft and revolutionizing air travel. As this book has argued, the Soviet Union succeeded in taking the lead mainly in those categories where the United States showed less enthusiasm in the early 1950s: intercontinental missiles and ballistic missile submarines. Yet even in areas where the competition was most intense, the Soviet Union's accomplishments were remarkable.

To understand how a formerly second-rate technological power had managed to tie the world's greatest aerospace power in the strategic arms race, it is informative to examine the long-term costs of the struggle. The Soviet Union's race to build strategic nuclear weapons was based on a massive and costly expansion of its scientific and engineering workforce. The Soviets were remarkably successful at doing this. From 1940 to 1964, the size of the Soviet scientific workforce expanded sixfold, from about 100,000 to 600,000 scientists.[8] By 1957, the number of Soviet scientists in the physical sciences and engineering outnumbered their American colleagues.[9] A very large portion of this newly created talent was absorbed into the design of both conventional and nuclear weapons.

Indeed, what is remarkable about the investment in science and engineering under Stalin and Khrushchev is the disparity in effect in the civil and military sectors of Soviet society. The disproportionate share of scientific and engineering talent going to the military had long-term, crippling effects on the development of Soviet industry and commerce outside of the military realm. A few crude measures of this can easily be made. In the area of basic science, Nobel prizes serve as a very rough gauge of basic scientific advances. From 1946 to 1960 the United States led by a substantial margin, followed by Britain and Germany. The USSR came in fifth, trailing Switzerland and narrowly beating out Italy and Argentina. An equally telling measure of the impact of the militarization of Soviet engineering is in the area of patents. In a recent study of major patent holdings, the United States was the leader, followed closely by Japan, and then Germany, Britain, and France. The Soviet Union's patents are about 1.5 percent of the American total, and only somewhat larger than Belgium's or Panama's.[10] These are, admittedly, very crude measures of technological prowess. Indeed, they fail to give a true picture of Soviet engineering capabilities because the Soviets do not patent many innovations in aerospace and defense technology for reasons of military secrecy. But they do provide a rough indication of the enormous diversion of technological talent from the civilian economy and into the arms race.

It was not the Soviet strategic weapons program alone that caused this trend, since some of this scientific and engineering talent was diverted into conventional weapons programs as well. But the strategic weapons program had its most dramatic impact on Soviet science and engineering in the period covered in this book—from 1945 to 1964. The massive growth in the scientific and engineering work force is heavily attributable to these programs, particularly during Stalin's final years. The creation of a uranium processing industry absorbed the attention of the Soviet chemical and electrical power industry, to say nothing of construction and mining. Much of the finest scientific talent was absorbed in the development of nuclear bombs and their delivery systems. With few exceptions, most of the prominent Soviet physicists, chemists, and mathematicians worked on aspects of the atomic bomb or other strategic weapons programs. Some indication of this is evident in the leadership of the Soviet Academy of Sciences. The head from 1961 to 1974, Mstislav Keldysh, devoted his talents in mathematics to assist Kurchatov in the development of the atomic bomb, helped Korolev calculate the ballistics of intercontinental missiles, and helped Myasishchev model the advanced aerodynamics of supersonic bombers. Anatoliy Aleksandrov, the president since 1975, was one of the original atomic bomb scientists and headed the Soviet atomic bomb program after Kurchatov's death in 1960.

Not only did the strategic programs absorb talent out of the civil sector, they drained talent out of other branches of military technology. The head of the bomb program after Stalin's death, Vyacheslav Malyshev, had been the head of the Soviet tank industry. The engineering director of the Arzamas-16 bomb design center, Nikolay Dukhov, was one of the most prominent tank designers of World War II. The young tank engineer Nikolay Shomin, who would design most of the Soviet Union's most advanced postwar tanks, including the T-64 and today's T-80, was taken off tank design in the 1950s to work on fuel pumps for intercontinental ballistic missiles.

During the Brezhnev years, with the main innovations in strategic weapons technology already made, the balance would shift. More technological talent would be directed toward conventional weapons, and some would return to the civil sector. By 1964 the strategic weapons race, from a technological standpoint, was cooling down.

With the advent of mature ICBM designs, safely ensconced in hardened silos, both sides had weapons that could withstand a surprise attack. This meant that any war involving thermonuclear weapons had become unthinkable. Even if the majority of an opponent's missiles and bombers were destroyed, a very unlikely eventuality given 1960s accuracies, there would still be a significant missile force able to kill most of the enemy's major cities. As the concrete hardened in the Sheksna silos buried in the Russian steppes and the Minuteman silos in the North Dakota plains, both sides had created the beginnings of an effective deterrent force. Nearly all of the contemporary tools of thermonuclear war were invented during the Stalin-Khrushchev years: the ICBM, the intercontinental bomber, the nuclear submarine, the air-launched cruise missile, and early forms of strategic defense systems. There would be innovations in the decade to come: MIRVs, FOBs (Fractional Orbiting Bombardment systems), and endoatmospheric ABMs. There would be further debates in nuclear doctrine: minimum deterrence versus mutually assured destruction. But the period of revolutionary technological change was over. So too was the bellicose relationship between Moscow and Washington. The shape of future nuclear forces would be sculpted by arms control agreements, pioneered by the Limited Test Ban Treaty of the Kennedy-Khrushchev years.

The militarization of Soviet science and engineering, however, remained a characteristic feature of the Stalinist economic system through the Brezhnev years and well into the Gorbachev years as well. The Brezhnev years saw a major modernization of Soviet conventional forces, as well as sizeable expansion in the strategic arsenal. This led an exasperated U.S. defense official in the 1970s to complain, "When we build, they build; when we stop building, they just continue to build!"

The collapse of the Soviet economy in the 1990s is in many ways a result of a strategic failure in the thinking of the Soviet leadership from Stalin through Gorbachev, tied to this militarization of the economy. Soviet economic policy was heavily shaped by the Soviet Union's amazing victory in World War II. The ability of the centrally planned, centrally controlled economy to outproduce Germany was the major success of the Stalinist system and the key ingredient in the Soviet victory. The militarization of the Soviet economy, begun by Stalin in the 1930s, continued in the postwar years thanks to Stalin's belief that the Soviets had to match the American nuclear arsenal. Ironically, during the Khrushchev years, the strategic weapons program was undertaken as a cheaper alternative to the bloated conventional forces left over from the Stalin regime. A generation of Soviet political, industrial, and military leaders was nurtured in a culture that afforded great prestige to the defense economy. Brezhnev himself was the contact point between the defense industries and the Communist party until the 1964 coup ousted Khrushchev. Marshal Ustinov, the defense minister under Brezhnev, was a leader of the Soviet military industries in World War II, not a combat soldier.

The nuclear arms race of 1945-64 was a remarkable achievement for a nation that had been bled white in the Second World War, and for a nation with such modest industrial and scientific resources. But it was an achievement whose legacy bears a large share of responsibility for the dire conditions in the former Soviet Union today.

Appendix A

Biographical Index

Anatoliy Petrovich **Aleksandrov** (1903–). Colleague of Igor Kurchatov at LFTI before the war and head of design group on naval antimine technology during World War II. After the war, associated with nuclear bomb effort. Aleksandrov headed the scientific aspects of the nuclear bomb program after Kurchatov's death in 1960 and was president of the Academy of Sciences from 1975 to 1986.

Abram Isaakovich **Alikhanov** (1904–1970). Highly regarded physicist who was considered for leadership of the Soviet atomic bomb program in 1943 in competition with Kurchatov. Developed the TVR heavy-water–moderated reactor at Laboratory No. 3 in Moscow, which first went into operation in 1949.

Manfred **von Ardenne**. Prominent wartime German physicist recruited by the Soviets in 1945 to help work on the A-bomb. He headed the Object A lab at Sinop involved in developing methods to extract uranium isotopes.

Lev Andreyevich **Artsimovich** (1909–1973). Worked on electromagnetic separation technology to acquire uranium for the Soviet atomic bomb program.

Vladimir Pavlovich **Barmin** (1909–). Headed the multiple rocket launcher design effort at NII-3 in the final years of World War II. After the war, headed the GSKB design bureau, which developed missile launch complexes such as the Tyulpan launcher for Korolev's R-7 ICBM.

Lavrentiy Pavlovich **Beria** (1899–1953). Head of the NKVD special police during World War II. In overall command of the atomic bomb program from 1945 until his execution in 1953 following a Kremlin power struggle.

Vladimir Nikolayevich **Chelomey** (1914–1984). Soviet missile designer who began by designing cruise missiles in 1944. His KB-2 design bureau was closed in 1953 by Stalin, but he continued to work under Admiral Kotov at MNII until 1959, when he took over the Moscow Machine Building Factory (named for M. V. Khrunichev) in Fili, formerly Myasishchev's OKB-23 bomber design bureau. Chelomey's new OKB-52 designed a number of ICBMs and other missiles during the Khrushchev years.

Nikolay Leonidovich **Dukhov** (1904–1964). Dukhov was the engineer in charge of adapting the atomic bomb to series production at Arzamas-16. General Dukhov had been a heavy tank designer in World War II, famous for the IS-2 Stalin tank.

Aleksandr Yevgenevich **Fersman** (1883–1945). Soviet geochemist who led the early uranium prospecting expeditions in Central Asia.

Arthur **Fielding**. Cover name for unidentified American atomic bomb spy working at Los Alamos. His code name was Perseus or Percy.

Georgiy Nikolayevich **Flerov** (1913–). Soviet physicist and colleague of Igor Kurchatov, best known for his letter to Stalin, which reportedly triggered the Soviet atomic bomb effort in 1942.

Klaus **Fuchs** (1911–). German physicist who spied for the Soviets while working on the Manhattan Project A-bomb effort in the United States in 1944–45. Convicted by Britain for spying, he lived in East Germany and the USSR after serving his prison sentence.

Valentin Petrovich **Glushko** (1908–1989). Soviet rocket engine designer. Glushko worked on early Soviet rocket engines in the 1930s. In the postwar years he headed the GDL-OKB (OKB-456) at Khimki in the Moscow suburbs and supervised the development of most of the major ballistic missile propulsion systems through the 1970s.

Gustav **Hertz**. German physicist recruited by the Soviets in 1946 to head the Object G lab at Agudzeri working on uranium processing.

Abram F. **Ioffe**. Soviet physicist at LFTI and mentor to many of the atomic bomb designers, including Kurchatov.

Nikolay **Isanin**. Soviet submarine designer. Developed the Project 611AB (Zulu V) submarine, the first ballistic missile submarine.

Sergey Vasiliyevich **Kaftanov** (1905–1978). Stalin's science adviser during World War II.

Mstislav Vsevolodovich **Keldysh** (1911–1978). Soviet mathematician who assisted Kurchatov in calculations for the atomic bomb, developed the mathematics of missile ballistics for Korolev, and was instrumental in early aerodynamic modeling techniques for supersonic aircraft such as Myasishchev's M-50 Bounder bomber. He was the director of the USSR Academy of Sciences from 1953 to 1978.

Petr Leonidovich **Kapitsa** (1894–1967). Prominent Soviet physicist who studied under Ernest Rutherford in England from 1921 to 1934. Kapitsa formulated the idea for a naval nuclear reactor, but he was never closely associated with the atomic bomb program. Although many in the West thought he might even be the head of the atomic program, his ties to Britain and his eccentric behavior led to his exclusion by Beria.

Yuliy Borisovich **Khariton** (1904–). Physicist and head of the KB-11 design bureau at Arzamas-16 that designed the first Soviet atomic bomb.

Vitaliy Grigoriyevich **Khlopin** (1890–1950). Soviet radiochemist who headed the embryonic atomic bomb program of 1940–41. After the war he headed the plutonium processing program at Chelyabinsk-65 in Kyshtym.

Mikhail Vasilevich **Khrunichev** (1901–1961). Assistant head of the Soviet munitions industry during World War II, instrumental in transferring factories from European Russia into the Urals refuge. He was primarily involved in the expansion of the aviation industry in the later years of the war, and in 1946 was appointed minister of aviation production.

Isaak Konstantinovich **Kikoin** (1908–1984). Soviet physicist who headed the effort to develop gaseous diffusion technology for uranium extraction.

Sergey Pavlovich **Korolev** (1907–1966). Soviet engineer who headed the main ballistic missile design bureau, OKB-1 in Kaliningrad. Korolev adapted the German V-2 ballistic missile to Soviet service and led the design of Soviet ballistic missiles, including the first nuclear-armed R-5M and the first intercontinental ballistic missile, the R-7. Died as a result of a botched operation.

Igor Vasiliyevich **Kurchatov** (1903–1960). Soviet physicist who headed the Soviet atomic bomb research program from 1943 until his death. He was succeeded by A. P. Aleksandrov.

Viktor Ivanovich **Kuznetsov** (1913–1991). Soviet naval engineer responsible for the development of gyroscopic systems and other devices for ballistic missile guidance. One of the "Council of Chief Designers" and chief designer at NII-944.

Semen Alekseyevich **Lavochkin** (1900–1960). Soviet aviation engineer who headed OKB-577. Best known for his World War II fighter aircraft, such as the La-5FN and La-7. After some work on postwar jets, Stalin assigned him to secret missile projects, including early Soviet air defense missiles and the Burya strategic cruise missile.

Viktor Petrovich **Makayev** (1925–1985). Soviet aerospace engineer who headed the missile design bureau in Chelyabinsk responsible for submarine-launched ballistic missiles. Makayev began his missile design work as part of Korolev's OKB-1 bureau.

Vyacheslav Aleksandrovich **Malyshev** (1902–1957). Head of the Ministry of Medium Machine Building (the atomic bomb program) after Stalin's death in 1953. Malyshev was an industrial administrator most famous for his leadership of the tank industry in World War II.

Vasiliy Pavlovich **Mishin** (1917–). Soviet aerospace engineer who headed the OKB-1 missile design bureau following Korolev's death in 1966. Mishin was fired following the failure of the N-1 lunar rocket program; his place was eventually taken by Valentin Glushko.

Vladimir Mikhaylovich **Myasishchev** (1902–1978). Soviet aerospace engineer best known for his postwar strategic bomber designs such as the M-4 Molot (Bison) and M-50 (Bounder) while head of OKB-23 at Fili. After OKB-23 was closed, he later directed TsAGI, the main Soviet aerospace research facility at Zhukovskiy in the Moscow suburbs. After Khrushchev was deposed in 1964, Myasishchev was allowed to form a small design bureau, OKB-1457, but it never achieved the prominence of OKB-23 during the Stalin and Khrushchev years.

Mitrofan Ivanovich **Nedelin** (1902–1960). Soviet artillery general who was responsible for supervising the ballistic missile program in the 1950s while serving as assistant defense minister for armaments. He was killed during the failed test firing of the R-16 ICBM.

V. N. **Peregudov**. Soviet naval engineer and submarine designer. Headed TsKB No. 143 after the death of Boris Malinin. Developed the Project 627 (November class) boats—the first Soviet nuclear-powered submarines.

Mikhail Georgiyevich **Pervukhin** (1904–1978). Head of the wartime Soviet chemical industry and administrative head of the Soviet atomic bomb program from 1943 to 1945. Later involved with the bomb program, heading the effort to build up the uranium and plutonium processing industry.

Georgiy Ivanovich **Petrov** (1912–1987). Soviet aerospace engineer and member of the "Council of Chiefs." Involved in the study of gas dynamics at high speed. Also involved in the development of ablative shielding for early Soviet ICBM reentry vehicles.

Nikolay Alekseyevich **Pilyugin** (1908–1982). Soviet aerospace engineer and member of the "Council of Chiefs." He supervised the design of missile inertial guidance systems while at NII-885 in Kharkov.

Julius **Rosenberg** (1918–1953). American convicted of espionage along with his wife, Ethel, in the highly publicized atomic spies case. He was charged with being a control agent for a network of spies working for the Soviet consulate in New York, specializing in advanced military technology, especially radar and nuclear developments.

Konstanin Nikolayevich **Rudnev** (1911–1980). Soviet administrator who headed the state commission that oversaw the ICBM program. During the war years Rudnev headed the Tula armaments plant, one of the largest Soviet small arms manufacturers.

Mikhail Sergeyevich **Ryazanskiy** (1909–1987). Soviet aerospace engineer and member of the "Council of Chiefs." He was responsible for radio-command guidance technology and space tracking on the ICBM program at NII-845.

Andrey Dmitriyevich **Sakharov** (1921–1989). Soviet physicist credited with inventing the Soviet H-bomb. A student of Ioffe's, Sakharov joined the KB-11 design bureau at Arzamas-16 in 1950 and became best known as the Soviet Union's most prominent dissident in the 1960s after his disenchantment with weapons work.

Aleksey Ivanovich **Shakurin** (1904–1975). Headed the Soviet aviation industry from 1940 to 1946. He was thrown in prison by Stalin in 1946 because of the failure of the Project 64 strategic bomber program. He was rehabilitated during the Khrushchev thaw in 1959.

Yefim Pavlovich **Slavskiy** (1898–1991). Soviet metallurgical engineer involved in developing technology to extract and process plutonium and uranium for nuclear weapons. He was chief engineer at Chelyabinsk-40 from 1946. Followed Pervukhin as minister of Medium Machine Building (the Soviet bomb program) from 1957 to 1989.

Max **Steenbeck**. German physicist recruited by the Soviets in 1946. He worked with Artsimovich on electromagnetic separation technology for uranium.

Igor Yevgeniyevich **Tamm**. Soviet physicist who first predicted that nuclear fission might make it possible to develop a uranium bomb of tremendous destructive power.

Peter-Adolf **Thiessen**. German physicist recruited by the Soviets in 1946. He helped develop the gaseous diffusion method for uranium separation at the Object A lab in Sinop.

Mikhail Klavdiyevich **Tikhonravov** (1900–1974). Soviet aerospace engineer and colleague of Sergey Korolev. He led the effort to adapt ballistic missiles to peaceful space applications.

Vladimir Fedorovich **Tolubko** (1914–1990). Soviet artillery marshal who headed the Strategic Missile Forces after Nedelin's death in the R-16 accident in 1960.

Mikhail Nikolayevich **Tukhachevskiy** (1893–1937). Soviet military leader who sponsored many of the early efforts in advanced military technology, including prewar rocket and bomber design. His execution during the Great Purge initiated the subsequent rampage through the ranks of the armed forces and military industries.

Andrey Nikolayevich **Tupolev** (1888–1972). Soviet aerospace engineer, considered to be the "father of Soviet aviation." Tupolev helped found TsAGI and headed the most important prewar aircraft design bureau. Imprisoned during the Purge and not freed until the war, he reestablished his reputation as the premier designer of strategic bombers and large passenger aircraft in the late 1940s at his OKB-116 design bureau in Moscow.

Dmitriy Fedorovich **Ustinov** (1908–1984). Soviet industrial administrator who headed the Second Chief Directorate (the development of nuclear weapons delivery systems) after 1945. Ustinov was the wartime head of the armaments industry. He held various high-level defense ministry positions connected with the defense industries until 1976, when Brezhnev named him to head the Ministry of Defense, the first civilian to hold the post.

Boris Lvovich **Vannikov** (1887–1962). Soviet industrialist who headed the First Chief Directorate (atomic bomb program) in 1945. Vannikov was a senior leader in the defense industries during the war and received state prizes in 1951 and 1953 for his management of the atomic bomb program.

Mikhail Kuzmich **Yangel** (1911–1971). Soviet aerospace engineer who led SKB-586 (later OKB-3), the second ICBM design bureau at Dnepropetrovsk. Yangel began his design work with Korolev in the early 1950s, and was assigned his own design bureau in 1954. He worked on intermediate-range ballistic missiles like the R-12 and R-14 and designed the first practical Soviet ICBM, the R-16 (SS-7 Saddler).

Yevgeniy Ivanovich **Zababakhin** (1917–1984). Soviet engineer appointed to head the second Soviet nuclear warhead development center, Chelyabinsk-70 near Kasli, in 1955.

Avraami P. **Zavenyagin** (1901–1956). Soviet metallurgist and NKVD officer who took over the Ministry of Medium Machine Building (atomic bomb program) in February 1955. Zavenyagin was one of Beria's aides on the A-bomb program during and after the war, responsible for overseeing conscripted German scientists.

Yakov Borisovich **Zeldovich** (1914–1987). Soviet physicist involved in theoretical work on A-bomb design. He is credited with many of the key discoveries leading to both the A-bomb and H-bomb.

Pavel M. **Zernov**. Administrative head of Arzamas-16, the A-bomb development center. In the mid-1950s he headed the state commission to adapt nuclear devices as missile warheads, beginning with the R-5M.

Appendix B

Weapons Data

R-1A (SS-1a Scunner) Tactical Ballistic Missile

R-1 was the Soviet designation for V-2 ballistic missiles assembled from German-manufactured components. These missiles were either captured intact in 1945 or assembled from captured components by Institut Rabe in occupied Germany in 1946–47. The first test launch took place on 18 October 1947. The R-1A was a slightly modified version of the German V-2 adapted for Soviet manufacturing practices. This missile was popularly called the *Yedinichka* (the Russian diminutive form for "one"). Production of the R-1A involved eighteen aviation factories and thirty-five research institutes. Quantity production of the R-1A did not begin until 1950 due to the novelty of the equipment. The first missiles entered service in the autumn of 1950. This permitted the formation of the first regular Soviet ballistic missile unit, the 23d Special Purpose Engineer Brigade, under the command of Col. M. G. Grigoryev. This unit was attached to the RVGK (High Command Reserve Forces) of the Soviet Army's artillery force. The R-1A remained in Soviet service into the late 1950s, gradually being replaced by the R-11 (SS-1b Scud A). There was no immediate American counterpart to the R-1A. The United States conducted a number of test launches of captured German V-2 missiles, but did not proceed with local manufacture, feeling that the technology was already outdated.

R-2 (SS-2 Sibling) Tactical Ballistic Missile

The R-2 was an evolutionary improvement on the R-1A aimed at increasing its range. The most significant technical change in the R-2 was the substitution of integral fuel tank construction for separate internal fuel tanks, as well as a lengthened fuselage to increase fuel capacity. The weight of the R-2 was only 151 percent of the R-1A, but its range was doubled, from 300 to 600 km. The most significant tactical change was the substitution of a separable warhead for greater accuracy. At the peak of its flight path, the warhead detached from the missile's fuselage, allowing it to descend by itself to the target. The combat support elements of the R-2 were essentially the same as for the V-2 and R-1A. The first test flight of an R-2 took place at Kapustin Yar on 26 October 1950. Series production began in August 1951 and the R-2 was accepted for Soviet Army service in 1952. As was the case with the R-1A, it was gradually replaced by the R-11 (SS-1b Scud A) in the late 1950s. The R-2 had no immediate American equivalent. The earliest U.S. attempt to progress beyond the V-2 was the experimental Convair MX-774. However, this was only a testbed for technologies applicable to an ICBM, and was never seriously considered for production. The U.S. Army did not adopt a tactical ballistic missile until the mid-1950s, and these were more comparable to the R-11 than to the R-2.

R-5 (SS-3 Shyster) Tactical Ballistic Missile

The R-5, which resembled a lengthened R-2, was the final Soviet elaboration on the German V-2 missile. Like the R-1 and R-2, it used cryogenic fuel, and the engine steering was by means of graphite vanes in the rocket efflux. Development was rapid, beginning in 1952. The first test flight was made on 2 April 1954. The R-5 had an effective range of 1,200 km, making it the first Soviet missile capable of reaching American bomber bases in Europe. Work on the R-5M nuclear-armed version began in 1954, with special emphasis on increased production quality and reliability. The successful test of an R-5M with a nuclear warhead at Kapustin Yar on 20 February 1955 led to the missile's official acceptance as the Soviet Army's first nuclear-armed missile. The R-5M subsequently entered small scale production at Dnepropetrovsk, eventually equipping four RVGK missile regiments, each armed with twelve launchers. The relatively small size of this force was probably due to continuing shortages of nuclear devices, as well as the perception that forthcoming missiles, including the new R-7 intercontinental missile, were a more prudent use of the nuclear weapons inventory. There was no immediate American counterpart to the R-5; it fell between the U.S. Redstone and Thor missiles in terms of range and capability.

R-12 (SS-4 Sandal) Tactical Ballistic Missile

The R-12 was the model the Soviets deployed during the 1962 Cuban missile crisis. Technically, it was the first major Soviet ballistic missile to depart from the basic German V-2 design. The R-12 was developed in the mid-1950s as an alternative to the cancelled R-3 project, and was intended as an "operational-strategic" missile aimed at targets in Europe and Asia, such as British and American bomber bases. Development was undertaken by the new Yangel

Comparative Technical Data
of Early Soviet Ballistic Missiles

U.S. designation	SS-1a	SS-2	SS-3	SS-4
NATO code name	Scunner	Sibling	Shyster	Sandal
Soviet code name	R-1A	R-2	R-5	R-12
Soviet industrial designation	8A11		8K38	8K63
Design bureau	Korolev	Korolev	Korolev	Yangel
First launch	10 Oct 48	26 Oct 50	2 Apr 54	22 Jun 57
Length (m)	14.96	17.65	20.75	22.7
Fuselage diameter (m)	1.65	1.65	1.65	1.65
Span diameter (m)	3.56	3.56	3.65	3.65
Warhead	HE	HE	HE/Nuke	Nuke
Warhead weight (metric T)	0.8	1.0	1.0	1.3
Launch weight (metric T)	13.9	20.4	28.6	28
Fuel weight (metric T)	9.44	15.5	24.3	23
Empty weight (metric T)	4	4.9	4.3	4.65
Engine designation	RD-100	RD-101	RD-103	RD-214
Fuel	alcohol	alcohol	alcohol	kerosene
Oxidizer	LOX	LOX	LOX	RFNA
Sea level thrust (kN)*	267	363	432	635
Vacuum thrust (kN)	307	415	500	730
Vacuum thrust (metric T)	28	35	44	74
Specific impulse (sec)**	204	210	219	264
Engine burn (sec)	65	85	120	140
Flight apogee (km)	100	210	510	
Range (km)	320	600	1,200	1,950

*kN = kilo-Newtons, a metric measure of the force required to give an acceleration of one meter per second to a mass of one metric ton.

**Specific impulse is an indicator of rocket engine efficiency measured in pounds of thrust per pound of propellant burned per second, and expressed in seconds. It is roughly comparable in concept to "miles per gallon" for an automobile engine. The greater the number of seconds, the greater the efficiency.

SKB-486 design bureau at Dnepropetrovsk, and was its first major effort. Due to army demands that the missile be suitable for mobile launchers, the engine requirement stressed the need for storable fuels, leading to the use of hypergolic fuel. The RD-214 rocket engine used four thrust chambers clustered around a common fuel turbopump. The use of a turbopump increased the cost and complexity of the system, but reduced overall fuselage weight by eliminating the need for a heavy gas pressure fuel-injection system like that used on earlier Soviet hypergolic-fueled missiles, such as the R-11 (SS-1b Scud A). Engine steering followed the German pattern of graphite vanes in the engine efflux, and stability was improved by the addition of four small stub fins at the rear of the missile. Missile guidance was originally by radio command, with inertial guidance systems added before production began. The R-12 was armed with a single nuclear warhead in the 1 megaton range. The missile's warhead detached during terminal approach to improve accuracy. The missile's first test flight was on 22 June 1957. The tests were prolonged, lasting well into 1960. The R-12 was widely used as a test platform for Soviet nuclear weapons trials. On 8 September 1961 a 16-MT device was first carried aloft by an R-12. The R-12 was also considered as an alternative to the R-7 to launch the first *Sputnik,* but this idea was later rejected.

The R-12 was designed as a mobile system, comparable to the earlier R-5. The missile was transported on a conventional trailer, and transferred to a special erector vehicle for launch preparation. The erector vehicle was fitted with a large H-frame assembly to load the missile vertically on its launch stand. A typical launch battery consisted of about twenty vehicles and trailers, including the erector, transporter, warhead vans, oxidant and fuel trailers, and pump equipment. The missile was launched from a simple stand reminiscent of the type used with the R-1. Siting, pad preparation, warhead fuzing, missile erection, and fueling took four to six hours. The entire launch cycle took about eight hours from notification to lift-off. R-12 regiments consisted of two battalions with four launch pads each, and shared a common nuclear warhead storage facility. The nuclear facility was controlled by a KGB OSNAZ nuclear security team, as was the practice in the Soviet armed forces at the time. The battalion launch sites were typically separated by a distance of about 5–8 km, with each battalion site having four connected launch pads.

The R-12 had no immediate American counterparts. Chronologically, its two closest American equivalents, the Jupiter and the Thor, were considerably heavier, longer ranged, and more sophisticated. For example, the Jupiter was 49 tons vs. the R-12's 28 tons, and had a range of 3,000 km vs. the R-12's 2,000 km. The American intermediate range missiles of this period were closer in performance to the later Soviet R-14 (SS-5 Skean), but preceded it by several years.

Korolev R-7 Semyorka (SS-6 Sapwood) Intercontinental Ballistic Missile

The R-7 was the first Soviet intercontinental ballistic missile. Development began in 1954 following the cancellation of the intermediate range R-3 missile. The R-7 used an unconventional configuration with a central core surrounded by four booster stages. On ignition, the engines in all five components were simultaneously fired. This avoided the uncertainties of igniting a second-stage engine in the vacuum of space. The four RD-107 engines in the first stage each consisted of four separate thrust chambers with two associated vernier chambers for steering. The central stage's single RD-108 sustainer was of nearly identical design, but with a total of four, rather than two, vernier chambers. After the RD-107 engines in the four booster stages had burned out, about 140 seconds after launch, they separated, and the main RD-108 core engine continued to fire, with a burn duration of about 320 seconds. Due to shortcomings in early inertial guidance technology, the R-7 used a mixed guidance approach. Following launch, the missile was tracked by radar, and radio command guidance signals were transmitted to the guidance unit to make modest corrections using the vernier chambers until the proper ballistic trajectory was reached. Inertial guidance provided sustained course correction to impact.

After three failed launch attempts, the first successful launch of an R-7 missile at full range took place on 21 August 1957 from Tashkent-50 (Baikonur). This was more than a month before the first successful flight of the Atlas, the first American ICBM. The final series of military acceptance trials for the R-7 took place at Tyuratam in March 1959. The R-7 was operationally deployed at the new Leningrad-300 base near Plesetsk and a total of four Tyulpan launchers were eventually erected there. The first successful test launch of an R-7 from Plesetsk took place on 15 December 1959, marking the operational readiness of the base. The four launchers remained in use until 1968.

Although the first R-7 was launched before its American counterpart, the SM-65 Atlas, the first Atlas squadrons were operational nearly a year earlier than the R-7, in February 1958. Technologically, the Atlas and R-7 reflected the different design styles of American and Soviet engineering, Gothic vs. Romanesque. The R-7 was designed to carry a much heavier warhead than the Atlas due to the Soviet lag in thermonuclear weapon miniaturization. The R-7 was burdened by a heavy structure due to Soviet backwardness in aviation materials and metallurgy. The Atlas design incorporated a lightweight stainless steel skin so thin that it had to be kept "inflated" by internal positive overpressure to keep it from collapsing. In contrast, Korolev's design was so robust that workmen could actually walk along the missile's outer skin. As a result of these factors, the R-7 was more than double the weight of the Atlas. The Atlas also enjoyed more advanced engine technology. The

Atlas's individual thrust chambers were 2.6 times more powerful than those on the RD-107 engines, so that the R-7 required twenty thrust chambers on lift-off, while the Atlas had only two (plus one sustainer).

Although the R-7 was soon overshadowed by more effective ICBM designs, notably the Yangel R-16, it remained in large-scale production for space missions. It served as the basis for the RN-*Sputnik* space booster, used to launch the first satellite, as well as later derivatives such as RN-*Vostok* and RN-*Soyuz*. More than a thousand R-7–derived space boosters have been launched since 1957, making it the most widely used space booster of all time.

Technical Data

Soviet designation	R-7
Soviet industrial designation	8K78
Soviet nickname	Semyorka
U.S. designation	SS-6
NATO code name	Sapwood
Design Bureau	Korolev OKB-1
First flight	15 May 1957
Length	33 m
Core diameter	2.95 m
Overall diameter	10.3 m
Guidance	radio command/inertial
Warhead	5-MT nuclear booster-fission device
Empty weight	23 metric tons
Fuel weight	250 metric tons
Launch weight	275 metric tons
Blok A propulsion	GDL-OKB RD-108 four-chamber rocket
Blok B propulsion (x four)	GDL-OKB RD-107 four-chamber rocket
Fuel	Kerosene
Oxidizer	LOX
Core RD-108 thrust	745 kN (sea level), 941 kN (vacuum)
Booster RD-107 thrust (x four)	821 kN (sea level), 1,000 kN (vacuum)
Total launch thrust	4,029 kN (504 metric tons)
Apogee	1,100 km
Range	6,200 km NRE*

*NRE = Non-Rotating-Earth. Because ICBMs fly around the globe, their range is affected by their orientation on launch relative to the earth's rotation. For comparison between different missiles, the data ignore the effects of earth rotation on range, hence NRE.

Yangel R-16 (SS-7 Saddler) Intercontinental Ballistic Missile

The R-16 missile was the first Soviet ICBM design to be deployed in large numbers. Development work began in 1958 by Mikhail Yangel's SKB-586 at the Yuzhmash Plant in Dnepropetrovsk. The primary design criterion of the SS-7 Saddler was the desire to reduce preparation and launch time to thirty minutes from time of warning. Its predecessor, the R-7, took nearly twenty hours to prepare and launch.

The R-16 used a conventional two-stage configuration. The first stage (Blok A) was powered by an RD-216 four-chamber liquid-fuel rocket engine. The second stage was powered by the related RD-219. The R-16 had a relatively high thrust-to-weight ratio for the time, 1.7 compared to the 1.3 more typical of the liquid-propelled missiles of the day. It reached its typical apogee of 650 km about fifteen minutes from time of launch. Flight time to a range of 11,000 km took fifty-four minutes.

The SS-7 used a fly-the-wire inertial guidance system. The guidance mode was typical of Soviet ICBMs of the period, using a preprogrammed variable thrust/attitude history so that the desired position and velocity profiles were maintained throughout the flight. This guidance technique did not require real-time solutions of elaborate guidance equations, and so permitted the use of simple analog computers and digital-differential analyzers rather than more sophisticated digital computers. During its thrust period, the guidance package controlled the missile to follow a preset attitude program in the pitch plane and zero velocity in the yaw.

The single reentry vehicle used by the R-16 was configured as a spherical cone. It was covered with an ablative material, presumably a glass phenolic material. System accuracy was related to warhead weight. The use of a heavier reentry vehicle on the SS-7 Saddler Mod 3 decreased the CEP by about 550 m compared to the lighter reentry on the Mod 2. There have been numerous reports of larger warheads being mounted on the SS-7, ranging from 6 to 25 megatons.

The first test launch on 24 October 1960 led to a pad explosion as described in the basic text. The R-16 began deployment in early 1962. Initial launch sites used simple, above-ground "coffin" launcher bins. These resembled those used with the early American Atlas ICBM and offered more protection against nuclear attack compared to the exposed launchers used with the R-7. The first bin launchers became operational in 1963, though small numbers of temporary launchers using simple blast deflection pads were operational in 1962 during the Cuban missile crisis. The launchers stored the missile in a horizontal position, elevating it out of the hardened structure for firing. Although the missiles used storable fuel, it would appear they had to be elevated before fueling as they could not withstand the dynamic pressures of being elevated fully fueled. This made the coffin launchers vulnerable to attack. Typically, two pads were located next to one another sharing a common fueling system, usually with a reload missile in the vicinity. These pairs formed clusters of eight or ten missiles.

Development of the Sheksna silo launch complexes had been initiated in 1960 at the KBSM design bureau in Leningrad. The Sheksna complex placed three missiles in neighboring silos, feeding fuel and other services to all three silos from a common protected bunker system in the complex. The first of the R-16 Sheksna silos became operational in 1964 at Yurya. At peak strength in 1968 there were twenty-three Sheksna silo complexes with sixty-nine missiles, and an additional 128 missiles in bin launchers. The R-16 remained in service until the 1970s. The first launchers were dismantled in 1971 and the process was completed by 1977.

Technical Data

Soviet designation	R-16
Soviet industrial designation	8K64
U.S. designation	SS-7
NATO code name	Saddler
Design Bureau	Yangel SKB-486
Production Facility	YMSZ, Dnepropetrovsk
Configuration	2-stage storable liquid fuel
Launch mode	Hot launch*
Launch preparation time	30 minutes
Fuel storage duration	2 days
Length	30.78 m
Diameter (Blok A)	3.05 m
Diameter (Blok B)	2.44 m
Max. dynamic pressure	8,050 kg/m^2
Max. staging dynamic pressure	975 kg/m^2
Max. angle of attack	8°
Launch weight	148.8 metric tons
Fuel (Blok A + B)	95 metric tons (55,500 + 39,500 kg)
Propulsion	liquid-fueled rocket
Fuel	RFNA and hydrazine (later IRFNA)

*Hot launch indicates that the missile engines are fired to push the missile out of the silo. Contemporary silo launchers use a "cold launch" technique, which employs compressed air or some other method to propel the missile from the launch tube. The missile engines ignite only after the silo is cleared.

Engine	RD-218 (Blok A), RD-219 (Blok B)
Block A thrust (sea level/vacuum)	266.3/302 metric tons
Block A burnout time	85 seconds
Thrust-weight ratio	1.7
Interstage coast	91 seconds
Block B thrust (sea level/vacuum)	79.4/100.25 metric tons
Block B burnout time	205 seconds
Range	10,200 11,650 km NRE
Guidance	Inertial, fly-the-wire
Payload	Single sphere-cone RV with ablator
Throw weight	1,360 kg @ 12,000 km–2,050 kg @ 9,900 km
Warhead	3-MT thermonuclear device
Accuracy	1.850 km @ 10,200 km

Variant Details	*Mod 2*	*Mod 3*
Reentry vehicle ballistic coefficient	3,400 kg/m^2	4,150 kg/m^2
Reentry vehicle weight	1,590 kg	1,950 kg
Warhead weight	1,135 kg	1,590 kg
Maximum range (NRE)	11,650 km	10,200 km

Lavochkin La-350 Burya Intercontinental Cruise Missile

In April 1953, the Myasishchev OKB-23 design bureau and the Lavochkin OKB-301 design bureau received orders to begin development of an MKR (intercontinental cruise missile). The idea for an intercontinental cruise missile stemmed from studies by Mstislav Keldysh and Sergey Korolev in 1951–52. This led to the Myasishchev Project 40 Sorokovka and the Lavochkin La-X Burya. They were both two-staged, being boosted to altitude by rocket engines, and then releasing a cruise missile upper stage, called the cruise stage, powered by a ramjet engine, called a PVRD. The Burya was the smaller of the two, the Sorokovka having one and a half times greater payload. The task of developing the ramjet engine was assigned to the M. M. Bondaryuk OKB. TsAGI was responsible for all related aerodynamic research, while Keldysh's RNII took care of interdepartmental issues as well as problems connected with thermal heat buildup. According to a study prepared by Keldysh's RNII, the missile would attain a velocity of 600–1,100 m/s at a height of 12–22 km.

The Myasishchev missile was given the code name 40, though it was more popularly called the Sorokovka in the bureau. Dmitriy F. Orochko was the principal designer on the program, and German M. Nazarov was appointed assistant main designer. System guidance and control for the Sorokovka was under the direction of R. G. Chachikyan. The triangular wing had a leading-edge sweep angle of 70 degrees with a straight trailing edge. The wing was "clean," that is, without internal fuel tanks. The liquid-fueled rocket engine for the boosters was assigned to the V. P. Glushko OKB-456 design bureau. The OKB-23 found that the original schemes of the Keldysh RNII were overly optimistic, but the bureau was able to rely on work earlier undertaken by L. L. Selyakov. Furthermore, the main designer for the cruising stage, code-named 42, G. D. Dermichev, had studied under Myasishchev's direction at the Moscow Aviation Institute (MAI) on the concept of a cruise missile. The OKB-23 also had a small "specialist brigade" of twenty-nine designers under K. S. Shpanko from the Chelomey OKB, who had been transferred in April 1951. They had been involved in both pulse-jet and ramjet propulsion for cruise missiles. Development of the booster, code-named 41, was under A. I. Elokazov. To assist in the calculations and analysis necessary for the project, a team under I. N. Moiseyev was transferred to OKB-23 from Korolev's design bureau.

The Sorokovka had a significantly different configuration from the Burya. The initial stage consisted of four identical boosters, nestled "under the armpits" of the ramjet cruise stage, which was situated between them. The missile would launch vertically, with the ramjet engine being ignited when the necessary speed was achieved.

The Lavochkin cruise missile system, designated La-X and later La-350, was also known as the Burya (Tempest). Aleksey M. Isayev was responsible for the booster. The Burya's cruise missile stage had a conventional aircraft layout with thin cross-section, swept wings. The ramjet engine provided 7 metric tons of thrust. In place of a manned cockpit, an astronavigation system was located in the upper center portion of the fuselage, the first use of this navigation technology in the USSR. The cruise missile was the first Soviet aerospace design to make extensive use of titanium in its airframe. A major design concern at this point in time was aerodynamic heating due to atmospheric friction. The cruise missile stage was mounted on a pair of liquid-fuel rocket boosters, each providing 68 metric tons of thrust. The missile was vertically launched from a conventional erector.

Flight tests began in 1957. During the course of 1957–1960, seventeen launches were conducted. The first launch was unsuccessful. A total of four of the launches were successful, with the cruise missile attaining speeds of 3,600 km/hr. In 1960, a flight at the maximum range of 9,000 km (5,600 miles) was finally achieved, which fulfilled the tactical-technical requirements (TTZ) for speed and flight range. However, following Lavochkin's death in June 1960, the project was cancelled. By this time, ICBMs were already a proven alternative.

The closest American technological counterpart to the Burya was the

SM-64 Navaho. Development of the Navaho began nearly a decade before the Burya, and it seems likely that the American program inspired the Soviet effort. The Navaho program was cancelled in favor of the Snark intercontinental cruise missile.

In November 1957, work on the Myasishchev Sorokovka was halted before any could be test launched. In August 1957, the Korolev OKB's R-7 intercontinental ballistic missile had been successfully test fired, reducing the need for a strategic cruise missile. The Lavochkin Burya, further along in development, was allowed to continue. In 1959, Myasishchev's bureau was tasked with assisting in the development of the PKA Lapotok space-plane, based on its research on Project 40. The Project 48 Lapotok (Wooden Shoe) program was an attempt to use the cruise missile research to develop an exoatmospheric space-plane as an alternative to conventional manned spacecraft. The Lapotok was probably intended as a reconnaissance platform. The program was a joint effort between P. V. Tsybin's OKB-256, Myasishchev's OKB-23, and Korolev's OKB-1.

The Lapotok was 9 meters long, with a fuselage width of 7.5 meters. It weighed 3.5 metric tons on launch, reduced to 2.6 metric tons by landing, due to fuel burn. Its aerodynamic surfaces were designed to withstand temperatures up to 1200° C. The Lapotok would have been launched into space on a modified R-7. It was cancelled in 1960 as part of the general consolidation of design bureaus. The research material was retained at OKB-1, where it served as the basis for later space-plane concepts, eventually leading to the contemporary *Buran* space shuttle. The Lapotok was an immediate counterpart to the American Dynasoar program. Like the Lapotok, the Dynasoar was cancelled and never flew.

Technical Data

Soviet designation	La-350 Burya
Design Bureau	OKB-301, Moscow

Cruise Stage

Wingspan	7.75 m
Fuselage length	18.04 m
Fuselage diameter	2.2 m
Wing area	60 m^2
Vertical tail area	7.1 m^2
Horizontal tail area	4.3 m^2
Guidance	astronavigation
Weight of cruise stage	35 metric tons
Cruise stage fuel weight	23.5 metric tons

Cruise stage flight altitude	18–20 km
Altitude on target approach	26–27 km
Cruise stage flight speed	Mach 3–3.2
Maximum guided range	7,500–8,000 km

Booster

Length	18.93 m
Diameter	1.453 m
Rudder area	3.0 m^2
Takeoff weight	97 metric tons

Tupolev Tu-4 Bull Strategic Bomber

The Tupolev Tu-4 was the Soviet copy of the American Boeing B-29A Superfortress bomber begun after the failure of the indigenous Project 64 bomber. Andrey Tupolev was in charge of the program, and nine hundred factories were at his disposal. The aim was to fly the first Soviet-built machines at the 1947 Aviation Day celebration.

The Tu-4 was similar in overall weight to the B-29A, 35.2 metric tons versus 34.9 metric tons for the B-29. There were several small changes to the design. The US IFF (Identification Friend or Foe) system was not adopted for obvious reasons. The B-29A's .50-caliber machine guns were replaced by 20mm B-20 cannon, and later by the improved 23mm NS-23. The first few production aircraft were not fitted with the Goodrich deicing system due to factory problems copying it, but it was later added when the technological hurdles were overcome. A Soviet VHF radio, based on U.S. Lend-Lease designs, was substituted for the UHF radio on the B-29A. The fuel tank design reverted back to separate fuel cells rather than the B-29A's integral fuel cells.

The first Tu-4 flight took place in July 1947, and the aircraft entered Soviet Air Force service in 1949. Peak strength of the Tu-4 in Soviet service was believed to be a thousand aircraft by 1952. Production was concentrated at the Kazan Aviation Plant and may have continued as late as 1954. In the early 1950s, Tu-4 regiments had tables of equipment calling for thirty-six bombers. However, U.S. intelligence agencies concluded that regimental strength was not always reached. In 1954, for example, Soviet Long-Range Aviation had thirty-four Tu-4 regiments, but only about 85 percent of the aircraft needed to reach full strength. At peak Tu-4 deployment, the Long-Range Aviation branch had three air armies, two in the western USSR and one in the Far East, plus an independent corps in the western USSR. The Far East Air Army had six regiments.

The Tu-4 did not possess adequate range to carry out round-trip attacks against the United States. However, it could reach most points in the United

States on one-way missions while carrying a 5-ton payload. Early U.S. estimates of Tu-4 performance in 1950 hinged on the assumption that it was
equivalent to the B-29. In fact, its performance was markedly less due to design
changes, notably the poorer fuel cell design. American assessments in 1950
credited the Tu-4 with a combat range of 4,500 miles with a 5-ton payload.
Soviet sources indicate a 3,170-mile range with a 6-ton payload. By 1953,
U.S. assessments were far more realistic, crediting the Tu-4 with a combat
radius of 1,700 nautical miles and a combat range of 3,100 nautical miles
with a 5-ton bomb load. The aircraft's maximum endurance was about sixteen hours for a 3,100-mile flight.

In the early 1950s, the Soviet Air Force developed an in-flight refueling
system to extend the effective range of the aircraft—using a hose system similar
to the early British and American approaches. It is unclear to what extent
this system was used operationally, what portion of the Tu-4 fleet was converted to tankers, how many Tu-4 bombers were modified for refueling, or
the actual Soviet tactical doctrine for employing refueling aircraft. For maximum
effectiveness, the refueling would have had to have been carried out over
the Gulf of Alaska.

American intelligence agencies expected that the Soviets would develop
a lightened version of the Tu-4 bomber that would have extended its range
(one-way) to 8,800 km (5,500 miles). However, there is no evidence of such
a program. The Soviet Air Force did modify a number of existing bombers
for nuclear delivery by adding suitable safety and arming systems, similar
to the the Il-28D nuclear strike modification of the Il-28 medium bomber or
the American B-29 Silverplate/Saddletree aircraft. The Soviets may have rejected
an extensive redesign of the Tu-4 for increased range, based on the poor
performance of American B-29 bombers over Korea when faced with MiG-
15 jet interceptors, opting instead to press ahead with faster, higher-altitude
bombers such as the M-4 (Bison) and Tu-95.

As an alternative to manned suicide missions to the United States, the Soviets
experimented with a remotely controlled Tu-4. This aircraft was tested outside of the Soviet Union on long-range flights, including to bases in Poland.
The program does not appear to have passed beyond trials due to technological limitations.

In February 1952 the USSR provided ten Tu-4A bombers to the People's
Republic of China. They were used to form the 4th Independent Air Regiment
near Peking, the main strategic strike force of the PRC through the 1960s.
In 1959–60, an additional three Tu-4As were provided to make up for attrition.

Two transport versions of the Tu-4 bomber were built, the Tu-70 in 1947
(based on B-29 components, but incorporating a new fuselage) and the
Tu-4T in 1954. Neither aircraft entered quantity production. The Tu-4 also

served as a testbed for the follow-on Tu-95 bomber, with the Tu-4LL version being used to examine the NK-6 and NK-12 turboprop engines. The principal Tupolev test-pilot, A. D. Perelyet, was killed during one of these tests when a propeller disintegrated and flew into the Tu-4LL cockpit.

Tupolev Tu-95M Bear A Strategic Bomber

The Tupolev Tu-95 strategic bomber was developed as an alternative to the preferred M-4 jet-propelled strategic bomber. It was the natural evolution of earlier Tupolev design efforts, the Tu-4, Tu-80, and Tu-85 bombers. Neither the Tu-80 nor Tu-85 bombers entered service, in spite of their performance advantages over the Tu-4, owing to the perception after the 1950–51 Korean air war that piston-engined bombers were doomed by the advent of jet interceptors. Indeed, it was this experience that so clearly shaped Stalin's decision to initiate a strategic jet bomber program in 1951 with the establishment of the new Myasishchev OKB-23 design bureau at Fili.

The Tupolev Tu-95 program began in 1949 as a long-term study, and transitioned to engineering design in 1950. Tupolev's experience with jet propulsion on his Tu-16 (Badger) medium bomber convinced him that existing Soviet jet-engine technology was too immature for an intercontinental strategic bomber. The new bomber was powered by a novel turboprop engine being developed by a German-Soviet team at Kuibyshev under Ferdinand Brandner and Nikolay Kuznetsov. A testbed version of the Tu-95, powered by NK-6 turboprop engines, made its first flight on 11 November 1952 with A. D. Perelyet at the controls. The NK-6 provided about 6,000 horsepower each. This aircraft proved woefully underpowered, leading to a major redesign. The new version, designated Tu-95M, awaited completion of the more powerful NK-12 12,000-horsepower turboprop engines. The initial test flights of the Tu-95M began in 1954.

The Tu-95M design straddled American bomber design in technology. It was a more advanced design than the decade-older B-36, maintaining a much higher cruising speed (440 mph vs. 225 mph), while having similar range. The Tu-95M resembled some early concepts for the B-52, such as the Model 464-35. The Tu-95M had flight performance similar in many respects to the Boeing B-52D. Their maximum speeds were similar, although the B-52 had the advantage of a higher cruising speed (510 mph vs. 440 mph). The B-52D had a slightly higher payload capacity in normal configurations, and both aircraft had similar range capabilities. It is believed that the B-52 enjoyed a considerably more sophisticated electronic warfare suite and radar navigation and bombing system, but details of the Tu-95M's avionics are lacking.

The Tu-95M became operational in April 1956. The strategic nuclear bomber version was called the Bear A by NATO. American intelligence estimates presumed that each bomber would carry four thermonuclear freefall bombs. In the late 1950s an improved strategic strike variant, the Tu-95K-20 (Bear B) was developed. This variant carried the Mikoyan Kh-20 (AS-3 Kangaroo) stand-off cruise missile, along with the associated *Crown Drum* strike radar. This variant was prompted by the deployment around key U.S. cities of air defense missiles such as the Nike Ajax and, later, the Nike Hercules missile. These missiles had a very high kill probability against large strategic bombers flying in the stratosphere, especially the Nike Hercules with its nuclear warhead. This meant that a strategic bomber would have to release its weapon before coming in range of the missiles, and that the stand-off weapon would have to be able to survive the antiaircraft missiles. The Mikoyan Kh-20 accomplished this by flying above the effective ceiling of the Nike missiles, then executing a very sharp dive over the target which would be difficult for the missile engagement radar to track. A total of fifteen Tu-95K-20 bombers were built, with the first being publicly displayed at the Tushino air show in 1961. The U.S. Air Force at the time was adopting the AGM-28 Hound Dog missile. In contrast to the Kh-20, the Hound Dog was mainly intended as a penetration aid, not for the delivery of a nuclear weapon against a primary target. A portion of the B-52 force would be armed with Hound Dogs (two per bomber), and directed against major air defense targets such as missile sites and key radars. The Kh-20 was oriented towards primary weapons delivery since it took up the entire weapons bay of the Tu-95K-20.

Rapid advances in U.S. continental air defense raised serious questions about the survivability of the Bear in the strategic strike role. Its cruising speed was only 710 km/hr (440 mph, Mach 0.67) at an altitude of 14,000 m (45,900 ft). On a typical strike mission based out of Anadyr in the Soviet Far East and aimed at targets in the Chicago area, the Tu-95M would have been inbound over American and Canadian territory for about eight hours. This was more than adequate time for interception, presuming, of course, detection was made early. Early detection was likely after 1956 due to upgrades in U.S./ Canadian air defense radars, as well as the continued backwardness of Soviet electronic warfare technology. Alternative approaches, such as low altitude tactics, would have been difficult due to the range reduction such tactics would have caused. Another tactic in the early 1960s might have been to try to swamp the NORAD defenses with additional aircraft, such as Tu-16 medium jet bombers and old Tu-4 bombers, which could penetrate the outer screens and dilute the defensive forces.

The shortcomings in the bomber force led the Khrushchev administration to back away from the employment of strategic bombers in favor of ballistic missiles in 1959. As a result, production of strategic bomber variants of the Bear were curtailed, and only fifteen Tu-95K-20 Bear Bs were fielded. By

1960, forty-eight Tu-95M bombers were in operational service, and peak Bear strength was reached in 1964 with 105 (three regiments) in service. Additional strategic aircraft were produced beyond these numbers for training and other purposes. Bear production was also diverted to other applications, such as the Tu-95RTs (Bear D), which were used by the Soviet Navy for providing targeting data for antiship missiles.

Tu-95 Bear strategic bomber regiments remained static in size. In the 1970s, the Tu-95M and Tu-95K-20 were gradually replaced by the Tu-95K-26 (Bear G) with the Kh-22 (AS-4 Kitchen) stand-off missile. Production was revived in 1983 for the Tu-95MS (Bear H). The advent of the more advanced RBV-500A (AS-15 Kent) stand-off cruise missiles gave the strategic bomber a new lease on life. A total of eighty-four Tu-95MS bombers were completed at the Kuibyshev Aviation Plant by 1991.

Technical Data: Kh-20 Strategic Cruise Missile

Soviet designation	Mikoyan Kh-20
U.S. designation	AS-3
NATO code name	Kangaroo
Carrier	Tu-95K-20 (Bear B)
Length	15 m
Wingspan	9.1 m
Launch weight	13.3 metric tons
Warhead	800-kt thermonuclear device
Propulsion	Tumanskiy R-11 turbojet
Range	350 km
Cruise speed	Mach 1.5–2
Launch height	10,700–11,900 m @ 800 km/h

Myasishchev M-4 Molot (Bison) Strategic Bomber

The Myasishchev M-4 Molot (Hammer) bomber was developed in response to the lessons of the 1950-51 air war in Korea. Development work on the M-4 (also designated the 2M, VM-25, and 103M) was begun in 1951 at the reconstituted OKB-23 at Fili in the Moscow suburbs. The program suffered from the shortcomings of existing Soviet jet engines. The weight and poor fuel economy of the Mikulin AM-3 turbojets meant that the initial production models of the Molot had inadequate range for round-trip strikes against the United States. The first flight took place on 20 January 1953.

Production of the M-4 was soon superceded by an improved version, the M-4A, which used the improved Mikulin AM-3D engine. Other changes included improvements to the wing and fuselage structure. This production variant still had inadequate range for the strategic strike mission, but was manufactured in spite of its obvious shortcomings. Its combat range with a 5-ton load was 8,000 km (4,970 miles). An early production batch of at least ten M-4 Bison As was completed by 1955, when they were flown in Aviation Day ceremonies.

The Dobrynin VD-7 turbojet finally became available in 1955, leading to the second strategic bomber variant, the M-6, also known as the 3M (Bison B in NATO). This more efficient engine boosted the plane's range from 8,000 to 13,000 km with a 5-ton payload. American intelligence agencies have traditionally estimated its range as being lower, about 11,000 km.

A final strategic bomber version, the 3MD (Bison C, 201M) was developed in the late 1950s. This version had a redesigned nose equipped with a new navigation radar, sometimes claimed to be the *Puff Ball*. This is unlikely, as the 3MD was never seen carrying the associated K-10 (AS-2 Kipper) missile. More likely, this was a navigation radar comparable to the *Short Horn* on the Bison A.

The 3M Bison B and 3MD Bison C were never entirely satisfactory. Their cruising speed was only about 10 percent better than the Tu-95M's, and their cruising altitude was only about 20 percent higher. This was not sufficient to substantially decrease the vulnerability of the bomber to U.S. interceptor aircraft or air defense missiles. Fewer Molots than Tu-95s were built, with only fifty-eight of the strategic bomber versions in service by 1961, their peak strength. Some of the older M-4 (2M) Bison As were converted to M-4TZ tankers to support the force and, in later years, the same fate befell some 3M variants, which were converted into the 3MS-2 and 3MN-2 tankers. By 1985 forty-eight bombers were still in service, mainly 3MD Bison C variants, and a further thirty tanker versions were flying. In 1986 the Bison force began to be retired, and the aircraft was entirely out of service by 1991 when the START treaty was signed.

The 3M was most comparable to the American Boeing B-52 Stratofortress. It was a far less successful design due to its range problems. Details of the radar/navigation system on the 3M are lacking, but it is believed to have been inferior to that on the B-52.

Myasishchev M-50 Bounder Strategic Bomber

The Myasishchev M-50 bomber was an attempt to circumvent the tactical shortcomings of the 3M Molot bomber with a major increase in speed. By increasing the cruising and dash speeds of the aircraft, it was presumed that its vulnerability to American interceptors could be reduced. Higher cruising speed would shorten the time needed to traverse North American airspace, and increased dash speed would allow the bomber to outrun fighters for short periods of time.

Design of the M-50 began in the mid-1950s after the first flight of the

M-4 Molot. Initial design studies were conducted at TsAGI, the Central Aerodynamic Institute. Various aircraft configurations were examined, including mounting the four engines on pylons with one above and one below each wing, or alternately two in the tail and two in underwing pods. Due to growing awareness of the area rule problem of drag management, the bureau engineers, Y. E. Ilyenko and V. A. Fedotov, came up with the final configuration: two engines under the wings on pylons and two in wing-tip pods. The efficiency of the design has been questioned by the Western aviation press.

As was the Molot, the M-50 was plagued with engine problems. The M-50 was supposed to employ a new, highly efficient *Izdeliye* 16–17 jet engine designed by P. F. Zubets at TsIAM (Central Aviation Engine Institute). This engine did not materialize in time, leading to the adoption of the far less satisfactory Dobrynin ND-7 turbojets.

The M-50 design was one of the most technologically ambitious Soviet programs of the time, and one of the first to make extensive use of computers in designing the aircraft and simulating its flight characteristics. The M-50 was to have been fitted with an early form of fly-by-wire control using remotely controlled electrical servo motors for actuating the control surfaces, but more conventional mechanical control was used on the first prototypes. Other advanced features on the bomber included a fuel trim management system to compensate for the changes in the center of pressure during transsonic flight. Another unusual feature, first pioneered on the 3M bomber, was the so-called leaping landing gear. On takeoff roll, the forward bicycle landing gear was hydraulically extended when a certain ground speed was reached, quickly increasing the wing incidence and accelerating the takeoff. The M-50 was intended to carry a stand-off cruise missile as its principal armament, but no information has been released about which system was to be employed.

The first test flight M-50 was conducted on 27 October 1959. The aircraft was disappointing in regards to both range and speed. The aircraft was barely capable of breaking the sound barrier and its range was far short of being intercontinental. A marginally improved version, designated the M-52, had afterburners added to the inner two engines. In view of the attitude of the Khrushchev administration towards bombers, the program was terminated and the OKB-23 design bureau was closed. The Fili plant was turned over to Vladimir Chelomey's OKB-52 missile design bureau, and Myasishchev was transferred to the Moscow Aviation Institute, where he continued to teach and design aircraft. He was allowed to maintain a small design staff, and proposed an alternative design to Tupolev's Tu-144 supersonic transport. Myasishchev was allowed to open the new OKB-1457 design bureau after Khrushchev's ouster. This bureau developed further strategic bomber ideas

Bomber Comparative Technical Data

	Tu-4A	Tu-95M	M-4A	3M	M-50
Soviet designation	Tu-4A	Tu-95M	M-4A	3M	M-50
NATO code name	Bull	Bear A	Bison A	Bison B	Bounder
Crew	11	8	8	6	6
Fuselage length (m)	30.2	49.5	47.2	53.4	57
Wingspan (m)	43.1	51.1	50.5	52.5	37
Number of engines	4	4	4	4	4
Engine type	ASh-73TK	NK-12M	AM-3D	VD-7	ND-7
Horsepower x 4	2,400	12,000	n/a	n/a	n/a
Max. thrust (kg) x 4	n/a	n/a	8,700	13,000	18,000
Empty weight (metric T)	35.2	86	82	90	74.5
Max. payload (metric T)	8	30	40	40	
Normal payload (metric T)	6	11.5	5	5	2
Normal loaded wt. (metric T)	47.5	154	160	165	165
Max. speed (sea level, km/h)	420	420	620	630	630
Max. speed (km/h)	550	950	900	950	1,950
Cruising speed (km/h)	315	710	835	860	860
Cruising altitude (m)	11,200	14,000	13,700	17,000	17,000
Range with normal payload (km)	5,100	12,550	8,000	13,000	6,000
Defensive weapons	10	6	6	6	0
Weapons type	B-20E	NR-23	NR-23	NR-23	n/a
Weapons caliber	20mm	23mm	23mm	23mm	n/a

including the M-56, M-60, and M-70, none of which materialized. During the competition for the supersonic strategic bomber in the late 1970s, the bureau developed the M-18 design, which lost to Tupolev's Izdeliye 70 (Tu-160 Blackjack).

The M-50's closest American counterpart was the Convair B-58 Hustler. The Hustler had shorter range than the claimed maximum range of the M-50, but there is little evidence that the M-50 actually was capable of these ranges. The B-58 first flew in 1956 and entered operational service in 1961. Like the M-50, it was a revolutionary advance in bomber design, but unlike the M-50, it proved successful enough to warrant quantity production.

Project 611AB (Zulu V) Ballistic Missile Submarine

The Project 611 (Zulu IV) class was developed as a conventionally powered attack submarine, with the first members of the class completed at the Sudomekh Shipyard in Leningrad in 1952. The class was developed by N. N. Isanin's design bureau in Leningrad. In 1955 a Zulu IV class submarine, hull number B-67 commanded by Capt. 2d Rank S. Kozlov, was converted as a test submarine for the R-11FM missile at Shipyard 402 in Severodvinsk. The first launch of the R-11FM from the B-67 took place in September.

Construction of five new Project 611AB (Zulu V) missile submarines followed at Sudomekh in 1955. The R-11FM was an adaptation of the army's R-11 (SS-1b Scud), with a range of 300 km. The missile was stowed in a fueled state, which would suggest either that its oxidizer tanks were specially lined to prevent the corrosive effects of the nitric acid oxidizer, or that the missile used an inhibited variety of the chemical. The missile was stowed inside the submarine's sail and then elevated to the top of the sail prior to launch. The launcher could be adjusted in azimuth, and the platform was gyrostabilized in two axes. To compensate for ship movements in the third axis, the missile would be launched only upon returning to true vertical, based on shipboard sensors.

The R-11FM naval missile was generally armed with a conventional warhead, though a nuclear warhead was available for the army version and could presumably be mounted on the naval version. It would appear that the Project 611AB gave the submarine force experience in handling submarine missiles rather than giving the navy significant strike capability.

The first Project 611AB submarine became operational with the Northern Fleet in August 1956, the second in April 1957, the third in December 1957, the fourth in September 1958, the fifth in March 1959, and the six (with the Pacific Fleet) in August 1959. Even though the submarines were deployed with the fleet, the new missile systems on board were not officially accepted by the Soviet government until early 1959 due to protracted development problems. During the Khrushchev years, the typical deployment pattern of the Project 611AB was four submarines with the Northern Fleet and two with the Pacific Fleet.

Project 629 (Golf I) Ballistic Missile Submarine

The Project 629 (Golf I) was the first class of submarines specifically designed to launch ballistic missiles. Designed by N. N. Isanin's bureau, it was based on the earlier Foxtrot attack submarine. The first Golf I submarine became operational with the Northern Fleet in October 1959. Twenty-three Golf I submarines were completed at Shipyard 402 in Severodvinsk and Shipyard 199 in Komsomolsk between 1958 and 1962 and were first based at Saida Tuba and Zapadnoe Litso. The final member of the class became operational with the Pacific Fleet in January 1963, at which point there were sixteen with the Northern Fleet and seven in the Pacific Fleet.

The Golf I was armed with the R-13 (SS-N-4) missile, developed by Viktor Makayev's design bureau in Chelyabinsk. This missile was a single-stage, liquid-fueled rocket design. Unlike the earlier Zulu V class, on the Golf the missile's fuel and oxidizer were stored in the submarine's sail until launch. The fuel was TG-02 (Tonka-250), a kerosene derivative, and the oxidizer was 80 percent nitric acid and 20 percent nitric tetroxide. The steering was provided by a series of small vernier rockets located at the base of the missile. It was surface launched, with the missile being erected above the sail on a Horn and Hoof launcher. The R-13 had an effective combat range of 1,200 km according to Soviet sources (Western sources claim 575 km). It was armed with a 500-kiloton thermonuclear reentry vehicle, weighing about 1.5 tons, which detached from the missile by a pneumatic separation system. The CEP for this missile is usually given as 3 km at a range of 575 km, but this would be much more variable than land-based missiles, dependent on the training and performance of the crew. The submarine was also fitted with six torpedo tubes. According to Soviet sources, a typical load was four conventional and two nuclear-armed torpedoes.

Thirteen Golf I's were later rebuilt as the Project 629M (Golf II). The Project 629M was armed with the improved R-21 missile (SS-N-5 Sark). The first Project 629M entered service with the Northern Fleet in March 1964. It was a Project 629M of the Pacific Fleet, PL 574 commanded by Capt. Vladimir I. Kobzar, that was lost in 1968 and later recovered by the CIA using the *Glomar Explorer* heavy lift ship.

The R-21 missile, also developed by the Makayev design bureau, was the first Soviet SLBM that could be launched from a submerged submarine. The submarine would rise to within 20 or 30 meters (65-100 feet) of the surface. Compressed air ejected the missile upward and when it breached the surface the rocket engine would ignite. The missile had an effective range of 2,000 km according to Soviet sources (Western sources credit it with a 1,200 km range.) According to Western sources, it had a CEP accuracy on the order of 2.5 km at a range of 1,200 km, but this figure would be much more prone to degradation due to the navigational uncertainties of the parent submarine than land-based missiles.

Project 658 (Hotel) Nuclear-Propelled Ballistic Missile Submarine

The Project 658 was developed by the V. N. Peregudov TsKB-143 design bureau in Leningrad, and was the world's first nuclear-propelled ballistic missile submarine. The design was derived from earlier work on the Project 627 (November) class attack submarine, the first Soviet nuclear-powered submarine.

The Hotel I submarine was a nuclear-powered counterpart to the Golf class, and was also armed with the Makayev R-13 ballistic missile. It was powered by a pair of nuclear reactors, dubbed HEN by NATO, referring to the Hotel-Echo-November submarine classes powered by this design. The cost of the HEN reactor and the larger size of the Hotel led to fewer of this design being built than the more economical Golf class.

The first Hotel I submarine, the K-19, went operational with the Northern Fleet in October 1960, the second in November 1960, the third in January 1961, the fourth in March 1961, the fifth in May 1961, the sixth in January 1962, the seventh in March 1962, and the eighth in May 1962. In October 1963 one of these submarines was transferred from the Northern Fleet to the Pacific Fleet. Like the November class which preceded it, the early Hotel class subs were plagued with design problems, some of them associated with the HEN reactors. In June 1961, the lead ship, K-19, suffered a major reactor failure, which led to the deaths of nine of the crew from radiation poisoning. K-19 later suffered a string of accidents, leading to its unofficial nickname, Hiroshima.

The Hotel class compared very unfavorably with contemporary American nuclear submarines of the George Washington class, which had preceded the Soviet type into service by several months. The George Washington class was 20 percent greater in displacement, but incomparably better armed. It carried sixteen solid-fueled Polaris missiles, compared to three R-13s on the Hotel. Not only were the missiles greater in number, they were of a more advanced design and could be fired submerged. The submarine was considerably more resistant to ASW attack since the missile launch process would take place underwater, and was much quicker than the R-13's launch. The R-13s had to be fueled, and then the submarine surfaced. At this point, the missiles would be laboriously erected above the sail. This was time consuming and made the submarine vulnerable to detection and attack. Little is known about the navigation systems on the Hotel, but it is believed that they lacked the sophisticated inertial guidance system of the Polaris submarines, which would contribute to the inaccuracy of their missiles. The first Soviet submarine comparable to the George Washington class was the Kovalev bureau's Project 667 Navaga class (Yankee I), which first appeared in service in 1967.

All eight Hotel class submarines were modernized to accommodate the Makayev R-21 missile in place of the earlier R-13. The main advantage of the R-21 was that it could be launched while submerged. These modified submarines were designated Project 659T (Hotel II by NATO). The first Hotel II submarine became operational with the Northern Fleet in April 1964, and the second in May 1965.

Ballistic Missile Submarine Comparative Data

Soviet designation	Project 611AB	Project 629	Project 658
NATO designation	Zulu V	Golf I	Hotel I
Crew	70	58	80
Length (m)	90	99	115
Beam (m)	7.5	8.1	9
Draft (m)	6	6.6	7
Surface displacement (tons)	1,900	2,900	5,000
Submerged displacement (tons)	2,350	3,600	6,000
Propulsion	Diesel-electric	Diesel-electric	Nuclear
Max. surface speed (knots)	18	17	20
Max. submerged speed (knots)	16	12	25
Max. operating depth (m)	200	300	300
Ballistic missiles	2	3	3
Missile type	R-11FM	R-13	R-13
Western missile name	SS-1b Scud A	SS-N-4	SS-N-4
Torpedo tubes	6 x 533mm	6 x 533mm	6 x 533mm
Surface search radar	*Snoop Plate*	*Snoop Tray*	*Snoop Tray*
Active sonar	*Tamir-5L*	*Hercules*	*Hercules*
Passive sonar	*Feniks*	*Feniks*	*Feniks*
Electronic warfare sensor	*Stop Light*	*Stop Light*	*Stop Light*

Notes

Chapter 1

1. GULAG is an acronym for *Glavnoe upravlenie ispravitelno-trudovikh lagerey*, the Main Administration for Corrective Labor Camps. The primary barrier to an adequate understanding of the Purge is the fact that the NKVD archives are still inaccessible to scholars. The classic study of the Purge is Robert Conquest's *The Great Terror*. First appearing in 1968, a revised edition was published in 1990. Recent revisionist studies have begun to question the role of factors other than Joseph Stalin himself in the Purge, for example: J. Arch Getty, *Origins of the Great Purges* (Cambridge: Cambridge University Press, 1985). But these organizational explanations describe the texture of the Purge more than the substance.

2. For an example of how the Purge was exploited to serve organizational ambitions, see: Steven J. Zaloga, "Soviet Air Defense Radar in the Second World War," *Journal of Soviet Military Studies,* 2, no. 1 (March 1989): 105–106.

3. Martin Gardner, *Fads & Fallacies in the Name of Science* (New York: Dover, 1952), 127.

4. K. Smirnov interview with A. P. Aleksandrov, "How We Made the Bomb," *Izvestiya,* 23 July 1988 (trans. JPRS-UMA-88-029, 55–56). For a more general overview of the politics of Soviet science in this period, see Paul Josephson, *Physics and Politics in Revolutionary Russia* (Berkeley: University of California Press, 1991).

5. Roy Medvedev, *Let History Judge: The Origins and Consequences of Stalinism* (New York: Columbia University Press, 1989), 440. Anton Antonov-Ovseyenko, *Portret Tirana* (New York: Khronika, 1980), 250–252.

6. This campaign is most thoroughly described in a three-part series: A. S. Sonin, "Soveshchanie, kotoroe ne sostoyalos," *Priroda,* no. 3 (1990): 91–102; no. 4 (1990): 91–98; and no. 5 (1990): 93–99.

7. Robert Conquest, *The Great Terror* (New York: Macmillan, 1968), 320.

8. G. E. Gorelik, "Ne uspershie stat akademkami," *Priroda,* no. 1 (1990): 123–128.

9. The most detailed account of the Uranium Commission's plans in 1940–41 is contained in the essay by L. V. Komlev et. al., "V. G. Khlopin i uranovaya problema," in A. M. Petrosyantsa, ed., *Akademik V. G. Khlopin: Ocherki, vospominaniya, sovremennikov* (Leningrad: Nauka, 1987), 37–52.

10. Tad Szulc, "The Untold Story of How Russia Got the Bomb," *Los Angeles Times,* 26 August 1984, Opinion (Part IV), 1.

11. D. Holloway, "Entering the Nuclear Arms Race: The Soviet Decision to Build the Atomic Bomb, 1939–45," *Social Studies of Science,* 11 (1981): 159–197.

12. Leonard Nikishin, "They Awakened the Genie," *Moscow News,* no. 41 (1989).

13. P. T. Astashenkov, *Academician Kurchatov: Hero in Science and Labour* (Moscow: Mir, 1981), 55.

14. Komlev, *V. G. Khlopin,* 45.

15. The budget included 225,000 rubles for the extraction and processing of the first 300 kilograms of uranium and a further commitment of 750,000 rubles to the 1941 goal of 1.5 metric tons. The RIAN cyclotron was allotted 970,600 rubles.

16. P. T. Astashenkov, *Akademik I. V. Kurchatov* (Moscow: Voenizdat, 1971), 147.

17. The full text of this letter was first printed in the newspaper *Moskovskie Novosti* and its English-language edition, *Moscow News,* no.16 (1988).

18. Nikishin, "They Awakened the Genie."

19. This account is based mainly on recent revelations by KGB historian Vladimir Chikov. The first accounts are excerpts from a forthcoming book which have appeared in the magazines *Novoe Vremya (New Times)* and *Soyuz.* Vladimir Chikov, "Ot Los Alamosa do Moskvy," *Soyuz,* no. 21 (May 1991); no. 22 (May 1991); no. 23 (June 1991) (trans. JPRS-UMA-91-023, 42–50).

20. Christopher Andrew and Oleg Gordievskiy, *KGB: The Inside Story* (New York: Harper-Collins, 1990), 311–312.

21. Andrei Nikolayev, "It Was Information of Inestimable Importance: How the Secret Materials Were Obtained on the First American Atomic Bomb," *Zhizn,* no. 15 (April 1992): 8–9 (trans. FBIS-USR-92-067, 5 June 1992). Details about this German officer vary. Some Soviet accounts, such as Chikov's, indicate that he was a prisoner. The more common and more likely accounts, such as Smirnov's, indicate the notebook was found on the body of a dead officer. Smirnov, "How We Made the Bomb."

22. Robert C. Williams, *Klaus Fuchs, Atom Spy* (Cambridge, Mass.: Harvard University Press, 1987).

23. Arnold Kramish, *Atomic Energy in the Soviet Union* (Palo Alto: Stanford University Press, 1959), 50–51.

24. Vladimir Chikov, "How the Soviet intelligence service 'split' the American atom," *New Times,* no. 16 (1991), 39.

25. The term *rezident* (resident) refers to a senior NKVD intelligence officer at a station.

26. A. P. Aleksandrov (ed), *Akademik A. I. Alikhanov: vospominaniya, pisma, dokumenty* (Leningrad: Nauka, 1989).

27. T. M. Chernoshchekov and V. Ya. Frenkel, *Lyudi nauki—I. V. Kurchatov* (Moscow: Prosveshcheniye, 1989), 100–101.

28. The fact that ninety-seven out of a hundred men in this age group were killed during the war seems hard to believe. But this statistic is frequently repeated by Soviets when explaining the magnitude of losses during the war. The author has heard it from Soviet military officers, as well as historians whose fathers served in the war.

29. The Russian word for this is *kotel*. This type of graphite-moderated reactor was called a nuclear "pile" in the United States at the time.

30. A. A. Logunov, ed., *Isaak Konstantinovich Kikoin* (Moscow: Nauka, 1988).

31. B. B. Kadomtsev, ed., *Reminiscences about Acadamecian Lev Artsimovich* (Moscow: Nauka, 1985).

32. Smirnov, "How We Made the Bomb."

33. I. Golovin, *Academician Igor Kurchatov* (Moscow: Mir, 1969), 64.

34. The story of Perseus was first revealed in 1991 by a KGB publicist, Col. Vladimir Chikov. His most detailed article to date appeared as a three-part series in the military journal *Armiya*, formerly *Kommunist Vooruzhenikh Sil*. V. Chikov, "Kak raskryvali 'atomnye sekrety'?" *Armiya*, nos. 18, 19, 20 (1991).

35. An article by Ronald Radosh, a scholar known for his book, *The Rosenberg File*, suggests that this unknown spy may have been University of Chicago physicist Clarence Hiskey, who had been the subject of a congressional investigation after the war and recommended for indictment on espionage charges. See also Ronald Radosh and Eric Breindel, "The KGB Fesses Up: Bombshell," *The New Republic* (10 June 1991): 11. Vladimir Chikov suggests that Perseus was a spy located at Los Alamos, but it is possible that Chikov has confused Los Alamos with the University of California at Berkeley as some of his descriptions of the spy seem more suited to scientists working at Lawrence's radiation laboratory. Several scientists at the radiation laboratory were under investigation for turning over material to Soviet agents, though none were tried. See Nuel Pharr Davis, *Lawrence & Oppenheimer* (New York: Simon & Schuster, 1968), 191–195.

36. The Eltenton recruitment attempt was made through a personal friend, Prof. Haakon Chevalier. Oppenheimer later reported the attempt to security at Los Alamos, but the incident came back to haunt him in the 1950s when it was used to impune his loyalty to the United States. The Oppenheimer controversy has been the subject of many books. For a look at the security issues at Los Alamos, and the problem of leaks to the Soviets, see Nuel Pharr Davis, *Lawrence & Oppenheimer*.

37. Kramish, *Atomic Energy,* 112.

38. Gregg Herken, *The Winning Weapon: The Atomic Bomb and the Cold War, 1945–1950* (Princeton, N.J.: Princeton University Press, 1988), 107.

39. Thaddeus Wittlin, *Commissar: The Life and Death of Lavrentiy Pavlovich Beria* (New York: Macmillan, 1972), 308.

40. Viktor Kravchenko, *I Chose Freedom* (New York: Scribner's, 1946).

41. Anglo-American military cooperation was rooted in similar efforts in World War I, particularly in the area of naval technology. The atmosphere for Anglo-American technological cooperation in World War II was set by the Tizard Mission. Sir Henry Tizard, who headed Britain's radar development effort, suggested in early 1940 that key British discoveries in radar technology, notably the magnetron, simply be given to the United States in the hopes that such unprecedented generosity would encourage further technological cooperation and lead to concrete American aid in quantity production of key radar components. Supported by Churchill, the Tizard Mission's 1940 visit to the United States was a seminal event in radar development, foreshadowing Anglo-American exploitation of the revolutionary centimetric radars made possible by the British invention of the magnetron. See for example E. G. Bowen, *Radar Days* (Bristol, U.K.: Adam Hilger, 1987).

42. A personal account of these relations can be found in Kemp Tolley, *Caviar and Commissars: The Experiences of a U.S. Naval Officer in Stalin's Russia* (Annapolis, Md.: Naval Institute Press, 1983). For a look at the institutional friction between the U.S. and Soviet military, see G. B. Infield, *The Poltava Affair* (New York: Macmillan, 1973).

43. The only known case of Soviet technological cooperation was in the matter of tanks. After repeated badgering for nearly two years, in 1943 the Soviet Union provided Britain and the United States each with one T-34 medium tank and one KV-1 heavy tank. These were not the latest versions; the Soviets were already switching to the T-34-85 and IS-2 tanks.

44. One of the clearest examples of American restrictions on technological sharing was the case of France and French atomic research. See Bertrand Goldschmidt, *Atomic Rivals: A Candid Memoir of Rivalries among the Allies over the Bomb* (New Brunswick, N.J.: Rutgers, 1990).

45. A. I. Perelman, *Aleksandr Yevgenevich Fersman* (Moscow: Nauka, 1984).

46. Some idea of how limited the wartime efforts were to exploit uranium deposits can be found in the standard account of the Soviet chemical industry during the war years. Only a few sentences are devoted to uranium efforts, even though the study was released in 1989 when the subject was no longer tightly classified. See N. M. Zhavoronkov, *Stranitsy geroicheskogo truda khimikov v gody VOV 1941–45* (Moscow: Nauka, 1989), 217–218.

47. Some Soviet scientists believe that Kurchatov's premature death in 1960 was due to the pressures of working with Beria. See for example Sergey Kapitsa's remarks in "Peter Kapitsa: The Scientist Who Talked Back to Stalin," *The Bulletin of Atomic Scientists* (April 1990), 31.

48. The NKVD went through several permutations during the war, including a division into the NKVD and NKGB in February 1941, a fusion back into a unified NKVD in July 1941, and another split in July 1943. Beria retained control of both organizations in practice, if not title, through most of the war. The size of the NKVD-NKGB forces is controversial, with estimates running from 750,000 to 2 million. See John Dziak, *Chekisty: A History of the KGB* (Lexington, Mass.: Lexington Books, 1988), 113–114.

49. There do not appear to have been nuclear physics prison design bureaus during the war as there were after 1945. However, a significant number of nuclear physicists, or scientists useful to the uranium program, were incarcerated in other prison design bureaus during the war. See "A. Charaguine" (Georgi Ozerov), *En prison avec Tupolev* (Paris: Editions Albin Michel, 1973), 41.

50. Williams, *Klaus Fuchs.*

51. Ronald Radosh and Joyce Milton, *The Rosenberg File* (New York: Vintage Books, 1984). Reproductions of the bomb component illustrations provided by Greenglass can be found in Elinor Langer, "The Case of Morton Sobell: New Queries from the Defense," *Science* (23 September 1966): 1501–1505. Details of the material provided by Greenglass can also be found in Roger M. Anders, "The Rosenberg Case Revisited: The Greenglass Testimony and the Protection of Atomic Secrets," *American Historical Review,* 83, no. 2 (April 1978): 388–400.

52. Chikov, *New Times,* no. 16 (1991): 37.

53. Chikov, *Soyuz,* nos. 22 and 23 (1991).

54. Avraham Shifrin, *The First Guidebook to Prison and Concentration Camps of the Soviet Union* (New York: Bantam Books, 1982), 230–231.

55. Georgi Zhukov, *The Memoirs of Marshal Zhukov* (New York: Delacorte Press, 1961), 674–675.

56. Chikov, *Soyuz,* no. 22 (1991).

57. Smirnov, "How We Made the Bomb."

Chapter 2

1. David Holloway, *Entering the Nuclear Arms Race: The Soviet Decision to Build the Atomic Bomb, 1939–45* (Washington, D.C.: The Wilson Center, 1979), 41.

2. *Foreign Relations of the United States,* 1945, vol. 2 (Washington, D.C.: 1967), 83.

3. Alexander Werth, *Russia at War, 1941–45* (New York: Carrol & Graf, 1964), 1037.

4. Szulc, "How Russia Got the Bomb," 3.

5. The issue of war casualties has remained a sensitive one for the Soviets, even after *glasnost*. The official figure is now put at 27 million, of which 8 million are military losses. However, some Russian historians have argued that the recent official commission cooked the books and lowered the real total of 34 million dead, which was deemed politically unacceptable by higher military officials, especially Marshal Yazov. Western assessments of Soviet war losses indicate that internal Soviet repression, especially the forced population transfers and labor camps, account for more than 8 million dead—the same order of magnitude as military losses. The Soviet military losses include more than 3 million prisoners of war in German POW camps. For the controversy over Soviet official figures, see Fyodor Setin, "How many did we lose in the war?" *New Times,* no. 7 (1990): 46–47. For assessments of Soviet losses, see R. J. Rummel, *Lethal Politics* (New Brunswick, N.J.: Transaction, 1990) and Iosif Dyadkin, *Unnatural Deaths in the USSR, 1928–1954* (New Brunswick, N.J.: Transaction, 1983).

6. Alec Nove, *An Economic History of the USSR* (London: Pelican, 1978), 285.

7. The GULAG population reached its wartime low of 1.1 million prisoners in 1944 due to the pressures to man the army. It increased to 2.5 million in 1950, its peak year. Documentation on GULAG prisoners can be found in A. H. Dugina and A. Malygina, "Solzhenitsin, Rybakov: tekhnologiya lzhi," *Voenno-istoricheskiy zhurnal,* no. 7 (1991): 71–73.

8. For a Soviet appreciation of the military industrial problem see N. Kozlov, *A Study of the Military Technical Supply of the Russian Army in the World War* (Leningrad: Government Military Publications Division, 1926; trans. by Charles Berman for the U.S. Army War College, 1931).

9. For example, the Soviet Union produced 112,000 combat aircraft to Germany's 92,000; 102,000 armored vehicles to Germany's 76,000; and 18.3 million small arms to Germany's 11.6 million. In terms of specific types, the figures are sometimes more dramatic. For example, by avoiding the production of armored cars, infantry vehicles, and self-propelled artillery, the USSR produced 79,000 tanks compared to only 25,000 by Germany. Nearly all of the Soviet aircraft production was combat types, while Germany's production included 17,000 trainers and support aircraft. However, it should be kept in mind that the Soviet advantages in these areas were offset by disadvantages in other areas. Soviet production of warships, military trucks, railroad equipment, and many other critical items virtually disappeared during the war.

10. Since the 1980s, American and British military historians specializing in Soviet tactical doctrine have begun to revitalize the study of Soviet World War II history. A particular focus of these historians has been Soviet concepts of "operational art," a level of military doctrine between tactics and grand strategy fostered by Soviet military thinkers. Other issues examined by this new generation of historians have been the role of tactical and operational intelligence, and its defensive counterpart, *maskirovka* (deception). The leading journal of these scholars is the *Journal of Soviet Military Studies*. A less sympathetic view of Soviet skills can be found in John Ellis, *Brute Force: Allied Strategy and Tactics in the Second World War* (New York: Viking, 1990).

11. In terms of coal, the life-blood of the heavy industries, Germany produced 422 million tons in 1941 compared to 151 million tons in the USSR. In terms of crude steel, German production was 20.8 million tons compared to 17.9 million tons in the USSR, and Soviet utilization was probably less efficient. German automotive production in 1940 was about 350,000 to 145,000 Soviet vehicles. Electricity was 70 billion kwh in 1941 compared to 46 billion in the USSR. The discrepancies were even greater in more advanced sectors of the economy. For example, German aluminum production was over 200,000 tons while Soviet production was less than 50,000.

12. Mark Harrison, *Soviet Planning in Peace and War, 1938–1945* (Cambridge: Cambridge University Press, 1985), 64.

13. Edward Homze, "The Luftwaffe's Failure to Develop a Heavy Bomber before World War II," *Aerospace Historian*, 24, no. 1 (Spring 1977): 20–26.

14. CIA, *A Summary of Soviet Guided Missile Intelligence* (US/UK GM 4-52, 20 July 1953), J-1.

15. For a recent assessment of the impact of strategic bombing on Germany, see Alfred Mierzejewski, *The Collapse of the German War Economy, 1944–1945* (Chapel Hill: University of North Carolina, 1988).

16. There has never been an adequate unclassified study of the postwar Soviet strategic defense program. For a short summary of the program, but one which focuses mainly on the missile programs of the 1950s, see Steven Zaloga, *Soviet Air Defense Missiles: Design, Development and Tactics* (Coulsdon, U.K.: Jane's, 1989).

17. Vojtech Mastny, *Russia's Road to the Cold War* (New York: Columbia University Press, 1979).

18. Andrew and Gordievskiy, *KGB*, 367.

19. There are dozens of fine studies on the origins of the Cold War. For a very succinct and pungent assessment, see the recent study by William Hyland, *The Cold War: Fifty Years of Conflict* (New York: Random House, 1991).

20. Costs associated with the atomic bomb program were estimated by the CIA to be 270 million rubles in 1946, rising to 7.5 billion rubles in 1950. This later figure would indicate that the program absorbed over 2 percent of the total Soviet GNP. Estimates of program costs and workforce size can be found in CIA, *National Intelligence Survey: USSR, Section 73, Atomic Energy* (NIS 26, January 1951).

21. Ustinov is well known in the Soviet Union since he went on to head the Ministry of Defense in the late Brezhnev years until his death in 1984. However, his wartime role is little known in the West due to the lack of attention paid to the role of the defense industries in the wartime victory.

22. David Irving, *The German Atomic Bomb* (London: Wm. Kimber, 1967); Mark Walker, *German National Socialism and the Quest for Nuclear Power, 1939–1949* (Cambridge: Cambridge University Press, 1989). For an illuminating debate on why the German program failed see "The Nazis and the Atom Bomb: An Exchange," *The New York Review of Books,* 27 June 1991, 62–64.

23. SVAG was the acronym for *Sovetskaya voennaya administratsiya-Germanii* (Soviet Military Administration-Germany). Two senior officials, both generals in the NKVD, were assigned the special responsibility for overseeing NKVD interests in the technological plunder: V. M. Nikoforov and M. Z. Saburov.

24. CIA, *The Problem of Uranium Isotope Separation by Means of Ultracentrifuge in the USSR* (EG-1802, 22 May 1957), 6.

25. Walker, *German National Socialism,* 184–185.

26. The name First Circle stems from Dante's descriptions in "Inferno" of the descending levels of hell. The term has become widely accepted for the network of *sharashki* and other special camps due to Aleksandr Solzhenitsyn's classic autobiographical novel of the GULAG, *The First Circle.*

27. The letter *G* in the bureau name stems from the fact that in Russian, there is no exact equivalent to *H. G* is used instead, so in Russian it is *Gertz* rather than Hertz, or *Gitler* rather than Hitler.

28. Robert Wilcox, *Japan's Secret War: Japan's Race Against Time to Build Its Own Atomic Bomb* (New York: Wm. Morrow, 1985).

29. GHQ, Far East Command, "Monazite Production in North Korea," *Far East Command Intelligence Digest,* no. 12 (2 December 1951): 12–16.

30. I. N. Golovin, *I. V. Kurchatov* (Bloomington, Ind.: Selbstverlag Press, 1968), 46.

31. R. Savushkin, "In the Tracks of a Tragedy," *The Journal of Soviet Military Studies,* 4 (June 1991): 235.

32. R. Lamphere and T. Shachtman, *The FBI-KGB War, A Special Agent's Story* (New York: Random House, 1986).

33. The U.S. Army found that it took eighteen times more conventional 90mm ammunition to down an aircraft than when using the VT fuze, even if the gun firing the conventional ammunition was radar directed. See *Air Defense: An Historical Analysis,* vol. 2 (Ft. Bliss, Texas: U.S. Army Air Defense School, 1965), 142–143, 146.

34. The best account of the Rosenberg case mentions the proximity fuze but fails to appreciate its significance. See Radosh and Milton, *The Rosenberg File,* 72. For an account of the proximity fuze during the war, see Ralph Baldwin, *The Deadly Fuze* (Novato, Calif.: Presidio Press, 1980).

35. The two engineers were Alfred Sarant and Joel Barr, who took the names F. G. Staros and J. B. Berg after their defections. See Henry Eric Firdman, *Decision Making in the Soviet Microelectronics Industry: The Leningrad Design Bureau, A Case Study* (Falls Church, Va.: Delphic Associates, 1985). Recent Russian accounts of the case have begun appearing in the technical journal *Inzhener.* See Va. Zavodinskiy, "U istokov novoi tekhnologii," *Inzhener,* no. 4 (1991): 2–4; and Yu. Ivashchenko, "Nevostrebovanniy intellekt," *Inzhener,* nos. 9 and 10 (1991).

36. H. M. Hyde, *The Atom Bomb Spies* (New York: Ballantine Books, 1981).

37. Andrew and Gordievskiy, *KGB,* 318.

38. Verne Newton, *The Cambridge Spies: The Untold Story of Maclean, Philby and Burgess in America* (Lanham Md.: Madison Books, 1990).

39. CIA, NIS 26, 73-19.

40. N. Khrushchev, *Khrushchev Remembers: The Glasnost Tapes* (New York: Little, Brown & Co., 1990), 194. In 1991, when asked to see the Rosenberg files at KGB headquarters in Moscow, a spokesman claimed that the files could not be found. It is not clear if this was due to the destruction of Beria's personal files after his execution in 1953 or their extreme degree of compartmentalization. See Uri Dan, "KGB Claims It Has No Record of Rosenbergs," *New York Post,* 25 November 1991, 5.

41. Chikov, "Soviet Intelligence Service," 37.

42. Jonathan Helmreich, *Gathering Rare Ores: The Diplomacy of Uranium Acquisition, 1943–54* (Princeton, N.J.: Princeton University Press, 1986). Most accounts of U.S. perceptions of the Soviet bomb program suggest that General Groves's skepticism was due to his belief that the Soviets lacked sufficient uranium deposits. However, a forthcoming book by Prof. Charles Ziegler of Brandeis University argues otherwise. Based on recently declassified material, Ziegler notes that Groves was aware of Soviet deposits but believed the ore to be of a very low grade. Assuming that the Soviet techniques were no better than American techniques for extracting uranium from low-grade ore, Groves predicted that it would take about ten years for the

Soviets to accumulate enough uranium for a single bomb. Groves underestimated the quality of Soviet deposits, as well as Soviet skill in developing better methods for extraction.

43. In yet another shake-up of the internal security organizations, in 1946 the NKVD became the MVD (Ministry of Internal Affairs) and the NKGB became the MGB (Ministry of State Security). In 1954, the MGB was renamed the KGB (Committee for State Security), a name which it has retained until this day.

44. Shifrin, *Guidebook to Prisons and Concentration Camps,* 230–231, 366. The initial mines in the Fergana Valley were located at Fergana, Tuya-Muyun, Uygur-Say, Mayly-Say, Chust, and Osh. They were mainly arid land deposits containing tyuyamunite and carnotite similar to the Colorado plateau deposits in the United States. A second set of deposits of the polymetallic and fissure-vein type was found in the Kara Mazar, with facilities at Taboshar, Adrasman, and Kansay.

45. CIA, NIS 26, 73-2.

46. Kramish, *Atomic Energy,* 112–113.

47. CIA, NIS 26, 73-6.

48. A. P. Aleksandrov. ed., *I. V. Kurchatov: izbrannie trudy v trekh tomakh, Tom 3—Yadernaya energiya* (Moscow: Nauka, 1984), 73.

49. Nikishin, "They Awakened the Genie," 8.

50. L. Nechayuk, "V gorode, u kotorogo net imeni," *Krasnaya Zvezda,* 19 October 1990.

51. T. B. Cochran and R. S. Norris, *Soviet Nuclear Warhead Production* (Washington, D.C.: National Resources Defense Council, 1990).

52. *Zek* is the Soviet slang word for a GULAG prisoner. Data presented here on Kyshtym comes primarily from declassified CIA reports which have been sanitized to the point that precise bibliographic data is lacking. The main source is a 1961 CIA plant summary report, IR Firm No. 8014401. Some of these documents are reprinted in Zhores A. Medvedev, *Nuclear Disaster in the Urals* (New York: Vintage Books, 1980).

53. Zhores Medvedev, *The Legacy of Chernobyl* (New York: Norton, 1990), 227.

54. I. Golovin, "The First Soviet A-Bomb," *Science in the USSR,* no. 6 (1990): 40.

55. A rem is a unit for measuring absorbed doses of radiation. Estimates for a dose likely to be fatal to half those exposed to it range from 250 to 600 rem. A study of the radiation exposure of Soviet nuclear workers in the late 1940s and early 1950s can be found in B. V. Nikipelov, et. al., "Opyt pervogo predpriyatiya atomnoy promyshlennosti," *Priroda,* no. 2 (1990): 30–38.

56. Cochran and Norris, *Soviet Warhead Production,* 20.

57. V. Beletskaya, "Ogonek Correspondent Vanda Beletskaya Talks with Academician Anatoliy Petrovich Aleksandrov," *Ogonek*, no. 35 (August 1990) (trans. JPRS-UST-90-012, 26).

58. A. Tarasov and D. Khrupov, "Spy satellites are made here: Report from a closed city," *Izvestiya*, 11 January 1992 (trans. JPRS-UMA-92-005, 12 February 1992, 71–72).

59. Moscow TASS Radio Broadcast, 09:18 GMT, 6 December 1990 (trans. FBIS-SOV-90-240, 13 December 1990, 63).

60. Zernov at the time was assistant minister of the Ministry of Transport Machinery Production. His appointment was typical of Soviet program management, teaming a scientist with an engineer with administrative background.

61. Yu. Chernyshev, "Nam dali vsego 5 let, k istorii sozdaniya pervoi sovetskoi atomnoi bomby," *Inzhener,* no. 12 (1991): 35.

62. The first public mention of this facility appeared in *Komsomolskaya Pravda* on 25 November, followed by another report in *Pravitelsyvenniy Vestnik* in December 1990.

63. Similar experiments at Los Alamos led to one of the few deaths of a scientist working on the program.

64. Vladimir Gubarev, "Nuclear Trace," *Pravda,* 25 August 1989, 1, 4 (trans. in JPRS-TND-89-021, 6 November 1989).

65. Smirnov, "How We Made the Bomb," 59.

66. Anatoliy Sonin, "How the A-Bomb Saved Soviet Physicists' Lives," *Moscow News,* no. 13 (1990): 16. Mathematicians were not so lucky. Boolean algebra and other advanced fields were deemed "idealistic" and otherwise unacceptable, leading to early delays in Soviet efforts to develop digital computers.

67. In fact, the new Tu-4 bomber, a copy of the American B-29, *could* lift such a weight. Probably the Soviet scientists, like their American counterparts in the Manhattan Project, believed that a ground-based test would reduce the chances for minor accidents spoiling the test.

68. By odd coincidence, the American bombs were also referred to as pumpkins, but because the bomb test casings were painted bright orange.

69. Gubarev, "Nuclear Trace," 15.

70. Igor Golovin, "A Crucial Moment," *Science in the USSR* (January-February 1991): 21.

Chapter 3
1. K. N. Finne, *Igor Sikorsky: The Russian Years* (Washington, D.C.: Smithsonian Institution, 1987).

2. Peter Korrell, *TB-3: Die Geschichte eines Bombers* (Berlin: Transpress, 1987).

3. In 1937 Tupolev reorganized his design bureau into separate elements.

KB-1 (Design Bureau-1), headed by Vladimir Petlyakov, was responsible for the ANT-42/TB-7 heavy bomber. KB-2, headed by A. P. Golubkov, was assigned a long-range, high-speed amphibious naval bomber. KB-3, headed by Pavel Sukhoy, was assigned the design of a high-speed attack aircraft, code-named Ivanov, which would later emerge as the Su-2. See G. P. Svishchev, et al., *Andrey Nikolayevich Tupolev: Grani derznovennogo tvorchestva* (Moscow: Nauka, 1988), 140.

4. Col. Yu. Tarasov, "Generalniy konstruktor," *Aviatsiya i kosmonavtika* (November 1988): 35. TsKB-29 later was transferred to the basement of KOSOS—*Konstruktorskiy otdel sektora opitnogo samoletostroyeniya*-TsAGI (Designers' unit of the experimental aircraft manufacturing sector of TsAGI) on Radio and Saltykovskaya streets. See A. Ponomarev, "Tu: Chelovek i samolety," *Krasnaya Zvezda,* 29 October 1988, 4.

5. I. Shelest, "Muzhestvo," *Krylya Rodiny* (November 1988): 24–26.

6. A history of the Red Air Force's strategic bomber force can be found in V. A. Vasilev, *Long Range, Missile-Equipped* (Washington, D.C.: U.S. Air Force, 1979).

7. Howard Moon, *Soviet SST: The Techno-politics of the Tupolev-144* (New York: Orion Books, 1989), 24.

8. Joan Beaumont, *Comrades in Arms: British Aid to Russia, 1941–1945* (London: Davis-Poynter, 1980), 190.

9. Steve Birdsall, *Superfortress: The Boeing B-29* (Carrollton, Tex: Squadron/ Signal, 1980), 77.

10. Otis Hays, *Home from Siberia: The Secret Odysseys of Interned American Airmen in World War II* (College Station: Texas A&M Press, 1990).

11. There is some dispute as to the reasons for the ouster of Novikov and Shakhurin. Traditional accounts, such as Khorobrykh's biography of Novikov, have attributed the imprisonment to delays in early Russian fighter efforts such as the MiG-9 and Yak-15. But recent accounts of the Tu-4 effort indicate that it was this program that was at the center of the trial. See L. Kerber & M. Saukke, "Ne kopiya, a analog: o samolete Tu-4," *Krylya Rodiny* (January 1989): 24–25 and (February 1989): 33–34; also A. M. Khorobykh, *Glavniy marshal aviatsii A. A. Novikov* (Moscow: Voenizdat, 1989), 267–268.

12. V. Suvorov, *The Liberators: Inside the Soviet Army* (London: Hamish-Hamilton, 1981), 128–129.

13. J. Nowicki and K. Ziecina, "Superkopia—superfortrecy," *Skrzydlata Polska,* no. 28 (9 July 1989): 12.

14. In 1947 the strategic aviation branch of the Soviet Air Force had 1,839 aircraft. However, only thirty-two were Pe-8 heavy bombers. The rest were medium Il-4 bombers, Lend-Lease medium bombers like the American B-25, and transport aircraft like the Li-2. See L. M. Sandalov, "Grif sekretnosti snyat—otkuda ugroza," *Voenno-istoricheskiy zhurnal,* no. 2 (1989): 24.

15. A. N. Ponomarev, *Sovetskie aviatsionnie konstruktory* (Moscow: Voenizdat, 1977), 36.

16. M. M. Lobanov, *Razvitie sovetskoi radiolokatsionnoi tekhniki* (Moscow: Voenizdat, 1982), 209. Work on the adaption of the American AN/APQ-13 radar bombsight was undertaken by a development institute under A. I. Kochmar and Ya. B. Shapirovskiy.

17. N. A. Grigoreva, *Radiolyubitel inzhener general* (Moscow: DOSAAF, 1985), 73.

18. Jean Alexander, *Russian Aircraft since 1940* (London: Putnam, 1975), 359.

19. CIA, *Soviet Capabilities for Attack on the U.S. through 1957* (SNIE 11-2-54, 24 February 1954), 3.

20. C. L. Grant, *The Development of Continental Air Defense to 1 September 1954* (Maxwell AFB, Ala.: USAF Historical Division, 1957), 7.

21. Timothy Osato, *Militia Missilemen: The Army National Guard in Air Defense, 1951–1967* (Washington, D.C.: Office of the Chief of Military History, 1968), 7.

22. The combat radius of a Tu-4 with a normal 5-ton bomb load was estimated at 1,700 nautical miles and a range of 3,100 nautical miles. This presumed that it maintained an optimal cruising speed of about 175 knots while flying at about 10,000 feet. Its range would have been substantially less with a larger payload, or at higher speeds, or if the attack profile was at a lower altitude intending to skirt under the Pinetree radar network. See *CIA, Soviet Capabilities for Attack on the United States through Mid-1955* (SE-36/1, 31 July 1953), 3.

23. Joint Intelligence Committee, *Magnitude and Imminence of Soviet Air Threat to the United States* (JCS 1924/95, 20 October 1953), 1206.

24. The fact that the Soviet Air Force had tested aerial refueling was disclosed as early as 1973 by one of the test pilots, Igor Shelest, in his memoirs *Lechu za mechtoi* (Moscow: Molodaya Gvardia, 1973). The first significant details appeared later in O. Alekseyev, "Perviy shag k paritetu," *Krylya Rodiny*, no. 4 (1989): 22–24. Operational details regarding the number of aircraft actually converted for tanker and refueling missions is still secret.

25. D. Harvey and V. Giroux, *Seventy Years of Strategic Air Refueling, 1918–1988* (Offutt AFB, Neb.: HQ, Strategic Air Command, 1990).

26. Zernov survived the incident. Y. Golovanov, "The Portrait Gallery," *Poisk*, 15–21 February 1990 (trans. in JPRS-UST-90-006, 31 May 1990, 90).

27. Stephen E. Ambrose, "Secrets of the Cold War," *New York Times*, 27 December 1990.

28. SNIE 11-2-54, 7.

29. B. Bruce Briggs, *The Shield of Faith: The Hidden Struggle for Strategic Defense* (New York: Simon & Schuster, 1988), 46–80.

30. Roy S. Barnard, *The History of the Army Air Defense Command: The Gun Era* (Washington, D.C.: HQ, ARADCOM, 1970), 132.

31. J. C. Hopkins and S. A. Goldberg, *The Development of Strategic Air Command, 1946–86* (Offutt AFB, Neb.: Office of the Historian, HQ, SAC, 1986), 42.

32. T. Cochran, W. Arkin, and M. Hoenig, *U.S. Nuclear Forces and Capabilities,* vol. 1 (Cambridge, Mass.: Ballinger, 1984), 15.

33. S. Zaloga, "The Russians in MiG Alley," *Air Force* (February 1991).

34. G. Lobov, "V nebe severnoi Korei," *Aviatsiya i Kosmonavtika,* no. 11 (1990): 31.

35. John Prados, *The Soviet Estimate: U.S. Intelligence Analysis and Russian Military Strength* (New York: Dial Press, 1982), 41–42.

36. CIA, *Main Trends in Soviet Capabilities and Policies, 1957–62* (NIE 11-4-57, 12 November 1957), 33.

37. Defense Intelligence Agency, *Intercontinental Strategic Forces Summary, USSR* (DDB-2680-253-85, August 1985), 7.

38. Boeing had proposed using turboprops in its 1946–48 design concepts for the U.S. Air Force strategic bomber program, but switched to turbojets by 1949. This resulted in the famous B-52 Stratofortress bomber. A subsequent design study for a heavy bomber in 1949, the Model 474/XB-55, had also contemplated turboprops as an option, but judged existing American turboprops to be insufficient for the task. See M. S. Knaak, *Encyclopedia of U.S. Air Force Aircraft and Missile Systems,* vol. 2, *Post–World War II Bombers, 1945-1973* (Washington, D.C.: Office of Air Force History, 1988), 208–209.

39. CIA, *Soviet Capabilities for Attack on the U.S. through 1957* (SNIE 11-2-54, 24 February 1954).

40. There is extensive and detailed study of American intelligence estimates and their problems during this period. See, for example, Lawrence Freedman, *U.S. Intelligence and the Soviet Strategic Threat* (Princeton, N.J.: Princeton University Press, 1986); John Prados, *The Soviet Estimate;* Raymond Garthoff, *Assessing the Adversary: Estimates by the Eisenhower Administration of Soviet Intentions and Capabilities* (Washington, D.C.: Brookings Institution, 1991).

41. Curtis Peebles, *The Moby Dick Project: Reconnaissance Balloons over Russia* (Washington, D.C.: Smithsonian Institution, 1991).

42. CIA, *Main Trends in Soviet Capabilities and Policies, 1957–62* (NIE 11-4-57), 33.

Chapter 4

1. Golovanov, "The Portrait Gallery."

2. These yield figures refer to an explosion comparable in energy to that of a given weight of TNT. A yield of 15 kilotons means an explosion equivalent to 15,000 tons of high explosives. By way of comparison, the U.S. atomic bombs dropped on Hiroshima and Nagasaki had yields of 15 and 21 kilotons.

3. The U.S. electromagnetic separation facility was the Oak Ridge Alpha calutron network. Due to shortages of copper during the war, the coils of the electromagnets were wound with silver—some 13,540 tons of it worth $300 million. The U.S. Treasury insisted on recovery of the silver after the war.

4. Vincent C. Jones, *Manhattan: The Army and the Atomic Bomb* (Washington, D.C.: Center for Military History, 1985).

5. The Smyth report was the first official unclassified report on the Manhattan Project published in the United States. It provided a broad look at the program, with significant detail on the various isotope separation approaches. See Henry DeWolf Smyth, *Atomic Energy for Military Purposes: The Official Report on the Development of the Atomic Bomb under the Auspices of the United States Government, 1940–45* (Princeton, N.J.: Princeton University Press, 1945).

6. CIA, *Status of the Soviet Atomic Energy Program* (SCI 2/50, 4 July 1950), 3.

7. CIA, *The Problem of Uranium Isotope Separation by Means of Ultracentrifuge in the USSR* (EG 1802, 22 May 1957).

8. *Ibid.,* 32. For his role in the effort, Kikoin received the prestigious Hero of Socialist Labor decoration, and a State Prize in 1951. See Logunov, *Isaak Konstantinovich Kikoin,* 4.

9. Some mark of their friendship can be found in the fact that in 1981, when the Soviet Academy of Sciences wanted to publish a small booklet on Artsimovich, Steenbeck, long since having returned to Germany, gladly penned a short essay as evidence of their friendship. See Kadomtsev, *Reminiscences about Artsimovich,* 26–29.

10. CIA, *Status of the Soviet Atomic Energy Program,* SI 13-52, 8 January 1953, 11.

11. Jeffrey Sands, R. S. Norris, and T. Cochran, *Known Soviet Nuclear Explosions 1949–1985: Preliminary List* (Washington, D.C.: Natural Resources Defense Council, 1986), 11.

12. Andrei Sakharov, *Memoirs* (New York: Knopf, 1990), 94.

13. Research into deuterium production in the USSR began in the prewar years, originally tied to other nuclear physics research such as a heavy-water–moderated nuclear reactor. A small-scale deuterium oxide (heavy water) system using electrolysis was installed by the Pisarzhevskiy Institute of Physical Chemistry at Dnepropetrovsk. A larger scale effort began in 1940 at the Chirchik Nitrogen Plant near Tashkent, but production was stymied by the outbreak of the war. Following the occupation of Germany in 1945, the German scientists of the Leuna Works at Merseberg were put under Soviet MVD control. In October 1946, they were tranferred to a research facility at Babushkin examining alternative production methods. The German contribution proved unimportant after 1946, as the Soviets began to modify several synthetic ammonia plants to produce deuterium by electrolysis. Production of suitable electrodes began at the Urals Chemical Machine Factory near Sverdlovsk in October 1946. Electrolytic cells were first installed at the Chirchik Nitrogen Plant, going into operation in 1948. This was followed by the installation of electrolytic hydrogen cells at three other plants, which went into operation in the early 1950s. Other applications for the deuterium produced by these plants included the fabrication of a heavy-water–moderated pile, the experimental TVR at Laboratory 3, the Institute of Theoretical Physics in Moscow, which first went critical in April 1949. It is unclear whether the Soviets ever intended to use the deuterium oxide for a "wet" hydrogen bomb of similar conception to the first American thermonuclear bomb of 1952. In the event, the first Soviet hydrogen bomb used lithium deuteride (lithium-6) in a "dry" bomb configuration.

14. In August 1990, the Soviet science journal *Priroda* published a special issue devoted to Andrei Sakharov, which contained more detailed notes on the early fusion bomb than Sakharov's own memoirs, especially the articles by V. E. Ritus and Yu. A. Romanov.

15. Sakharov, *Memoirs,* 135.

16. James Hansen, "The Kremlin Follies of '53 . . . the Demise of Lavrenti Beria," *International Journal of Intelligence and Counterintelligence,* 4, no. 1 (Spring 1990): 101–114.

17. Ye. Klimchuk, "How Beriya Was Tried and Executed," *Soviet Soldier,* no. 5 (1990): 59.

18. Herbert York, *The Advisors: Oppenheimer, Teller and the Superbomb* (Palo Alto: Stanford University Press, 1989). See also D. Hirsch and W. Matthews, "The H-Bomb: Who really gave away the secret?" *Bulletin of the Atomic Scientists* (February 1990) and the letter to the editor response in the November 1990 issue, 45–46.

19. Joint Intelligence Committee, *Magnitude of Soviet Air Threat,* 1210.

20. What might have been learned from the samples is discussed in detail in Lars-Erik De Geer, "The Radioactive Signature of the Hydrogen Bomb," *Science & Global Security,* 2 (1991): 351–363.

21. By 1957 the Soviet Union had about 45,000 scientists with the *kandidat* degree (equivalent to the Ph.D.), compared to 37,000 Americans in the physical sciences and engineering with doctorates. This scientific manpower was the result of a major effort in the postwar years to build up the Soviet Union's scientific workforce. It was far more heavily committed to the defense

effort than was the case with its American counterpart. It is unclear that sheer numbers are an adequate measure of the scientific potential, but the Soviet potential was far stronger than in 1945. See CIA, *Main Trends in Soviet Capabilities and Policies, 1958–1963* (NIE 11-4-58, 23 December 1958): 1920.

22. Steven Zaloga and James Grandsen, *Soviet Tanks and Combat Vehicles of World War II* (London: Arms & Armour Press, 1984).

23. Iosif Zorich, "Victim of his Principles," *Science in the USSR* (May-June 1991): 100–103.

24. CIA, SCI 2/50, 5.

25. For a history of early Soviet computers, see A. Kondalev, "In the World of Science: Information, Reexamination and Prospects," *Pod Znamen Leninizma,* no. 20 (October 1989) (trans. JPRS-UST-90-002, 6–12).

Chapter 5

1. The RNII also had a military designation: NII-3 NKOP—Scientific Research Institute-3, State Commissariat for Defense Production. The history of the early Soviet rocket teams is covered in many Soviet accounts of the Soviet space program. A good English language account can be found in Frank H. Winter, *Prelude to the Space Age, The Rocket Societies: 1924–1940* (Washington, D.C.: Smithsonian Institution, 1983). More detailed articles on individual aspects of the rocket programs can be found in the essay collections of the American Astronautical Society's History Series, *History of Rocketry and Astronautics,* particularly volumes 6, 7, and 9. See especially I. A. Merkulov, "Organization and Results of the Work of the First Scientific Centers for Rocket Technology in the USSR," *History of Rocketry and Astronautics,* vol. 9 (San Diego: American Astronautical Association Publications, 1989), 63–77.

2. Mikhail Tsypkin, *"The Origins of Soviet Military Research and Development, 1917–1941,"* Ph.D. Diss., Harvard University, 1985, 183–233.

3. M. Rebrov, "Udelnyi impuls: stranitsy iz zhizni Generalnogo konstruktora V. P. Glushko," *Krasnaya Zvezda,* 26 August 1989, 4.

4. Kostikov's role in the decimation of the RNII was the source of lasting bitterness to the later heads of the Soviet space program. Especially galling was the fact that Kostikov was given credit for the rocket weapons pioneered by the RNII before he was a worker in the institute. Recent revelations in the case can be found in N. L. Anisimov and V. G. Oppokov, "Proisshestvie v NII-3," *Voenno-istoricheskiy zhurnal,* no. 10 (1989): 81–87; and no. 11 (1989): 65–71. See also I. I. Kleimenova, "Proisshestviya posle Proisshestviya," *Voenno-istoricheskiy zhurnal,* no. 3 (1991), 78–81.

5. Aleksandr Romanov, *Korolev* (Moscow: Molodaya Gvardiya, 1990), 138.

6. Robert Conquest, *Kolyma: The Arctic Death Camps* (Oxford: Oxford University Press, 1979).

7. Although there are many Soviet biographies of Korolev, until recently his wartime experiences were omitted or sanitized. One of the more detailed recent accounts is in A. Yu. Ishlinskiy, ed., *Akademik S. P. Korolev: ucheniy, inzhener, chelovek* (Moscow: Nauka, 1986). A more candid treatment is offered by an émigré Soviet science writer in Leonid Vladimirov, *The Russian Space Bluff* (London: Tom Stacey Ltd., 1973).

8. M. Rebrov, "Lider: maloizvestnye stranitsy iz zhizni S. P. Koroleva," *Krasnaya Zvezda*, 1 July 1989, 4.

9. Besides attempts at rocket assistance for fighter aircraft, there was also a ramjet program and a pulse-jet program. The ramjet programs have been amply dealt with, even in English. See F. C. Durant, ed., *The First Steps Toward Space* (San Diego: American Astronautical Society Publications, 1985), 167–184 and Richard Hallion, "Soviet Stovepipes," *Air Enthusiast*, no. 9 (1979).

10. Soviet wartime artillery rocket development has been covered in dozens of Russian language accounts. See, for example, V. N. Novikova, *Oruzhie pobedi* (Moscow: Mashinostroenie, 1985), 98–126. For an English language survey see Steven J. Zaloga, "Soviet Rocket Artillery," *Military Journal*, 1, nos. 2 and 4 (1977).

11. F. S. Alymov, ed., *Zagadki zvezdnikh ostrovov*, vol. 3 (Moscow: Molodaya Gvardiy, 1986), 114.

12. Khorobykh, *Glavniy marshal aviatsii A. A. Novikov*, 222.

13. Chelomey had been working since 1942 at TsIAM, the Central Aviation Propulsion Institute, on the pulse-jet idea as a possible source of auxiliary power for propeller driven aircraft. See A. I. Shakhurin, *Krylya pobedy* (Moscow: Politizdat, 1983), 196.

14. The Soviets have not yet published a comprehensive account of their wartime guided missile programs. A brief description of this project appeared in Valeriy Rodikov, "Pod shifrom 10Kh," *Tekhnika Molodezhi*, no. 6 (1985), and in V. Shcherbakov, ed., *Zagadki zvezdnikh ostrovov* (Moscow: Molodaya Gvardiya, 1987), 80–81.

15. Rodikov, "Pod Shifrom 10Kh," 35. The literal translation of the missile designation is 10Kh, the Cyrillic letter "Kh" resembling the Roman X. The X translation has been used here, as Chelomey's missiles were unofficially called the "Iks" (X) series. See also V. Rodikov, "Iksy Vladimira Chelomeya," *Krylya Rodiny*, no. 8 (1989): 6–7.

16. The most detailed account of Chelomey's early cruise missile efforts appears in F. S. Alymov, ed., *Zagadki zvezdnikh ostrovov*, 5. The photos in the book show the later 14Kh and 16Kh missiles, both of which are obviously derivatives of the German V-1.

17. The British mistake was based on the fact that test versions of the V-2 *did* use a radio command link. But the actual weapons used against England used only inertial guidance, making them unjammable.

18. Frederick Ordway and Mitchell Sharpe, *The Rocket Team* (Cambridge, Mass.: MIT, 1982), 158.

19. *Raketa* is often mistranslated into English as rocket. In fact, a more appropriate translation is missile. A rocket in English refers to a reactive propulsion system which contains an integral oxidant as well as fuel; a missile is a guided projectile using either rocket or jet propulsion. *Raketa* is used in the latter sense in Russian, since non-rocket–powered devices are called *raketa*, for example, jet-powered cruise missiles (*krylata raketa*).

20. G. Tyulin, "The 'Seven' Years—Accomplishments, People," *Krasnaya Zvezda*, 1 April 1989, 3–4 (trans. JPRS-UMA-89-013, 55–61).

21. George Cully, "A Kind of Déjà Vu: Some Historical Perspectives on Cruise Missile Defense," *Airpower Journal* (Spring 1990): 47–60; Roland Beamont, "Defence against Flying Bombs," *Putnam Aeronautical Review* (June 1990): 75–82.

22. The principal members at the time were G. A. Tyulin (a rocket artillery officer and liaison with the army artillery branch); V. P. Glushko (rocket engine specialist); V. P. Barmin (Katyusha launcher designer and head of the Kompressor Factory artillery rocket design group after the removal of Kostikov in 1944); M. S. Ryazanskiy and V. I. Kuznetsov (missile guidance); and E. Ya. Boguslavskiy. See Romanov, *Korolev*, 183.

23. For a sense of the German attitudes towards the Russians in the last months of the war, see Erich Kuby, *The Russians and Berlin 1945* (New York: Ballantine, 1969).

24. Ordway and Sharpe, *The Rocket Team*, 307.

25. Romanov, *Korolev*, 187–88.

26. CIA, *Scientific Research Institute and Experimental Factory 88 for Guided Missile Development, Moskva/Kaliningrad* (OSI C-RA/60-2, 4 March 1960).

27. Germany was prohibited from the test and manufacture of many types of weapons by the Versailles Treaty ending the First World War. In the 1920s, the Germans worked out an arrangement with the Soviets, providing the Soviets with military technology in return for allowing the German army, the *Reichswehr*, to develop and test new weapons secretly in the Soviet Union. See Willi Esser, *Dokumentation uber die Entwicklung und Erprobung der ersten Panzerkampfwagen der Reichswehr* (Munich: Krauss-Maffei, 1979).

28. The GAU (*Glavnoye artilleriskoye upravleniye* or Main Artillery Directorate) was headed by Gen. N. D. Yakovlev at the time, and traced its ancestry back to a Tsarist organization of the same name. It was one of the oldest and most prestigious organizations in the Tsarist, and later Red, Army.

29. The new bureau was code-named OKB-1 by the military, but was more popularly known as the Korolev OKB or TsKBEM (*Tsentralnoye konstruktorskoye biuro eksperimentalnogo mashinostroitelstva* or Central Experimental Design

Bureau of Machine Manufacturing). One of the more detailed accounts of this design bureau from the civilian viewpoint is offered by an émigré who worked in the ablative materials section. See Viktor Yevsikov, *Re-entry Technology and the Soviet Space Program* (Falls Church, Va.: Delphic Associates, 1982).

30. Following the debriefing of returning German scientists in the mid-1950s by U.S. intelligence agencies, a top secret interagency study was prepared under the auspices of the CIA as *A Summary of Soviet Guided Missile Intelligence.* It was downgraded to secret in 1975, and declassified in 1978. A more readily available account of the activities of the German scientists, which combines the CIA study with later German autobiographical accounts, can be found in Ordway and Sharpe's excellent study, *The Rocket Team.*

31. Irene Sanger-Bredt, "The Silver Bird, A Memoir," *History of Rocketry and Astronautics,* vol. 7, part 1 (San Diego: American Astronautical Society, 1986).

32. "O silovoi ustanovke stratosfernogo sverkhskorostnogo samoleta." The summary of the report is reprinted in V. S. Aleksandrov, ed., *M. V. Keldysh: izbrannie trudy, raketnaya tekhnika i kosmonavtika* (Moscow: Nauka, 1988), 22–34.

33. Those present at the meeting included M. V. Khrunichev, the minister of the aviation industry; Col. Gen. A. Yakovlev, the wartime aviation industry leader and fighter designer; Artem Mikoyan, a fighter designer soon to become famous for his MiG fighters; and Lt. Gen. Timofey Kutsevalov, the head of the air force department of the Soviet Military Administration in occupied Germany. G. A. Tokady-Tokayev, *Comrade X* (London: Harvill Press, 1956), 312.

34. The STK-2 commission, also called the PKRDD (State Commission on Intercontinental Missiles) was headed by Col. Gen. I. A. Serov, Beria's first deputy chairman of the NKVD special police, and also included Gen. Maj. V. I. Stalin, son of Joseph Stalin. STK-2 was formed on the basis of an existing state commission (*Goskomitet*) under Serov responsible for overseeing the ballistic missile program. The principal engineers added to STK-2 were G. A. Tokady-Tokayev of the Soviet Air Force, Prof. M. V. Keldysh, postwar head of the RNII, and Prof. M. A. Kishkin.

35. Tokady-Tokayev, *Comrade X,* 319.

36. Following his defection, G. A. Tokady-Tokayev gave numerous speeches and interviews, and wrote several books on his experiences in Soviet missile development. A good overview of his efforts can be found in: G. A. Tokady-Tokayev, "Surveying Soviet Space Technology," *The Aeroplane and Astronautics,* 28 September 1961. The details of his defection can be found in his *Comrade X.*

37. Dennis Newkirk, "Soviet Space Planes," *Spaceflight,* 32 (October 1990): 350–355.

38. There has been some uncertainty regarding the first launch date, with some Soviet sources stating 10 October, others 18 October. The date of 18 October is now generally accepted. See Ye. Bokhanov, "Pervaya ballisticheskaya," *Krasnaya Zvezda,* 18 October 1987.

39. The accounts by Germans who witnessed the launchings mention twenty launchings, but Soviet accounts list eleven, with the last on 12 November. The discrepancy may be due to the fact that the Soviets counted only successful launches. See Lt. Gen. G. Tyulin, "The 'Seven' Years."

40. "Slagayemie kosmicheskogo podviga," *Krasnaya Zvezda,* 13 January 1987.

41. M. Rebrov, "Sovet glavnykh," *Krasnaya Zvezda*, 8 April 1989. Details of the roles played by these chief designers have been provided in a recent series of articles in *Krasnaya Zvezda,* all by Colonel Rebrov. "Delo na zavtra" (V. P. Barmin), 22 October 1988; "Sem likov sudbi" (V. I. Kuznetsov), 7 January 1989; "Sutki pered startom" (N. A. Pilyugin), 25 February 1989; "Marcianskikh morei belizna" (M. S. Ryazanskiy), 11 March 1989.

42. One of the few areas where these programs led to actual results was in scientific rockets. Increasing interest in upper atmospheric and meteorological research led to the development of a series of small sounding rockets in the late 1940s for the Academy of Sciences. The first of these, the MR-1, was test fired in 1949 and led to a succession of other types. These rockets were used primarily by the TsAO (*Tsentralnaya aerologicheskaya observatroria*) of the Soviet Weather Service, and the Academy of Sciences. See V. Mishin ed., "Pervie meteorologicheskie," *Tekhnika Molodezhi,* no. 6 (1981): 41.

43. The RVGK is the artillery force's high command reserve, controlling all long-range artillery. Until the formation of the Strategic Missile Forces in 1959, the RVGK controlled all Soviet Army ballistic missile units. The 23d Brigade is covered in Col. A. Belousov, "They were conceived at Kapustin Yar," *Krasnaya Zvezda,* 3 January 1991, 2 (trans. JPRS-UMA-91-005, 115).

44. Y. Golovanov, "Portrait Gallery: Underwater Thunder," *Poisk,* nos. 18–19 (May 1990) (trans. JPRS-UST-90-011, 38–39).

45. Present at the meeting were the head of the Soviet Army's artillery branch, N. N. Voronov; the head of the nuclear weapons program, I. V. Kurchatov; the armaments minister, D. F. Ustinov; assistant minister of the armed forces N. D. Yakovlev; and the head of the Soviet Army's artillery directorate, M. I. Nedelin. See Romanov, *Korolev,* 201.

46. Romanov, *Korolev,* 201–202.

47. Because the Soviet designations for their missiles are usually not determined by Western intelligence until years after their first deployment, a system has been developed over the years to give them a reporting name. The U.S. armed forces use an alphanumeric descriptor, which in the case of the R-11 was SS-1b. This stood for Surface-to-Surface Missile-1b. At first, it was thought that the R-11 was simply a modified version of the R-1A, which was known in the West by its U.S. designation, SS-1a. Besides the U.S. designator, NATO assigns a code name, based on a system similar to that used for Soviet aircraft. Surface-to-surface ballistic missiles are given names starting with S. Hence, the R-1 was called Scunner; the R-2, Sibling; and the R-11, Scud. The names have no particular significance, and in fact come from a prepared list of words chosen for their distinctiveness and clarity.

48. V. I. Prishchepa, "History of the Development of the First Space Rocket Engines in the USSR," *History of Rocketry and Astronautics,* vol. 9 (San Diego: American Astronautics Society, 1989), 89–104.

49. The 100-ton–thrust engine is not mentioned in Glushko's history of his design bureau, nor in his other writings. Yet the general outlines of the program are known from CIA interviews with German rocket engine designers who worked on the program.

50. Report to the V. A. Steklov Mathematical Institute of the Soviet Academy of Sciences (MIAN): "Ballisticheskie vozmozhnosti sostavnykh raket," excerpted in V. S. Avduyevskiy, ed., *M. V. Keldysh: Izbrannye trudy,* 39–140.

51. Peter Stache, *Sowjetische Raketen* (Berlin: Militärverlag der DDR, 1987), 160–164.

52. The first-stage engine would offer 1,000 to 1,600 kN of thrust (kN= kilo-Newton, a unit of force equal to 100,000 dynes), lifting the missile to an altitude of 15–25 km. The ramjet would then be ignited, proving a thrust of 75–100 kN giving the second-stage cruise missile portion a top speed of about Mach 3.

53. Chelomey's bureau was involved in exploiting the German V-1 buzz bomb cruise missiles. Chelomey ran into political trouble in the early 1950s and his bureau was absorbed into the Mikoyan design bureau, home of the legendary MiG fighters. Before being absorbed by Mikoyan, some of his cruise missile engineers were lured over to the Myasishchev bureau and formed the core of the new intercontinental cruise missile project. Chelomey's story is covered in detail in later chapters.

54. Additional details of the program can be found in Appendix B. P. Ya. Kozlov, *Konstruktor* (Moscow: Mashinostroenie, 1989).

55. N. Khrushchev, *Khrushchev Remembers: The Last Testament* (New York: Bantam Books, 1984), 47.

56. Keldysh's study on this issue was entitled: "Teoreticheskie issledovaniya dinamiki poleta sostavnyikh krylatyikh raket dalnego deistviya," and can be found in *Aleksandrov, M. V. Keldysh: Izbrannie trudy.*

57. Details of the Burya are from a Lavochkin OKB data sheet provided to the National Air and Space Museum.

58. With the successful completion of the R-1A and R-2 development programs, the Soviet Academy of Sciences requested governmental permission to use modified ballistic missiles for geophysical research. As early as 1945, M. Tikhonravov had proposed the development of the VR-190 capsule for the A-4/R-1 ballistic missile, which would be launched to an altitude of 190 km, carrying two "stratonauts" in a sub-orbital flight. This did not pass beyond paper studies. In 1947, S. N. Vernov began to design instrumentation for the measurement of cosmic rays in the upper atmosphere using sounding rockets. On 24 May 1949, a modified R-1A missile, designated the V-1A (also 1 VA) was first launched with an instrumentation package in the nose. Korolev's personal enthusiasm for space research, an interest shared by many of the other key engineers in the army program, was instrumental in gaining approval for scientific applications of missile technology. The Academy of Sciences formed a "Commission for Research into the Upper Atmosphere," headed by A. A. Blagonravov, to coordinate further requests for the use of scientific rockets. See B. N. Kantemirov, "Ideya kosmicheskogo poleta v tvorchestve M. K. Tikhonravov," in: B. V. Raushenakh, ed., *Issledovaniya po istorii i teorii razvitiya aviatsionnoi i raketno-kosmicheskoi nauki i tekhniki— Vypusk 6* (Moscow: Nauka, 1988), 87–93. Also K. V. Frolov, et al., *Anatoli Arkadevich Blagonravov* (Moscow: Mir, 1986), 140–155.

59. Stache, *Sowjetische Raketen*, 151–158.

Chapter 6

1. Tyulin, "The 'Seven' Years" (trans. JPRS-UMA-89-013, 55–61).

2. The thrust of the V-2 engine (and its Soviet copy, the RD-100) was 28 tons versus 23 tons for each of the four chambers in the new RD-107 engines. The old V-2 combustion chamber weighed 450 kg versus 143 kg for the RD-107 chambers. The efficiency of the engine, technically referred to as its specific impulse, was 314 seconds on the RD-107, compared to only 204 seconds on the old V-2 engine. Specific impulse is the measure of thrust per mass of propellant per second of burning time. See Prishchepa, "First Space Rocket Engines in the USSR," 100.

3. B. Pokrovskiy, "Glavniy konstruktor sistem radioupravleniya," *Krylya Rodiny* (April 1989): 44–45.

4. K. Brown, ed., *Ground Support Systems for Missiles and Space Vehicles* (New York: McGraw-Hill, 1961), 3.

5. B. Konovalov, "How will we split up Baikonur?" *Izvestiya,* 4 October 1991 (trans. FBIS-SOV-91-198, 26).

6. Nicholas Johnson, "The Baikonur SS-6 Space Launch Facilities," *Spaceflight,* 23, no. 4 (April 1981): 109–116.

7. A. Abramov, "Glavniy konstruktor stratovikh sistem," *Aviatsiya i Kosmonavtika,* no. 3 (1989): 44–45.

8. The construction of the massive structure under the Tyulpan launcher was under the direction of A. A. Nitochkin. For an overview of the considerable architectural challenge posed by the construction of the R-7 launch facility, see Sergey A. Alekseyenko, "Vzglyad iz kotlovana: na stroitelstvo pervogo kosmischeskogo starta," *Tekhnika Molodezhi,* no. 4 (1991): 30–36.

9. I. V. Meshcheryakov and B. A. Pokrovskiy, "Razvitie komandno-izmeritelnogo kompleksa," in Raushenakh, ed., *Issledovaniya po istorii,* 93–116.

10. Ya. Golovanov, "The Beginning of the Space Era," *Pravda,* 4 October 1987 (trans. JPRS-USP-88-001, 26 February 1988, 50).

11. A. Zakharov, "V nachale puti," *Aviatsiya i Kosmonavtika,* no. 10 (1990): 13.

12. MIK-KA stands for *Montazhno-Ispytatelniy Korpus-Kosmicheskiy Apparat* and has become the standard Russian term for the large assembly hangars where the missiles are prepared prior to launch.

13. Johnson, "Baikonur SS-6 Launch Facilities."

14. Curtis Peebles, "Tests of the SS-6 Sapwood ICBM," *Spaceflight,* 22, no. 11–12 (November-December 1980): 340–342.

15. Valentin Bobkov, "Kosmicheskiy Lapotok," *Krylya Rodiny,* no. 11 (1991): 25. Korolev tried to redeem the investment in the cruise missile research program by converting it into the Project 48 Lapotok space-plane, which could be used for reconnaissance. See Appendix B for further details of this final evolution of the cruise missile program.

16. Stache, *Sowjetische Raketen,* 154–155.

17. Golovanov, "The Beginning of the Space Era," 48.

18. V. S. Avduyesvskiy, "Osnovnie etapy razvitiya v SSSR kosmicheskikh issledovanii (1957–1982)," in: Raushenakh, ed., *Issledovaniya po istorii i teorii,* 4 (Moscow: Nauka, 1985), 17.

19. Yu. Mozzhorin and A. Yeremenko, "Ot pervykh ballisticheskikh do . . . ," *Aviatsiya i Kosmonavtika,* no. 8 (1991): 34.

20. The modified version of the R-7 ICBM was designated RN-*Sputnik* (*Raketa nositel-Sputnik* or Rocket booster-*Sputnik*).

21. Marina Marchenko, "Pervie ISZ," *Tekhnika Molodezhi,* no. 1 (1979).

22. F. C. Durant, ed., *Between Sputnik and the Shuttle: New Perspectives on American Astronautics* (San Diego: American Astronautical Society, 1981),

19; Rip Bulkeley, *The Sputniks and Early United States Space Policy* (Bloomington: Indiana University Press, 1991).

23. Luna 1 was launched using a heavily modified version of the R-7, called RN-Vostok. The RN-Vostok had a new upper stage added with its own RO-7 rocket engine. This was a significant technical advance in Soviet missile technology since it represented the first successful demonstration of a true two-stage missile, with the upper stage capable of being ignited in the vacuum of space.

24. M. Rebrov, "Subject to Special Order: Chief of the USSR Ministry of Defense Space Units Discusses Career," *Krasnaya Zvezda*, 8 September 1990 (trans. JPRS-UMA-90-026, 20–21).

25. Yu. Zaitsev, "Kosmicheskaya gaban Plesetsk," *Krasnaya Zvezda*, 15 July 1987; V. Gorkov, "Mesto starta-Plesetsk," *Aviatsiya i Kosmonavtika* (April 1989): 44–45; James Oberg, "The Plesetsk Cosmodrome," *Final Frontier* (May-June 1992): 36–50.

26. Peebles, *The Moby Dick Project*.

27. The M-17 resembles the American U-2 spy-plane. This has led most observers to assume it was built as a reconnaissance aircraft. In fact, the prototype was configured with a gun turret to shoot down the balloons. Its similarity to the U-2 was due to the fact that, like the U-2, it was designed to operate in the thin upper atmosphere where enormous wing surfaces were needed to keep the aircraft aloft. After the cessation of the Moby Dick balloon flights, the program proceeded aimlessly, looking for another sponsor.

28. Jay Miller, *Lockheed U-2* (Austin, Tex.: Aerofax, 1983), 29.

29. The R-11 was known in NATO as the SS-1b Scud A. The more common type was an improved version, the R-17 Zemlya, known to NATO as the SS-1c Scud B. The Iraqis used modified versions of this type of missile in the Gulf War.

30. For recent Soviet accounts of the U-2 shootdown, see Anatoliy Dokuchayev, "Operatsiya Overflayt," *Krylya Rodiny*, no. 10 (1990): 26, and no. 11 (1990): 19; also Boris Balkarey, "Drakon prikazyvaet umeret," *Novoye Vremya*, no. 3 (1991): 38–40.

31. For an excellent account of the political ramifications of the shootdown, see Michael Beschloss, *May-Day: Eisenhower, Khrushchev and the U-2 Affair* (New York: Harper & Row, 1986).

32. Anatoliy Dokuchayev, "Duel in the Stratosphere, How the Spy Flight of F. Powers Was Stopped," *Krasnaya Zvezda*, 27 April 1990 (trans. JPRS-UMA-90-021).

Chapter 7

1. Piotr Butowski, "Cold War Warrior," *Flypast* (October 1991): 11–12.

2. In order to cover all targets in the United States from forward bases in the Soviet arctic, a Soviet strategic bomber needs a range of about 8,200 miles (a combat radius of 4,200 miles). Combat radius is not necessarily half of combat range, however, since an aircraft consumes a disproportionate amount of fuel during takeoff and the initial climb to cruising altitude. The original M-4A version of the Molot could only reach targets in the northwestern United States using bases in the Far East. The improved 3M version could reach nearly all targets while carrying a 5-ton payload. A further improvement of the 3M in 1964 resulted in the 3MD (Bison-C). Molot performance data is based partly on that in Wilfried Kopenhagen, *Sowjetische Bombenflugzeuge* (Berlin: Transpress, 1989), 199.

3. Defense Intelligence Agency, *Intercontinental Strategic Forces Summary, USSR* (DDB-2680-253-85, August 1985), 7.

4. Richard Kohn and Joseph Harahan, "U.S. Strategic Air Power, 1948–1962," *International Security* (Spring 1988): 86.

5. Edward Longacre, *Strategic Air Command: The Formative Years, 1944–49* (Offutt AFB, Neb.: HQ, SAC, 1990).

6. Moon, *Soviet SST*, 37.

7. The Yu-R would eventually emerge as the Tu-22 *Shilo* (Blinder). Its intended KGB spy-plane variant did not live up to expectations and it was produced mainly as a medium-range strike aircraft.

8. Vyacheslav Kazmin, "Kometa pochti ne vidna," *Krylya Rodiny*, no. 6 (1991): 22–23.

9. *Flugkorper des Sowjetblocks* (Porz-Wahn, FRG: Luftwaffenamt, 1970).

10. Piotr Butowski, *OKB MiG: A History of the Design Bureau and Its Aircraft* (Stillwater, Minn.: Specialty Press, 1991), 84.

11. Roy Braybrook, "A Mighty Failure—The Bounder," *Flying Review International*, 20, no. 3: 32–34. There is still some controversy on this point. Braybrook's later writing discounts the area rule problems. Roy Braybrook, *Soviet Combat Aircraft: The Four Postwar Generations* (London: Osprey, 1991), 102.

Chapter 8
1. An analysis of the Soviet Navy's combat performance by one of its German adversaries can be found in Fredrich Ruge, *The Soviets as Naval Opponents, 1941–1945* (Annapolis, Md.: Naval Institute Press, 1979).

2. A critical analysis of the Soviet Navy's submarine force by a Swiss naval historian can be found in Jurg Meister, *Soviet Warships of the Second World War* (New York: Arco, 1977). Meister concludes that Soviet submarines sank only 108 merchant ships and transports during the war, about 27 percent of what is claimed in official Soviet histories. The Soviets claim to have sunk

94 Axis warships, including 3 destroyers, but Meister found that records prove
the loss of only 28 minor warships and auxiliaries, none of which were destroyers. Soviet submarine successes for the whole war were similar to *monthly*
German U-boat sinkings in 1941–42. A less critical assessment of Soviet
submarine performance in the war is offered in Jan Breemer, *Soviet Submarines: Design, Development and Tactics* (London: Jane's, 1989), 75–76. Recent
Soviet writing on their submarine forces has concentrated on the previously
secret issue of submarine design. See, for example, V. I. Dmitriev, *Sovetskoe
podvodnoe korablestroenie* (Moscow: Voenizdat, 1990).

3. E. Klee and O. Merk, *The Birth of the Missile: The Secrets of Peenemünde*
(London: George Harrap & Co., 1965), 105–108.

4. Jan Breemer, "Soviet Navy Submarine Missile Developments 1947–62,"
Navy International (March 1985): 174.

5. Several Soviet accounts of submarine development mention the Test
Stand XII program, but give no details of Soviet exploitation of the idea. The
most detailed account appeared in a three-part article: M. Rebrov, "O proekte
X-11 nikto ne dolzhen znat," *Krasnaya Zvezda*, 29 August, 31 August, and
4 September 1990.

6. Norman Polmar and Jurrien Noot, *Submarines of the Russian and
Soviet Navies, 1918–1990* (Annapolis, Md.: Naval Institute Press, 1990),
149.

7. Fritz Kohl and Eberhard Rossler, *The Type XXI U-Boat* (London: Conway
Press, 1991).

8. Yu. Stvolinskiy, "Konstruktor podvodnogo atomkhoda," *Krasnaya Zvezda*,
15 October 1988.

9. This bureau is called TsKB No. 143 in Russian, and was headed by
V. N. Peregudov. Peregudov first proposed the idea of a nuclear-powered
submarine as early as 1947. His efforts were encouraged by Boris Malinin,
who headed TsKB No. 143 until his death in 1949. Lacking official support,
Peregudov was forced to turn his attention to conventional diesel-powered
submarines. After a short stint at a research institute in the late 1940s, Peregudov
was brought back to TsKB No. 143 with the intention of developing a nuclear
submarine, the Project 627.

10. S. Bystrov, "A Reactor for Submarines," *Krasnaya Zvezda*, 21 October 1989 (trans. JPRS-UMA-89-029, 20 December 1989, 43).

11. The R-P designation stands for *Raketa-Podvodnaya,* or Submarine Missile.

12. Discussion of submarine ballistic missiles appeared in an article on
new naval technology by the admiral in charge of the warship construction
program. See Adm. L. A. Vladimirskiy, "Novaya tekhnika na korablyakh,"
Komsomolskaya Pravda, 23 July 1955.

13. Robert Herrick, *Soviet SSBN Roles in Strategic Strike, Part 1: Final*

Report on Soviet Naval Mission Assignments (Report to the Assistant Director for Net Assessment, Office of the Secretary of Defense, April 1979).

14. Harvey Sapolsky, *The Polaris System Development* (Cambridge, Mass.: Harvard University Press, 1962).

15. This class of submarines is called Zulu by NATO, and B-67 was sometimes called the Zulu IV 1/2 because it was based on a Zulu IV configuration.

16. One of the most illuminating discussions of early submarine missile guidance design can be found in Norman Friedman, *World Naval Weapon Systems, 1991/1992* (Annapolis, Md.: Naval Institute Press, 1991), 117–119.

17. Steven Zaloga, "The Development of Soviet Operational-Tactical Ballistic Missiles," Unpublished manuscript, 1989.

18. D. Mackenzie, *Inventing Accuracy: A Historical Sociology of Nuclear Missile Guidance* (Cambridge, Mass.: MIT Press, 1990).

19. This problem was not solved until the 1970s with the advent of Soviet navigation satellites. The program began in 1967 and mirrored the earlier American Transit network. See Nicholas Johnson, *Soviet Military Strategy in Space* (London: Jane's, 1987), 65–66.

20. The main limitation of hard-wired guidance systems for land-based ICBMs was the inability to retarget the missile. This became a problem in later years when there were sufficient missiles to consider the need for changing the missiles' targets during protracted nuclear conflicts. In the 1950s and early 1960s, however, there were insufficient missiles to worry about such contingencies.

21. A missile become stuck in its elevated position at least twice. Once, during the test program for the R-11FM, the missile failed to fire. Lacking a warhead, it was dumped overboard. Later, during an operational patrol by a Project 629 (Golf) submarine carrying an R-13 (SS-N-4) SLBM, the missile failed to retract after a test erection. The submarine was unable to dispose of it, due either to technical reasons or perhaps the political consequences of dumping a missile with a nuclear warhead. The submarine apparently traveled back to its base in the Northern Fleet area with the missile awkwardly riding on top of the sail.

22. By far one of the most detailed looks into the early Soviet missile program has been provided by an émigré Soviet naval officer who took part in the Northern Fleet's test programs. See Mikhail Turetsky, *The Introduction of Missile Systems into the Soviet Navy, 1945–1962* (Falls Church, Va.: Delphic Associates, 1983).

23. Acceptance of the missiles into navy use was contingent on approval by a special state commission headed by Admiral Chabanenko. It would appear that all five of the Project 611 submarines were being modified before the system was even approved.

24. B. D. Bruins, "U.S. Navy Bombardment Missiles, 1940–1958: A Study of the Weapons Innovation Process," (Ph.D. Diss., Columbia University, 1981).

25. "Soviet Modified Z Class Submarine Missile Launching System," *ONI Review*, April 1960.

26. The Project 629 submarine was known in the West as the Golf class and the Project 658 as the Hotel. These names are arbitrarily assigned to Soviet submarines by NATO intelligence for reporting purposes, since the actual Soviet names for the submarines are often not known for decades after their first encounter.

27. V. Zdanyuk, "Ivan Kulakov vs. a Nuclear Reactor," *Soviet Soldier*, no. 4 (1991): 28.

28. Ian Hogg, *Anti-Aircraft: A History of Air Defence* (London: MacDonald & Jane's, 1978), 133–134.

29. Valeriy Rodikov, "Iksy Vladimira Chelomeya," *Krylya Rodiny*, no. 8 (1989): 6–7.

30. This was probably the Main Directorate for Artillery, later called the Main Directorate for Missiles and Artillery, and finally, NII-4.

31. S. Bystrov, "Podnyataya iz glubin," *Krasnaya Zvezda*, 28 September 1990.

32. In 1958, Chelomey received authority to begin development of a submarine-launched ballistic missile that would later emerge as the SS-N-6. See Mikhail Turetsky, "Development and Deployment of Missile Systems in the Soviet Navy: Administrative Decision Flows," in Andreas Tamberg, ed., *Soviet Defense Decision-Making: An Integrated View*, vol. 1 (Falls Church, Va.: Delphic Associates, 1989).

33. Interestingly enough, a study of Soviet naval policy in this period found that Soviet naval writing focused on the aircraft carrier and paid little attention to missile submarines. See Robert W. Herrick, *Soviet Naval Theory and Policy: Gorshkov's Inheritance* (Newport, R.I.: Naval War College Press, 1988).

34. This analysis is argued most strenuously in Robert Herrick's *Soviet SSBN Roles*. But it is also found in most other analyses of the period, such as Norman Friedman's *Submarine Design and Development* (Annapolis, Md.: Naval Institute Press, 1984), 101–103.

35. Zdanyuk, "Kulakov vs. a Nuclear Reactor," 28.

36. Mikhail Turetsky, "Case Study: R&D Cycle of the SS-N-6," *USSR Technology Update*, 5 November 1986, 9,12.

Chapter 9

1. Jacob Neufield, *Ballistic Missiles in the United States Air Force, 1945–60* (Washington, D.C.: Office of Air Force History, 1990), 149–184.

2. E. Michael Del Papa, et al., *From Snark to Peacekeeper* (Offutt AFB, Neb.: Office of the Historian, HQ, SAC, 1990), 51–59.

3. *Ibid.,* 11–13.

4. J. C. Hopkins and S. A. Goldberg, *The Development of Strategic Air Command, 1946–86* (Offutt AFB, Neb.: Office of the Historian, HQ, SAC, 1986).

5. Sapolsky, *The Polaris System Development.*

6. Steven Zaloga, *Soviet Air Defense Missiles,* 118–126.

7. A. Rodionov, "It Happened at Baikonur," *Krasnaya Zvezda,* 24 October 1990 (trans. JPRS-USP-91-002).

8. S. Averkov, "Top Secret: The Explosion at the Baikonur Cosmodrome," *Rabochnaya Tribuna,* 6 December 1990 (trans. JPRS-USP-91-002, 76–78).

9. A. Bolotin, "Site 10," *Ogonek,* no. 16 (15–22 April 1989) (trans. JPRS-UMA-89-015, 41).

10. DIA estimates of Soviet missile strength in the early 1960s estimate the total number of R-16 (SS-7 Saddler) ICBMs at 23 in 1960, 86 in 1961, and 144 in 1962. These numbers appear to be improbably high. See *Intercontinental Strategic Forces Summary, USSR* (DDB-2860-253-85, August 1985). Other intelligence estimates from the time of the Cuban missile crisis in October 1962 put the total at 44 operational ICBMs plus 6 training launchers at Baikonur (including 4 R-7 launch sites. See Raymond Garthoff, *Reflections on the Cuban Missile Crisis* (Washington, D.C.: Brookings Institution, 1987), 141–142. However, Soviet historians who have had the opportunity to study Soviet archives indicate that the actual number of operational missiles in October 1962 was even smaller, only about 20. See Bill Keller, "Soviets Say Nuclear Warheads Were Deployed in Cuba in '62," *New York Times,* 29 January 1989.

11. M. N. Cuich, *Armes Secretes et Ouvrages Mysterieux de Dunkerque à Cherbourg* (Tourcoing, France: Imp. Jean Bernard, 1984), 65–88.

12. KBSM in Russian is *Konstruktorskoe Biuro Sredstv Mekanizatsiy.* See Irukhim Smotkin, *Hardening Soviet ICBM Silos* (Falls Church, Va.: Delphic Associates, 1991).

13. Raymond L. Garthoff, "Cuban Missile Crisis: The Soviet Story," *Foreign Affairs,* no. 72 (Fall 1988): 64.

14. Oleg Penkovskiy, *The Penkovskiy Papers* (New York: Doubleday & Co., 1965), 345.

Chapter 10

1. The Soviet Air Force had fifty-eight M-4 Bison and seventy-six Tu-95M Bear A strategic bombers, but these would suffer significant attrition from U.S. continental air defenses. See DIA, *Intercontinental Strategic Force Summary, USSR* (DDB-2680-253-85), 7.

2. Khrushchev's memoirs suggest that the idea came to him later, when he visited Bulgaria in May 1962. But Soviet officials close to Khrushchev have recently suggested that the discussions began in late April-early May, not as late as the Bulgaria trip in the third week of May. See, for example, Garthoff, "Cuban Missile Crisis," 64.

3. Khrushchev himself argued that the defense of Cuba was his primary rationale for deploying the missiles. See Khrushchev, *Khrushchev Remembers,* 488–500. There is by no means any consensus over the relative importance of the various motives for deploying the missiles. Two recent studies examine this complex issue: Garthoff, *Reflections on the Cuban Missile Crisis,* 5–22; and James Blight and David Welsh, *On the Brink: Americans and Soviets Reexamine the Cuban Missile Crisis* (New York: Hill and Wang, 1989), 293–305.

4. Michael Beschloss, *The Crisis Years: Kennedy and Khrushchev, 1960–63* (New York: Harper Collins, 1991), 380. Beschloss argues that Khrushchev's desire to install the missiles in Cuba was closely connected with his own failures in correcting the weaknesses of the USSR's strategic forces. The subject of the motivations of Khrushchev and the Kremlin leadership in placing missiles in Cuba has been the subject of considerable scholarship over the years. Two of the classic studies of Soviet intentions are Graham Allison, *Essence of Decision: Explaining the Cuban Missile Crisis* (Boston: Little, Brown & Co., 1971) and A. L. Horelick and M. Rush, *Strategic Power and Soviet Foreign Policy* (Chicago: University of Chicago Press, 1965). For a Soviet view by one of Khrushchev's aides, see Fedor Burlatsky, *Khrushchev and the First Russian Spring* (New York: Charles Scribner's Sons, 1992).

5. Letter from Thomas L. Hughes, Office of the Director of Intelligence & Research, Department of State, to the Secretary of State, 16 April 1963. The source of this information was a report by a U.S. Air Force officer stationed at the Moscow embassy in 1963. Moskalenko was rehabilitated in November 1962 after the failure of the Cuban deployment.

6. G. Bolshakov, "Times, Events and People: The Kennedy-Khrushchev Secret Channel," *Kommunist Vooruzhennykh Sil,* no. 21 (November 1989) (trans. JPRS-UMA-90-007, 115).

7. Soviet accounts indicate that the Defense Council meeting was held in June. More likely, it was held in late May, as several of the attendees had already been dispatched to Cuba on 30 May 1962. Anatoliy Dokuchayev, "Operatsiya 'Anadyr'," *Krasnaya Zvezda,* 4 February 1990, 2.

8. In 1989, Gen. Dmitri Volkogonov of the Moscow Military History Archives revealed that, in 1962, the Soviet RVSN had only twenty missiles deployed capable of hitting the United States. Previous U.S. estimates had been far higher. See Keller, "Nuclear Warheads Deployed in Cuba," *New York Times,* 29 January 1989.

9. Suvorov, *Inside the Soviet Army,* 57–58; R. Berman and B. Gunston, *Rockets & Missiles of World War III* (New York: Exeter Books, 1983), 82.

10. CIA, "The Crisis USSR/Cuba," memorandum dated 26 October 1962. The CIA estimated that the deployment of Soviet forces and equipment to Cuba cost $750 million to $1 billion, of which about a third was the cost of the MRBM/IRBM force.

11. This is the viewpoint of the Soviet ambassador in Cuba at the time, A. Alexeyev, as cited in Bruce Allyn, et al., "Essence of Revision: Moscow, Havana and the Cuban Missile Crisis," *International Security*, 14, no. 3 (Winter 1989): 151.

12. Nestor Carbonell, *And the Russians Stayed: The Sovietization of Cuba* (New York: Wm. Morrow & Co., 1989), 227, and Allyn, et al., "Essence of Revision." Among the command staff under Pliyev were Col. Gen. Viktor Davidkov, deputy for PVO air defense aviation units; Gen. N. Peregudov, PVO chief of staff; Gen. Stepan N. Grechko, deputy for PVO air defense missile forces; Maj. Gen. Leonid Garbuz, deputy for PVO training; Lt. Gen. Sergey F. Ushakov, deputy for the Strategic Missile Forces; Lt. Gen. Pavel B. Dankevich, deputy for VVS aviation units; Col. Gen. N. I. Gusev, commander of VVS air force units; Maj. Gen. Fedor M. Bendonesko, in charge of the Ground Forces contingent; and Maj. Gen. A. A. Dementev, Cuban forces adviser.

13. CIA, Office of Current Intelligence, "Current Intelligence Memorandum," 23 October 1962.

14. The presence of the tactical nuclear warheads in Cuba was first revealed at the Tripartite Conference on the October 1962 Crisis held at the Palace of Conferences in Havana beginning 9 January 1992. The revelations about the weapons came from Gen. Anatoliy Gribkov.

15. Peter Usowski, "John McCone and the Cuban Missile Crisis: A Persistent Approach to the Intelligence-Policy Relationship," *International Journal of Intelligence and Counterintelligence*, 2, no. 4 (1990).

16. This type of site was first spotted by U.S. intelligence in May 1958 near Bina airfield outside Baku in the USSR. By the fall of 1959, these sites had been identified as having the SA-2 Guideline missile system. See, for example, "Baku's Surface-to-Air Missile Sites," *ONI Review*, 14, no. 9 (September 1959) and "Guided Missile Activities in the European Satellites," *ONI Review*, 14, no. 10 (October 1959).

17. CIA, "The Crisis USSR/Cuba," memorandum dated 3 November 1962.

18. Steven Zaloga, "The Missiles of October: Soviet Ballistic Missile Forces during the Cuban Crisis," *The Journal of Soviet Military Studies*, 3, no. 2 (June 1990).

19. Neither system was accurate enough to threaten the hardened silos used by the newer Titan and Minuteman ICBMs.

20. CIA, "The Crisis USSR/Cuba," memorandum dated 24 October 1962.

21. Penkovskiy provided Western intelligence with technical manuals for the R-12, as well as a manual entitled "Methods of Protecting and Defending Strategic Missile Sites." These documents assisted the CIA in determining the nature of the Soviet construction. See, for example, Gordon Brook-Shepherd, *The Storm Birds* (New York: Weidenfeld & Nicolson, 1989), 163. The most thorough account of the Penkovskiy affair is Jerrold Schecter and Peter Deriabin, *The Spy Who Saved the World: How a Soviet Colonel Changed the Course of the Cold War* (New York: Charles Scribner's Sons, 1992).

22. Carbonell, *And the Russians Stayed,* 228, 236.

23. The first nuclear storage shelter is evident on several reconnaissance photos taken by U.S. Air Force RF-101C aircraft, the best unclassified view being 167743 USAF, Defense Audio Visual Agency Still Photo Repository, U.S. Naval Air Station, Anacostia, Virginia.

24. CIA, "The Crisis USSR/Cuba," memorandum dated 28 October 1962.

25. CIA, "The Crisis USSR/Cuba," memorandum dated 24 October 1962.

26. Gen. D. A. Volkogonov, an army historian from the Soviet military archives, first confirmed the presence of the nuclear warheads in 1988 at a conference on the Cuban missile crisis. See Bill Keller, "Nuclear Warheads Deployed in Cuba," *New York Times,* 29 January 1989. Further details were provided in an interview with A. Burlov in the Dokuchayev article mentioned in note 7 above.

27. The alert included the first R-16 launchers, R-7 launchers at Plesetsk, and test launchers at Baikonur. See Smotkin, *Hardening Soviet ICBM Silos,* 27.

28. Recent revelations by Khrushchev confidants have permitted a clearer understanding of Khrushchev's thinking on American reactions. See Beschloss, *The Crisis Years,* 382–387.

29. Arthur Schlesinger, Jr., "Four Days with Fidel: A Havana Diary," *New York Review of Books,* 26 March 1992, 23.

30. The CIA estimated at the time of the crisis that the Soviets had 60–65 ICBMs operational, with 125–175 expected by mid-1963. CIA, "Subject SNIE 11-18-62: Soviet Reactions to Certain U.S. Courses of Action on Cuba," 19 October 1962. Later assessments reduced this estimate to 44 operational plus six training launchers with some operational capability. See Garthoff, *Reflections on the Cuban Missile Crisis,* 141–142. Other recent official sources place the total even higher. For example, the standard DIA reference tool places the 1962 Soviet ICBM force at 148 (4 R-7, 144 R-16). See *Intercontinental Strategic Force Summary, USSR,* 3.

31. Garthoff, *Reflections on the Cuban Missile Crisis,* 142. Garthoff presents the figures regarding both American and Soviet nuclear strength available to Kennedy in 1962. From subsequent evaluations, we now know that Soviet missile and bomber strengths were markedly lower than 1962 estimates: only 20 missiles instead of 44, and only about 100 bombers instead of 155.

32. CIA, "The Crisis USSR/Cuba," memorandum dated 1 November 1962. However, in later statements to U.N. officials, Gen. Igor D. Statsenko indicated that only six to eight missile launchers had actually reached operational status before the dismantling order arrived at 1300–1500 hours on Sunday, 28 October.

33. CIA, *Major Consequences of Certain U.S. Courses of Action on Cuba* (SNIE 11-19-62, 20 October 1962).

34. Beschloss, *The Crisis Years,* 532.

35. Allyn, et al., "Essence of Revision," 153.

36. For further details of the operational parameters of the V-75 Volkho system (SA-2 Guideline), see Zaloga, *Soviet Air Defense Missiles,* 36–76.

Chapter 11

1. Vladimir Gubarev, "Nuclear Trace" (trans. JPRS-TND-89-021, 11).

2. Zhores A. Medvedev, who emigrated to Britain in 1973, casually mentioned the disaster in a 1976 article on dissidence in Soviet science. He had heard of the accident from fellow scientists, although details were very sketchy. Medvedev's claims were rebutted by experts in the nuclear power industry, prompting him to undertake more extensive research on the subject, including attempts to obtain CIA files on the subject. His conclusions appeared in a 1979 book, which was the first detailed look at the extent of the disaster. See Zhores Medvedev, *Nuclear Disaster in the Urals.*

3. Recent studies indicate that about 2.76 million Curies of fluid radioactive waste was released during this period. See A. G. Nazarov, et al., *Rezonans zaklyuchenie obyedinennoy ekspertnoy gruppy po okhrane okruzhayushchey sredy ekspertnoy podkomissiy Gosudarstvennoy ekspertnoy komissiy Gosplana SSSR i postoyannoy ekspertnoy gruppy Verkhovnogo Soveta SSSR* (Chelyabinsk: Yuzhno-Uralskoe Knizhnoe Izdatelstvo, 1991), 22.

4. Thomas Cochran and R. S. Norris, *Soviet Nuclear Warhead Production* (Washington, D.C.: National Resources Defense Council, 1991).

5. The effect of radiation on human tissue is dependent on the absorbed dose of ionizing radiation (measured in rads) multiplied by the relative biological effectiveness (RBE) of the particular type of radiation. The biological dose of rads x RBE is expressed in rems. Scientists generally distinguish between two types of doses, acute and chronic. Acute means a dose received over a short period of time, usually twenty-four hours, while chronic refers to doses received over a prolonged period of time. There is a significant difference in effect between acute and chronic radiation doses, even though the size of the rem dose is the same. Acute doses have far more detrimental effects. Those in excess of 500 rems almost invariably cause severe radiation sickness, and acute doses over 1,000 rems are often fatal. Those of more than 5,000 rems are generally fatal within a day or two. Samuel Glasstone and Philip Dolan, *The Effects of Nuclear Weapons* (Washington, D.C.: DA Pamphlet 50-3, 1977).

6. Andrei Borodenkov, "Chernobyl wasn't the first," *Moscow News,* no. 19 (1991).

7. Estimates of the size of the explosion vary from 5–10 tons (Soviet sources) to 70–100 tons of TNT (U.S. Department of Energy).

8. Moscow Radio Domestic Service, 1030 GMT, 28 March 1990 (trans. JPRS-TND-90-007, 26).

9. A. Lyaputin, "Thirty Years Have Passed," *Trud,* 21 June 1989 (trans. JPRS-TND-89-014, 22).

10. N. Terekhin, "The Echo of an Accident Passed Over in Silence for More Than 30 Years," *Sotsialisticheskaya Industriya,* 18 June 1989 (trans. JPRS-TND-89-014, 24.)

11. A. Illesh, "Thirty Years before Chernobyl," *Izvestiya,* 13 July 1989 (trans. FBIS-SOV-89-152, 52–53).

12. Moscow Central Television, *Vremya,* 1800 GMT, 12 September 1991 (trans. FBIS-SOV-91-179, 44).

13. Nazarov, et al., *Rezonans,* 24.

14. *Ibid.,* 52.

15. Thomas Heurlin, "The Atom Bomb's Guinea Pigs," *Berlingske Tidende Sondag,* 17 December 1989 (trans. JPRS-TND-90-003, 20).

16. D. Yefremov, "Training under a Mushroom Cloud," *Izvestiya,* 14 October 1989 (trans. Current Digest of the Soviet Press, no. 41, 41).

17. N. Ostroumov, "In the Zone of a Nuclear Strike," *Aviatsiya i Kosmonavtika,* September 1990 (trans. JPRS-UAC-91-002, 23).

18. Moscow Radio Domestic Service, 0600 GMT, 3 January 1991 (trans. FBIS-SOV-91-003, 19).

19. Futher tests were conducted with bunkers, weapons, and buildings to more precisely determine the nuclear effects on weaponry. See "Iz istorii sovremennosti: Ostrov," *Tekhnika Molodezhi,* no. 3 (1990): 13–16.

20. Susan Reed, "Atomic Lake," *The New Republic,* 28 October 1991, 12–13.

21. Joshua Handler, *Preliminary Report on Greenpeace Visit to Vladivostok and the Areas around the Chazma Bay and Bolshoi Kamen Submarine Re-*

pair and Refuelling Facilities, October 1991 (Washington, D.C.: Greenpeace, 1991), 16.

22. Zdanyuk, "Kulakov vs. a Nuclear Reactor," 28–30.

23. Scott McMichael, "Service in the Soviet Armed Forces—Dangerous Duty?" *Jane's Intelligence Review* (November 1991): 512.

24. An informative account from an engineer inside the Soviet nuclear program can be found in Grigori Medvedev, *The Truth about Chernobyl* (New York: Basic Books, 1991).

Chapter 12

1. Thomas Cochran, et al., *Soviet Nuclear Weapons* (New York: Ballinger, 1989), 373.

2. Iosif Shklovskiy, *Five Billion Vodka Bottles to the Moon: Tales of a Soviet Scientist* (New York: Norton, 1991), 222–230.

3. Sergey Khrushchev, (ed. & trans. William Taubman, *Khrushchev on Khrushchev* (Boston: Little, Brown & Co., 1990), 106.

4. Phillip Clark, "The Soviet Manned Lunar Programme and Its Legacy," *Space Policy* (August 1991): 221–232.

5. Andrei Tarasov, "Space Science of the Future," *Pravda,* 17 May 1990 (trans. FBIS-SOV-90-103, 89).

6. The N-1 lunar program began in 1960 with Khrushchev's support. Chelomey managed to get involved in the program as well, offering his own UR-700 rocket booster. This diversion of funds into two separate booster programs, combined with the propulsion squabbles, seriously delayed the program. Chelomey's UR-700 program was finally axed, but the damage had been done. Korolev died in 1966 and direction of the program fell to V. Mishin. Testing of the N-1 began in February 1969. The first four test launches were failures. Mishin did not have Korolev's enormous political clout and the program had little priority after it failed to beat the United States to the moon. The N-1 was cancelled and Glushko was allowed to merge his engine design bureau with OKB-1 in order to begin work on a new program to build a space shuttle. See V. Pikul, "How We Conceded the Moon: A Look by One of the Participants of the N-1 Drama and the Reasons Behind It," *Izobretatel i Ratsionalizator,* no. 8 (August 1990) (trans. JPRS-USP-91-002, 73). Also M. Rebrov, "But Things Were Like That—Top Secret: The Painful Fortune of the N-1 Project," *Krasnaya Zvezda,* 13 January 1990 (trans. JPRS-USP-90-002, 46–47).

7. Michael Getler, "Arms Control and the SS-9," *Space/Aeronautics* (November 1969): 38–47.

8. Trevor Williams, *Science: A History of Discovery in the Twentieth Century* (Oxford: Oxford University Press, 1990), 126.

9. In mid-1957 there were about 45,000 Soviet vs. 37,000 Americans with doctorates or their equivalents in the physical sciences or engineering. Since the 1950s the Soviet Union has often outstripped the U.S. in the numbers of scientists, but it has long been argued that the Soviet scientific workforce is substantially less productive. Figures on the size of the scientific force come from a CIA study: *Main Trends in Soviet Capabilities and Policies, 1958–1963* (NIE 11-4-58, 23 December 1958).

10. Robert Wright, "Why Soviet Science Collapsed: The Experiment That Failed," *The New Republic,* 28 October 1991, 21.

Glossary

Arzamas-16: Main Soviet atomic bomb development institute in Sarova.

Atomic bomb: Nuclear weapon using the fission of the nucleus of heavy metals such as uranium or plutonium as the source of its energy.

Baikonur: Official Soviet name for the missile and space launch center in Kazakhstan, also code-named Tashkent-50. In fact, the facility is closer to the town of Tyuratam, so U.S. intelligence agencies often refer to it by that name. To further confuse matters, the site was renamed by the Soviets in the 1980s and is now officially referred to as Leninsk.

Ballistic missile: A surface-to-surface missile that follows a predicted ballistic flight path.

Bear: NATO code name for the Tupolev Tu-95 bomber.

Bison: NATO code name for the Myasishchev M-4 and 3M jet bombers.

Boiler: Early Russian expression (*kotel*) for a nuclear reactor.

Borodino: Code name for the Soviet atomic bomb program. Named after famous battle with Napoleon.

Buzz bomb: Anglo-American slang for a cruise missile propelled by a pulse-jet engine, so named for the sound it makes. The term usually refers to the German V-1 Fiesler Fi-103 missile.

Chelyabinsk-65: Soviet reactor complex near Kyshtym for the production of weapons' grade plutonium. Chelyabinsk-40 is the neighboring chemical processing facility.

Cruise missile: A winged missile that gains an appreciable amount of lift from its flying surfaces.

Cryogenic fuel: A type of rocket fuel in which the fuel or oxidizer is a gas at room temperature and which must be kept in a supercooled state near absolute zero when stored in the missile. A typical combination was liquid oxygen (oxidizer) and alcohol (fuel). The alcohol was kept at ambient air temperature, but the oxygen had to be kept supercooled. The cooling allows a much greater mass of the material to be stored in a rocket than would be practical if it was kept in its normal gaseous state.

FIAN: Physics Institute of the Soviet Academy of Sciences in Leningrad.

First Chief Directorate: Cover name for the administration of the Soviet atomic bomb program headed by Lavrentiy Beria.

GDL-OKB: Gas Dynamics Laboratory—Special Design Bureau. In the postwar years, headed by Glushko. This was the main Soviet rocket engine development center.

GKO: State Defense Committee. The government organization headed by Stalin which led the Soviet Union during World War II.

GULAG: Soviet acronym for the Main Directorate of Labor Camps. Generally used to refer to the forced labor camps themselves.

GRU: Main Intelligence Directorate. The Soviet Army's main intelligence service, comparable to the U.S. Defense Intelligence Agency. This organization is separate from the better-known special police intelligence organizations of the NKVD or KGB.

Hydrogen bomb: Nuclear weapon using the fusion of hydrogen isotopes as the source of its energy. Also called thermonuclear bomb or superbomb.

Hypergolic fuel: A type of rocket fuel combination that derives its energy from the chemical reaction between a chemical oxidant and hydrocarbon fuel, often a form of nitric acid (oxidant) and kerosene (fuel).

ICBM: Intercontinental ballistic missile.

Inertial guidance: A type of guidance or navigation system that relies on gyroscopes to serve as a reference in measuring the deviation of a missile from its intended flight path.

IRBM: Intermediate-range ballistic missile.

Isotopes: Different forms of an element that share the same atomic number but have different atomic weights and slightly different physical properties due to differing numbers of neutrons in the nucleus.

KB-11: Design Bureau-11, headed by Khariton, at Arzamas-16. Developed the first Soviet A-bomb and H-bomb.

KGB: Committee for State Security. The final evolution of the Soviet NKVD in 1954 gave intelligence/counterintelligence and political control functions to the KGB, while the MVD was given traditional state police functions.

Laboratory No. 2: Code name for Igor Kurchatov's atomic research facility in Moscow.

Leningrad-300: Code name for the ICBM base at Plesetsk.

LFTI: Leningrad Physics Technology Institute.

Los Alamos: New Mexico site of the U.S. atomic bomb development center.

Moby Dick: Code name for U.S. reconnaissance balloon program of the 1950s.

NII: Scientific Research Institute. The usual progression of weapons' research in the Soviet Union since the 1940s was: the Academy of Sciences (basic research), NII (advanced research), Design Bureau (engineering development and experimental production).

NKVD: State Committee for Internal Affairs, the Soviet special police organization responsible for intelligence as well as internal repression from 1938 to 1943. During World War II it was renamed and reorganized several times as NKGB/SMERSH (1943), MGB (1946), MVD (1953), and, finally, KGB (1954). To avoid confusion, this book refers to the wartime special police as the NKVD. The term "special police" is used in this book since the NKVD's roles combined "secret police" intelligence/counterintelligence functions with internal political control and repression and traditional state police functions.

OKB-1: Special Design Bureau-1. The main Soviet missile development center located in Kaliningrad in the Moscow suburbs. Headed by Sergey Korolev until 1966.

Oxidizer: A chemical used in a rocket engine to combust the fuel.

Poligon: Russian word for a proving ground. Often applied to the Semipalatinsk-21 nuclear test site.

Pu-239: Fissile isotope of plutonium used in nuclear weapons.

RFNA: Red fuming nitric acid, a type of rocket fuel oxidizer.

RNII: Scientific Research Institute for Jet Propulsion, also called NII-3.

RVSN: Soviet Strategic Missile Forces. A branch of the Soviet armed forces controlling strategic missiles, including ICBMs and IRBMs.

SAC: The U.S. Air Force's Strategic Air Command.

Second Chief Directorate: Cover name for the military industrial administration developing delivery systems for nuclear weapons in the late 1940s and early 1950s. Headed by Dmitriy Ustinov.

Semipalatinsk-21: Main Soviet nuclear test site in Kazakhstan.

Semyorka: Russian for "little seven." Nickname for the R-7 ICBM.

SVAG: Soviet Military Administration for Germany. The Soviet military government in postwar East Germany.

Tashkent-50: Code name for the Baikonur missile test center.

TsAGI: Central Aerohydrodynamics Institute in Zhukovskiy, outside Moscow. TsAGI is the main research center for the Soviet aviation industry and somewhat similar to NASA in the United States.

Tushino: Location of one of the major Soviet air bases near Moscow. Frequent site of air shows in the later 1940s and early 1950s.

Tyuratam: See Baikonur.

U-235: Fissile isotope of uranium used in nuclear weapons.

U-238: Isotope of uranium most commonly found in nature.

V-2: First successful military ballistic missile. Developed by Germany in World War II, its official designation was A-4.

V-75: The Soviet Volkhov air defense missile, also called S-75 in its strategic defense version and SA-2 Guideline by Western intelligence.

zek: Russian slang for a prisoner in the GULAG.

Selected Bibliography

This bibliography lists the most relevant books and government studies used in researching this study. I have avoided listing many of the more general historical accounts of this period of Soviet history, as well as general surveys of weapons' history, for reasons of space. Likewise, articles are not listed, although they will be found in the chapter notes. I have provided references to English translations of many of these articles. These translations generally refer to the JPRS (Joint Publications Research Service) or FBIS (Foreign Broadcast Information Service), U.S. government organizations that translate foreign publications of interest to other government agencies. Not all these documents are generally available, some being "For Official Use Only." These are obtainable under the Freedom of Information Act (FOIA). However, many JPRS and FBIS translations are available at regional Federal Records depositories, either in hard copy or on microfiche. These depositories are often collocated at major university libraries. Some of the Russian books mentioned in this bibliography have been translated for U.S. government use and, where the author is familiar with such examples, the translations are identified. Those dealing with missiles and aircraft are translated primarily by the U.S. Air Force's Foreign Technology Division, and are identified "FTD." In recent years, distribution of these translations has been limited by the "For Official Use Only" restriction, mainly for copyright reasons rather than security concerns.

Russian language books cited in this bibliography were mainly located by the author during trips to eastern Europe, or obtained through Victor Kamkin Books of Rockville, Md., the largest distributor of Russian language publications in the United States.

A few words are in order regarding formerly classified government studies cited in this bibliography, especially those from the CIA and DIA. The CIA documents were obtained from three sources: requests to the Information and Privacy Office of the CIA, documents in presidential libraries, and documents contained in the "Declassified Documents" microfiche collection. This latter source is available at many large university libraries. The DIA documents in nearly all cases were obtained through FOIA requests.

DECLASSIFIED GOVERNMENT REPORTS

Central Intelligence Agency
"The Crisis USSR/Cuba." Memorandum, 19 October 1962.
"The Crisis USSR/Cuba." Memorandum, 24 October 1962.

"The Crisis USSR/Cuba." Memorandum, 25 October 1962.

"The Crisis USSR/Cuba." Memorandum, 26 October 1962.

"The Crisis USSR/Cuba." Memorandum, 28 October 1962.

"The Crisis USSR/Cuba." Memorandum, 29 October 1962.

"The Crisis USSR/Cuba." Memorandum, 1 November 1962.

"The Crisis USSR/Cuba." Memorandum, 3 November 1962.

"The Crisis USSR/Cuba." Memorandum, 5 November 1962.

Current Intelligence Memorandum. 23 October 1962.

"Current Status of Soviet and Satellite Military Forces and Indications of Military Intentions." Memorandum, 6 September 1961.

Estimate of the Effects of the Soviet Possession of the Atomic Bomb upon the Security of the United States and upon the Probabilities of Direct Soviet Military Action. ORE 91-49, 6 April 1950.

German Scientists at Sukhumi. OSI/SR-2/49, 31 October 1949.

Impact of a September 1958 Nuclear Test Moratorium on Soviet Nuclear Weapons Capabilities. 18 March 1958.

Main Trends in Soviet Capabilities and Policies, 1958–1963. NIE 11-4-58, 23 December 1958.

Major Consequences of Certain U.S. Courses of Action on Cuba. SNIE 11-19-62, 20 October 1962.

National Intelligence Survey USSR, Section 73, Atomic Energy. NIS 26, January 1951.

The Problem of Uranium Isotope Separation by Means of Ultracentrifuge in the USSR. EG-1802, 22 May 1957.

Scientific Research Institute and Experimental Factory 88 for Guided Missile Development, Moskva/Kaliningrad. OSI-C-RA/60-2, 4 March 1960.

Semi-Annual Estimate of Status of the Soviet Atomic Energy Program. CIA/SCI-2/50, 10 July 1950.

Soviet Capabilities for Attack on the Continental United States before July 1952. SE-10, 15 September 1951.

Soviet Capabilities for Attack on the United States through Mid-1955. SE-36/1, 31 July 1953.

Soviet Capabilities for Attack on the U.S. through 1957. SNIE 11-2-54, 24 February 1954.

Soviet Capabilities and Probable Course of Action through Mid-1959. NIE 11-4-54, 13 August 1954.

Soviet Capabilities and Probable Course of Action through 1960. NIE 11-3-55, 17 May 1955.

Soviet Capabilities and Probable Course of Action through Mid-1962. NIE 11-4-57, 12 November 1957.

Soviet Reactions to Certain U.S. Courses of Action on Cuba. SNIE 11-18-62, 19 October 1962.

The Soviet Weapons Industry, An Overview. 1986.
Status of the Soviet Atomic Energy Program. SCI-2/50, 4 July 1950.
Status of the Soviet Atomic Energy Program. 27 December 1950.
Status of the Soviet Atomic Energy Program. SC 118-51, 6 March 1952.
Status of the Soviet Atomic Energy Program. SI 13-52, 8 January 1953.
A Summary of Soviet Guided Missile Intelligence. US/UK GM 4-52, 20 July
    1953.

Department of Defense
Defense Intelligence Agency. *Intercontinental Strategic Forces Summary, USSR.*
    DDB-2680-253-85, August 1985.
————. *Missile Industry Design and Development Resources—USSR.* DST-
    1830S-289-80-SAO. April 1980.
————. *Aviation Industry Design and Development Resources—USSR.* DST-
    1830S-104-81. July 1981.
————. *Soviet Submarine Order of Battle, 1950–1974.* DDB-1220-14-78. 1978.
Defense Nuclear Agency. *Measures and Trends of U.S. and USSR Strategic
    Force Effectiveness.* 1978.
Far East Command. "Monazite Production in North Korea," *Far East Com-
    mand Intelligence Digest,* no. 12 (2 December 1951).
Joint Intelligence Committee. *Soviet Intentions and Capabilities, 1949.* JIC
    435-12, 3 December 1948.
————. *Magnitude and Imminence of Soviet Air Threat to the United States.*
    JCS 1924/75, 20 October 1953.
————. *Soviet Capabilities and Probable Course of Action against North America
    in a Major War Commencing during the Period 1 January 1958 to 31
    December 1958.* JIC 491/122, 29 January 1957.
Joint Intelligence Staff. *Soviet Capabilities.* JIS 80/15, 9 November 1945.
Military Liaison Committee. *Basis for Estimating Maximum Soviet Capabilities
    for Atomic Warfare.* 20 February 1950.
Office of the Secretary of Defense. "Memorandum for the President: The Missile
    Gap Controversy." 4 March 1963.
Office of the Secretary of Defense. Director for Net Assessment. *Soviet SSBN
    Roles in Strategic Strike, Part 1, Final Report on Soviet Naval Mission
    Assignments.* 1979.

UNPUBLISHED SOURCES

Barnard, Roy. "The History of Army Air Defense Command: The Gun Era."
    Washington, D.C.: U.S. Army Air Defense Command, 1970.
Bruins, B. D. "U.S. Navy Bombardment Missiles, 1940–1958: A Study of
    the Weapons Innovation Process." Ph.D. diss., Columbia University, 1981.

Grant, C. L. "The Development of Continental Air Defense to 1 September 1954." Maxwell AFB, Ala.: USAF Historical Division, 1957.

Kalish, Jack. "Performance Characteristics of an SS-7 in a Depressed Trajectory Mode of Operation." Washington, D.C.: Institute for Defense Analyses, 1972.

Laird, Gerald P. "North American Air Defense, Past, Present, and Future." Maxwell AFB, Ala.: Air University, 1975.

Luftwaffenamt. "Flugkorper des Sowjetblocks." Porz-Wahn, FRG: 1970.

Osato, Timothy. "Militia Missilemen: The Army National Guard in Air Defense, 1951–1967." Washington, D.C.: Chief of Military History, 1968.

Tsypkin, Mikhail. "The Origins of Soviet Military Research and Development, 1917–1941." Ph.D. diss., Harvard University, 1985.

Vick, C. P. "The Soviet Civil/Military Space, Missile, and Aircraft Industry." Privately published, 1992.

BOOKS

Afanasev, A. L. *Sovetskie Inzhenery*. Moscow: Molodaya Gvardiya, 1985.

Alexander, Jean. *Russian Aircraft since 1940*. London: Putnam, 1975.

Aleksandrov, A. P., ed. *Akademik A. I. Alikhanov: vospominaniya, pisma, dokumenty*. Leningrad: Nauka, 1989.

———. *I. V. Kurchatov: izbrannie trudy v trekh tomakh, Tom 3—Yadernaya energiya*. Moscow: Izd. Nauka, 1984.

Aleksandrov, V. S., ed. *M. V. Keldysh: izbrannie trudy, raketnaya tekhnika i kosmonavtika*. Moscow: Nauka, 1988.

Allison, Graham. *Essence of Decision: Explaining the Cuban Missile Crisis*. Boston: Little, Brown & Co., 1971.

Almquist, Peter. *Red Forge: Soviet Military Industry since 1965*. New York: Columbia University Press, 1990.

Alymov, F. S., ed. *Zagadki zvezdnikh ostrovov*. Moscow: Molodaya Gvardiya, vol. 3, 1986; vol. 4, 1987; vol. 5, 1989; vol. 6, 1990.

Amann, R., et al. *The Technological Level of Soviet Industry*. New Haven, Conn.: Yale University, 1977.

Andrew, Christopher and Oleg Gordievskiy. *KGB: The Inside Story*. New York: Harper-Collins, 1990.

Antonov-Ovseyenko, Anton. *Portret Tirana*. New York: Khronika, 1980.

Arlazorov, Mikhail. *Doroga na Kosmodrom*. Moscow: Pollit, 1984.

Astashenkov, P. T. *Academician Kurchatov: Hero in Science and Labour*. Moscow: Mir, 1981.

———. *Akademik I. V. Kurchatov*. Moscow: Voenizdat, 1971.

———. *Sovetskiye Raketniye Voiska*. Moscow: Voenizdat, 1967. Trans. FTD-MT-24-20-68.

Babanskiy, Yu. I., et al. *Nauka i tekhnika SSSR, 1917–1987*. Moscow: Nauka, 1987.

Baldwin, Ralph. *The Deadly Fuze*. Novato, Calif.: Presidio Press, 1980.

Ball, Desmond. *Politics and Force Levels: The Strategic Missile Program of the Kennedy Administration*. Berkeley: University of California Press, 1980.

Batekhin, L. L. *Vozdushnaya moshch rodiny*. Moscow: Voenizdat, 1988.

Beaumont, Joan. *Comrades in Arms: British Aid to Russia, 1941–1945*. London: Davis-Poynter, 1980.

Benecke, T., et al. *Die deutsche Luftfahr:t Flugkorper und Lenkraketen*. Koblenz: Bernard & Graefe, 1987.

Berman, R. and Bill Gunston. *Rockets & Missiles of World War III*. New York: Exeter Books, 1983.

Beschloss, Michael. *The Crisis Years: Kennedy and Khrushchev, 1960–63*. New York: Harper-Collins, 1991.

———. *May-Day: Eisenhower, Khrushchev and the U-2 Affair*. New York: Harper & Row, 1986.

Birdsall, Steve. *Superfortress: The Boeing B-29*. Carrollton, Tex.: Squadron/ Signal, 1980.

Blight, James and David Welsh. *On the Brink: Americans and Soviets Reexamine the Cuban Missile Crisis*. New York: Hill and Wang, 1989.

Bloomfield, L. P., et al. *Khrushchev and the Arms Race*. Cambridge, Mass.: MIT Press, 1966.

Bluth, Christopher. *Soviet Strategic Arms Policy before SALT*. Cambridge: Cambridge University Press, 1992.

Bolonkin, Alexander. *The Development of Soviet Rocket Engines for Strategic Missiles*. Falls Church, Va.: Delphic Associates, 1991.

Bowen, E. G. *Radar Days*. Bristol, U.K.: Adam Hilger, 1987.

Brown, Kenneth and Peter Weiser. *Ground Support Systems for Missiles and Space Vehicles*. New York: McGraw-Hill, 1961.

Breemer, Jan. *Soviet Submarines: Design, Development and Tactics*. London: Jane's, 1989.

Briggs, B. Bruce. *The Shield of Faith: The Hidden Struggle for Strategic Defense*. New York: Simon & Schuster, 1988.

Brook-Shepherd, Gordon. *The Storm Birds*. New York: Weidenfeld & Nicolson, 1989.

Brookes, Andrew. *V-Force: The History of Britain's Airborne Deterrent*. London: Jane's, 1982.

Brugioni, Dino. *Eyeball to Eyeball: The Inside Story of the Cuban Missile Crisis*. New York: Random House, 1990.

Bulkeley, Rip. *The Sputniks and Early United States Space Policy*. Bloomington: Indiana University Press, 1991.

Burlatsky, Fedor. *Khrushchev and the First Russian Spring.* New York: Charles Scribner's Sons, 1992.

Butowski, Piotr. *OKB MiG: A History of the Design Bureau and Its Aircraft.* Stillwater, Minn.: Specialty Press, 1991.

Carbonell, Nestor. *And the Russians Stayed: The Sovietization of Cuba.* New York: Wm. Morrow & Co., 1989.

Chernoshchekov, T. M. and V. Ya. Frenkel. *Lyudi nauki—I. V. Kurchatov.* Moscow: Prosveshcheniye, 1989.

Clark, Ian and N. Wheeler. *The British Origins of Nuclear Strategy, 1945–1955.* Oxford, U.K.: Clarendon, 1989.

Cochran, Thomas B. and R. S. Norris. *Soviet Nuclear Warhead Production.* Washington, D.C.: Natural Resources Defense Council, 2d ed., 1990; 3d ed., 1991; 4th ed., 1992.

———, et al. *Soviet Nuclear Weapons.* New York: Ballinger, 1989.

———, W. Arkin, and M. Hoenig. *U.S. Nuclear Forces and Capabilities,* vol. 1. Cambridge, Mass.: Ballinger, 1984.

Conquest, Robert. *The Great Terror.* New York: Macmillan, 1968.

———. *Kolyma: The Arctic Death Camps.* Oxford: Oxford University Press, 1979.

Cuich, M. N. *Armes Secretes et Ouvrages Mysterieux de Dunkerque à Cherbourg.* Tourcoing, France: Imp. Jean Bernard, 1984.

Daniloff, Nicholas. *The Kremlin & the Cosmos.* New York: Knopf, 1972.

Davis, Nuel Pharr. *Lawrence & Oppenheimer.* New York: Simon & Schuster, 1968.

Del Papa, E. Michael, et al. *SAC Missile Chronology, 1939–1988.* Offutt AFB, Neb.: Office of the Historian, HQ Strategic Air Command, 1990.

———, *From Snark to Peacekeeper.* Offutt AFB, Neb.: Office of the Historian, HQ Strategic Air Command, 1990.

Dmitriev, V. I. *Sovetskoe podvodnoe korablestroenie.* Moscow: Voenizdat, 1990.

Durant, F. C., ed. *Between Sputnik and the Shuttle: New Perspectives on American Astronautics.* San Diego: American Astronautical Society, 1981.

———. *The First Steps Toward Space.* San Diego: AAS Publications, 1985.

Dyadkin, Iosif. *Unnatural Deaths in the USSR, 1928–1954.* New Brunswick, N.J.: Transaction, 1983.

Dziak, John. *Chekisty: A History of the KGB.* Lexington, Mass.: Lexington Books, 1988.

Eglin, James. *Air Defense in the Nuclear Age: Postwar Development of American and Soviet Strategic Defense Systems.* New York: Garland, 1988.

Evangelista, Matthew. *Innovations and the Arms Race.* Ithaca, N.Y.: Cornell University Press, 1988.

Fagan, M. D., ed. *A History of Engineering and Science in the Bell System:*

National Service in War and Peace, 1925–1975. New York: Bell Telephone Labs, 1978.

Finne, K. N. *Igor Sikorsky: The Russian Years*. Washington, D.C.: Smithsonian Institution, 1987.

Firdman, Henry Eric. *Decision Making in the Soviet Microelectronics Industry: The Leningrad Design Bureau, A Case Study*. Falls Church, Va.: Delphic Associates, 1985.

Fortesque, Stephen. *Science Policy in the Soviet Union*. London: Rutledge, 1990.

Freedman, Lawrence. *The Evolution of Nuclear Strategy*. New York: St. Martin's, 1983.

———. *U.S. Intelligence and the Soviet Strategic Threat*. Princeton, N.J.: Princeton University Press, 1986.

Friedman, Norman. *Submarine Design and Development*. Annapolis, Md.: Naval Institute Press, 1984.

———. *World Naval Weapon Systems, 1991/1992*. Annapolis, Md.: Naval Institute Press, 1991.

Frolov, K. V., et al. *Anatoli Arkadevich Blagonravov*. Moscow: Mir, 1986.

Garthoff, Raymond L. *Reflections on the Cuban Missile Crisis*. Washington, D.C.: Brookings Institution, 1987.

Getty, J. Arch. *Origins of the Great Purges*. Cambridge: Cambridge University Press, 1985.

Glushko, V. P. *Kosmonavtika-Entsiklopediya*. Moscow: Sov. Entsiklopediya, 1985.

———. *Razvitie Raketostroeniya i Kosmonavtiki v SSSR*. Moscow: Mashinostroenie, 1981.

———. *Rocket Engines of the GDL-OKB*. Moscow: Novosti, 1975.

Goldschmidt, Bertrand. *Atomic Rivals: A Candid Memoir of Rivalries among the Allies over the Bomb*. New Brunswick, N.J.: Rutgers University Press, 1990.

Golovin, I. N. *Academician Igor Kurchatov*. Moscow: Mir, 1969.

———. *I. V. Kurchatov*. Bloomington, Ind.: Selbstverlag Press, 1968.

Green, William. *Soviet Nuclear Weapons Policy: A Research and Bibliographic Guide*. Boulder, Colo.: Westview, 1987.

Grigoreva, N. A. *Radiolyubitel inzhener general*. Moscow: DOSAAF, 1985.

Grigoryev, M. G., et al. *Vom Raketengerat zur Interkontinentalrakete*. Berlin: Militärverlag der DDR, 1980.

Gunston, Bill. *Aircraft of the Soviet Union*. London: Osprey, 1983.

Hall, R. Cargill, ed. *History of Rocketry & Astronautics*, vol. 7. San Diego: American Astronautical Society, 1986.

Hansen, Chuck. *U.S. Nuclear Weapons: The Secret History*. New York: Orion, 1988.

Harrison, Mark. *Soviet Planning in Peace and War, 1938–1945.* Cambridge: Cambridge University Press, 1985.

Harvey, D. and V. Giroux. *Seventy Years of Strategic Air Refueling, 1918–1988.* Offutt AFB, Neb.: HQ Strategic Air Command, 1990.

Hays, Otis. *Home from Siberia: The Secret Odysseys of Interned American Airmen in World War II.* College Station: Texas A&M Press, 1990.

Helmreich, Jonathan. *Gathering Rare Ores: The Diplomacy of Uranium Acquisition, 1943–54.* Princeton, N.J.: Princeton University Press, 1986.

Herken, Gregg. *The Winning Weapon: The Atomic Bomb and the Cold War, 1945–1950.* Princeton, N.J.: Princeton University Press, 1988.

Herrick, Robert W. *Soviet Naval Theory and Policy: Gorshkov's Inheritance.* Newport, R.I.: Naval War College Press, 1988.

Hewlett, R. and J. Holt. *Atoms for Peace and War, 1953–1961.* Berkeley: University of California Press, 1989.

Hogg, Ian. *Anti-Aircraft: A History of Air Defence.* London: MacDonald & Jane's, 1978.

Holloway, David. *The Soviet Union and the Arms Race.* New Haven, Conn.: Yale University Press, 1983.

Hopkins, J. C. and S. A. Goldberg. *The Development of Strategic Air Command, 1946–86.* Offutt AFB, Neb.: Office of the Historian, HQ Strategic Air Command, 1986.

Horelick, A. L. and M. Rush. *Strategic Power and Soviet Foreign Policy.* Chicago: University of Chicago Press, 1965.

Hyde, H. M. *The Atom Bomb Spies.* New York: Ballantine Books, 1981.

Hyland, William. *The Cold War: Fifty Years of Conflict.* New York: Random House, 1991.

Infield, G. B. *The Poltava Affair.* New York: Macmillan, 1973.

Iorysh, A. I. *Rakety dolzhny sluzhit miru.* Moscow: Mezh. Otnosheniya, 1985.

Irving, David. *The German Atomic Bomb.* London: Wm. Kimber, 1967.

Ishlinskiy, A. Yu. *Akademik S. P. Korolev: ucheniy, inzhener, chelovek.* Moscow: Nauka, 1986.

Ivanovskiy, Oleg. *Naperekor zemnomu prityazhenyu.* Moscow: Pollit, 1988.

Johnson, Nicholas. *Soviet Military Strategy in Space.* London: Jane's, 1987.

Josephson, Paul R. *Physics and Politics in Revolutionary Russia.* Berkeley: University of California Press, 1991.

Kadomtsev, B. B., ed. *Reminiscences about Academician Lev Artsimovich.* Moscow: Nauka, 1985.

Kazaryan, P. E. *Stranitsy geroicheskogo truda khimikov v gody VOV 1941–45.* Moscow: Nauka, 1988.

Kedrov, F. B. *Kapitza: Life and Discoveries.* Moscow: Mir, 1984.

Khorobykh, A. M. *Glavniy marshal aviatsii A. A. Novikov.* Moscow: Voenizdat, 1989.

Khrushchev, Nikita. *Khrushchev Remembers*. Boston: Little, Brown & Co., 1970.

———. *Khrushchev Remembers: The Last Testament*. New York: Bantam Books, 1984.

———. *Khrushchev Remembers: The Glasnost Tapes*. Boston: Little, Brown & Co., 1990.

Khrushchev, Sergey, ed. & trans. by William Taubman. *Khrushchev on Khrushchev*. Boston: Little, Brown & Co., 1990.

Kintner, William, et al. *The Nuclear Revolution in Soviet Military Affairs*. Norman: University of Oklahoma Press, 1968.

Klee, E. and O. Merk. *The Birth of the Missile: The Secrets of Peenemünde*. London: George Harrap & Co., 1965.

Knaak, M. S. *Encyclopedia of U.S. Air Force Aircraft and Missile Systems*, vol. 2: *Post–World War II Bombers, 1945–1973*. Washington, D.C.: Office of Air Force History, 1988.

Knight, Michael. *Strategic Offensive Air Operations*. London: Brassey's, 1989.

Kokin, Lev. *Yunost Akademikov*. Moscow: Sov. Rossiya, 1970.

Kolkowicz, R. and E. P. Mickiewicz. *The Soviet Calculus of Nuclear War*. Lexington, Mass.: Lexington Books, 1986.

Konstantinovskiy, Vladimir. *Ballistic Missile Engine Production in the USSR*. Falls Church, Va.: Delphic Associates, 1991.

Kopenhagen, Wilfried. *Sowjetische Bombenflugzeuge*. Berlin: Transpress, 1989.

Korrell, Peter. *TB-3: Die Geschichte eines Bombers*. Berlin: Transpress, 1987.

Kosmodemiansky, A. *Konstantin Tsiolkovskiy*. Moscow: Nauka, 1985.

Kozlov, P. Ya. *Konstruktor*. Moscow: Mashinostroenie, 1989.

Kramish, Arnold. *Atomic Energy in the Soviet Union*. Palo Alto: Stanford University Press, 1959.

Kravchenko, Viktor. *I Chose Freedom*. New York: Charles Scribner's Sons, 1946.

Laird, Robbin and D. Herspring. *The Soviet Union and Strategic Arms*. Boulder, Colo.: Westview, 1984.

Lamphere, Robert J. *The FBI-KGB War: A Special Agent's Story*. New York: Random House, 1986.

Linden, Carl. *Khrushchev and the Soviet Leadership*. Baltimore, Md.: Johns Hopkins University, 1990.

Lobanov, M. M. *Razvitie sovetskoi radiolokatsionnoi tekhniki*. Moscow: Voenizdat, 1982.

Lockwood, Jonathan. *The Soviet View of U.S. Strategic Doctrine*. New Brunswick, N.J.: Transaction, 1985.

Logunov, A. A., ed. *Boris Nikolayevich Petrov*. Moscow: Nauka, 1984.

———. *Isaak Konstantinovich Kikoin*. Moscow: Nauka, 1988.

Longacre, Edward. *Strategic Air Command: The Formative Years, 1944–49.* Offutt AFB, Neb.: Office of the Historian, HQ Strategic Air Command, 1990.

Lee, William and Richard Staar. *Soviet Military Policy since World War II.* Palo Alto, Calif.: Hoover Institution, 1986.

Lewytzkyj, Boris. *Who's Who in the Soviet Union.* Munich: K. G. Saur, 1984.

Lysenko, V., ed. *Three Paces beyond the Horizon.* Moscow: Mir, 1989.

McDougall, Walter. *The Heavens and the Earth: A Political History of the Space Age.* New York: Basic Books, 1985.

McGwire, Michael. *Military Objectives in Soviet Foreign Policy.* Washington, D.C.: Brookings Institution, 1987.

Mackenzie, D. *Inventing Accuracy: A Historical Sociology of Nuclear Missile Guidance.* Cambridge, Mass.: MIT Press, 1990.

McLean, Scilla, ed. *How Nuclear Weapons Decisions Are Made.* New York: St. Martin's, 1986.

Martel, William and Paul Savage. *Strategic Nuclear War.* Westport, Conn.: Greenwood, 1986.

Mastny, Vojtech. *Russia's Road to the Cold War.* New York: Columbia University Press, 1979.

Medvedev, Roy. *Let History Judge: The Origins and Consequences of Stalinism.* New York: Columbia University Press, 1989.

Medvedev, Zhores A. *Nuclear Disaster in the Urals.* New York: Vintage Books, 1980.

———. *The Legacy of Chernobyl.* New York: Norton, 1990.

Meister, Jurg. *Soviet Warships of the Second World War.* New York: Arco, 1977.

Mierzejewski, Alfred. *The Collapse of the German War Economy.* Chapel Hill, N.C.: University of North Carolina, 1988.

Miller, Jay. *Lockheed U-2.* Austin, Tex.: Aerofax, 1983.

Mitroshenkov, V. *Pioneers of Space.* Moscow: Progress, 1989.

———. *Sozvezdie.* Moscow: Moskovskiy Rabochiy, 1989.

Moon, Howard. *Soviet SST: The Techno-politics of the Tupolev-144.* New York: Orion Books, 1989.

Nazarov, A. G., et al. *Rezonans zaklyuchenie obyedinennoy ekspertnoy gruppy po okhrane okruzhayushchey sredy ekspertnoy podkomissiy Gosudarstvennoy ekspertnoy komissiy Gosplana SSSR i postoyannoy ekspertnoy gruppy Verkhovnogo Soveta SSSR.* Chelyabinsk: Yuzhno-Uralskoe Knizhnoe Izdatelstvo, 1991.

Newton, Verne. *The Cambridge Spies: The Untold Story of Maclean, Philby and Burgess in America.* Lanham, Md.: Madison Books, 1990.

Neufield, Jacob. *Ballistic Missiles in the United States Air Force, 1945–60.* Washington, D.C.: Office of Air Force History, 1990.

Nisbet, Robert. *Roosevelt and Stalin: The Failed Courtship*. Washington, D.C.: Regnery Gateway, 1988.

Nobel, Erika. *Soviet Defense Decision Making: An Integrated View*. Falls Church, Va.: Delphic Associates, 1989.

Nove, Alec. *An Economic History of the USSR*. London: Pelican, 1978.

Novikova, V. N. *Oruzhie pobedi*. Moscow: Mashinostroenie, 1985.

Oberg, James. *Red Star in Orbit*. New York: Random House, 1981.

Ordway, Frederick, ed. *History of Rocketry & Astronautics,* vol. 9. San Diego: American Astronautical Society, 1989.

———and Mitchell Sharpe. *The Rocket Team*. Cambridge, Mass.: MIT Press, 1982.

Parrott, Bruce. *Politics and Technology in the Soviet Union*. Cambridge, Mass.: MIT Press, 1983.

Parry, Albert. *The Russian Scientist*. New York: Macmillan, 1973.

Peebles, Curtis. *The Moby Dick Project: Reconnaissance Balloons over Russia*. Washington, D.C.: Smithsonian Institution, 1991.

Penkovskiy, Oleg. *The Penkovskiy Papers*. New York: Doubleday & Co., 1965.

Perelman, A. I. *Aleksandr Yevgenevich Fersman*. Moscow: Nauka, 1984.

Petrosyantsa, A. M., ed. *Akademik V. G. Khlopin: Ocherki, vospominaniya, sovremennikov*. Leningrad: Nauka, 1987.

———. *Atomnaya nauka i tekhnika SSSR*. Moscow: Energoatomizdat, 1987.

Polikanov, Sergey. *Nuclear Physics in the Soviet Union*. Falls Church, Va.: Delphic Associates, 1984.

Polmar, Norman and Jurrien Noot. *Submarines of the Russian and Soviet Navies, 1918–1990*. Annapolis, Md.: Naval Institute Press, 1990.

Ponomarev, A. N. *Sovetskie aviatsionnie konstruktory*. Moscow: Voenizdat, 1977.

Prados, John. *The Soviet Estimate: U.S. Intelligence Analysis and Russian Military Strength*. New York: Dial Press, 1982.

Radosh, Ronald and Joyce Milton. *The Rosenberg File*. New York: Vintage Books, 1984.

Rhodes, Richard. *The Making of the Atomic Bomb*. New York: Simon & Schuster, 1986.

Rowen, Henry, et al. *The Impoverished Superpower: Perestroika and the Soviet Military Burden*. San Francisco: ICS, 1989.

Riabchikov, Yevgeniy. *Russians in Space*. New York: Doubleday, 1971.

———. *Zvezdniy Put*. Moscow: Mashinostroenie, 1986.

Richelson, Jeffrey. *American Espionage and the Soviet Target*. New York: Wm. Morrow, 1987.

Romanov, Aleksandr P. *Konstruktor kosmicheskikh korabley*. Moscow: Politizdat, 1971.

—— and V. S. Gubarev. *Konstruktory.* Moscow: Politizdat, 1989.
——. *Korolev.* Moscow: Molodaya Gvardiya, 1990.
Ruge, Fredrich. *The Soviets as Naval Opponents, 1941–1945.* Annapolis, Md.: Naval Institute Press, 1979.
Rummel, R. J. *Lethal Politics.* New Brunswick, N.J.: Transaction, 1990.
Sakharov, Andrei. *Memoirs.* New York: Knopf, 1990.
Sands, Jeffrey, R. S. Norris, and T. Cochran. *Known Soviet Nuclear Explosions, 1949–1985: Preliminary List.* Washington, D.C.: Natural Resources Defense Council, 1986.
Sapir, Jacques. *The Soviet Military System.* Cambridge, Mass.: Polity Press, 1991.
Sapolsky, Harvey M. *The Polaris System Development: Bureaucratic and Programmatic Success in Government.* Cambridge, Mass.: Harvard University Press, 1962.
Schroeer, Dietrich. *Science, Technology and the Nuclear Arms Race.* Boston: John Wiley, 1984.
Shakhurin, A. I. *Krylya pobedy.* Moscow: Polizdat, 1983.
Sharagin, A. Georgi Ozerov. *Tupolevskaya sharashka.* Frankfurt: Possev, 1971.
Shavrov, B. V. *Istoriya konstruktsiy samoletov v SSSR 1938–1950gg.* Moscow: Mashinostroenie, 1988.
Shcherbakov, V. ed. *Zagadki zvezdnikh ostrovov.* Moscow: Molodaya Gvardiya, 1987.
Schecter, Jerrold L. and Peter S. Deriabin. *The Spy Who Saved the World: How a Soviet Colonel Changed the Course of the Cold War.* New York: Charles Scribner's Sons, 1992.
Sheldon, Charles. *Review of the Soviet Space Program.* New York: McGraw-Hill, 1968.
Shelest, Igor. *Lechu za mechtoi.* Moscow: Molodaya Gvardia, 1973.
Shifrin, Avraham. *The First Guidebook to Prisons and Concentration Camps of the Soviet Union.* New York: Bantam Books, 1982.
Shklovskiy, Iosif. *Five Billion Vodka Bottles to the Moon: Tales of a Soviet Scientist.* New York: Norton, 1991.
Smith, Myron. *The Soviet Air and Strategic Rocket Forces, 1939–1980: A Guide to Sources.* Santa Barbara, Ca.: ABC-Clio, 1981.
Smotkin, Irukhim. *Hardening Soviet ICBM Silos.* Falls Church, Va.: Delphic Associates, 1991.
Smyth, Henry DeWolf. *Atomic Energy for Military Purposes: The Official Report on the Development of the Atomic Bomb under the Auspices of the United States Government, 1940–45.* Princeton, N.J.: Princeton University Press, 1945.
Stache, Peter. *Sowjetische Raketen.* Berlin: Militärverlag der DDR, 1987.

Starostin, Aleksandr. *Korolev: Admiral vselennoi*. Moscow: Molodaya Gvardiya, 1982.

Steinhaus, Alexander. *The Beginnings of Soviet Military Electronics, 1948–1961*. Falls Church, Va.: Delphic Associates, 1986.

Suvorov, Victor. *Inside the Soviet Army*. London: Hamish-Hamilton, 1982.

———. *The Liberators: Inside the Soviet Army*. London: Hamish-Hamilton, 1981.

Svishchev, G. P., et al. *Andrei Nikolayevich Tupolev: Grani derznovennogo tvorchestva*. Moscow: Nauka, 1988.

Taubman, William. *Stalin's American Policy*. New York: W. H. Norton, 1982.

Thomas, Hugh. *Armed Truce: The Beginnings of the Cold War, 1945–46*. New York: Atheneum, 1987.

Tokady-Tokayev, G. A. *Comrade X*. London: The Harvill Press, 1956.

Tolley, Kemp. *Caviar and Commissars: The Experiences of a U.S. Naval Officer in Stalin's Russia*. Annapolis, Md.: Naval Institute Press, 1983.

Tolubko, V. F. *Nedelin Perviy glavkom strategicheskikh*. Moscow: Molodaya Gvardiya, 1979.

———. *Raketniye Voiska*. Moscow: Znaniya, 1977. Trans. FTD-IDRST-0501-79.

Turetsky, Mikhail. *The Introduction of Missile Systems into the Soviet Navy, 1945–1962*. Falls Church, Va.: Delphic Associates, 1983.

Ulam, Adam. *The Rivals: America & Russia since World War II*. New York: Viking, 1971.

Umanski, S. P. *Realnaya Fantastika*. Moscow: Moskovskiy Rabochiy, 1985.

Vasilev, V. A. *Long Range, Missile-Equipped*. Washington, D.C.: U.S. Air Force, 1979.

Vladimirov, Leonid. *The Russian Space Bluff*. London: Tom Stacey Ltd., 1973.

Volkogonov, Dmitri. *Stalin: Triumph & Tragedy*. New York: Grove Weidenfeld, 1991.

Walker, Mark. *German National Socialism and the Quest for Nuclear Power 1939–1949*. Cambridge: Cambridge University Press, 1989.

Werth, Alexander. *Russia at War, 1941–45*. New York: Carrol & Graf, 1964.

Wilcox, Robert. *Japan's Secret War: Japan's Race Against Time to Build Its Own Atomic Bomb*. New York: Wm. Morrow, 1985.

Williams, Robert Chadwell. *Klaus Fuchs, Atom Spy*. Cambridge, Mass.: Harvard University Press, 1987.

Williams, Trevor. *Science: A History of Discovery in the Twentieth Century*. Oxford: Oxford University Press, 1990.

Winter, Frank H. *Prelude to the Space Age: The Rocket Societies, 1924–1940*. Washington, D.C.: Smithsonian Institution, 1983.

Wittlin, Thaddeus. *Commissar: The Life and Death of Lavrentiy Pavlovich Beria*. New York: Macmillan, 1972.

Wukelic, George. *Handbook of Soviet Space-Science Research*. New York: Gordon and Breach, 1968.

Yevsikov, Viktor. *Re-entry Technology and the Soviet Space Program*. Falls Church, Va.: Delphic Associates, 1982.

York, Herbert. *The Advisors: Oppenheimer, Teller and the Superbomb*. Palo Alto: Stanford University Press, 1989.

Zaloga, Steven. *Soviet Air Defense Missiles: Design, Development and Tactics*. Coulsdon, UK: Jane's, 1989.

—— and James Grandsen, *Soviet Tanks and Combat Vehicles of World War II*. London: Arms & Armour Press, 1984.

Zhukov, Georgi. *The Memoirs of Marshal Zhukov*. New York: Delacorte Press, 1961.

Index